CompTIA.

MW00607855

when you purchase your exam voucher from CompTIA.org.

Use code:
COMPTIA10

Your Next Move Starts Here!

Get CompTIA certified to help achieve your career goals and gain a powerful, vendor-neutral credential that is trusted by employers.

WHY GET CompTIA CERTIFIED?

Increase your confidence
91% of certification earners show increased confidence.*

Earn more money
77% of IT pros got a raise within six months of earning their certification.*

Stand out to employers
64% of IT decision makers say certified employers add additional value.**

Join a global community
92% of IT professionals hold at least one certification.**

GET READY FOR EXAM DAY.

- **Download the exam objectives:** Visit CompTIA.org to find the exam objectives for your IT certification and print them out. This is your roadmap!

- **Create your study plan:** Decide how many hours each week you are going to dedicate to studying, choose your preferred study tools and get to work. Studying is a unique experience. Download a study plan worksheet on CompTIA.org.

- **Get certified:** If you haven't already, use the coupon on this page when you purchase your exam voucher and schedule your exam. CompTIA offers flexible testing options to fit your busy life.

CHOOSE YOUR TESTING OPTION.

Online testing
Earn a CompTIA certification online, from your home – or any quiet, distraction-free, secure location – at a time that's convenient for you.

In-person testing
Test at any of the Pearson VUE test centers around the world, where you can use their equipment under the supervision of a proctor.

To purchase your exam voucher and learn how to prepare for exam day, visit CompTIA.org.

*Pearson VUE 2021 Value of IT Certifications
**2021 Global Knowledge IT Skills and Salary Report

The Official
CompTIA
Linux+
Study Guide
(Exam XK0-005)

Course Edition: 1.0

Acknowledgments

CompTIA.

Damon Garn, Author

Becky Mann, Director, Product Development

James Chesterfield, Senior Manager, User Experience and Design

Katherine Keyes, Senior Specialist, Product Development

Notices

Disclaimer

While CompTIA, Inc. takes care to ensure the accuracy and quality of these materials, we cannot guarantee their accuracy, and all materials are provided without any warranty whatsoever, including, but not limited to, the implied warranties of merchantability or fitness for a particular purpose. The use of screenshots, photographs of another entity's products, or another entity's product name or service in this book is for editorial purposes only. No such use should be construed to imply sponsorship or endorsement of the book by nor any affiliation of such entity with CompTIA. This courseware may contain links to sites on the Internet that are owned and operated by third parties (the "External Sites"). CompTIA is not responsible for the availability of, or the content located on or through, any External Site. Please contact CompTIA if you have any concerns regarding such links or External Sites.

Trademark Notice

CompTIA®, Linux+®, and the CompTIA logo are registered trademarks of CompTIA, Inc., in the U.S. and other countries. All other product and service names used may be common law or registered trademarks of their respective proprietors.

Copyright Notice

Copyright © 2022 CompTIA, Inc. All rights reserved. Screenshots used for illustrative purposes are the property of the software proprietor. Except as permitted under the Copyright Act of 1976, no part of this publication may be reproduced or distributed in any form or by any means, or stored in a database or retrieval system, without the prior written permission of CompTIA, 3500 Lacey Road, Suite 100, Downers Grove, IL 60515-5439.

This book conveys no rights in the software or other products about which it was written; all use or licensing of such software or other products is the responsibility of the user according to terms and conditions of the owner. If you believe that this book, related materials, or any other CompTIA materials are being reproduced or transmitted without permission, please call 1-866-835-8020 or visit **https://help.comptia.org**.

Table of Contents

About This Course

CompTIA is a not-for-profit trade association with the purpose of advancing the interests of IT professionals and IT channel organizations; its industry-leading IT certifications are an important part of that mission. CompTIA's Linux+ certification is an intermediate-level certification designed for professionals with at least 12 months of hands-on experience working with Linux servers in a junior Linux support engineer or junior cloud/DevOps support engineer job role. In addition, the knowledge gained in CompTIA's A+, Network+, and Server+ courses, or the equivalent, is strongly recommended.

> The CompTIA Linux+ certification exam will verify the successful candidate has the knowledge and skills required to configure, manage, operate, and troubleshoot Linux in on-premises and cloud-based server environments while using security best practices, scripting, containerization, and automation.
>
> *CompTIA Linux+ Exam Objectives*

Course Description

Course Objectives

This course can benefit you in two ways. If you intend to pass the CompTIA Linux+ (Exam XK0-005) certification examination, this course can be a significant part of your preparation. But certification is not the only key to professional success in the field of systems administration. Today's job market demands individuals with demonstrable skills, and the information and activities in this course can help you build your sysadmin skill set so that you can confidently perform your duties in any intermediate-level Linux systems administration role.

On course completion, you will be able to:

- Configure, manage, and troubleshoot Linux systems.

- Operate Linux in both on-premises and cloud-based server environments.

- Implement security best practices.

- Use scripting, containerization, and automation to optimize a Linux system.

Target Student

The Official CompTIA Linux+ (Exam XK0-005) is the primary course you will need to take if your job responsibilities include Linux system administration, installation, and security within your organization. You can take this course to prepare for the CompTIA Linux+ (Exam XK0-005) certification examination.

Prerequisites

To ensure your success in this course, you should have at least 12 months of hands-on experience working with Linux servers. CompTIA A+, Network+, and Server+ certifications, or the equivalent knowledge, are strongly recommended.

The prerequisites for this course might differ significantly from the prerequisites for the CompTIA certification exams. For the most up-to-date information about the exam prerequisites, complete the form on this page: www.comptia.org/training/resources/exam-objectives.

How to Use the Study Notes

The following notes will help you understand how the course structure and components are designed to support mastery of the competencies and tasks associated with the target job roles and will help you prepare to take the certification exam.

As You Learn

At the top level, this course is divided into **Lessons,** with each representing an area of competency within the target job roles. Each Lesson is composed of a number of topics. A **Topic** contains subjects that are related to a discrete job task and mapped to objectives and content examples in the CompTIA exam objectives document. Rather than follow the exam domains and objectives sequence, lessons and topics are arranged in order of increasing proficiency. Each topic is intended to be studied within a short period (typically 30 minutes at most). Each topic is concluded by one or more activities, designed to help you apply your understanding of the study notes to practical scenarios and tasks.

In addition to the study content in the lessons, there is a glossary of the terms and concepts used throughout the course. There is also an index to assist in locating particular terminology, concepts, technologies, and tasks within the Lesson and topic content.

 In many electronic versions of the book, you can click links on key words in the topic content to move to the associated glossary definition and on page references in the index to move to that term in the content. To return to the previous location in the document after clicking a link, use the appropriate functionality in your eBook viewing software.

Watch throughout the material for the following visual cues.

Student Icon	Student Icon Descriptive Text
	A **Note** provides additional information, guidance, or hints about a topic or task.
	A **Caution** note makes you aware of places where you need to be particularly careful with your actions, settings, or decisions so that you can be sure to get the desired results of an activity or task.

As You Review

Any method of instruction is only as effective as the time and effort you, the student, are willing to invest in it. In addition, some of the information that you learn in class may not be important to you immediately, but it may become important later. For this reason, we encourage you to spend some time reviewing the content of the course after your time in the classroom.

Following the lesson content, you will find a table mapping the lessons and topics to the exam domains, objectives, and content examples. You can use this as a checklist as you prepare to take the exam and review any content that you are uncertain about.

As a Reference

The organization and layout of this book make it an easy-to-use resource for future reference. Guidelines can be used during class and as after-class references when you're back on the job and need to refresh your understanding. When taking advantage of the glossary, index, and table of contents, you can use this book as a first source of definitions, background information, and summaries.

Lesson 1

Introducing Linux

LESSON INTRODUCTION

Working with Linux begins with an understanding of licensing and the operating system's history. The open-source nature of Linux has resulted in many different distributions, so it's important to understand how distributions differ from each other. Linux servers are primarily managed from the command line, using shells such as Bash. Bash enforces a particular syntax, or way of structuring commands. In addition, Linux holds its configurations in text files, so it's critical that sysadmins can edit these files to manage system settings. Man pages are available as quick reference documents to help administrators recall the function of specific commands and any available options.

Misconfigurations or physical failures may provide troubleshooting opportunities, so sysadmins should follow a standard methodology to help narrow the scope of problems, solve the root cause of the issue, and manage documentation related to configuration issues.

Lesson Objectives

In this Lesson, you will:

- Identify Linux characteristics.

- Understand basic interaction with Linux.

- Use help documentation in Linux.

- Identify the troubleshooting methodology.

Topic 1A

Identify Linux Characteristics

EXAM OBJECTIVES COVERED
This topic provides background information about the history and features of Linux and does not cover a specific exam objective.

Linux is characterized by a free and open-source software licensing approach, which makes the operating system freely distributable and encourages the release of modified versions. These versions are known as distros or distributions. Distros are purpose-specific combinations of the Linux OS and particular applications geared toward supporting defined goals, such as enterprise services, database management, or virtualization hosting. Finally, Linux is distinctive for frequently being managed from a command-line interface, which is often more efficient and easier on resources, rather than a graphical interface.

Characteristics of Free and Open-Source Software

Much of today's software is closed-source software, or proprietary software that's released under copyright law. These laws restrict intellectual property, such as closed-source software, from duplication and re-release by competitors. **Open-source** software takes a different approach.

In general, software licensed as open-source can be duplicated, shared, and modified, and the modified versions can be released to consumers. Code licensed as **free and open-source software (FOSS)** can be used and changed without cost. In fact, changes are encouraged as a form of improvement, even by individuals who do not work for the original developers. Any changes must also be made available and released for free.

Some examples of open-source licenses include the Apache License 2.0, the GNU General Public License, and Mozilla's Public License. While the exam does not focus on the specifics of these licenses, they are a good sample of the open-source requirements and permissions.

The History and Philosophy of Unix and Linux

Unix is one of the oldest operating systems still in use. It was created in 1969, and it was not released as open-source software. Instead, Unix versions were associated with many different tech organizations, including IBM, Hewlett-Packard, and AT&T. These various Unix versions are referred to as Unix "flavors" and were proprietary to each company.

In 1991, Linus Torvalds created a new Unix-like operating system kernel. He released this kernel, which he called **Linux**, under the GPL license. The **Linux kernel**, as well as much of the software released with it, is open-source; it can be modified, shared freely, and re-released. This collaborative approach allows Linux to grow and evolve rapidly. As a result of this approach, there are now more than 200 Linux versions, or distributions (abbreviated "distros").

Of the three primary operating systems in the marketplace today (Linux, macOS, and Windows), two can trace their roots back to Unix. The macOS kernel evolved from a Unix flavor named BSD and shares many of the same standards and some software as Linux. However, Apple's OS is not FOSS. Microsoft Windows also uses a proprietary kernel with a more restrictive licensing method.

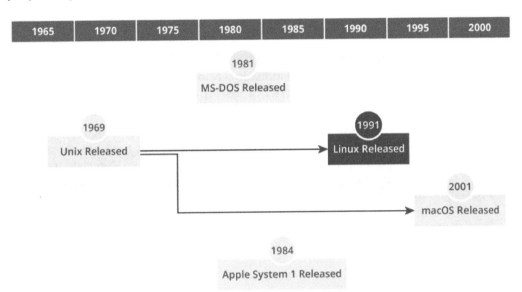

The timeline of early OS development. Unix, released in 1969, directly generated the Linux and the macOS systems.

Traits of the Linux Operating System

Like any operating system, Linux has characteristics that may or may not fit the needs of a given organization. Here are a few general considerations:

- **Free:** No licensing fees or tracking associated with most Linux distributions.

- **Security:** Because of the open-source nature of Linux and its associated software, many developers can and do review code for vulnerabilities. Such vulnerabilities tend to be addressed quickly.

- **Support:** Community-driven support may provide easy, efficient, and cost-effective solutions. However, support may be limited to the community, without a strong corporate support structure implemented by the distribution's vendor.

- **Performance:** Linux often provides greater performance and stability compared to other operating systems.

- **Software availability:** Fewer or less familiar software options may exist, especially for nonbusiness applications, such as games.

- **Hardware requirements:** Linux may consume fewer hardware resources, making it easier to retain older systems for longer.

- **Hardware flexibility:** Linux runs on a wide variety of hardware platforms, adding to its flexibility in areas such as Internet of Things (IoT). Specialized hardware may require specific drivers that may not exist for Linux.

- **Learning curve:** Some find that Linux has a steeper learning curve than Windows or macOS does.

- **Distribution creation:** If existing Linux distributions do not fit your needs, you are welcome (and encouraged) to create your own. The sheer number and purpose of Linux distributions can be confusing and overwhelming. There is not a big name in the marketplace that represents Linux and lends it a sense of stability.

Understand Linux Distributions

Because anyone can create and release their own version of Linux, there are thousands of different options. These individual releases are called distributions (or "**distros**" for short). Distributions are purpose-specific versions of Linux that address a specific need, such as system security or application hosting.

Many distributions trace their history back to one of two specific Linux distributions: Red Hat Linux or Debian Linux. One of the main differentiators between these two distros is how they manage software. Those distros derived from Red Hat Linux use different software managers than those derived from Debian Linux. The software is also packaged differently.

 Software management, including more differences between the Red Hat method and the Debian method, are discussed in a later section.

Some of the most common distros include:

- Fedora Linux

- Ubuntu Desktop, Server, Core

- Red Hat Enterprise Linux (RHEL)

- Linux Mint

- Debian

- openSUSE

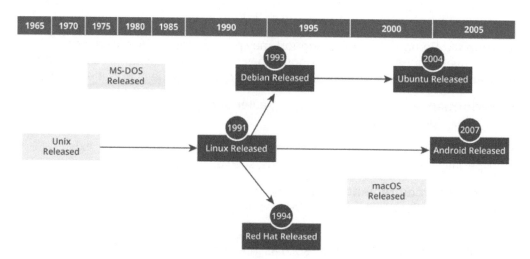

After the release of Linux in 1991, the two major branches, Debian and Red Hat, followed quickly and generated hundreds of distros.

Many of these distributions fulfill specific roles in the marketplace, including desktop or workstation computer, server, IoT device, mobile device, or other functions. While mobile and IoT implementations are common, the focus of this course is on server deployments. One of the most important characteristics of a distribution is its included software.

Some distributions contain end-user applications, such as word processors or presentation software. Others contain server services, such as web services or file storage. Still other distributions include security software or creative applications, such as music editing.

Linux server deployments are put to use in the following ways:

- **Webserver:** Hosts one or more websites.

- **Name resolution:** Hosts Domain Name System (DNS) name resolution services.

- **File:** Stores business data, usually in some form of text document.

- **Print:** Manages the print process and access to print services.

- **Log:** Centralizes and stores log files from other systems.

- **Virtualization/container:** Hosts virtual machine or container virtualization software.

- **Database:** Hosts one or more databases.

- **Cluster:** Works with other cluster nodes to host high-performance, fault-tolerant services.

Linux is heavily involved in newer forms of infrastructure management. A DevOps approach to the management of such Linux servers and services works toward high quality, iterative, and frequent updates and releases. Linux tends to include security in design and implementation throughout the development lifecycle (this approach is sometimes called DevSecOps).

Most commands are consistent across distributions. A few commands, such as those for software management, may be specific to one group of distributions or another. For example, Red Hat Linux uses the rpm *command to manage software, while Debian Linux uses* apt.

The Command-Line Interface

One distinguishing characteristic of Linux compared to other operating systems is its reliance on the **command-line interface (CLI)**. Linux administrators frequently use the CLI for everyday tasks, while administrators of other platforms often use **graphical user interface (GUI)** utilities. In fact, the installation of a GUI is often optional with Linux and may be frowned upon for performance and security reasons.

A GUI consumes a great many hardware resources, specifically memory and processor time. On a server, these resources should be dedicated to the service provided, such as handling database queries or managing print jobs. Desktop systems might need a user-friendly GUI but servers usually do not.

CLI advantages:

- **Quicker:** It's usually quicker to execute a series of commands at the CLI (assuming you know the commands).

- **Performance:** CLI environments consume fewer hardware resources, leaving those resources free to support the server's purpose.

- **Scriptable:** CLI commands can be written into a text file, which the system then reads and executes in a consistent, efficient, repeatable, and scheduled manner.

CLI disadvantages:

- **Learning curve:** Remembering many different commands and their related options is difficult.

- **Nonintuitive:** Commands are often difficult to relate to or understand, with no apparent logic.

- **Inconsistent:** Many commands differ from each other in small but distinctive ways, making it difficult to recall exactly how to use them.

Common CLIs

Command-line interfaces are available in Linux, Windows, and macOS. Users type commands using a specific syntax, and the system processes the commands. At first, such input may seem intimidating or difficult, but CLI environments get easier with use. These environments are usually faster and offer automation options that are not available in GUIs.

```
student@ubuntu20:~$ whoami
student
student@ubuntu20:~$ pwd
/home/student
student@ubuntu20:~$ date
Fri 12 Nov 2021 11:36:22 AM MST
student@ubuntu20:~$ █
```

Several sample commands and their output, including whoami, pwd, *and* date.

Shells provide the CLI. Each shell has its own syntax, or way of structuring commands.

Common Linux shells:

- **Bash:** Default Linux shell

- **ksh:** Korn shell

- **zsh:** Z shell

These shells are differentiated by their syntax and user-friendly features.

 The Bash shell is covered in more detail later in this Lesson. It is the only shell covered by the CompTIA Linux+ exam objectives.

Common GUIs

Just as there are many different Linux distributions, there are also many different Linux graphical environments. Windows and macOS users have one GUI available to them—whatever graphical environment Microsoft and Apple choose to provide. Linux users have the freedom to install zero, one, or many GUI environments and switch between them.

These GUIs are usually distinguished by two characteristics: user-friendly interface and performance. Some users like the look and feel of a particular GUI over others. In addition, some GUIs consume more processor time and memory than others do. Luckily, many options are available in the Linux world.

Common GUI environments include **GNOME**, **KDE Plasma**, **Cinnamon**, and **MATE**.

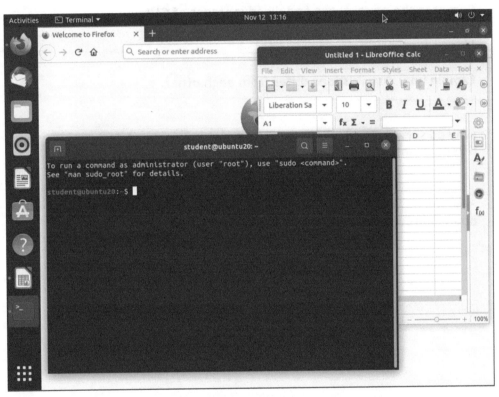

Example of a GUI with running apps and menus.

Another important attribute of Linux GUIs is support for graphics-based applications, such as web browsers, presentation software, and image-editing programs. These types of software are critical to today's business environments and users.

Linux graphical interfaces provide many accessibility features that are worth exploring. Some of these include high-contrast displays, screen readers, magnifiers, visual alerts, and keyboard sticky keys.

Review Activity:

Linux Characteristics

Answer the following questions:

1. Compare the advantages and disadvantages of GUI and CLI environments.

2. Explain how distributions differ from each other.

3. Why do servers tend to rely on CLI administration and desktops rely on GUI environments?

4. How might anyone contribute improvements to a piece of free and open-source software?

Topic 1B

Understand Bash Interaction with Linux

EXAM OBJECTIVES COVERED
1.2 Given a scenario, manage files and directories.

Command-line administration relies on interfaces called shells. The default Linux shell is Bash, which has a particular syntax, or way of structuring commands. The syntax includes commands, command modifiers called options, and arguments. Bash also includes features such as tab completion and a history file. There are several common commands, directories, and applications available on most Linux systems, including the Vim and Nano text editors. Bash also supports privilege escalation. A solid understanding of Bash and its syntax makes Linux administration much easier.

Command Shells

The CLI is provided by software called a **shell**. The shell accepts user input, processes the input for syntax, and provides output back to the user. The default shell for most Linux distributions is **Bash**, and this is the shell that sysadmins should be prepared to work with.

Other common Linux shells include ksh, or KornShell, which is common among Unix servers; Zsh, or Z Shell, with quite powerful scripting capabilities; and Fish, or friendly interactive shell, an interface that provides a user-friendly experience and web-based configurations.

By way of comparison, Windows Server also uses shells: the traditional, DOS-like cmd.exe shell and Microsoft PowerShell. The current (at the time of this writing) default shell for macOS is the Zsh.

Bash is the Linux default and the only shell to concern yourself with for CompTIA Linux+.

Bash Characteristics and Syntax

Commands must be entered into Bash using a specific structure, or **syntax**. Each component of the syntax has a name to make it easier to understand.

The syntax components are:

- **Command:** The primary instruction given to the system.
  - **Subcommand:** A secondary, more detailed instruction supporting the primary command.

- **Option:** A command modifier that slightly changes the way a command is processed.
- **Argument:** The object on which the command acts. For example, in a command to delete a file, the argument is the name of the file to be deleted.

There are two basic forms, normal command and command-subcommand, to this syntax.

Normal Command Syntax

The normal command syntax relies on the three primary components of the Bash syntax: the command, options to modify the command, and an argument for the command to act upon.

 Observe that there is a space between each of the three components!

As an example, here are several ways to use the list (`ls`) command with options and arguments.

Normal Command Syntax for the ls Command	Purpose
`ls`	List directory contents.
`ls -la`	List all (`-a`) directory contents in long format (`-l`).
`ls /var/log`	List the contents of the `/var/log` directory.
`ls -la /var/log`	List all contents of the `/var/log` directory in long format.

 Most Bash error messages are descriptive, so be careful to read the error message to understand what went wrong.

Command-Subcommand Syntax

Many Linux commands support subcommands to specify particular information that the sysadmin needs. These commands rely on a different syntax from the basic format in normal command syntax. The sysadmin enters the primary command, then follows it with a space and a subcommand, and then a space and argument.

The `ip` command uses this format.

Command-Subcommand Syntax for the ip Command	Purpose
`ip addr`	Display all IP addresses for all interfaces.
`ip addr show eth0`	Display only IP address information for the eth0 interface.
`ip help`	Display basic help about the `ip` command.
`ip link help`	Display help about the `ip link` subcommand.

```
$ ip addr show eth0
```

The ip command showing address information for the eth0 interface.

Use Basic Bash Commands

There are many Bash commands. Some of the most often-used commands deal with file management functions, such as displaying files and file contents, moving from one directory (or folder) to another, or editing files.

 It is customary in Linux to refer to folders as "directories."

Use Common Commands

The following commands exemplify the Bash syntax and enable users to begin working with the files and directories that make up Linux. These commands are used throughout this course and will quickly become familiar.

Command	Purpose	Example with Options	Result
ls	List the contents of the current directory	ls /tmp	List the contents of the /tmp directory
touch	Create a new empty file or update the timestamp on an existing file	touch newfile.txt	Create a new file named newfile.txt
cd	Change from one directory to another	cd /etc	Changes the current directory to /etc
cat	Display the contents of a text file on the screen	cat data.txt	Display the contents of the data.txt file
less	Display the contents of a file in windows that fit on the screen	less data.txt	Display the contents of the data.txt file screen at a time when the file would not normally fit on one screen
tree	Display the directory structure in a tree format	tree /etc	Display the subdirectories and files in the /etc directory in a tree structure
shutdown	Shut down the system	shutdown -r now	Restart the system immediately

Two common commands do not use options to generate an output. Use `whoami` to display the current user, and use `pwd` to display the present working directory.

```
student@ubuntu20:~$ ls
Desktop  Documents  Downloads  Music  Pictures  Pu
student@ubuntu20:~$ pwd
/home/student
student@ubuntu20:~$ whoami
student
student@ubuntu20:~$ touch fileA
student@ubuntu20:~$
```

Command line interface showing the output of `ls`, `pwd`, `whoami`, *and* `touch`.

The number of Bash commands can be overwhelming. Start by using a few commands at a time, and make them a habit. The longer you work with Linux, the more comfortable you'll become with the commands.

Use Bash Tab Completion and History

Bash supports **tab completion**. Users can type in enough of a command to make it unique from any other command. Select the Tab key, and Bash automatically completes the command. This feature also works with file and directory names. Tab completion reduces typographical errors and increases speed at the CLI.

Bash also keeps a record of previously entered commands in a history file. This file can be referenced and used to repeat or edit commands.

The simplest way to work with history is by using the Up and Down Arrow keys. Select the Up Arrow key one time to recall the most recently used command. You can cycle through the command history by pressing Up Arrow or Down Arrow multiple times. Select Enter once the appropriate command is displayed.

Typing the history command displays the contents of the history file. Each entry in the file is numbered. Type `!` and the command number executes that command.

```
11  pwd
12  whoami
13  touch fileA
14  clear
15  touch /hme/student/fileZ
16  touch /home/student/fileZ
17  ls
18  rm fileZ
19  ls
20  clear
21  touch /hme/student/fileZ
22  touch /home/student/fileZ
23  clear
24  history
25  pwd
26  clear
27  history
28  clear
29  history
student@ubuntu20:~$ !12
whoami
student
student@ubuntu20:~$
```

Retrieving a past command with the `history` *command.*

Some shells cache command history in memory. When the system is rebooted, the commands are no longer available. Bash writes the command history to a file stored on the hard disk. The commands are available even after multiple reboots.

Shell Tips and Tricks

Tab completion and history can make working in Bash far more efficient and less frustrating. Try to get comfortable using both features as quickly as possible, along with trying these other tips for easier use:

- **Tab completion:** Get in the habit of using tab completion for speed and to minimize typographical errors.

- **Use command history instead of rewriting long commands:** When you make a typographical error in a command or file name, do not manually retype the entire line. Repeat the line with the mistake by hitting the Up Arrow key one time, and then use the Left and Right Arrow keys to move to the mistake so that you can correct it.

- **Read the command backward:** When troubleshooting your commands, start from the right and read to the left. This method makes it a great deal easier to notice missing or duplicate characters.

- **Clear the screen:** Enter the `clear` command to clear the CLI of all text. This is useful when you're starting a new task and want to eliminate any distracting information from past command entries.

Introducing Vim and Nano

Linux stores its configurations in text files. When a sysadmin needs to change system settings, these text files must be edited. There are many familiar text editors in GUIs, but what about Linux systems that do not have a graphical interface available, such as Linux server installations?

Two standard text editors exist that are run from the CLI and do not need a mouse or graphical interface: Vim and Nano. Here is a very brief overview of using these two editors.

Vim

Vim is very powerful and complex. It uses three different modes, where each mode maps keyboard keys to different functions. For example, in **Insert mode** the keyboard acts as normal, inserting text into the file. If you're in Insert mode and type "abc," those three characters appear in the file's content. In **Command mode**, pressing a key on the keyboard issues commands to Vim instead of entering text in the file. Selecting the `i` key tells Vim to switch from Command mode to Insert mode. The third mode is **Execute**. This mode is entered by selecting the colon character, `:`, and it provides a command prompt to Vim where additional commands can be issued. For example, `:wq` places Vim in Execute mode, writes the files to the disk (save), and then quits Vim (q).

The many modes and commands can make Vim a little confusing. Strive to understand four basic functions: create/open, edit, save, close.

Function	Command	Result
Create/Open	`vim filename`	Create a new empty file, or open an existing file in Vim.
Edit	`i`	Enter Insert mode, and begin making edits.
Save	`ESC` and `:w`	Move out of Insert mode and into Command mode, and then save (write) changes.
Close	`ESC` and `:q`	Move to Command mode, and then exit.

 For efficiency, type `:wq` *to combine the save and close options.*

The Vim editor. Note the INSERT flag in the lower left corner.

Vim is covered in more detail in Lesson 5. A summary is provided here to permit immediate editing of text files if necessary.

Nano

Nano is a popular and common alternative to Vim. It's simpler but less powerful. However, in many cases sysadmins don't need the power offered by Vim, which makes Nano a useful choice for basic editing functions.

Nano does not have modes. Pressing keys on the keyboard inserts text into the file, just as expected with most editors. To save and close the file, use keyboard shortcuts using the `Ctrl` meta key. For example, `Ctrl+O` saves the file, and `Ctrl+X` exits the file. You may have used similar keyboard shortcuts in other applications.

As with Vim, it's critical that you are capable of using Nano to create or open, edit, save, and close files.

- Type `nano filename` to create a new empty file or open an existing file with Nano.

- To edit the file, simply begin typing. Use the arrow keys to move the cursor.

- Type `Ctrl+O` to save changes.

- Type `Ctrl+X` to exit Nano after saving changes.

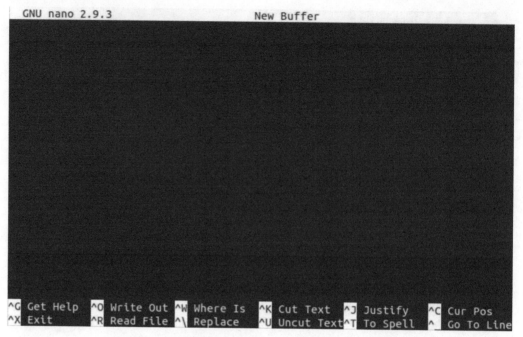

The Nano editor. Note the menu at bottom of the window.

 Nano is covered in more detail in Lesson 5. A summary is provided here to permit immediate editing of text files if necessary.

Some Linux distributions install both Vim and Nano by default, while others will include only one or the other. It is essential for you to be able to use both editors at a very basic level (open, edit, save, close) so that you are capable of editing files with whichever tool is available.

Introducing su and sudo

There are three types of accounts on Linux systems: root, standard user, and service.

The administrator account in Linux is called root. Logging in to the system with administrator access is frowned upon. The security best practice is to log on with a standard **user account**, and then, if necessary, switch your user account to root. The command to accomplish this is `su`.

Type `su root` to switch from the standard user to root.

Type `exit` to leave the root user and return to the standard user.

Type `su - root` to switch from the standard user to root with the root profile. Note that there is a space on each side of the dash character. Again, type `exit` to close the root login and return to the standard user account login.

```
student@ubuntu20:~$ whoami
student
student@ubuntu20:~$ su - root
Password:
root@ubuntu20:~# whoami
root
root@ubuntu20:~# exit
logout
student@ubuntu20:~$ whoami
student
student@ubuntu20:~$ ▮
```

Elevate privileges from standard user to root, and confirm the change with the whoami *command.*

The problem with the `su - root` command is that it grants all administrative privileges to the escalating user, assuming the user knows the root password. In other words, the user is either a non-privileged account with almost no administrative authority or the full root user account with all possible administrative authoring—and nothing in between. Sometimes, administrators want to delegate specific, defined activities that require root authority, but only those particular activities.

Sysadmins can edit a file named `/etc/sudoers` to delegate specific tasks to individual users and groups. The specified identity may exercise that task as if they are root, but nothing else. This is a much safer alternative than giving full root privileges to individuals who may not be fully qualified to run the system. This delegation concept is critical to good security.

To accomplish a delegated task, simply precede the command with `sudo`. You will usually be prompted for your password and given a warning to be careful on the system. The command then executes.

As a security measure, some distributions disable the root user account and force the use of `sudo` on specific user accounts.

 Privilege escalation using su *and* sudo *are covered in more detail in a later Lesson. A summary is provided here in case it's needed for hands-on activities.*

Identify Common Directories

With so many Linux distributions available, administrators rely on the Filesystem Hierarchy Standard to understand the default location of particular resources. There are three common directories that administrators work with on a regular basis.

- **/home/username:** Each standard user has a specific and private directory used to store personal files, profile settings, and other data. These user directories are subdirectories of /home.

- **/etc:** Most system configuration files are stored in the /etc directory.

- **/var/log:** Log files for the system and applications are stored in the /var/log directory.

```
student@ubuntu20:~$ ls /home
student
```

Use the command `ls /home` *to display a few existing user directories.*

There are many other standard directories, and they are covered in a later Lesson.

Log In Using the GUI and CLI

If the Linux system is configured to boot to the CLI (or doesn't have a GUI at all), users are prompted for a username and password. After entering these two values, the system authenticates the account and loads profile settings from files stored in the user's **home directory**.

```
localhost login: root
Password:
Last login: Tue Mar  8 16:25:14 on tty1
[root@localhost ~]#
```

Logging in from the command line.

If the system boots to the GUI, a login prompt is displayed that may show available user accounts. A password is entered, and then the user is authenticated. Profile settings related to the GUI—such as desktop backgrounds and menu items—are then loaded.

Logging in from a GUI.

Review Activity:

Interact with Linux

Answer the following questions:

1. **An administrator asks you to make a change to the system's configuration. Why would you need to use Vim or Nano to accomplish this task?**

2. **What types of files will be found in the /etc directory?**

3. **Explain the difference between the su and sudo commands.**

Topic 1C

Use Help in Linux

EXAM OBJECTIVES COVERED
This topic covers the foundational concepts of documentation and does not address a specific exam objective.

Linux includes strong built-in documentation in the form of manual pages, which provide brief explanations of the command, available options, and a few examples. They are short, concise references. It is essential that sysadmins become comfortable accessing and using manual pages. More significant documentation may be built into applications, stored on the system, or available online at vendor websites.

Linux Documentation

There are several ways of getting help in Linux. The most common are the manual pages, referred to as "man pages" for short. There is built-in documentation for the system and some applications, too. Many online resources also exist, and they are often the most up to date.

Because there are so many commands, and because each command has so many options, it's very common to use the man pages as a quick reference for displaying the available options.

Manual Pages

It's common for new Linux users to ask for help and then be asked, "Did you check the man pages?" That's because man pages are the primary reference for standard Linux commands. The man pages provide syntax information and usage examples. Perhaps most important, the available options are displayed. Because of the number of options for each command, and the fact that many options differ from command to command, the man pages provide an essential quick reference.

The syntax for using man pages is `man {command}`.

For example, to display help for the `ls` command, type `man ls`.

Obtaining help for the `ls` command, using the man pages.

Man Page Sections

Man pages are organized into eight sections. A section defines what category the command belongs to. These sections are displayed by a number following the command. For example, `fsck (8)` indicates that the `fsck` command is found in section eight.

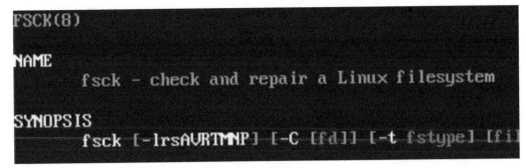

The man page for `fsck`.

Note that the numbers in this list are man page section numbers, not merely part of the list. In other words, "System calls" is in **Section 2** of the man pages documentation, not just the second item in this grouping.

Section eight is probably the most commonly used section for administrators.

 It is not necessary to memorize the section numbers. Sometimes it can be useful to recognize what section might contain the man page for a given command. If you're interested in a deeper dive into the conventions and configurations of man pages, take a look at the man-pages project website.

man Page Navigation

You can use several different keys to navigate through the man pages, all mapped to specific actions.

`Home` -- Move to the beginning of the man page.

`End` -- Move to the end of the man page.

`Page Up` -- Scroll up one page.

`Page Down` -- Scroll down one page.

`/` -- Begin a search for a term or text string.

`n` -- Move to the next occurrence of the search term.

`p` -- Move to the previous occurrence of the search term.

`q` -- Exit the man page, and return to the shell.

For example, to search for the string "directory" in the ls man page, open the man page and then type a forward slash character and the word "directory."

```
$ man ls
/directory
```

The first line opens the man page for `ls`, and the second line searches the keyword directory.

Built-In Documentation

Most commands include help references. Add the `-h` option, or `help` after the command to display this reference material.

The `whatis` command provides a brief description of the specified command.

The syntax for `whatis` is `whatis {command}`.

Finally, built-in documentation can be found at `/usr/share/doc`. This directory contains some Linux and application help files. Not all applications store documentation at this location, but it's worth checking.

Online Documentation

There is a great deal of information available online that covers Linux administration, applications, security configurations, and network services. This documentation may be provided by vendors, community groups, online forums, article repositories, and other sites.

- **Linux distribution vendors:** Vendors such as Red Hat and Ubuntu have large repositories of reference information.

- **Linux application vendors:** Vendors for products such as Apache web server, Vim, and Firefox provide many references for their applications.

- **Linux Documentation Project:** This is a community project dedicated to providing documentation for Linux, including how-to documents, man pages, and guides. These references are found at https://tldp.org/.

Review Activity:

Help in Linux

Answer the following questions:

1. Name three things a man page might provide a user.

2. Why might vendor websites be the best source of information about an application or service?

Topic 1D

Identify the Linux Troubleshooting Methodology

EXAM OBJECTIVES COVERED
This topic covers the foundational concepts of troubleshooting and does not address a specific exam objective.

One of the primary skills and duties of a systems administrator is to troubleshoot problems with servers, the network, and data access. It is important to have a methodology for troubleshooting. You should also recognize that troubleshooting methods may change by situation, skill level, and experience with the network environment.

Troubleshooting Methodology

A formalized and consistent **troubleshooting methodology** can make identifying issues and discovering fixes more efficient. While the steps can vary depending on the actual issue and components involved, there are several universal troubleshooting steps.

The following list represents the basic steps in a troubleshooting methodology:

- Identify the problem.

- Determine the scope of the problem.

- Establish a theory of probable cause/question the obvious.

- Test the theory to determine the cause.

- Establish a plan of action.

- Implement the solution or escalate the issue.

- Verify full system functionality.

- Implement preventive measures.

- Perform a root cause analysis.

Throughout the process you will find it helpful to document findings, actions, and outcomes of the various steps.

Identify the Problem and Determine the Scope

Identify the Problem

The first troubleshooting phase is to identify the problem. The problem may be discovered for you by the end users you support, exposed by log files, identified by monitoring software, or indicated by lights on the server. There are many ways through which the problem may be detected. Once a problem is identified, a service desk ticket is used to track it.

Determine the Scope of the Problem

Once a problem is identified, gather additional information to determine the scope of the problem. Start this process by asking users for additional details or examining log files. Attempt to replicate the problem by asking users to show you what they were doing when the problem was encountered or to try to recreate the situation where the problem first arose. It is a good practice to back up data if there is any risk to the data during the troubleshooting phase. You must use your own judgment as to whether a data backup is necessary before you begin troubleshooting. Finally, consider whether you have the skills to address the problem or if you need to escalate the service desk ticket to another administrator.

One of the most important steps is to determine whether the problem exists on only one server or on multiple servers. The scope of the problem could be hardware based and, if so, may be isolated to that device. It could be network based, in which case, multiple devices may be affected. It could be software based, such as a misconfiguration or a bug. This also may impact multiple servers.

For example, if one workstation cannot access a file server, but all other workstations can, the problem likely lies with that workstation. If many workstations cannot access the file server, the problem likely lies with that server or with the network between the workstations and the server.

 In Linux, the log file service is named "rsyslog." Services are covered in Lesson 9.

Establish and Test a Theory of Probable Cause

Establish a Theory of Probable Cause: Question the Obvious

The next troubleshooting phase is to establish a probable cause for the problem. It is essential to keep this step as simple as possible. Troubleshooting often begins with very basic steps, such as confirming that the system is plugged in and powered on. More complex problems may require you to examine log files, talk to users or other administrators, or check the hardware.

When troubleshooting, identify any common elements or similar problems that might span multiple servers or network devices. Such common elements might include a new or updated piece of software, a new device driver, or a new configuration.

Check for any recent changes to the environment. These changes may have been implemented by another IT staff member or a stakeholder, such as a manager or other user. Recent changes are common culprits for issues.

Test the Theory to Determine the Cause

Next, test the theory by verifying that the likely cause is indeed the culprit. This phase involves research or other testing. Very simple problems may actually be solved during this step. If your theory is confirmed, then move on to the next phase, which is to establish a plan of action. If your theory is not confirmed, then you must establish and test a new theory.

Establish and Implement a Plan of Action

Establish a Plan of Action

The plan of action for addressing the problem must recognize that service interruptions and data loss should be avoided. If a server needs to be brought down to replace hardware, or if data has been lost due to a HDD failure, the end users must be notified. The plan of action defines the steps to be taken. These steps should be defined ahead of time rather than created during the implementation of the solution. It is useful to provide the impacted users with an expected duration of the outage.

Implement the Solution or Escalate

In this phase, follow the plan of action established earlier. It is important not to deviate from the plan. You may not have the knowledge to implement the plan and need to escalate the problem to the vendor's support team or other members of your own team.

When following a plan of action, be sure to only make one change at a time, and then test the result. If you make multiple changes simultaneously, it is difficult to identify exactly which change corrected the problem. If a given change does not solve the problem, reverse that change, and then try another option.

Verify, Prevent, Analyze, and Document

Verify Full System Functionality

Once the potential solution has been implemented, the next phase is to test for functionality. Your goal is to ensure that the server has returned to the service levels that are defined by the system parameters. The server performance baseline that you performed during the deployment portion of the server lifecycle will be very useful as a comparison.

Implement Preventive Measures

It may be possible to preemptively reconfigure other servers to avoid a repeat of the same problem. It may also be possible to implement additional technologies (such as a redundant array of independent/inexpensive disks [RAID]) or additional practices (such as backups) to prevent future instances of failure. In some cases, additional training or documentation may also be necessary.

Perform a Root Cause Analysis

Once service is restored to your users, it is time to evaluate why the problem occurred. Identifying the root cause permits you to change processes or implement different technologies to avoid the problem in the future.

Document Findings, Actions, and Outcomes Throughout the Process

Documenting the symptoms of the problem, the results of research into potential solutions, and the results of each step of the plan of action (whether the step was successful or not) permits you to understand your environment better and therefore helps to prevent possible future problems. Note that documentation is not a separate step but rather a good practice used during each phase of the troubleshooting process.

 Some service desk management software requires the use of tickets. Such software may require that troubleshooting documentation be entered before the ticket can be closed.

Review Activity:

Troubleshoot in Linux

Answer the following questions:

1. **A user contacts you to find out why they cannot access a directory. Using the troubleshooting methodology, how would you narrow the scope of the problem?**

2. **When should you escalate a problem?**

3. **True or False? Documentation should be created only at the end of the troubleshooting process.**

Lesson 1

Summary

By understanding how open-source licensing allows many Linux distributions to exist, it is easier to differentiate between Linux and other operating systems. Linux is widely used with various hardware, but one of its most common roles is as a server OS. Servers need to maximize the use of available hardware resources, so Linux is often managed via the Bash shell rather than a graphical interface. Bash is more hardware-efficient and allows tasks to be scripted and scheduled.

Command-line administration has its challenges, however, especially when managing system configurations through text files. Applications such as the Vim text editor are used to edit these files, resulting in updated settings. Text editors and Bash commands may be difficult to remember and often rely on one or more options to modify their behavior. Administrators use built-in man pages to reference command functions and options. Often, such references are made as part of a larger troubleshooting methodology that attempts to provide comprehensive and effective problem-solving.

Guidelines

These best practices and guidelines are provided for your use as revision tools or as quick references in your job role.

- **FOSS**: Recognize and describe free and open-source software, including advantages and disadvantages.

- **GPL**: Understand how the GPL influences the development and availability of the Linux OS.

- **Distributions**: Understand what a distribution is and how distributions differ from each other.

- **GUI vs CLI**: Understand the advantages and disadvantages of each environment.

- Use Vim and Nano to open, edit, save, and close files.

- Recognize both command syntax structures:

  - command -option argument

  - command subcommand argument

Command Reference Table

This list of commands and their associated syntax can also be found in Appendix B.

Command	Syntax	Purpose	Covered in
ls	ls [option]	List the contents of the current directory.	Lesson 1, Topic B
cat	cat [file-name]	Display the contents of a text file on the screen.	Lesson 1, Topic B
cd	cd /etc	Change from one directory to another.	Lesson 1, Topic B
pwd	pwd	Displays the present working directory.	Lesson 1, Topic B
whoami	whoami	Displays the username of the current user.	Lesson 1, Topic B
touch	touch [file-name]	Create a new empty file or update the timestamp on an existing file.	Lesson 1, Topic B
man	man [command]	Display manual, or help, pages for a specific command.	Lesson 1, Topic C
whatis	whatis [command]	Provides a brief description of the specified command.	Lesson 1, Topic C

Lesson 2
Administering Users and Groups

LESSON INTRODUCTION

Modern operating systems require users to prove their identity. This identification process, referred to as authentication, provides access to major functions. First, the user's identity can be used to control access to resources via permissions and other rules. Second, the user's environment can be customized to fit that individual's work style and habits.

The first task is to understand user account management, including its related configuration files and commands. However, managing individual users can be inefficient, so users are often placed into groups for simplicity. Group management involves a different set of configuration files and commands. Next, administrators should log on to the server with non-privileged accounts and then elevate privileges only when necessary. The administration of privilege elevation and its related commands is covered in the third Topic. Finally, this lesson will cover applying configuration files and commands in troubleshooting and security auditing.

Lesson Objectives

In this lesson, you will:

- Manage user accounts.

- Manage group accounts.

- Configure privilege escalation.

- Troubleshoot user and group issues.

Topic 2A

Manage User Accounts

EXAM OBJECTIVES COVERED
2.2 Given a scenario, implement identity management.

Sysadmins are responsible for, among other things, managing user accounts. These accounts customize the user environment and provide access to resources. It's difficult to administer user accounts effectively without a solid understanding of the files and tools used to manage accounts. This Topic covers user configuration files and management commands.

User Configuration Files

Like most Linux settings, user accounts are stored in text files. However, administrators do not simply edit these text files directly to manage user accounts. Instead, specific applications are used to create, modify, and remove user accounts on the Linux system. It's still important to know what files maintain user account information.

User Account Storage

Two files store user account data: `/etc/passwd` and `/etc/shadow`. Note that both of them are stored in the /etc directory, where most Linux configuration files reside. The `/etc/passwd` file stores the actual user account and maintains various settings related to accounts. The `/etc/shadow` file stores password information for the accounts.

```
student@ubuntu20:~$ tail /etc/passwd | grep student
student:x:1000:1000:student,,,:/home/student:/bin/bash
student@ubuntu20:~$ █
```

Field	Content
User Name	The name the user logs into the system with
Password	User password represented as an x; the actual password is stored elsewhere
User ID	Unique number representing the user to the system
Group ID	Unique number representing the user's primary group
Comment	Typically displays the user's full name
Home directory	Absolute path to the user's home directory
Login shell	Absolute path to the user's default shell (usually `/bin/bash`)

```
student@ubuntu20:~$ sudo tail /etc/shadow | grep student
student:$6$XYM8.t73X57Xq/NH$IN5RCtXNyaf4RE4yn5.4Tf464W0AR
IQWRGt/UW.U92/qAK2TqjVj5V9WdmUSQSWoMqfFXljRGyflfUxDxeeCf0
:18942:0:99999:7:::
student@ubuntu20:~$ 
```

The /etc/shadow file. Note the long string representing the hashed password.

Field	Content
User name	The name the user logs into the system with
Password	Hash value of the user's password
Days since last password change	Number of days since the last password change; counted from January 1, 1970
Days before password may be changed	Minimum changeable period, typically set at 1 day
Days before password must be changed	Maximum number of days since the last password change before the password must be changed again; a value of 99999 means the password never needs to be changed, but often set at 90 days
Days until the user is warned to change password	Days before the date the password must be changed that the warning is issued, often set to 7 days
Days after password expires that the account is disabled	Number of days after the password expires until the account is disabled; should be immediate
Days until account expires	Number of days until the account expires and cannot be used
Unused field	Reserved for potential future use

It may seem odd that account information is distributed across two files and that specifically password information is stored in a different file than user accounts. Passwords were originally stored in the second field of the /etc/passwd file. This file, however, is "world-readable," meaning that all users have read permissions to the file. The password itself, or the encrypted version of it, could be viewed by all users. To increase security, the password was moved to the /etc/shadow file, which only the root user (administrator) can access.

The default shell setting, defined in the last field of the /etc/passwd file, specifies which shell will launch when the user logs in. There are many different shells, and some users may prefer one over another. Bash is the default shell and therefore the most common.

For example, User1 has experience with several Unix flavors and is already familiar with the Korn shell (ksh). The sysadmin may install ksh and set it as the default shell for this user. The last field of the User1 line in /etc/passwd will read /bin/ksh. User2, however, might be more comfortable with the Bash shell. In that case, the sysadmin leaves the default shell value as /bin/bash.

System and User Profiles

Users are allowed to define preferred settings within a CLI environment. Each user may have a custom profile tailored to their unique preferences. System administrators may also define profiles to provide required settings to all users on the system. Additionally, shell features such as command history are unique to each user and stored in the individual user's home directories.

As a sysadmin, you can use a few different files to set the system up the way your institution prefers. Use /etc/profile to set system-wide environment **variables** and startup programs for new user shells. Use /etc/bashrc to establish system-wide functions and aliases for new user shells.

Users can customize their preferred settings as well. The ~/.bash_profile sets user-specific environment variables for new Bash shells, and ~/.bashrc runs when noninteractive shells are launched.

The tilde character (~) represents the current user's home directory. For example, the ~ character means the same as /home/user1 (assuming user1 is the currently logged-in user).

The system-wide files process first, and then the user-specific files are executed. The user-specific configuration files take precedence over system files, allowing users to customize their environments to suit their needs.

Finally, a sysadmin can store files in the /etc/skel directory and have those files copy automatically to the home directory of any new user. This feature is useful for pre-populating configuration files such as .bashrc with suggested settings for users or for distributing policy documents all users should have access to.

Account Management Commands

There are three primary commands for managing user accounts in Red Hat–based distributions. The useradd command creates users, while usermod modifies existing users and userdel removes existing users. Many Debian-based distributions also recognize these commands, but they support the adduser command as well.

```
student@ubuntu20:~$ sudo useradd student10
student@ubuntu20:~$ sudo usermod -c "Student Ten" student10
student@ubuntu20:~$ tail /etc/passwd | grep student10
student10:x:1002:1002:Student Ten:/home/student10:/bin/sh
student@ubuntu20:~$ sudo userdel student10
student@ubuntu20:~$ 
```

The user management lifecycle, including adding, modifying, and deleting a user.

Options for useradd

By default, the user management commands rely on the /etc/login.defs file to define default account settings, including home directory location, preferred shell, and account expiration values.

The /etc/login.defs file contains the user mailbox location, password aging values, the UID and GID ranges, home directory creation, the default umask, and the password encryption hash.

The default values found in the `/etc/login.defs` file can be overridden with various options, providing administrators with flexibility. Common options include the comment field or default shell settings.

Some common options for the `useradd` command include:

Option for the useradd Command	Purpose
`-c`	Set the comment value, usually the user's full name.
`-e`	Set an expiration date for the user account, format YYYY-MM-DD.
`-m`	Create a user home directory in /home.
`-s`	Set a default shell for the user.
`-u`	Set a specific user ID value.
`-D`	Display the default settings.

The syntax for using `useradd` is `useradd -options argument`

For example, if you are asked to create a new user account; define its full user name; set it to expire on December 31, 2025; and configure the Korn shell as the default, the command would look like this:

```
useradd -c "Kai Garcia" -e 2025-12-31 -s /bin/ksh
kgarcia
```

Confirm that the new user has been created by displaying the last line in the `/etc/passwd` file.

Observe that the comment value is enclosed in double quotes. The quotes cause Bash to recognize the enclosed information as a single object. If the quotes did not exist, the first name would be seen as a separate item from the last name, resulting in an error.

Set a Password

The `useradd` command creates the user but does not set a password. Most Linux systems will not allow a user to log in with a blank password, so while the account exists, it is not yet usable. The `passwd` command sets passwords for user accounts.

The syntax for using `passwd` is `passwd [username]`

Helpdesk Ticket #01982

Submitted by:	Department:	Assigned to:	Date Opened:
Kai Garcia	**Engineering**	*you*	**2024-03-08**

Subject	Forgot Password
Ticket Detail	Hi, can you please reset my password? Thank you, KG
Date last updated	2023-03-08

For example, to reset Kai Garcia's password, type `passwd kgarcia`

```
student@ubuntu20:~$ sudo passwd kgarcia
New password:
Retype new password:
passwd: password updated successfully
student@ubuntu20:~$
```

Resetting the password for the kgarcia account.

You are prompted to enter a new password twice. Use the `passwd` command to configure a password for a new account as well as to reset a forgotten password for an existing user.

The adduser Command

Some Linux distributions use the `adduser` command instead of `useradd`. Some systems recognize both. The `adduser` command prompts administrators for details, including home directory locations and full names. Perhaps most importantly, `adduser` prompts sysadmins to set a user password. The `adduser` command can be added to a Linux system.

```
student@ubuntu20:~$ sudo adduser student12
Adding user `student12' ...
Adding new group `student12' (1004) ...
Adding new user `student12' (1004) with group `student12' ...
Creating home directory `/home/student12' ...
Copying files from `/etc/skel' ...
New password:
Retype new password:
passwd: password updated successfully
Changing the user information for student12
Enter the new value, or press ENTER for the default
        Full Name []: Student Twelve
        Room Number []:
        Work Phone []:
        Home Phone []:
        Other []:
Is the information correct? [Y/n] Y
student@ubuntu20:~$ █
```

The `adduser` command walks the admin through each field of the user account information.

Modify and Delete User Accounts

Of course, the sysadmin doesn't only make new accounts. A new policy might require sysadmins to update some users' accounts from time to time, or a user's preference might change. Just as you add new users when they onboard, you must remove user accounts during the offboarding process to ensure the integrity of the system.

The usermod Command

Helpdesk Ticket #01983

Submitted by:	Department:	Assigned to:	Date Opened:
Anna Tanaka	HR	*you*	2024-03-29

Subject	Account changes
Ticket Detail	A recent security audit shows that the account for temporary employee Alex Lee should expire on December 31, 2025.
	Another finding is that the comment field for Joseph Deng's account is blank but should be populated in the usual manner, "firstname lastname." Please update.
Date last updated	2024-03-30

Modify these existing user accounts by using the `usermod` command. In these two cases, the commands will look like this:

```
# usermod -e 2025-12-31 alee
# usermod -c "Joseph Deng" jdeng
```

Helpdesk Ticket #01984

Submitted by:	Department:	Assigned to:	Date Opened:
Kai Garcia	Engineering	*you*	2024-04-01

Subject	Change default shell
Ticket Detail	Can you change my default shell to Ksh? I'm much more comfortable with Unix and Ksh over Bash.
	Thank you, KG
Date last updated	2024-04-01

You'll update Kai Garcia's default shell like this:

```
# usermod -s /bin/ksh kgarcia
```

The userdel Command

Helpdesk Ticket #01985

Submitted by:	Department:	Assigned to:	Date Opened:
Anna Tanaka	HR	*you*	2024-11-25

Subject	Personnel update
Ticket Detail	Effective today, Alex Lee is no longer with the company. Please disable Alex's account, but hold on to the data until we can reassign it to other team members.
Date last updated	2024-11-25

The `userdel` command removes existing users from the system. By default, the command does not remove the user's home directory. This is important, as the user data may need to be assigned to other users. However, the `-r` option can be added to the command to remove the account and its associated home directory.

The syntax for using `userdel` is `userdel {user-name}`

For example, to delete the Alex Lee account, type `userdel alee`

Neither the `usermod` nor `userdel` commands will modify users if the accounts have running processes.

The `deluser` command removes user accounts from the system on some distributions.

Deleted user accounts cannot be recovered. They can be recreated, but they will be a different identity (unless created with the same UID value). It is often better to disable a user account rather than delete it.

Verification

When you use the `useradd`, `usermod`, or `userdel` commands to manage users, the result of the command is recorded, even if nothing is displayed on the screen. For example, when you create a user, there is no message displayed. When something goes wrong, an error is displayed explaining the issue. While the messages are self-explanatory, such as "Username already in use" informing you that the username you tried to set exists already, the results are actually labeled using an exit code number. Display the results of the most recent command by typing the following:

```
# echo $?
0
```

A zero indicates success; any other value indicates an error of some sort.

Some examples of those exit codes are provided here.

Exit Code for the useradd Command	Result
0	Success
1	Couldn't update the passwd file
9	Username is already in use
12	Couldn't create the home directory

The error values differ slightly for the `usermod` and `userdel` commands.

Exit Code for the usermod and userdel Commands	Result
0	Success
1	Couldn't update the passwd file
2	Invalid command syntax
6	Specified user doesn't exist
8	Cannot delete user because the specified user is currently logged in

There are many other exit codes, with some shared among the three user management commands and some unique. View the man page for the command to see its specific exit values.

 All Executables have exit codes. Use the `echo $?` *command to display the exit status of the most recent command.*

Account Configuration Commands

Linux includes many additional account management and configuration commands. Several commands display account information, while others configure password settings and other default values. Finally, configuration files set default values for new user accounts.

Display Account Information

The Bash command prompt can be configured to display the current user, but that setting is optional. Typing the `whoami` command displays the current username and is useful when the prompt does not display this information.

The `w` and `who` commands display all current logins on the system, including those that might have remote terminal connections. Suppose you've decided to restart a Linux server, but you wish to know whether any users are currently on the system. Type the `w` command to display the users so you can warn them of the impending restart.

You can also display account information with the `id` command. Typing `id` with no argument displays information for the current user. An existing username is added to `id` to display information about that account, including user ID, group ID, and group memberships.

The syntax for using the `id` command is `id {user-name}`

For example, to gather account information for the Kai Garcia account, type `id kgarcia`

General password settings are pulled from `/etc/login.defs`, and specific passwords are managed with the `passwd` command. Password requirements are also configured by using the `chage` command.

Option for the passwd Command	Purpose
-d	Delete a password and disable the account.
-e	Immediately expire a password, forcing a password change by the user.
-l	Lock the account (for example, during a leave of absence).
-u	Unlock a locked account.

To set a password for your own account, type:

```
$ passwd
```

As the root user, you can change a password for any account. The syntax is `passwd username`

You will be prompted to type the password twice. Note that no characters will show in the Terminal while entering the new password.

Values displayed by the `chage -l` command:

- Last password change date

- Password expiration date

- Account inactive date

- Account expiration date

- Minimum days between password changes

- Maximum days between password changes

- Number of days before password expiration a warning is displayed

The `chage` command options:

Option for the chage Command	Purpose
-l	Display the current values.
-M	Specify the maximum number of days between password changes.
-m	Specify the minimum number of days between password changes.
-W	Specify the number of warning days before a password expires.
-E	Lock an account after a specified date.

Helpdesk Ticket #01986

Submitted by:	Department:	Assigned to:	Date Opened:
Anna Tanaka	HR	*you*	2024-04-12

Subject	Account settings updates
Ticket Detail	Tuesday's security audit showed that some accounts are out of compliance.
	Can you please adjust Ali Selassi's account password settings for a 5 day warning, change required within four months, and change not allowed within 1 day of a new password?
Date last updated	2024-04-12

Your response will look like this:

```
# chage -l aselassi
# chage -m 1 -M 120 -W 5 aselassi
```

Pluggable Authentication Models

Standard Linux **authentication** relies solely on the `/etc/passwd` and `/etc/shadow` files. Often, more flexible authentication standards are needed. Pluggable Authentication Modules (PAM) supplement authentication methods. Modules provide additional options and flexibility.

Two PAM modules help administrators manage authentication. The first is `pam_tally2`, and the second is `faillock`.

The `pam_faillock` module tracks login attempts and can block authentication if too many attempts fail. Sysadmins may configure the `pam_faillock` module to lockout a user account after three failed login attempts. The root user can display login attempt tally information by using the `faillock` command.

The `pam_tally2` module is deprecated and should only be used if `pam_faillock` is not available on the system.

Lesson 12 contains additional details on Pluggable Authentication Modules (PAM).

Review Activity:

User Account Management

Answer the following questions:

1. **Why are user passwords stored in the** `/etc/shadow` **file and not the** `/etc/passwd` **file?**

2. **What is the purpose of the** `/etc/skel` **directory?**

3. **Why might an administrator change a user's default shell?**

Topic 2B

Manage Group Accounts

EXAM OBJECTIVES COVERED
2.2 Given a scenario, implement identity management.

Like the management of user accounts in the previous section, managing groups requires an understanding of the configuration files and commands used to govern groups. Groups simplify the process of granting access to resources to multiple users.

Group Configuration Files

Groups associate user accounts that have similar security requirements. For example, it is easier to grant permissions to a resource to a single group with five members than it is to individually grant access to each user account. Groups are a standard administrative tool for controlling access to resources.

Like user accounts, groups are stored in a configuration file. The file is `/etc/group`, and displaying its contents shows existing groups and any user accounts that are a member of those groups.

One way of displaying the contents of `/etc/group` is to use the `tail` command. For example, type `tail /etc/group`. The output displays the last 10 entries in the file, including the most recently added groups.

```
student@ubuntu20:~$ tail /etc/group
pulse-access:x:129:
gdm:x:130:
lxd:x:131:student
student:x:1000:
sambashare:x:132:student
systemd-coredump:x:999:
student999:x:1001:
student10:x:1002:
abc:x:1003:
student12:x:1004:
student@ubuntu20:~$ 
```

Output of the `tail /etc/group` *command, showing the most recently added groups.*

Group Management Commands

The commands to manage groups are similar to user management commands. Groups have a standard life cycle, including creation, modification, and deletion.

Group Management Command	Purpose
groupadd	Create a new group.
groupmod	Modify an existing group.
groupdel	Remove an existing group.

Helpdesk Ticket #01987

Submitted by:	Department:	Assigned to:	Date Opened:
Anna Tanaka	HR	*you*	2024-04-18

Subject	group updates
Ticket Detail	The group named Marketing is evolving to handle publicity only. Please update the group name.
	We're also starting a new Sales group and need a group for that.
Date last updated	2024-04-19

As the help desk tech, you run the following two commands to complete the service request:

```
# groupmod -n publicity marketing
# groupadd sales
```

The `-n` option changes the group name.

Deleting a group does not delete the user accounts that are a member of that group. A group is a separate object from the user.

Note that you cannot remove the primary group of an existing user. You must remove the user account first by using the `userdel` command.

Some distributions rely on `addgroup` and `delgroup` to manage groups. These commands are more interactive than `groupadd` and `groupdel`. If the commands are not installed on the system, they can be added.

 Be sure to search for files or other resources that may be associated with the group before deleting it. Configure another group with access to those resources before deleting the original group.

Verification

Group management commands are usually straightforward, but things can go wrong. The messages printed on the screen should be plenty to guide you toward a solution. However, you can also display the exit values by using `echo $?`

 Exit codes were discussed in additional detail in Topic 2A.

Exit Code for the groupadd Command	Result
0	Success
2	Invalid argument syntax
4	GID not unique
9	Group name not unique

Exit Code for the groupmod and groupdel Commands	Result
0	Success
2	Invalid command syntax
6	Specified group doesn't exist
8	Can't remove user's primary group (for `groupdel` only)
10	Can't update group file

There are many other exit codes; some shared among the three user management commands and some unique. View the man page for the command to see its specific exit values.

Add Users to Groups

Adding a user to a group is a modification of the user, not the group. Use the `usermod` command covered earlier to add a user to an existing group.

Two specific options are used with `usermod` to manage group membership:

Option for the usermod Command	Purpose
`-a`	Append the user to the group, and maintain any existing group memberships.
`-G`	Specify a group to which the user will be added.

If the `-a` option is not selected, the user is removed from all other groups and added only to the specified group. Users can be a member of multiple groups, so such a mistake could have drastic consequences.

The syntax for using the `usermod` command is `usermod -options argument`

For example, the command to add Joseph Deng to the sales group while retaining membership in all other groups is:

```
usermod -aG sales jdeng.
```

```
student@ubuntu20:~$ sudo useradd jdeng
student@ubuntu20:~$ sudo groupadd sales
student@ubuntu20:~$ sudo usermod -aG sales jdeng
student@ubuntu20:~$ sudo tail /etc/group | grep sales
sales:x:1003:jdeng
```

The group management lifecycle.

Review Activity:

Group Account Management

Answer the following questions:

1. **Suggest at least two ways to display group membership information.**

2. **What command adds a user to a group?**

3. **What is the result if an administrator forgets to add the -a option when adding a user to a group?**

4. **Why might a user be a member of multiple groups?**

Topic 2C

Configure Privilege Escalation

EXAM OBJECTIVES COVERED
2.4 Given a scenario, configure and execute remote connectivity for system management.
4.4 Given a scenario, analyze and troubleshoot user access and file permissions.

One should avoid logging on to a system as the root user. The root user's broad privileges are unnecessary for most day-to-day user tasks, such as managing data or browsing the Internet. If the standard practice is to log on with a non-privileged standard account, then what about situations where administrative privileges are required? Instead of logging off and then logging back on as root, Linux provides ways of switching identities or running commands as a different user.

This section introduces privilege escalation and then covers tools such as `su`, `sudo`, and `pkexec`. Proper use of privilege escalation helps to maintain the security of the system and satisfy security policy requirements.

What is Privilege Escalation?

The root user is the system's administration account. It has full privileges to do anything on the system. This is both necessary for managing the system and dangerous in the hands of malicious or inexperienced users. Logging in as root is frowned upon.

Standard user accounts typically have privileges to manage their own data and some basic system settings and preferences. Most standard accounts cannot run commands that would damage or disable the system, which also means they cannot usually make the configuration changes necessary to administer Linux.

Service accounts represent services running on the system that consume resources. Because the services are represented by service accounts, their ability to consume system resources can be controlled. This helps prevent a service from overwhelming the system or blocking other services from accessing resources.

A common idiom for privilege escalation is "get root."

Understand a Disabled Root Account

Your organization's security policy may require that you log on to server systems with a non-privileged account. This is a very good practice to keep in mind; however, it often isn't possible to execute administrative tasks with nonadministrative privileges. Logging on with a standard user account and then changing your identity to one with administrative privileges is referred to as **privilege escalation**. There are two ways of managing privilege escalation: `su` and `sudo`.

Many Linux distributions disable the root user account by default. During the OS installation, an "admin" account is created that has privileges delegated via `sudo`.

Those distributions that do not disable the root user still suggest that sysadmins log in with non-privileged accounts and then elevate privileges by using `su`.

Avoiding signing in as the root user is an example of the principle of least privilege. This principle states that the minimum level of access should be granted to accomplish a given task.

Elevate Privileges with su

The `su` utility provides the ability to "switch user" to another account. The most common example is a sysadmin that follows proper security practices by signing in as a standard user and then switches to the root user to accomplish system administration tasks.

The syntax for using `su` is `su {user-name}`.

For example, to switch to the root user, type `su root`.

The `su` command, without an option, enables a user to switch their identity to that of another user, but it retains the original user's profile and variables. The switched user also remains in the home directory. Anyone using `su` except the root user will be challenged for the password of the user account they are switching to.

Note that in this discussion, the string "su - {user-name}" has a space on each side of the dash. This is a rare instance in Linux where this is true; the majority of other commands are spaced as "command -option," which has a space only on the left side of the dash.

Using `su` with a hyphen following it enables a user to change users and launch a new shell under the context of that new user. This is a much better practice. Anyone using the `su -` except the root user will be challenged for the password of the user they are switching to. It is most common to switch to the root user, but any user can switch to any other user as long as they know that user's password.

Without a user name argument, the `su -` command will assume you mean to sign in as root.

Elevate Privileges with sudo

With the `su` command, any user who knows the root password can "get root" and do anything the root user can do. An account using `su - root` essentially is the server administrator. This is often much more power than should be delegated to users. A better practice is to delegate specific functions to users, rather than granting system-wide root privileges.

The `sudo` command enables the server administrator to delegate specific commands to specific users, without granting them full privileges on the server. Delegation is done in the `/etc/sudoers` file by using the `visudo` editor. Users and groups may be given specific commands to run in order to fulfill their responsibilities without having full administrator privileges.

The syntax for using the `sudo` command is `sudo -options command`.

For example, to run a command by using sudo, type `sudo shutdown -h now`. Recall that you will be prompted for your password.

You can check your sudo privileges by using the -l option. For example, type
sudo -l, and your privileges are displayed.

 It may be difficult to get into the habit of using sudo *before each command. Recall that Bash keeps a history of recent commands and that* !! *repeats the most recent command. If you forget to type* sudo *in front of a command, rerun the command by typing* sudo !!.

Understand visudo

While the /etc/sudoers file is a normal text file, it is essential not to directly edit it with a standard text editor like Vim or nano. The /etc/sudoers file controls access to all elevated privileges, and a mistake in this file can render it impossible to gain root privileges on the server. Most distributions will set a default editor (usually Vim or nano) for /etc/sudoers. When using the visudo command, the system verifies the syntax of the /etc/sudoers file before committing changes, enabling the administrator an opportunity to correct mistakes before they become part of the running configuration.

```
student@ubuntu20:~$ sudo tail /etc/sudoers

# Members of the admin group may gain root privileges
%admin ALL=(ALL) ALL

# Allow members of group sudo to execute any command
%sudo    ALL=(ALL:ALL) ALL

# See sudoers(5) for more information on "#include" directives:

#includedir /etc/sudoers.d
student@ubuntu20:~$
```

A portion of the /etc/sudoers *file displaying delegated privileges.*

The following are some options you can use with the visudo command:

Option for the visudo Command	Purpose
-c	Check the existing sudoers file for errors.
-f	Edit or check a sudoers file in a different location than the default.
-s	Check the sudoers file in strict mode—any aliases that are used before being defined will result in errors.
-x	Output the sudoers file to the specified file in JavaScript Object Notation (JSON) format.

Because the /etc/sudoers file is sensitive to misconfigurations that could result in not being able to elevate privileges, it's critical to check the file after edits. The visudo editor does this automatically, but various types of checks can be run with the -c, -f, or -s options.

The syntax for `/etc/sudoers` entries is `username hostname = (user) command` where `username` is the user to whom privileges are being given, `hostname` is the terminal from which commands can be run, `user` is the level of access, and `command` is the delegated executable.

For example, to grant full administrative privileges to Kai Garcia, type:

```
kaigarcia ALL=(ALL:ALL) ALL.
```

The user will be prompted for their password. Be very careful with this level of delegation!

Additionally, assuming that `SHUTDOWN_CMDS` is aliased to all related options for the `shutdown` command, to delegate the ability to execute these shutdown commands without entering a password, type:

```
KAIGARCIA ALL=(ALL) NOPASSWD: SHUTDOWN_CMDS.
```

 The `/etc/sudoers` file contains aliases, or combinations of commands. For example, an alias of `SHUTDOWN_CMDS` is associated with several commands that manage system reboot or shutdown.

The wheel Group

The root account is used for a great deal more than just administrative tasks. Some parts of the actual Linux operating system run under root credentials. Many distributions disable the root account for users, preventing sysadmins from logging on as root. Instead, these distros allow administrative functions based on membership in the `wheel` group.

Members of the `wheel` group exercise the administrative privileges of root with less potential for damaging the system. For example, members of the `wheel` group use the `sudo` command to avoid having to sign in as the root user. Add users to the `wheel` group to give them the privileges necessary to complete administrative tasks, but be very cautious about this membership.

Use the `visudo` command to edit the privileges of the `wheel` group, if necessary.

The sudoedit Command

Some Linux files require root user privileges to edit. This could be accomplished with a `sudo` configuration, but a simpler and more secure option is to use the `sudoedit` command. This command permits a user to edit a file with their own credentials, even if the file is only available to the root user. In addition, the user can use their preferred text editor.

To use `sudoedit`, you must make an entry in the `sudoers` file. For example, the following line could be added to the `sudoers` file:

```
%editors ALL = sudoedit /path/to/file
```

Any member of the editors group could then enter the following command to edit a file: `sudoedit /path/to/file`.

The `sudo` configuration is appropriate for commands that need to be executed with elevated privileges, while the `sudoedit` option is appropriate for files that need to be edited with elevated privileges.

PolicyKit Rules

The polkit (PolicyKit) toolkit provides a different way of delegating privileges than `sudo` does. The polkitd daemon works with systemd to permit administrators to delegate more granular control to users than `sudo` allows. Unlike `sudo`, polkit does not grant full root access to a process but instead grants specific access to defined actions.

One example of polkit's benefits is software management. Using polkit rules, sysadmins can permit a user to update existing software but prevent the installation of new software. Other delegated tasks include system shutdown or hibernation, configuring network devices, controlling device access, and mounting or unmounting filesystems on removable media.

 Some topics in this section, such as systemd and software management, are covered in more detail elsewhere.

Configure polkit Rules

Rules are written that define what actions can be performed by what users. The actions, or specified processes, are written into text files. The rules are also text files that reference the actions.

Actions are defined in XML files stored at `/usr/share/polkit-1/actions`. These files have a .policy file extension. Rules files are stored in two different directories: `/etc/polkit-t/rules.d` for local policies and `/etc/share/polkit-1/rules.d` for third-party policies. Rules use a .rules file extension. Administrators write rules in JavaScript notation to reference actions defined in the actions files. When a user attempts an action, the rules are checked to determine success or failure.

pkexec and Other polkit Commands

Four commands are associated with polkit. These commands display details, authorization information, or enable a user to execute a command with elevated privileges.

polkit Command	Purpose
`pkexec`	Allows an authorized user to execute an action.
`pkaction`	Displays details about an action.
`pkcheck`	Displays whether a process is authorized.
`pkttyagent`	Provides a text-based authentication agent.

```
student@ubuntu20:~$ sudo pkexec useradd student5
student@ubuntu20:~$ tail /etc/passwd | grep student5
student5:x:1007:1008::/home/student5:/bin/sh
student@ubuntu20:~$
```

Use of `pkexec` *to create a user account with confirmation that the account has been created.*

The syntax for using `pkexec` is `pkexec program argument`.

For example, to launch nano with `pkexec` and edit the `/etc/named.conf` configuration file, type:

```
pkexec nano /etc/named.conf.
```

Recall that the `su - root` command actually changes the user identity to root, with all related privileges. This could be dangerous. The `sudo` and polkit utilities allow administrators to delegate specific tasks to specific users without granting complete administrative privileges to the system.

Troubleshoot Privilege Escalation Issues

You field the following four phone calls in the course of your week.

Phone Call 1: su

A user calls and says that the `su` command is not responding as expected. You ask the user to type `whoami` and the user reports the result is root. You also ask the user to type `pwd` and the user reports the result is their own home directory. When the user switches identities, they remain in their own home directory with their own profile settings. The user wants to know what is preventing them from switching to root and gaining the root user's profile.

In this case, it's likely that they are using the incorrect syntax. The user failed to include the space on both sides of the dash between the `su` command and the username, `su - root`.

Phone Call 2: sudo

A user calls and says `sudo` is broken on their system after they edited the `/etc/sudoers` file with Nano. The user wants you to fix it.

Open `/etc/sudoers` with `visudo`, and allow it to identify syntax errors that Nano would not have caught. Let the user know to use `visudo` in the future.

Phone Call 3: Authorization

A user indicates they cannot accomplish administrative tasks that they are authorized for.

The likely problem is that they are not a member of the wheel group or they have not been delegated the tasks directly via `/etc/sudoers`. The easiest solution is to add them to the wheel group.

Phone Call 4: New Command

A user calls after attempting to run a command that was referenced on an Internet website. The user preceded the command with `sudo` and with `pkexec`, as suggested on the site. The command failed to run, however.

The likely problem is that the privilege has not been delegated via either `sudo` or `polkit`.

Review Activity:

Privilege Escalation

Answer the following questions:

1. **A developer at your organization needs the ability to reboot a test server, but their account's standard privileges do not permit this. The developer requests the system's root user password in order to use su to reboot the server. Is there a more secure option that aligns with the principle of least privilege?**

2. **How are the su root and su - root commands different?**

3. **You must delegate the shutdown -h privilege to SOMEUSER. What tool is used to modify the /etc/sudoers file, and what line must be added to that file?**

4. **Whose password must be entered with sudo? Whose password must be entered with su?**

Topic 2D

Troubleshoot User and Group Issues

EXAM OBJECTIVES COVERED

4.4 Given a scenario, analyze and troubleshoot user access and file permissions.

User and group management is a straightforward task, but troubleshooting opportunities still arise. Sysadmins must review configuration files and individual user account settings to help identify and resolve login or configuration issues. In addition, security audits or troubleshooting may require a record of when users attempted to log in and whether the attempts were successful.

Troubleshoot User Management Issues

User account management involves creating, modifying, and deleting user accounts. Group account management is similar, though there are some additional restrictions, such as deleting a user's primary group. The following scenarios define some common user management issues.

Account Management Issues

Only authorized users may create, modify, or remove user and group accounts. The root user can do this, as can anyone else delegated such privileges via `sudo`. If you cannot create or modify a user or group, ensure you're using an account with the proper authorization.

Account management problems often relate to whether the account or group exists. Recall that each user account is assigned a unique user ID. New groups are also given a unique group ID. One way to view these identifiers is to check the `/etc/passwd` or `/etc/group` files. If a user account or group cannot be created, check to see if the name or ID is already in use.

Halt any active processes associated with the user. If the delete attempt fails, check for any running processes belonging to the user. The `ps` command can be helpful for identifying processes. The command to halt or kill all processes for the user is:

```
sudo killall -u {username}
```

When you create a user account, an associated group may also be created. Whether this occurs depends on the Linux distribution. This group, known as the user's primary group, cannot be deleted unless the user is also deleted.

Be sure to add the `-r` option to the `userdel` command if you want the user's home directory deleted when the account is created.

Troubleshoot User Login Issues

Like other troubleshooting opportunities, begin solving login issues by starting with basic checks. Ensure accounts exist and have a valid password. Consider the login procedure and the order in which profile files are processed. Linux has several commands to help administrators gather information about login attempts and current user sessions.

Users may fail to authenticate to the system. These failures are often associated with user account and password misconfigurations. Recall that account information is stored in the `/etc/passwd` and `/etc/shadow` files.

User Login Attempt Failures

Confirm the user has an account on the system by displaying the contents of `/etc/passwd`. If necessary, create an account for the user by using the `useradd` command.

If the account exists, confirm that a password is set. Display the contents of `/etc/shadow`, and verify a hashed password exists. Use the `passwd` command to set a password if one did not exist.

If the account exists and a password is set, the user may have forgotten the correct password. Reset the password with the `passwd` command.

If the account exists and a password is set, the password may be expired. Reset the password by using the `passwd` command.

If the account exists and a password is set, the account may be locked. Unlock the account by using the `chage` command.

Review the Login Process

Refer to the login process to help pinpoint specific issues. The system goes through a logical order, and understanding where in that process a failure could occur is a great place to begin troubleshooting.

1. The operating system boots and the kernel is loaded. Assume the system boots to the CLI and displays an authentication prompt.

2. The user enters a name and password combination. These are checked against the `/etc/passwd` and `/etc/shadow` files. Settings such as expired passwords and locked accounts are checked for at this point.

3. System and user profile files are processed, and the user is presented with an authenticated and customized environment.

The boot process is covered in a future Lesson.

Use User Login Commands

Administrators need to know who has tried to log in and succeeded as well as who has tried to log in and failed. Linux tracks this information, and it can be displayed by using several different commands.

The `lastlog` command displays the last login times for accounts. This information allows administrators to know who was logged in at any given time. Use this information in system audits and security reviews. The lastlog utility uses its own log file (usually found at `/var/log/lastlog`).

The `last` command displays the contents of the `wtmp` file, which includes every login and logoff event on the system. The output can be filtered by timestamp and even displays information for remote users. The `wtmp` file is usually found at `/var/log/wtmp`.

```
student@ubuntu20:/etc/polkit-1$ last
student  :1              :1              Thu Dec  9 08:34   still logged in
reboot   system boot 5.8.0-43-generic Thu Dec  9 08:27   still running
student  :1              :1              Thu Nov 11 14:45 - 14:47 (00:01)
reboot   system boot 5.8.0-43-generic Thu Nov 11 14:44 - 14:48 (00:03)

wtmp begins Thu Nov 11 14:44:38 2021
student@ubuntu20:/etc/polkit-1$
```

The `last` *command displays the most recent logins and logouts.*

It is a good security practice to delete unused user accounts, and these tools help identify such accounts.

While the historical data displayed by `last` and `lastlog` can be helpful, it's also useful to know what users are currently on the system. Both the `w` and `who` commands display this information. The `w` command is particularly useful because it shows the user idle time, which indicates the user may be logged on but no longer interacting with the session.

Review Activity:

User and Group Troubleshooting

Answer the following questions:

1. List at least three scenarios where you might need records of who logged in to a Linux system.

2. Another administrator asks you to explain the value of editing the /etc/sudoer's file with visudo rather than a traditional text editor. What is your response?

3. List at least three reasons a user account might be locked.

4. During a security audit it is discovered that a user does not have a password set. When you check the /etc/passwd file, the password field is properly populated with the x character. What file would actually display whether a password has been set for the user?

5. A user places sudo before a command, but the command still fails to run. What might be the cause?

6. An administrator asks you how to delegate Linux administrative privileges to a specific user. What group is used for such delegation?

Lesson 2

Summary

Observe how user authentication allows the system to uniquely identify the logged-on user. The primary purpose of this identification is to enforce permissions on files and directories. Permissions can be granted (or denied) to identities, allowing tasks such as read-only file access, script execution, or application execution. Users are placed into groups when more than one user must be restricted by permissions.

The use of user identities is further exemplified by considering privilege escalation. What privilege escalation actually provides is the ability to move from one user identity to another to exercise different levels of resource access.

Command Reference Table

This list of commands and their associated syntax can also be found in Appendix B.

Command	Syntax	Purpose	Covered in
passwd	passwd [user-name]	Manage user passwords.	Lesson 2, Topic A
chage	chage -options	Manage password settings.	Lesson 2, Topic A
w	w	Display current users on the system.	Lesson 2, Topic A
who	who	Display current users on the system.	Lesson 2, Topic A
useradd	useradd -options argument	Add a user.	Lesson 2, Topic A
usermod	usermod -options argument	Modify a user.	Lesson 2, Topic A
userdel	userdel [user-name]	Delete a user.	Lesson 2, Topic A
id	id [user-name]	Gather and display account information.	Lesson 2, Topic A
groupadd	groupadd [group-name]	Create a new group.	Lesson 2, Topic B
groupmod	groupmod -options argument	Modify an existing group.	Lesson 2, Topic B
groupdel	groupdel [group-name]	Remove an existing group.	Lesson 2, Topic B

Command	Syntax	Purpose	Covered in
su	su - [user-name]	Switch user to the specified user or account name.	Lesson 2, Topic C
sudo	sudo -options [command]	Exercise delegated privileges.	Lesson 2, Topic C
pkexec	pkexec program argument	Allows an authorized user to execute an action.	Lesson 2, Topic C

Lesson 3

Configuring Permissions

LESSON INTRODUCTION

The identity of an authenticated user provides context for enforcing permissions. Once the system knows which user is logged on, it can limit the actions that user can take. Linux relies on a simple yet effective permissions structure that recognizes three identities (users, groups, and all others) and provides three access levels (read, write, and execute). More complex permissions options exist, including special permissions and access control lists (ACLs).

Administrators manage group membership, file ownership, and group association to control access to resources. As such, the permissions discussion in this Lesson is a natural extension of the account management subject of the previous lesson.

Lesson Objectives

In this lesson, you will:

- Configure standard Linux permissions.
- Configure special Linux permissions.
- Configure access control lists.

Topic 3A

Configure Standard Linux Permissions

EXAM OBJECTIVES COVERED
2.5 Given a scenario, apply the appropriate access controls.
4.4 Given a scenario, analyze and troubleshoot user access and file permissions.

The authentication process provides users with an identity on the system. Based on this identity, the system can enforce levels of access to system resources, such as processes and files. This type of access control allows users to share systems and resources with the appropriate levels of confidentiality and privacy.

Sysadmins rely on default Linux settings, such as `umask`, to define some levels of access. Administrators also define explicit controls by associating specific access levels with particular identities. Linux has several permissions structures, including standard, special, and access control list mechanisms. Users are organized into groups to make access control more efficient. Proper permissions settings and owner/group associations are critical to Linux security and administration.

Understand Permissions Concepts

Standard permissions provide a way for sysadmins to enforce levels of access on users for files and directories. Standard **permissions** are relatively simple, with three identities given up to three levels of access. Permissions and file ownership are managed with the `chmod` and `chown` commands, and permissions are displayed by using the `ls -l` command.

Principle of Least Privilege

The **principle of least privilege** enforces the idea that users should be given as little access to resources as necessary for them to do their jobs, with no additional unneeded access.

Two scenarios illustrating this concept are provided here.

Kai Garcia needs to be able to read file1.

- **Proper:** They are granted the read permission only.

- **Improper:** They are granted the read, write, and execute permissions and could potentially change the file.

Joseph Deng needs to create files associated with their own job but doesn't need to perform system administrative tasks.

- **Proper:** Joseph logs on with a standard user account.

- **Improper:** Joseph logs on with the root user account.

Keep the principle of least privilege in mind in all access control configurations, especially those involving file permissions.

Access Levels

Standard Linux permissions define three levels of access: read, write, and execute (rwx). These permissions perform differently depending on whether they are applied to files or directories.

	Files	Directories
Read (r)	The ability to access and view the contents of a file.	The ability to list the contents of a directory.
Write (w)	The ability to save changes to a file.	The ability to create, rename, and delete files in a directory. Requires the execute attribute to also be set.
Execute (x)	The ability to run a script, program, or other software file.	The ability to access a directory, execute a file from that directory, or perform a task on that directory (e.g., a search).

 The three permissions levels are abbreviated with r, w, and x. These abbreviations are used in conjunction with permissions management commands, so be able to recognize them.

Access Identities

Standard Linux permissions define three identities to which permissions can be applied: user (owner), group, and others.

The user (u) identity is a single resource owner. Only one user identity is associated with the resource with standard permissions, and specific permissions are applied to this identity. By default, the user is the identity of the account that created the resource, but that can be changed. This user identity is referred to as the resource "owner."

 The chown *command allows administrators to change the associated user (and group). The* chown *command is covered later in this Topic.*

The group (g) identity is a single group of users associated with the resource. In standard Linux permissions, only one group is assigned to the resource and a specific set of permissions is assigned. By default, the creator's group is set on the resource, but that can be changed.

A group allows multiple users to access the resource at a given level. For example, a sales group consisting of several user accounts can be granted read access to a sales file, allowing all members of the group to view the contents of the file.

The others (o) identity represents all accounts that are not the user (u) identity or a member of the one associated group (g). The others identity means "everyone else" who is not the user and not a member of the group. These other accounts are granted a level of access. Frequently, that permissions level is either read or no access.

Linux permissions are enhanced with special permissions and access control lists (ACLs), which are both covered later in this Topic.

View Permissions

The `ls` command, introduced earlier, relies on the `-l` option to display permissions. Think of the `ls -l` command as "list in long format," where the long format includes the display of permissions. Sysadmins use this command frequently to confirm permissions settings.

```
student@ubuntu20:/projects$ ls -l
total 4
drwxr-xr-x 2 root      root         4096 Dec  9 11:11 old-projects
-rwxrw-r-- 1 root      root            0 Dec  9 11:11 project1.txt
-rw-rw---- 1 student5  2022projects    0 Dec  9 11:11 project2.txt
-r-------- 1 student9  2022projects    0 Dec  9 11:11 project3.txt
student@ubuntu20:/projects$
```

The `ls -l` command displays details about permissions, owner, group, size, and more.

In the following example, note that the resource is a file (based on the leftmost dash character), the owner (root) has rwx, the group (grp) has rwx, and all others have r only.

```
-rwxrwxr-- root grp fileA
```

Interpreting Permissions Strings

The permissions string consists of 10 fields, with each field containing different information.

The first field defines whether the resource is a file or a directory. A file is identified by a dash character (`-`), while a directory is identified by a `d` character.

```
student@ubuntu20:/projects$ ls -l
total 4
drwxr-xr-x 2 root      root         4096 Dec  9 11:11 old-projects
-rwxrw-r-- 1 root      root            0 Dec  9 11:11 project1.txt
-rw-rw---- 1 student5  2022projects    0 Dec  9 11:11 project2.txt
-r-------- 1 student9  2022projects    0 Dec  9 11:11 project3.txt
student@ubuntu20:/projects$
```

The first column of the permission string, listing one directory and three files.

The next three fields are related and identify the permissions assigned to the resource for the user identity. If a permission is granted, it is identified with one of three characters: r, w, or x. If the permission is not granted, the dash character is used as a placeholder.

For example, if the user is granted read but not write or execute, the three fields appear like this: r--. If the user is granted read and write, but not execute, the three fields appear as rw-. Note that the permissions are always displayed in the rwx order, and the - is a placeholder for any unassigned permission.

```
student@ubuntu20:/projects$ ls -l
total 4
drwxr-xr-x 2 root      root        4096 Dec  9 11:11 old-projects
-rwxrw-r-- 1 root      root           0 Dec  9 11:11 project1.txt
-rw-rw---- 1 student5 2022projects    0 Dec  9 11:11 project2.txt
-r-------- 1 student9 2022projects    0 Dec  9 11:11 project3.txt
student@ubuntu20:/projects$
```

The second three columns list the permissions assigned to the user identity. Here the user has rwx access to the directory and the first file, rw access to the second file, and read only access to the third file.

The same structure applies to permissions assigned to the group, in the fifth, sixth, and seventh fields.

```
student@ubuntu20:/projects$ ls -l
total 4
drwxr-xr-x 2 root      root        4096 Dec  9 11:11 old-projects
-rwxrw-r-- 1 root      root           0 Dec  9 11:11 project1.txt
-rw-rw---- 1 student5 2022projects    0 Dec  9 11:11 project2.txt
-r-------- 1 student9 2022projects    0 Dec  9 11:11 project3.txt
student@ubuntu20:/projects$
```

The group permissions are outlined here. The group has r-x access to the directory, rw access to the first and second files, and no access at all to the third file.

And the final three fields use the same structure for others.

```
student@ubuntu20:/projects$ ls -l
total 4
drwxr-xr-x 2 root      root        4096 Dec  9 11:11 old-projects
-rwxrw-r-- 1 root      root           0 Dec  9 11:11 project1.txt
-rw-rw---- 1 student5 2022projects    0 Dec  9 11:11 project2.txt
-r-------- 1 student9 2022projects    0 Dec  9 11:11 project3.txt
student@ubuntu20:/projects$
```

The final three columns show permissions for others not in the user or group identity. Permissions are more stringent here, with others having r-x access to the directory and read only access to the first file, with no access at all to the last two files.

Some other examples are provided here.

A file named fileA, with the user having read, write, and execute; the group having read and write; and others having read-only would appear as:

```
-rwxrw-r-- fileA
```

 Additional fields, such as owner, group, and file size, have been removed from these examples to provide clarity.

A file named file A, with the user having read, the group having read, and others having no access would appear as:

```
-r--r----- fileA
```

A directory named dir1, with the user having read, write, and execute; the group having read and execute; and others having read and execute would appear as:

```
drwxr-xr-x dir1
```

A directory named dir1, with the user having read and execute, the group having read and execute, and others having no access would appear as:

```
dr-xr-x--- dir1
```

 Recall that the execute (x) permission is required for the user to use cd *to move into the directory. If a user does not have execute to a directory, they cannot change into that directory.*

Default Permissions

The ls -l command displays the existing permissions, but what if permissions need to be changed? Administrators can set file and directory permissions for all resources, and resource owners (the account identified by the user (u) permissions) can also configure permissions.

A value named umask defines default permissions on a per-user basis. The "change mode" or chmod command changes permissions settings from the default values.

Configure Default Permissions

The umask command alters the default permissions on newly created files and directories. Changing default permissions can be useful if you'd like to automatically control how new objects can be used, rather than changing these permissions manually on every new object.

With umask, you set default permissions using an octal numeric format. However, instead of specifying which permissions to set, you specify which permissions to mask, or clear, from the default. For example, the default permissions for non-executable files in Linux are 666 (rw-rw-rw-). If you want the owner to retain these permissions, but you want the group and others to only have read access, you'll need to set the umask to 022. Each number is explained as follows, in order from left to right:

- 0 means that the current owner permissions should not be masked at all (i.e., left as read and write).

- 2 means that the group permissions should be masked by 2 (i.e., subtract 2 from the default [6] and you get 4). Group members now only have read access.

- 2 does the same thing as the previous number, but it does so for other users.

You can use the umask command directly in the CLI to set the default permissions for that session, or you can set the default permissions for each user in their .bashrc or .profile file.

The syntax of the umask command is umask {number}.

 Because it subtracts from the default (666), the umask *command cannot force newly created files to set the execute bit.*

Absolute and Symbolic Modes

The chmod command enables you to modify the permissions of a file or directory. Only the owner of the file or directory or the system administrator can change the permissions of the object. This command has several options and may be configured by using two different modes.

The syntax of the `chmod` command is `chmod [options] {mode} {file/ directory name}`

The `chmod` command supports different options to modify permissions. One or more of these options may be used at a time.

Option for the chmod Command	Purpose
`-c`	Report changes that are made in permissions.
`-f`	Hide most error messages.
`-v`	Display a diagnostic entry for every file processed.
`-R`	Modify permissions of files and directories recursively.

The `chmod` command has two different syntaxes for setting permissions: absolute mode and symbolic mode. Both approaches provide the same results. Some administrators find one approach more logical than the other, and it does not really matter which is used. Sysadmins should understand and be able to use both modes.

Absolute Mode

Absolute mode uses octal (base-8) numbers to specify permissions. Each permission (r/w/x) has an associated number.

Absolute mode octal values:

- Read = 4

- Write = 2

- Execute = 1

By adding the **octal numbers** for the permissions you want to grant, you get the overall permission number to assign to a directory or file. For example, full permissions (read, write, and execute) are equivalent to 4 + 2 + 1, or 7. Read and write permissions are equivalent to 4 + 2, or 6. Complete permissions are expressed as a three-digit number, where each digit corresponds to the owner, the group, and others, respectively.

In absolute mode, the syntax of the `chmod` command is `chmod {number} {file/directory name}`

Three-digit and Four-digit Modes

When written in octal, numeric format, file permissions typically have three digits, with each digit corresponding to the user, group, and others permissions. However, file permissions may also be written with four digits, with the new, leading digit signifying any advanced permissions to be defined (or 0, for none). For example, the permissions for a non-executable file in Linux might be rw-rw-r--, or 664. This is equivalent to the octal format of 0664.

Symbolic Mode

Symbolic mode enables you to set permissions using three components, namely:

- Permission contexts: u/g/o/a (a applies the permissions to all three contexts)

- Permission operators: +/-/=

- Permission attributes: r/w/x

Permission **operators** determine whether a permission is to be granted or removed.

The operator **+** (plus sign) grants permissions. The operator **-** (minus sign, or hyphen) denies permissions. Operator **=** (equal sign) assigns permissions exactly as provided, rather than being additive or subtractive.

In symbolic mode, the syntax of the `chmod` command is: `chmod {access context}{operators}{permission attributes} {file/ directory names}`

As an example, to add read and write permissions to myfile for the owner and the group: `chmod u+rw,g+rw myfile`

Permission	Absolute Mode	Symbolic Mode
User has read-write-execute. Group has read and execute. Others have read and execute.	755	u=rwx,g=rx,o=rx
User has read-write-execute. Group has no permissions. Others have no permissions.	700	u=rwx,g=,o=
User has read and write. Group has write. Others have write.	644	u=rw,g=r,o=r
User has read and write. Group has no permissions. Others have no permissions.	600	u=rw,g=,o=
User has read and write. Group has read. Others have no permissions.	640	u=rw,g=r,o=

Some common permissions and their representations in absolute and symbolic modes.

While sysadmins tend to prefer one mode or the other, it is worthwhile to understand both modes. Documentation, online resources, and other administrators may provide permissions settings using either mode, so you must be able to interpret whichever mode is presented.

Set Permissions in a GUI

In most GUI **desktop environments**, right-click a file or directory, select Properties, and select the Security tab. Check the appropriate permissions boxes for the identity and access level you wish to set.

	file2 Properties	⊗
Basic	**Permissions**	Open With

Owner: `Me`

Access: Read and write ▼

Group: student ▼

Access: Read and write ▼

Others

Access: Read-only ▼

Execute: ☐ Allow executing file as program

Security context: unknown

GUI environment permissions output.

Configure Ownership

Although you've restricted access to your data by assigning permissions, you may need to allow users to modify those permissions for certain files and directories. This is where the concept of ownership comes into play.

As you've seen, the first permission context is the owner or user. In Linux, **ownership** refers to the property by which a user can apply and modify the permissions of a file or directory. By default, the owner of a file or directory is the user who created that file or directory. Other than the **superuser**, no other user can change the permissions of an object that is owned by someone else. While the most common application of ownership is the changing of read, write, and execute permission attributes, owners can also alter advanced and special permissions of the objects they own.

Use the chown Command

Helpdesk Ticket #01988

Submitted by:	Department:	Assigned to:	Date Opened:
Kai Garcia	Engineering	*you*	2024-04-22

Subject	Ownership change
Ticket Detail	Hello, can you please update the Projects directory and set Joseph Deng as the owner? Joseph will be taking over that duty now that Alex has left.
Date last updated	2024-14-22

The `chown` command is used to change the owner, the group, or both for a file or directory. At times, you may wish for someone else to manage an object's permissions other than the user who created that object.

```
student@ubuntu20:/projects$ ls -l
total 0
-rw-r--r-- 1 root root 0 Dec  9 10:55 project1.txt
-rw-r--r-- 1 root root 0 Dec  9 10:55 project2.txt
-rw-r--r-- 1 root root 0 Dec  9 10:55 project3.txt
student@ubuntu20:/projects$ sudo chown student5:2022projects project1.txt
student@ubuntu20:/projects$ ls -l
total 0
-rw-r--r-- 1 student5 2022projects 0 Dec  9 10:55 project1.txt
-rw-r--r-- 1 root     root         0 Dec  9 10:55 project2.txt
-rw-r--r-- 1 root     root         0 Dec  9 10:55 project3.txt
student@ubuntu20:/projects$
```

Changing the owner with `chown`. *The file named "project1.txt" was owned by root, but is now owned by student5 in this example.*

The `chown` command syntax varies based on the desired outcome:

- Change the owner but not the group: `chown {newowner} {filename}`

- Change both the owner and the group: `chown {newowner}:{newgroup} {filename}`

- Change the group but not the owner: `chown :{newgroup} {filename}`

You can also combine the `chown` command with the `-R` option to recursively change ownership through a directory structure.

Use the chgrp Command

The `chgrp` command is used to change the group ownership of a file or directory. Changing the group ownership of an object ensures that the group permissions are applied to the specific group.

The syntax of the `chgrp` command is `chgrp {group name} {file/directory name}`

Configure Attributes

Files can have one or more attributes set on them that define how the system interacts with those files. These attributes go beyond typical permissions and enable you to more granularly customize what the system is and is not allowed to do with a file.

There are many such attributes. Some examples include:

- Only allow the file to be open for writing in append mode (i.e., don't allow the file to be overwritten).

- Set the file to be automatically compressed.

- Save the file if it is deleted, providing an opportunity for it to be recovered.

- Make the file immutable.

The Immutable Flag

The **immutable flag** is an attribute of a file or directory that prevents it from being modified, even by the root user. In other words, no one can delete, rename, or write to an immutable file. Setting the immutable flag is useful for files with a high degree of sensitivity and importance (and with the unlikelihood of changing any time soon). A careless user or an errant process will be unable to delete the immutable file.

The immutable flag is not set on all files. A single directory can have a mix of mutable and immutable files and subdirectories. Also, an immutable subdirectory can have mutable files.

When viewing file attributes, the lowercase `i` character indicates that the immutable flag is set.

Attribute Management with lsattr

Administrators use the `lsattr` command to list the attributes of a file or directory.

The `lsattr` *command displays current attribute settings, such as this immutable flag.*

Some of the options for the `lsattr` command are:

Option for the lsattr Command	Purpose
`-R`	Recursively list the attributes of directories and their contents.
`-a`	List all files in directories.
`-d`	List directories like files, instead of listing their contents.
`-v`	List the version number of the file.

The syntax of the `lsattr` command is `lsattr [options] {file/directory names}`

Attribute Management with chattr

The `chattr` command is used to change the attributes of a file or directory.

The `chattr` *command modifies attribute settings.*

The `chattr` command includes these options:

Option for the chattr Command	Purpose
`-R`	Recursively change the attributes of directories and their contents.
`-v {version}`	Set the version number of a file.
`+i`	Mark the file as read-only, or immutable. Requires superuser privileges.
`-i`	Remove the read-only, or immutable, attribute of the file. Requires superuser privileges.

The syntax of the `chattr` command is `chattr [-R] [-v {version}]` `[+-{attributes}] {file/directory names}`

Troubleshoot Access Issues

Permission-based access problems usually consist of misapplied permissions or misunderstood identities.

Helpdesk Ticket #01989

Submitted by:	Department:	Assigned to:	Date Opened:
Ali Selassi	**Marketing**	*you*	**2024-04-25**

Subject	Access issues
Ticket Detail	Hi, can you help me with access to File1? I'm in the Sales group, which manages DirectoryA, and should be able to get into File1, but I can't get in. Thanks, Ali
Date last updated	2024-04-25

Is the user actually a member of the sales group?

Confirm the user's membership in sales with the `group` or `id` commands, and confirm the permissions applied to sales for the file by using `ls -l`

Are the permissions set correctly?

Display permissions with `ls -l`, and check permissions of the file.

Are permissions set recursively from the parent directory?

Use `su` to test access, then reapply permissions, being careful of your absolute or symbolic mode syntax.

Attribute Issues

Attribute problems are typically related to whether or not the attribute is set. Often the solution is to either set or unset the value.

If the file can be deleted and should not be, set the immutable attribute with `chattr +i {filename}`

If the file cannot be deleted and should be, unset the immutable attribute with `chattr -i {filename}`

Review Activity:

Standard Linux Permissions

Answer the following questions:

1. How does the principle of least privilege help mitigate threats and mistakes?

2. What octal value is used in absolute mode to set permissions at all access for all identities?

3. Write the command by using symbolic mode that removes the read permission from others for fileA without impacting other permissions.

4. Interpret the results of the following command: chown -R USERA:sales dirA

Topic 3B

Configure Special Linux Permissions

EXAM OBJECTIVES COVERED
2.5 Given a scenario, apply the appropriate access controls.
4.4 Given a scenario, analyze and troubleshoot user access and file permissions.

The standard read, write, and execute permissions are good enough in most circumstances. However, there are additional permissions and attributes that you can use to restrict access in a more specialized way. These permissions permit users to run software as someone else or allow directory contents to inherit group associations, providing default access control settings.

Understand User and Group ID

Special permissions are used when normal permissions become inadequate. With special permissions, less-privileged users are allowed to execute a file by assuming the privileges of the file's owner or group. This enables the user to temporarily take on these higher-level privileges in a limited context.

In Linux, two main special permissions are **set user ID (SUID)** and **set group ID (SGID)**. SUID, or setuid, is the permission that allows a user to have similar permissions as the owner of the file. Certain executable files and commands, such as `passwd`, require access to additional resources that the user may not have explicit permissions to. Instead of granting those permissions individually, the `passwd` command is configured so that any user will execute it as root (the owner), giving them permission to the additional resources.

SGID, or setgid, is the permission that allows a user to have permissions that are similar to those of the file's group owner . In addition to files, SGID can also be set on directories. Any subdirectories created in this directory will automatically inherit the SGID permission. Likewise, all new files and subdirectories created in this directory will inherit the directory's group ID, rather than the group ID of the user who created the object. This inheritance is useful because users in a shared environment don't need to change their group when they create objects in the directory. Note that the SGID permission is not applied to existing objects in the directory, nor is it applied to objects that are moved from other locations into the directory.

SUID and SGID are both set using the `chmod` command, and you can do so using either symbolic mode or absolute mode. When using `ls  -l` to see permissions, the execute permission for the owner will appear as `s` for the SUID, and the execute permission for the group will appear as s for the SGID.

Set Special Permissions with Absolute and Symbolic Modes

Symbolic mode uses this syntax:

- To set the SUID: `chmod u+s {file-names}`

- To set the SGID: `chmod g+s {directory-names}`

Absolute mode uses this syntax:

- To set the SUID: `chmod 4--- {file-names}`
- To set the SGID: `chmod 2--- {directory-names}`

Note the last three bits in absolute mode are whatever standard permissions you choose.

Removing the SUID and SGID is as simple as using the - (minus) operator in symbolic mode or setting the first permission bit to 0 in absolute mode.

Understand the Sticky Bit

A **sticky bit** is a special permission bit that protects files in a directory. It ensures that only the owner of a file or directory (or root) can delete the file or directory. Without the sticky bit, any user with write and execute permissions on an object can delete that object. The sticky bit ensures that these users do not have delete privileges but still have the rest of the privileges that come with writing and executing files and directories.

Like SUID and SGID, you set a sticky bit using the `chmod` command. Using `ls -l` you can see the sticky bit in the execute position for other users (the last position) as the lowercase letter `t` or the capitalized letter `T` if the execute permission is not set for others.

In older versions of the kernel, a sticky bit could force a program or file to remain in memory so that it wouldn't need to be reloaded when it was invoked again. A sticky bit on a file indicated to the operating system that the file would be executed frequently. Modern versions of the Linux kernel ignore the sticky bit on files; if you want to protect specific files, you need to apply the sticky bit on the directory that contains them.

Setting the sticky bit uses this syntax in symbolic mode:

```
# chmod +t {directory names}
```

Setting the sticky bit uses this syntax in absolute mode:

```
# chmod 1--- {directory names}
```

As with SUID and SGID, use `-` or `0` to clear the sticky bit.

Troubleshoot Special Permissions Access

Troubleshooting special permissions is more difficult than finding issues with standard permissions, but the steps are much the same. First, confirm any identities and group memberships. Next, ensure permissions are set correctly by using `ls -l`, and make any updates with `chmod`.

- Confirm the SUID permission is set correctly for executable files.
- Confirm the SGID permission is set correctly for directories to permit files created in the directory to inherit the group association.
- Confirm the sticky bit permission is set correctly.

Review Activity:

Special Linux Permissions

Answer the following questions:

1. How would SGID benefit users when set on the /projects directory where multiple users are members of the associated group and need access to each other's files in the directory?

2. Why might a sysadmin set the sticky bit on a configuration file?

Topic 3C

Configure Access Control Lists

EXAM OBJECTIVES COVERED
2.5 Given a scenario, apply the appropriate access controls.
4.4 Given a scenario, analyze and troubleshoot user access and file permissions.

One weakness of standard Linux permissions is that only a single user, a single group, and all others who are not that user or a member of that group can be granted access. With standard permissions, a sysadmin cannot provide UserA with rw- and UserB with r--. Nor can GroupA be given rwx to a directory while GroupB is given r-x.

Access control lists, a feature of the filesystem, do permit the system to recognize multiple identities and enforce different levels of access on those identities. In other words, with ACLs the scenarios above are possible.

ACLs do not replace standard permissions, but rather they enhance them. Everything you know about standard permissions still applies and is then supplemented with additional ACL features.

Access Control List Concepts

An **access control list (ACL)** is a list of permissions attached to an object. ACLs can be used for situations where the traditional file permission concept does not suffice. ACLs enable you to assign permissions to individual users or groups even if these do not correspond to the object's owner or group.

For example, members of two department groups may need different levels of access to the same resource. Group 1 might need rwx to a directory, whereas Group 2 only needs r-x access. By using ACLs, you can grant different levels of access to different users, groups, and even processes. ACLs enable a more granular level of control.

Configure Access Control Lists on Files

Two commands are the basis for ACL configuration. The first is `getfacl`, which is used to display existing ACL settings. The `setfacl` command configures ACL permissions.

Display ACL Entries

The `getfacl` command is used to retrieve the ACLs of files and directories.

The basic output format of the `getfacl` command shows metadata about the object, including its owner, its group, any SUID/SGID/sticky bit flags set, the standard permissions associated with the object, and the individual permission entries for users and groups. Directories can also have default ACL entries that pertain to any new files or subdirectories created within them.

The syntax of the `getfacl` command is `getfacl {filename}`

```
student@ubuntu20:/projects$ getfacl project1.txt
# file: project1.txt
# owner: student5
# group: 2022projects
user::rw-
user:student9:r--
group::r--
mask::r--
other::r--

student@ubuntu20:/projects$
```

The `getfacl` command output shows the file owner, group, and standard permissions.

Configure ACL Entries

The `setfacl` command is used to change the permissions associated with the ACL of a file or directory. This command has several options. Some of the most common options are:

Option for the setfacl Command	Purpose
-R	Recursively set ACL options for directories and their contents.
-s	Set the ACL of an object, replacing any existing ACL.
-m	Modify the existing ACL of an object.
-x	Remove entries from an existing ACL.
-b	Remove all ACL entries (not including the standard permissions).

The syntax of the `setfacl` command is `setfacl [-bR] [-mx {acl_spec}] {file/directory names}`

The ACL specification can be formatted in one of several ways:

* When working with users, the format is `u:{user name}:{permissions}`

* When working with groups, the format is `g:{group name}:{permissions}`

```
student@ubuntu20:/projects$ sudo setfacl -m u:student9:r project2.txt
student@ubuntu20:/projects$ getfacl project2.txt
# file: project2.txt
# owner: root
# group: root
user::rw-
user:student9:r--
group::r--
mask::r--
other::r--

student@ubuntu20:/projects$ ▮
```

The `setfacl` command uses the `-m` option to modify the access control list already in place.

ACL Entry Examples

Consider the following examples. Note the ability to manage users, groups, or both.

To set an ACL entry for usera with rwx access:

```
# setfacl -m u:usera:rwx fileA
```

To set an ACL entry for groupa with rwx access:

```
# setfacl -m g:groupa:rwx fileA
```

To set an ACL entry usera with rwx access and group sales with rw access:

```
# setfacl -m u:userA:rwx,g:sales:rw fileA
```

To remove an ACL entry for usera for fileA:

```
# setfacl -x u:usera fileA
```

 ACL settings do not replace standard permissions. Standard permissions are still enforced as described earlier in this Lesson, but they are further enhanced by ACL capability.

Troubleshoot ACL Issues

Like troubleshooting standard permissions issues, ACL troubleshooting involves displaying the existing ACL entries by using the `getfacl` command and ensuring they are set as expected. If they are not, use `setfacl` to configure the correct entries in the ACL.

It is also common to see access control issues based on identities and group memberships, so be sure to confirm the user is signed in with an identity that should have access. Adjust group memberships as needed with the `usermod` command.

Review Activity:

ACL Configuration

Answer the following questions:

1. Explain the benefit offered by ACLs compared to standard Linux permissions.

2. What commands are used to set ACL entries for USERA with rwx and USERB with r-- for fileA?

3. Does the ACL structure replace standard permissions?

Lesson 3

Summary

The identity of a user or a user's membership in a particular group governs access to files and directories. This access control, provided mainly by permissions, allows the possible viewing, editing, or running of files. Additional controls, such as attributes, default permissions, and access control lists, permit administrators to exercise more granular control over resources.

Guidelines

These best practices and guidelines are provided for your use as revision tools or as quick references in your job role.

- Understand the principle of least privilege, which enforces the idea that users should be given as little access to resources as necessary for them to do their jobs, with no additional unneeded access.

- Recognize access levels and identities.

- Absolute mode and symbolic mode provide the same information in different ways. Absolute mode displays in octal numerals, while symbolic mode displays information using operators.

- The immutable flag is an attribute of a file or directory that prevents it from being modified, even by the root user.

Command Reference Table

This list of commands and their associated syntax can also be found in Appendix B.

Command	Syntax	Purpose	Covered in
umask	`umask {number}`	Alter the default permissions on newly created files and directories.	Lesson 3, Topic A
chmod	`chmod [options] {mode} {file/directory name}`	Modify the permissions of a file or directory.	Lesson 3, Topic A
chown	Varies based on desired outcome: • Change the owner but not the group: `chown {newowner} {filename}` • Change both the owner and the group: `chown {newowner}:{newgroup} {filename}` • Change the group but not the owner: `chown :{newgroup} {filename}`	Change the owner, the group, or both for a file or directory.	Lesson 3, Topic A

Command	Syntax	Purpose	Covered in
chgrp	chgrp {group name} {file/directory name}	Change the group ownership of a file or directory.	Lesson 3, Topic A
lsattr	lsattr [options] {file/directory names}	List attributes of a file or a directory.	Lesson 3, Topic A
chattr	chattr [-R] [-v {version}] [+- {attributes}] {file/directory names}	Change attributes of a file or a directory.	Lesson 3, Topic A
getfacl	getfacl {filename}	Retrieve the ACLs of files and directories.	Lesson 3, Topic C
setfacl	setfacl [-bR] [-mx {acl_spec}] {file/directory names}	Change the permissions associated with the ACL of a file or directory.	Lesson 3, Topic C

Lesson 4

Implementing File Management

LESSON INTRODUCTION

This Lesson covers the Filesystem Hierarchy Standard (FHS) that defines consistent locations for data across the various Linux distributions and makes it easier for users to navigate among directories to find and manage files and directories. Users rely on an understanding of the FHS to perform file management tasks such as creating and deleting resources. This Lesson covers the necessary commands to perform these file operations. In addition, commands such as find and locate are used to search for resources using many different parameters.

Lesson Objectives

In this lesson, you will:

- Understand the Linux file system.

- Use file management commands.

- Locate files.

Topic 4A

Understand the Linux File System

EXAM OBJECTIVES COVERED
1.1 Summarize Linux fundamentals.
1.2 Given a scenario, manage files and directories.
3.1 Given a scenario, create simple shell scripts to automate common tasks.

Linux relies on a standardized series of directories to organize data into a filesystem. The benefit of such standardization is that both administrators and applications know where to find specific types of data. Configuration files are held in one consistent location, and log files are held in a different consistent location. This filesystem is named the Filesystem Hierarchy Standard (FHS). Sysadmins must understand what types of files are held where. Navigate to these locations utilizing paths, which may be defined from the root of the filesystem (represented by the forward slash character) or from the user's present location. Files may also be linked, making their contents accessible from multiple locations within the filesystem. This is usually done for convenience.

Linux File Organization

While there are a great many Linux distributions—thousands of them with varied utilities for varied uses—there are a few things the distros have in common. These common features allow compatibility between Linux offers and permit a certain amount of comfort and standardization with regard to where to find specific types of files. For example, Linux distributions store most configurations in the `/etc` directory, most users have a private directory in the `/home` directory, and log files are found in `/var/log`. Such standardization allows software installers to expect resources in certain locations and sysadmins to anticipate where particular settings can be found.

This standardization is achieved via the Filesystem Hierarchy Standard (FHS).

The Filesystem Hierarchy Standard

The **Filesystem Hierarchy Standard (FHS)** is a collaborative document that specifies a set of guidelines for the names of files and directories and their locations on Linux systems. Most Linux distributions are FHS-compliant and therefore support compatibility with other systems. The FHS also creates a naming convention that helps administrators, users, and applications consistently find the files they are looking for as well as store files where other entities can easily find them.

As defined in the FHS, the top-most directory in a Linux **file system** is the root directory, indicated by a single forward slash (/). Below the root directory are various subdirectories that are standardized as part of the FHS.

Standard Subdirectories

`/bin` - Stores essential command-line utilities and binaries. For example, the **/bin/ls** is the binary for the `ls` command.

`/boot` - Stores the files necessary to boot the Linux operating system.

`/dev` - Stores hardware and software device drivers. This directory maintains file system entries that represent the devices connected to the system (for example, the `/dev/sda1` partition).

`/etc` - Stores basic configuration files. For example, the `/etc/ samba/smb. conf` file stores Samba configuration data.

`/home` - Stores users' home directories, including personal files.

`/lib` - Stores shared program libraries required by the kernel, command-line utilities, and binaries.

`/media` - Stores mount points for removable media such as CD-ROMs and floppy disks.

`/mnt` - This is the mount point for temporarily mounting file systems.

`/opt` - Stores optional files of large software packages. These packages normally create a subdirectory bearing their name under the `/opt` directory and then place their files in the subdirectory. For example, the `/opt/nessus` subdirectory contains files for the Nessus vulnerability scanning program.

`/proc` - This is a **virtual file system (VFS)** that represents continually updated kernel information to the user in a typical file format (for example, the `/proc/mounts` file).

`/root` - The home directory of the root user.

`/sbin` - Stores binaries that are used for completing the booting process and also the ones that are used by the root user. For example, the `/sbin/ifconfig` file is the binary for the `ifconfig` command that is used to manage network interfaces on the system.

`/sys` - This is another VFS, and it primarily stores information about devices. For example, `/sys/block` includes links to devices that are stored in various subdirectories under the `/sys/ devices/` location, which presents a hierarchy of devices in the kernel.

`/tmp` - Stores temporary files that may be lost on system shutdown.

`/usr` - A read-only directory that stores small programs and files accessible to all users.

> The `/usr` directory contains some important subdirectories.
> - `/usr/bin` - Includes executable programs that can be executed by all users.
> - `/usr/local` - Includes custom build applications that are stored here by default.
> - `/usr/lib` - Includes object libraries and internal binaries that are needed by the executable programs.
> - `/usr/lib64` - Serves the same purpose as `/usr/lib`, except it is meant only for 64-bit systems.
> - `/usr/share` - Includes read-only architecture independent files. These files can be shared among different architectures of an operating system.

`/var` - Stores variable files, or files that are expected to constantly change as the system runs. Examples include log files, printer spools, and some networking services' configuration files.

 The FHS is displayed by running the following command: `ls /` *(recall that the forward slash represents the root of the filesystem).*

Key Directories

The critical directories to know from the FHS are `/etc`, `/home`, `/root`, and `/var/log`.

/etc

The `/etc` directory contains files and subdirectories that hold configuration information for the system and its services. It's reasonable to assume that if you need to adjust firewall rules, manage **Secure Shell (SSH)** access, or configure software-management settings, you will need to work with files stored in `/etc`.

/home

The home directory contains a user's personal files or files that are otherwise specific to that user. The home directory is where you are placed when you log in to the system. In Linux, by default, every user except the root user is assigned a subdirectory in `/home` that corresponds to their user name. A user can create subdirectories and files within this directory.

The home directory path is set to a variable named $HOME. When the string $HOME is used, it references the path to the current user's home directory, such as `/home/student-user`. This text will often reference the home directory using the $HOME variable. In many shells, including KornShell, C shell, and Bash, the tilde character (~) represents your home directory.

```
student@ubuntu20:~$ ls -a
.                  .bashrc    Documents   Music      .ssh
..                 .cache     Downloads   Pictures   .sudo_as_admin_successful
.bash_history      .config    .gnupg      .profile   Templates
.bash_logout       Desktop    .local      Public     Videos
student@ubuntu20:~$
```

Output of the `ls -a` command.

/root

The home directory of the root user is `/root`. This is not to be confused with the root directory (/), which is the top-most part of the file system hierarchy.

/var/log

Linux and installed services typically write to log files stored in the `/var/log` directory. As a sysadmin investigating a system issue or auditing system access, you will likely find the information required in log files stored at `/var/log`.

Familiarity with all of the directories is important, but the directories listed above are more commonly used and accessed.

Display File Metadata

When examining files it can be useful to display information such as permissions, size, storage location, modification times, etc. The `ls` command has options that provide much of this data, but the output may not be very clear. The `stat` and `file` commands provide good information about file properties.

Use the stat and file Commands

The `stat` command displays file metadata in a relatively user-friendly structure. File size, access information, storage data, and more are displayed. Use the man page to display various options that supplement `stat`.

The syntax for the `stat` command is `stat {filename}`

The `file` command displays different metadata. Specifically, it examines the file type and provides information based on that. It may show PDF version information for .pdf files or image information for .jpg files. Such information is used to ensure compatible applications are available to work with the files.

The syntax for the `file` command is `file {filename}`

```
student@ubuntu20:~$
student@ubuntu20:~$ file test
test: ASCII text
student@ubuntu20:~$ stat test
  File: test
  Size: 5            Blocks: 8          IO Block: 4096    regular file
Device: 805h/2053d       Inode: 4984263      Links: 1
Access: (0664/-rw-rw-r--)  Uid: ( 1000/ student)   Gid: ( 1000/ student)
Access: 2021-12-31 12:14:22.467906100 -0700
Modify: 2021-12-31 12:14:18.235906100 -0700
Change: 2021-12-31 12:14:18.235906100 -0700
 Birth: -
student@ubuntu20:~$
```

Output of the `file` and `stat` commands.

File Naming Conventions

A file name is a string of characters that identify a file. By using the right combination of characters in file names, you can ensure that the files are unique and easy to recognize. On an ext4 file system, a file name may be up to 255 bytes long and contain any byte except NULL (\0) and the forward slash (/). File names of user files may not be a single dot . or two dots .. because these are special, reserved file names. Various file systems may enforce different requirements for file names. Although file names may contain a space, convention on Linux systems dictates that words in a file name are more frequently demarcated by a hyphen or an underscore, as these are easier to manage on the command-line. For example, `auditfile`.txt or `audit_file`.txt are acceptable

Absolute and Relative Paths

A **path** defines the series of directories to be traversed to find a specific file (or subdirectory). For example, if a text file is stored in the resources directory of your home directory, the path defines what directories to travel through to arrive at the file. There are two types of paths: absolute and relative.

Absolute Path

The **absolute path** defines the directories to traverse, starting from the root of the filesystem. Recall that the filesystem root is depicted using a forward slash character (/). The absolute path is the complete path from the top of the directory structure.

Suppose a user named student-user wants to find the `widgets.txt` file, which is stored in the inventory subdirectory of the resources directory of their home folder. The absolute path is:

`/home/student-user/resources/inventory/widgets.txt`

Relative Path

A **relative path** is dependent upon the user's current location in the filesystem. Using the above scenario, if the user is already in their home directory, then the entire path is unneeded, and all that needs to be specified is the remainder of the path from the current location. Assuming the user is in their home directory, the relative path is:

`resources/inventory/widgets.txt`

In other words, relative to your current location, what's the rest of the path?

 It is a good practice to use absolute paths in resources such as scripts and configuration files. Relative paths may be different depending on where the file resource executes from.

Configure File Links

The `ln` command creates a link to a file. Linking enables a file name in one directory (the link) to point to a file in another directory (the target). A link does not contain data of its own. It only contains a reference to the target file. Any changes to the link will reflect in the target file. If you don't specify the link name, the `ln` command will create the link in your **current working directory (CWD)**.

Helpdesk Ticket #01990

Submitted by:	Department:	Assigned to:	Date Opened:
Ali Selassi	**Marketing**	*you*	**2024-05-02**

Subject	Shorter path option?
Ticket Detail	Hello, I'm regularly using a file that is buried in a bunch of subfolders (the path is: /projects/2022/finance/YTDsales/Final/salesdata.txt). Can you help me with an easier way to access this file rather than drilling down the directory branches over and over?
Response	Sure, I've set up a soft link in your home directory.
	Look for the file at /home/aselassi and let me know if you need anything else.
Date last updated	2024-05-03

Understand Inodes

An **index node (inode)** is an object that stores metadata about a file or directory on a file system. This metadata can include time-based values such as when a file was created and last modified, permission and ownership information, the block locations of a file's data on a storage device, and other miscellaneous information.

Each inode on a file system is identified by a unique integer called an inode number. Whenever the system or an application tries to access a file, it searches for the appropriate inode number in a data structure called an inode table. The inode table maps an inode number to its corresponding file or directory name.

Some file systems set a maximum number of inodes when that file system is created, usually by considering the overall size of the file system. The total number of files and directories cannot exceed this inode maximum. However, some file system types, such as **XFS**, use a dynamic inode allocation system that scales as a percentage of the file system's capacity. In other words, these file systems do not set a strict inode limit.

 Use the `ls -i` *command to list the inode numbers for files and directories.*

Link Types

Using the `ln` command, you can create two types of links: hard and symbolic (soft). Hard and symbolic links are a feature of the file system and are common in most file systems supported by Linux. The **ext2**, **ext3**, **ext4**, and XFS file systems all support hard and symbolic links.

The syntax of the `ln` command is `ln [options] {target name} {link name}`

The `ln` command has various options. Some of these options include:

Option for the ln Command	Purpose
`--backup`	Back up existing destination files.
`-f`	Remove existing destination files.
`-s`	Make symbolic links instead of hard links.
`-i`	Prompt to remove destination files.
`-v`	Print the name of a file before linking.

Configure Hard Links

A **hard link** is a reference to another file; it enables the file's data to have more than one name in different locations in the same file system. Applications treat a hard link as a real file. If the original file is deleted after a hard link is created, all its contents will still be available in the linked file. This is because the inode of a hard link is the same as its target; in other words, it points to the same object on the file system. Hard links cannot be created between two directories, nor can they be created between two files in different file systems.

The syntax for hard links is `ln /business-docs/current-projects.txt ~/projects.txt`

Configure Symbolic Links

A **symbolic link** is a reference to a file or directory that can span multiple file systems. If the original file or directory is deleted after a symbolic link is created, then the original content is lost. This is because the inode of a symbolic link is different from its target; in other words, it points to a different object on the file system. A symbolic link is also known as a soft link.

The syntax for symbolic links is `ls -s /business-docs/current-projects.txt ~/projects.txt`

Use the long format display of the list command to view link information: `ls -l`

Symbolic links are often referred to as "sym links" for short.

```
student@ubuntu20:~/linkdemo$ ls -il
total 0
395726 -rw-rw-r-- 2 student student 0 Dec 31 12:15 file1
395726 -rw-rw-r-- 2 student student 0 Dec 31 12:15 fileA
395758 lrwxrwxrwx 1 student student 5 Dec 31 12:16 sym-file1 -> file1
student@ubuntu20:~/linkdemo$ ▮
```

Symbolic link output, showing the "sym-file1" string.

Review Activity:

The Linux File System

Answer the following questions:

1. **You are installing a new application on your Linux system. The documentation states that configuration files and log files will be added to your system. Where will these files likely be stored, and how does the FHS make such installations easier?**

2. **You are in the new-projects directory, which is stored in the projects directory within your home directory. What is the absolute path to the new-projects directory?**

3. **A user submits a ticket regarding a file access issue. The first file, projectA.txt, had a second hard link named my-project.txt. The same data was available via either link. The user deleted the my-project.txt file, and the data was still available via projectA.txt. The second file, projectB.txt, had a sym link that pointed to the projectB.txt link. When the projectB.txt link was deleted, the data was no longer available via the sym link. The user wants to know why the first file is still available after a link deletion but the second is not.**

Topic 4B

Use File Management Commands

EXAM OBJECTIVES COVERED
1.2 Given a scenario, manage files and directories.
3.1 Given a scenario, create simple shell scripts to automate common tasks.

Once the FHS is familiar, navigation among directories is much easier. Commands such as `pwd` and `cd` allow users to understand where in the filesystem they are and how to move to another location. Over the years, shortcuts have been added to reduce the amount of typing at the command prompt. Users must manage file operations—tasks such as moving, copying, creating, and deleting files and directories—to manage their data correctly. Users must also be able to redirect information into or out of files.

Navigate Directories

Directories store system configuration files, user data, log files, and other resources. Linux users move from directory to directory by using various navigation commands. Shortcuts make the navigation process quicker and simpler.

Knowing how to navigate through the directories allows Linux users to understand specific directory navigation information such as:

- Where in the file system you are.

- How to change where in the filesystem you are.

- How to use shortcuts to get where you want to go.

Navigation Shortcuts

Absolute and relative paths clearly delineate how to travel from one directory to another, but over the decades, shortcuts have been established to make common tasks easier.

The single dot character (represented by " . ") means "here" or this directory. If your present working directory is `/home/USERNAME/resources`, then that path can be abbreviated as a dot: .

The term **parent directory** refers to whatever directory is above the current directory. If your current location is `/home/USERNAME/resources/inventory`, then the parent directory of inventory is resources. The parent directory of resources is USERNAME. The parent directory is often referenced in commands (particularly with `cd`), and it has been abbreviated as two dots (represented by " . . "). In the above scenario, the result of typing `cd . .` is to move to the resources directory. This is far less typing than the absolute path of `/Home/USERNAME/resources`.

One of the most useful shortcuts is the tilde symbol (~). This abbreviation means the home directory of the currently logged-in user. This is incredibly handy. A user could type `cd ~` instead of `cd /home/USERNAME` to jump to their home directory. The ~ can be combined with many other commands covered below, including copy and paste functions.

Using the `cd` *command to return to your home directory is so common that even the* `~` *is strictly necessary. If you type* `cd` *with no argument (path), Bash assumes you wish to return to your home directory.*

```
student@ubuntu20:~$ cd /tmp
student@ubuntu20:/tmp$ pwd
/tmp
student@ubuntu20:/tmp$ cd /home/student/
student@ubuntu20:~$ pwd
/home/student
student@ubuntu20:~$ cd /tmp
student@ubuntu20:/tmp$ pwd
/tmp
student@ubuntu20:/tmp$ cd ~
student@ubuntu20:~$ pwd
/home/student
student@ubuntu20:~$ cd /tmp
student@ubuntu20:/tmp$ pwd
/tmp
student@ubuntu20:/tmp$ cd
student@ubuntu20:~$ pwd
/home/student
student@ubuntu20:~$
```

A command-line output showing all three ways (`/home/student/`*, *`~`*, and *`cd`*) of getting "home."*

Change Directories

The `cd` command moves your present working directory to another directory. For example, if you type `pwd` and discover you are currently in your home directory, then you could type `cd /etc` to move to the `/etc` directory, where many configuration files are stored.

The `cd` command is the primary filesystem navigation command in Bash.

The syntax for the `cd` command is `cd {path}`

Note that either an absolute or relative path can be specified, depending on your current location in the filesystem and the desired destination. To traverse the filesystem to the inventory subdirectory in the resources directory of your home directory, type the following:

```
cd /home/USERNAME/resources/inventory
```

Know Your Location

The critical piece of knowledge for navigation is to know your current location. In Linux, this is referred to as the "present working directory," and the `pwd` command displays that. The output is an absolute path from the root of the filesystem to the directory the shell is currently focused on. The output from `pwd` may be used to confirm your location before a backup job, a file transfer, or the deletion of files.

The syntax for the `pwd` command is `pwd`

```
[student@fedora ~]$ pwd
/home/student
[student@fedora ~]$ ▮
```

Output of the `pwd` command, showing that the user is in the /home/student directory.

 Some Linux distributions are configured to display the name of the current directory as part of the command prompt. Note that this is not the absolute path but merely the name of the current directory. The prompt configuration can be changed.

It may be difficult to visualize a location in the filesystem with a text-based path. This is especially true for users who are more familiar with graphical user interfaces. The `tree` command displays the filesystem in a more familiar structure, perhaps making it easier to understand a directory's location relative to other directories.

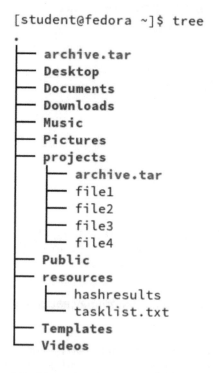

```
[student@fedora ~]$ tree
.
├── archive.tar
├── Desktop
├── Documents
├── Downloads
├── Music
├── Pictures
├── projects
│   ├── archive.tar
│   ├── file1
│   ├── file2
│   ├── file3
│   └── file4
├── Public
├── resources
│   ├── hashresults
│   └── tasklist.txt
├── Templates
└── Videos

10 directories, 8 files
```

Output of the `tree` command, showing a hierarchical representation of the directories' relationship to each other.

The syntax for the `tree` command is `tree {dirname}`

Some options commonly used with `tree` are:

Option for the tree Command	Purpose
`-a`	Display all files, including hidden files.
`-d`	Display directories only.
`-s`	Display file size.
`-D`	Display last modification date.

File Management Scenario: Starting the Project

In order to illustrate how these commands can be used, you'll walk through a common workplace scenario. In this scenario, you are responsible for managing a project through file management tasks and use of commands. You, the project manager, decide to create the appropriate directories and files to store the project. In some cases, those files will need to be copied, moved, or renamed. Once the project concludes, the files will be removed from the system. Throughout this section, observe how file management commands are used to facilitate the project management requirements.

What Directories Currently Exist?

You will store project files in your home directory. Before creating a directory structure to store the files, you want to see what directories currently exist. The command for displaying directory contents is `ls` (list).

You move to your home directory and then type `ls`. If no argument is included with `ls`, it displays the contents of the current directory. However, you can display the contents of the /etc directory by specifying the path to it.

For example, to display the contents of /etc, type:

```
# ls /etc
```

Options commonly used with `ls` include:

Option for the ls Command	Purpose
`-a`	Lists all contents, including hidden resources.
`-l`	Lists contents in long format, most useful for displaying permissions.
`-d`	Limits the output to directories but not files.
`-R`	Lists the contents of subdirectories.
`-s`	Displays the file sizes.

Two of the most useful options are `-a` and `-l`. The two can be combined, such that `ls -al ~` displays all contents of the home directory in long format (showing permissions for all files, including hidden ones).

Files where the first character is a dot (" . ") are hidden by Bash. This isn't a security feature, but rather a way of keeping some files out of the user's way. Profile files are often hidden. Use `ls -a` to display all files, including hidden files.

Create a Directory Structure

Now that you, the project manager, understand what directories currently exist, it's time to create a directory structure to hold the files and subdirectories associated with the project. The `mkdir` command creates directories along the specified path.

The syntax for `mkdir` is `mkdir {new-directory-name}`

You decide to create a single project directory, and inside that project directory you create three subdirectories:

- `$ mkdir project`
- `$ mkdir project/drafts`
- `$ mkdir project/final`
- `$ mkdir project/resources`

You'll use the `ls` or `tree` commands to display these directories.

```
student@ubuntu20:~$ mkdir project
student@ubuntu20:~$ mkdir project/drafts
student@ubuntu20:~$ mkdir project/final
student@ubuntu20:~$ mkdir project/resources
student@ubuntu20:~$ ls project
drafts   final   resources
student@ubuntu20:~$ █
```

Commands used to create a project directory with three subdirectories, and use of the `ls` command to display the directories.

Create Project Files

Files can be created using multiple methods, including text editors and copy commands. To create a simple empty file, use the `touch` command. The original purpose of `touch` is to update a file's timestamp (useful for backup programs), but one effect of the command is if the specified file doesn't already exist, it then gets created.

The syntax for `touch` is `touch {filename}`

You're now ready to create project files. First, the user types the `cd project` command to move into the project directory. Next, project files are created with touch by typing:

```
# touch newprojects.txt completedprojects.txt
timeline.txt
```

File Management Scenario: Working the Project

As project manager in our scenario, you now work through the tasks and deliverables involved in the project, having established your directories and project files.

Copy and Move Project Files

The files created in the previous section now exist in the project's directory, but they aren't well organized. The `cp` (copy) and `mv` (move) commands allow users to place files in the directory structure.

Duplicating files allows multiple copies of the same file. A common use for copying a file is as a backup. For example, before making a configuration change to a service such as SSH, it is prudent to copy the original configuration file. Doing so provides the opportunity to return the service to its original configuration if necessary.

The syntax for `cp` is `cp {sourcefile} {newfile}`

It is a common practice to copy or back up a configuration file before making significant changes to it. Doing so allows the sysadmin to return the system to an earlier configuration. For example, before making major configuration changes to the SSH service, the sysadmin might use the `cp` *command to copy the* `/etc/ssh/sshd_config` *file to* `/root/sshd_config.old`. *The .old file extension is a common way of identifying such files.*

While copying a file creates a new file (a duplicate of the original), moving a file typically places the file elsewhere in the filesystem. While the file itself may not move from its location on the hard drive, pointers to the file will be updated with a new location.

The `mv` command moves one or more files from one location to another. Like `cp`, the `mv` syntax is to specify the source location first and the destination location second.

The syntax for the `mv` command when moving a file is `mv {source-location} {destination-location}`

For example, to move a fileA from your home directory to the Projects directory in your home folder type:

```
$ mv fileA Projects
```

However, the `mv` command has a second function. It also serves as the rename command in Bash. The syntax is the same, but the terms shift to original-filename and new-filename. The syntax for the `mv` command when renaming a file is `mv {original-name} {new-name}`

For example, to rename an existing file named "sales-project.txt" to "marketing-project.txt", type:

```
$ mv sales-project.txt marketing-project.txt
```

In the project management scenario, the `cp` and `mv` commands are very useful for organizing files.

First, you'll copy the timeline.txt file to the resources directory:

```
$ cp timeline.txt resources/
```

Next, you move the newprojects.txt file to the drafts subdirectory:

```
$ mv newprojects.txt drafts/
```

Finally, the completedprojects.txt file is renamed to oldprojects.txt:

```
$ mv completedprojects.txt oldprojects.txt
```

Display Project File Contents

The `cat` command (short for concatenate) is used to combine file contents from multiple sources into one. It's much more common, however, to use the command to display file contents. This is especially useful for content that consumes less than one screen's worth of space.

The syntax for the `cat` command is `cat {filename}`

You'll use the echo command and a redirector to add some text to a file:

```
$ echo "Q1 goals" > drafts/newprojects.txt
```

Confirm the text exists in the newprojects.txt file by using the cat command:

```
$ cat drafts/newprojects.txt
```

```
student@ubuntu20:~/project/drafts$ cat newprojects.txt
Build new web site
Update inventory database
Upgrade dev workstations
```

Using the `cat` command to confirm the newly created text exists in the newprojects text file.

Redirectors such as > are covered later in this Topic.

There are many ways to display file contents besides using `cat`. A text or configuration file may be opened with a text editor such as Vim or Nano, or database resources may be accessed via database programs such as MariaDB.

File Management Scenario: Closing the Project

The final step in the life cycle of data is to dispose of the files and directories. Once a project is completed it may no longer be necessary to retain the files. The `rm` and `rmdir` commands delete files and directories.

Remove Directories and Files

At this point you wish to delete one of the directories. The directory delete command is `rmdir` with the directory name as the argument: `rmdir {dir-name}`.

If the final directory is empty, you type:

```
$ rmdir final
```

The `rm` command deletes files. Many Linux distributions are preconfigured to ask for confirmation before deleting a file (there is no undo for the `rm` command!).

You may be prompted to enter Y or N to complete the deletion process. Common options for the `rm` command include:

Option for the rm Command	Purpose
`-f`	Never prompt for confirmation (this is a dangerous course of action).
`-i`	Interactive mode, prompt for confirmation before deleting (this is usually set by default with an alias).
`-R`	Recursively removes a non-empty directory and its contents.

To delete the file, you type `rm timeline.txt`, and a `ls` of the project directory shows the file is now gone.

The `rmdir` command works on empty directories but fails with directories that contain files. The `rm` command, however, may be used to remove non-empty directories. To remove the newprojects directory and the files in it, type:

```
$ rm -fR newprojects
```

Observe that to delete an empty directory, the command is `rmdir`, but to remove a non-empty directory, the `rm` command is combined with the `-R` (recursive) option.

If the user is in their home directory, the entire project directory structure can be deleted by using the `rm` command and the `-R` option. Again, be very certain about what's being deleted before running this command:

```
$ rm -fR project
```

Use the `ls` command to confirm the project directory and its contents are gone.

Files are not recovered from the CLI. There is no concept of a trash can from which to recover deleted files. Be careful before using the `rm` and `rmdir` commands!

Summarizing the File Management Scenario

In this scenario, the project manager creates a hierarchical directory structure to store project data. The `mkdir` command creates the directories. The `touch` command creates sample text files to simulate project data. Commands such as `mv` and `cp` allow for file management, while `cat` provides a look at file contents. Finally, the `rm` and `rmdir` commands delete the resources once the project is complete.

Display Files with Additional Commands

The `cat` command is just one of the ways to display file contents. Many other commands both display the contents and permit more focus on exactly which data you wish to see. Commands such as `less` and `more` allow paging through text, while `head` and `tail` show just the beginning or end of files. The `grep` command allows for keyword searching within files or other output.

Display File Contents with less and more

Helpdesk Ticket #01991

Submitted by:	Department:	Assigned to:	Date Opened:
Kai Garcia	Engineering	*you*	2024-05-04

Subject	can't view reports
Ticket Detail	I'm pulling up a report that covers 3 years of projects, and it's impossible to read. How can I shorten the display?
Date last updated	2024-05-06

Not all file contents fit on the display. When using `cat` to display a long file, only the contents at the bottom of the file may fit on the monitor. The remainder scrolls upward, off the screen. The `less` command breaks the output into pages that fit on the screen and can be cycled through.

There are two ways of using `less`. The first is directly, as a primary command to display file contents. An example is `less long-file.txt`. The second way to use `less` is to better organize the output of other commands. For example, the /etc directory has many subdirectories and files—too many to display on the screen simultaneously. The output of a `ls` command can be redirected into `less`, which allows pagination through the output of `ls`.

The syntax for this example is `ls /etc | less`

The pipe character | is discussed later in this Topic in the redirectors section.

The `more` command is similar to `less`. The primary difference between the two commands is that with `less`, you can paginate up and down, while with `more` you can only paginate downward.

Display File Contents with head and tail

Sometimes it's useful to see only the beginning or the end of a particular file. As a general rule, configuration files have comments and instructions at the beginning or top of a file. These comments may provide guidance, version information, and examples for the file. The `head` command displays the first 10 lines of a file, giving administrators valuable information about the file.

The syntax for the `head` command is `head {filename}`

Few options exist to modify the head command. The most common option is to change the number of lines displayed from the default of 10. For example, typing `head -n 15 {filename}` will display the first 15 lines of the file.

Log files, however, have the newest information appended at the end of the file. Hence, if an administrator wishes to see the most recent log file entries, the bottom of the file must be displayed. The `tail` command, by default, shows the last 10 lines of a file. This is incredibly helpful for troubleshooting.

The `tail` command also has some very practical options. Like `head`, the `tail` command accepts the `-n` option to modify the number of displayed lines. In addition, the `-f` (or follow) option updates the output whenever the bottom of the file changes. This is useful for following log files, as the display will update whenever the log file changes.

The basic syntax for the `tail` command is `tail {filename}`

To display the last 15 lines of the file, type `tail -n 15 {filename}`. However, to follow a log file and see updated output whenever the log file changes, type `tail -f {filename}`.

Display Strings with grep

You've received a helpdesk ticket from a user who requests a keyword search of a report. Your solution in this case is to teach them `grep`.

Helpdesk Ticket #01992

Submitted by:	Department:	Assigned to:	Date Opened:
Joseph Deng	Engineering	*you*	2024-05-05

Subject	Engineering project report - search?
Ticket Detail	I need some help in searching this report by a few key terms, can you help?
Date last updated	2024-05-06

Commands such as `less` and `tail` display the specified file contents, regardless of whether it contains the data administrators or users need. These commands don't search for particular information within the file, they simply display its existing content.

The `grep` command is a pattern matcher, which is a complex way of saying it searches for strings of characters within a data stream. For text files, `grep` is a find utility that displays the specified string or search term in the output.

The grep Command

The `grep` command can be used directly on a file. For example, the command `grep error /var/log/messages` searches the messages log file for the combination of characters that spell "error." Any lines of the file containing that combination of characters in that order are displayed.

Note that `grep` is case-sensitive, so in the above example, it would match the string "error," but it would fail to display the string with a capital E "Error." The `-i` option makes `grep` case insensitive. Modifying the above example to `grep -i error /var/log/messages` would display both "error" and "Error" if those strings exist in the file. It would also match any other combination of uppercase and lowercase characters in that string.

The `grep` command provides even more functionality when combined with other commands. Many commands produce a significant amount of output, which users then have to browse through to find what they need.

The pipe character | takes the output of one command and makes it the input of another. One of the most common uses of pipe is in combination with `grep`.

The syntax for these combinations can take on several different forms.

To list all files in the /etc directory that contain the string "net" in either uppercase or lowercase:

```
student@ubuntu20:~$ ls /etc | grep -i net
issue.net
netplan
network
networkd-dispatcher
NetworkManager
networks
```

To list all files in the /home/student directory that contain the string ".txt":

```
student@ubuntu20:~$ ls /home/student | grep .txt
file1.txt
file2.txt
file3.txt
```

To check for the string "jdeng" in the /etc/passwd file:

```
student@ubuntu20:~$ grep jdeng /etc/passwd
jdeng:x:1002:1002::/home/jdeng:/bin/sh
```

To check for the string "localhost" in the /etc/hosts file:

```
student@ubuntu20:~$ grep localhost /etc/hosts
127.0.0.1       localhost
::1       ip6-localhost ip6-loopback
```

 The pipe (|) character is covered in more detail in the next section of this lesson. The ps *command is also covered later in the course.*

The egrep command is a modified version of grep and functions similarly from the user perspective, but this utility is deprecated in favor of grep -E.

Redirectors

All of this management and manipulation of files is useful for more than just looking at the results in a terminal. When you use the terminal, or log out entirely, you'll want to ensure that crucial information is stored in a file for later retrieval and analysis. In addition, you'll benefit from combining multiple commands in conjunction, making your administrative duties more efficient and powerful.

Understand Text Streams

A text stream is a sequence of one or more lines of text that applications can leverage to read from or write to a particular device or system component. This enables the application to interface with components such as the CLI, files, network sockets, and more while hiding those components' details from the application. In most Linux shells, there are three stream types: standard input, standard output, and standard error.

Standard input, or stdin, is a text stream that acts as the source for command input. Standard input for the Linux command-line is usually generated from the keyboard. In the case of the GUI, the standard input can also come from the mouse.

Standard output, or stdout, is a text stream that acts as the destination for command output. By default, standard output from a Linux command is directed to the CLI.

Standard error, or stderr, is a text stream that is used as the destination for error messages. By default, the standard error stream prints error messages at the CLI.

Redirection is the process of accepting input data from a source other than the keyboard and sending output data to a destination other than the display device. In other words, you can use redirection to bypass the default devices when working with input/output (I/O). Redirection is commonly used to accept input from files or send output to files using the stdin, stdout, and stderr streams.

Use Redirection Operators

Sysadmins use several operators to redirect input or output.

Redirection Operator	Action	Example	Results
>	Redirect the standard output to a file.	ls > file1.txt	The output of the ls command is redirected to a file named file1.txt
>>	Append the standard output to the end of the destination file.	ls >> file1.txt	The output of the ls command is appended to a file named file1.txt
2>	Redirect the standard error message to a file.	ls file3.txt 2> errorfile.txt	The output will not be displayed on the screen but is redirected to a file named errorfile.txt
2>>	Append the standard error message to the end of the destination file.	ls file3.txt 2>> errorfile.txt	The output will not be displayed on the screen but is appended to a file named errorfile.txt
&>	Redirect both the standard output and the standard error message to a file.	ls file1.txt file3.txt &> errorfile.txt	The output will not be displayed on the screen but is redirected to a file named errorfile.txt

Redirection Operator	Action	Example	Results
<	Read the input from a file rather than from the keyboard or mouse.	mail user@ address < myletter.txt	The myletter.txt file is taken as the input and attached to the email message.
<<{string}	Provide input data from the current source, stopping when a line containing the provided string occurs. When placed in a script, this is called a here document.	cat <<EOF This is a here document. EOF	The cat command will use the rest of the lines in this file as input. It will stop accepting that input when it reaches the string EOF. This string can be named anything you want. The output of the cat command would therefore be: This is a here document.

Redirection operators, their syntax, and results.

Command Modifiers

Several command modifiers exist that allow users to run combinations of commands. These commands differ from redirectors in that they manipulate the command, not the output. Learning to use these effectively makes command-line administration more efficient.

Background a Command

The single ampersand & causes the command to execute in the background. Normally, when a command is executed, it consumes the shell until it completes. Some commands, such as backup scripts, may take a very long time to finish, and until the script is done, the user cannot type in additional commands or accomplish additional tasks in that shell instance. If the command runs in the background, however, it executes while the user continues to work within the shell. Such commands are referred to as jobs.

 Process and job management is covered in a later section.

The syntax is the command, followed by a space, followed by an ampersand:

```
$ sudo backupscript.sh &
```

Chain Commands

Many Linux users will simply enter one command at a time. In some cases, however, it is useful to enter multiple commands at a single command prompt. This approach is known as "chaining," and there are several tools in Bash to help you with this process.

Standard interaction with the Bash shell involves typing a command, executing the command, and then typing another command for execution. Commands can be written sequentially at a single command prompt to be processed in order. There are multiple ways of doing this.

Piping is the process of combining the standard I/O streams of commands. It uses the standard output of one command as the standard input for another command. The output format of the first command should be compatible with the format that the second command works with. The pipe operator (|) can be used with most commands in Linux.

```
$ ls -l | grep audit
```

This command, which searches for files named "audit," is an example of using a pipe. The standard output of the `ls -l` command is fed as standard input into the `grep audit` command so that `grep` searches for the term within the directory listing.

Chain Operator Character	Common Name	Results
;	semicolon	If the semi-colon character is placed between commands, they are run one after another, regardless of whether the previous command completed successfully.
&&	logical AND	If the logical AND is placed between commands, the following command is only run after the previous command completed successfully. Useful for commands that rely on each other's success.
||	logical OR	If the logical OR is placed between commands, the following command is only run if the previous command fails.
!	bang	If the bang is placed in a command expression, it negates the expression. Used as a way of stating "except this."

 Many of these command chains and redirectors are used in scripts. Scripts are covered in a later section.

These command modifiers do not use a typical or regular syntax. Instead, they are used between commands to modify certain portions of the command expressions.

To run a series of commands one after another:

```
$ backupscript.sh;rmdir /projects;mkdir holidays.txt
```

To run a series of commands that rely on the success of the previous command:

```
$ backupscript.sh && rmdir /projects
```

To run a second command only if the first command fails:

```
$ backupscript.sh || cp projects /tmp
```

The tee Command

The `tee` command reads the standard input, sends the output to the default output device (the CLI), and also copies the output to each specified file. This command enables you to verify the output of a command immediately as well as store that output in a file for later reference. It accepts input from another command using the pipe operator. When used with the `-a` option, tee appends the output to each output file instead of overwriting it.

The general syntax of the `tee` command is `command [options] [arguments] | tee [options] {file names}`

Let's say you want to check the contents of a directory and also output those contents to a file to process later. You could issue separate commands to do this, or you can use the `tee` command in the following manner: `ls -l | tee listing.txt`

The xargs Command

The `xargs` command reads from standard input and executes a command for each argument provided. Each argument must be separated by spaces. The pipe operator is used to make the output of the first command the input for the second command. The `xargs` command is commonly used with the `find` command to operate on each result that is found within the file or directory search.

The general syntax of the `xargs` command is `command [options] [arguments] | xargs [options] {command}`

Let's say you want to delete all of the files in the `/projects` directory that have a .pdf extension. You can use `xargs` to automate the process: `find /projects -type f -name "*.pdf" | xargs rm`. The `find` command searches for all files in `/projects` that have a .pdf extension, then pipes the result to the `xargs` command. Because the results are delimited by a space, the `xargs` command will execute the `rm` command for each file in the results— removing all PDF files in the directory.

The `xargs` command has several common options.

Option for the xargs Command	Purpose
`-I {replacement string}`	Consider each line in the standard input as a single argument.
`-L {number of lines}`	Read a specified number of lines from the standard input, and concatenate them into one long string.
`-p`	Prompt the user before each command.
`-n {number of arguments}`	Read the maximum number of arguments from the standard input, and insert them at the end of the command template.
`-E {end of string}`	Represent the end of the standard input.
`-t`	Write each command to the standard error output before executing the command.
`-s {max size}`	Set the maximum allowable size of an argument list to a specified number of characters.

Review Activity:

File Management Commands

Answer the following questions:

1. You have been assigned a helpdesk ticket to answer a user question. The user is attempting to rename files but cannot find the rename command. What command do you teach the user?

2. A user asks how to delete a directory named /projects containing 100 directories. The user does not want to delete the files individually and does not want to be prompted to confirm the deletion of each file. What is the appropriate command expression, and why?

3. A user complains that they redirected the output from several commands into a text file, but the only content that appears in the file is the output from the most recent command. How would you explain to the user what happened and how to correct the problem?

Topic 4C

Find File Locations

EXAM OBJECTIVES COVERED
3.1 Given a scenario, create simple shell scripts to automate common tasks.

Users and sysadmins may struggle to find older files managed by the system and applications. The `find` command permits users to search for files based on specific parameters such as name, ownership, permissions, and more. Users can use commands such as `which` to discover where files were executed. Finally, many file manipulation commands, such as `sed`, `awk`, `wc`, `echo`, and others, help sysadmins find data available within files.

Search Commands

Even though the Linux filesystem is fairly well organized by the Filesystem Hierarchy Standard, and users have file management options with `mkdir`, `mv`, and `grep` commands, sometimes files are lost or their location is unknown. The primary command for searching for files using parameters is the `find` command. The `locate` command is an alternative that may make searching easier in a very large filesystem. Finally, the `which` command displays where a command executable file is stored.

The find Command

Helpdesk Ticket #01993

Submitted by:	Department:	Assigned to:	Date Opened:
Joseph Deng	**Engineering**	*you*	**2024-05-10**

Subject	lost file - help!
Ticket Detail	I cannot find my file NICspecs.txt, it's just gone. How can I get it back?
Response	Hi Joseph, you can search by the file name or by the file owner using the `find` command.
Date last updated	2024-05-10

The `find` command searches the filesystem for files that match the given parameters. These parameters might be file size, modification date, owner, or even permissions. The `find` command is a powerful tool for managing files.

The syntax for `find` is more complicated than some other commands. The general syntax is:

```
# find {where to search} {search criteria}
```

For example, to search for a file named "business-plan.txt" in the projects directory within your home directory, type:

```
# find -name business-plan.txt /home/USERNAME/
projects
```

The `-name` option specifies to search by name.

Option for the find Command	Purpose
`-name`	Search by name.
`-type f`	Search by resource type file.
`-type d`	Search by resource type directory.
`-perm`	Search by permissions level.

For example, to search for any files in the `/etc` directory with the rwx permissions for ugo, type:

```
# find /etc -perm 777
```

Though this example uses absolute mode, `find` is capable of interpreting symbolic mode as well.

```
[student@fedora ~]$ find /home/student/ -perm 664
/home/student/.config/enchant/en_US.dic
/home/student/.config/enchant/en_US.exc
/home/student/archive.tar
/home/student/projects/archive.tar
/home/student/projects/file1
/home/student/projects/file2
/home/student/projects/file3
/home/student/projects/file4
/home/student/resources/tasklist.txt
/home/student/resources/hashresults
[student@fedora ~]$ █
```

A search by permissions of the `/home/student` *directory returns only those files with the 664 access level.*

The locate and updatedb Commands

The `find` command is not the only search option for the filesystem. The `locate` command can also search for files and directories along a specified path. `Locate` relies on an index database for its search. While locate may be quicker due to this index, it's only accurate when the index is current.

The syntax for the locate command is `locate [options] {string}`

Sometimes the search you're doing should ignore uppercase and lowercase characters. The `-i` option disables case sensitivity.

For example, to search for a file named "reports.txt" in the current directory, type:

```
# locate reports.txt.
```

The `updatedb` command is used to both build and update a database of files based on the `/etc/updatedb.conf` file. The database itself is located at `/var/lib/mlocate/mlocate.db`. The configuration file can be set to exclude particular directories that should not be indexed by the utility.

Comparing find and locate Commands

The `locate` command searches a database and retrieves information on files present on the system. However, failure to keep this database updated may produce outdated results. The `find` command, on the other hand, performs a live search of the filesystem and may concentrate on a specific location. The `find` command may take more time to complete a search than the locate command.

The which Command

The `which` command displays the complete path of a specified command by searching the directories assigned to the PATH variable. For example, upon entering `which cat`, the following output is displayed: `/bin/cat`.

The `which` command can help you locate where a program has been installed. It can also help identify which version of a command you're using if there are multiple binaries of the command stored in different locations. By identifying where a command is running, you can troubleshoot unexpected behavior more easily.

The syntax for the `which` command is `which {command}`

```
[student@fedora ~]$ which cat
/usr/bin/cat
[student@fedora ~]$ which tail
/usr/bin/tail
[student@fedora ~]$
```

Using the `which` *command to display the complete path of a command.*

File Manipulation Commands

Various commands are available to manipulate existing files or to display file information. These commands might append text to files, conduct find-and-replace operations, count words or characters in a file, sort file contents, or compare the contents of two files.

The echo Command

The `echo` command is used to display a line of text on the terminal. You can also use the `echo` command to write text to a file by providing the string after the `echo` command and redirecting to the file.

The syntax of the `echo` command is `echo {string}`

The printf Command

The `printf` command is similar to `echo` but provides the user with much more control over how the output is formatted. You can supply various format characters within the text you want to output, using a backslash (\) to indicate when they are being used. For example,

```
$ printf "Hello.\nWhat's your name?"
```

will print:

```
Hello.
What's your name?
```

This is because `\n` is the newline format character, and it automatically adds a new line wherever it is placed.

The `printf` command also supports conversion characters, which use a percent sign (%) to indicate when they are being used. Conversion characters are typically used in scripts to change the output of a variable, like dictating the number of decimal places to print after a precise calculation.

The tr Command

The `tr` command is used to translate a string of characters. It is predominantly used to change the case of letters in a file. This command acts only on a stream of characters and does not accept file names as arguments. You must use redirection to actually change a file.

The syntax of the `tr` command is `tr {character 1} {character 2}` where {character 1} is the character to be replaced.

The wc Command

The word count (`wc`) command is used to count the number of lines, words, and characters in a text file. If multiple files are specified, then the command displays the counts for each file and the total count for all files.

The syntax of the `wc` command is `wc [options] {file-names}`

The `wc` command provides various options that enable you to specify the nature of the output.

Option for the wc Command	Purpose
`-c`	Display the byte count.
`-m`	Display the character count.
`-l`	Display the newline count.
`-w`	Display the word count.

Here is an example of combining the find command with `wc` to display how many files in the `/sales` directory match the search parameters of 775 permissions:

```
$ find /sales -perm 775 | wc -l
```

The sort Command

The `sort` command arranges the lines within a file. Some of the most common `sort` command options are in this table.

Option for the sort Command	Purpose
`-k{column numbers]`	Specify field values. For example, -k2 indicates the second field.
`-n`	Compare and sort lines based on the string numerical value.
`-r`	Sort fields in descending order. By default, the fields are sorted in ascending order.
`-t{delimiter}`	Separate one field from another.

The syntax of the `sort` command is `sort [options] {file-names}`

The cut Command

The `cut` command extracts the specified lines of text from a file using any of the common options found in this table.

Option for the cut Command	Purpose
`-c`	Specify the number of the character to cut from each line.
`-d{delimiter}`	Separate one field from another.
`-f{field numbers}`	Specify the field numbers to cut, as separated by the delimiter. For example, -f2 indicates the field between the first and second instances of the delimiter.
`-s`	Suppress a line if the delimiter is not found.

The syntax of the `cut` command is `cut [options] {file-names}`

The paste Command

The `paste` command is used to merge lines from text files horizontally. Each line of an initial file is a row in the first column; using `paste`, you specify a second file, and every line of the second file becomes a row in a newly created second column. By default, the `paste` command uses a tab space delimiter to separate each column. You can use the `-d` option to specify a different delimiter.

For example, you have a file named `cities` that contains the city names New York, Tokyo, London, and Lima. You have a second file named `countries` that lists the four corresponding countries United States, Japan, United Kingdom, and Peru. The output of `paste -d , cities countries` merges the two:

- New York,United States

- Tokyo,Japan

- London,United Kingdom

- Lima,Peru

The diff Command

The `diff` command is used to compare text files. The command displays the two files and the differences between them. Using various symbols, the output suggests how you can change one file to make it identical to the other. Each symbol has a special meaning. The less-than symbol (<) with a line after it means that line should be removed from the first file because it doesn't appear in the second. The greater-than symbol (>) with a line after it means that line should be added from the second file. In addition, the `diff` command also denotes the line numbers for each file that would be affected by deletion, addition, and change operations.

The syntax of the `diff` command is `diff {file-name 1} {file-name 2}`

You can specify the nature of the output with these options:

Option for the diff Command	Purpose
`-b`	Ignore spacing differences.
`-i`	Ignore case differences.
`-t`	Expand tab characters in output lines.
`-w`	Ignore spacing differences and tabs.
`-c`	Display a list of differences with three lines of context.
`-u`	Output results in unified mode, which presents a more streamlined format.

The awk Command

The `awk` command performs pattern matching on files. It is based on the AWK programming language. The `awk` keyword is followed by the pattern, the action to be performed, and the file name. The action to be performed is given within curly braces. The pattern and the action to be performed should be specified within single quotes. If the pattern is not specified, the action is performed on all input data. Similarly, if the action is not specified, the entire line is printed.

The `awk` command can be executed from the command-line or from within an AWK script file. The `awk` command can be used to process text files in a variety of ways, such as extracting text matching a certain pattern, deleting text matching a certain pattern, adding text matching a certain pattern, and many more.

The syntax of the `awk` command is `awk [options] ['patterns {actions}'] {file-names}`

In `awk` scripts, you can provide patterns along with blocks of code. If a pattern matches any line in the input file, the code block in the script will be executed.

For example, the following `awk` query retrieves all records in the `example.txt` file beginning with "a", "b", or "c":

```
$ awk '/[abc]/' example.txt
```

To retrieve all records whose first field contains the value "abc" from the example.txt file, type `awk awk "abc" example.txt`

The sed Command

The `sed` or stream editor command is a program that you can use to modify text files according to various parameters. The `sed` command can also be used for global search and replace actions.

Some of the more common options for `sed` are:

Options for the sed Command	Purpose
d	Delete the lines that match a specific pattern or line number.
-n,p	Print only the lines that contain the pattern.
s	Substitute the first occurrence of the string in the file.
s,g	Globally substitute the original string with the replacement string for each occurrence in the file.

The general syntax of the `sed` command is `sed {'option/address/action'} {file-names}`

Addresses tell `sed` to act only on certain lines or to act only on text that matches a given regular expression pattern. They are optional. Addresses are followed by the action to be performed when a match is found. The last argument is the name of the input file. The option, address, and action parameters are typically enclosed within single quotation marks.

Review Activity:

File Location

Answer the following questions:

1. You are conducting a security audit and need to document user access to log files—specifically whether any files are world-readable or whether any allow rwx access to all users. How can the find command be used in such a project, and what specific command might you use?

2. A coworker on the helpdesk team is troubleshooting an issue where a user is attempting to run a command, but the command is not executing. Your coworker needs to discover where the command executes from as part of the troubleshooting process. What command(s) can you suggest?

3. A senior sysadmin suggests that commands such as sed, awk, and sort are just as useful in automation as at the command-line. How might commands such as these be used in automation?

Lesson 4

Summary

Data stored on a Linux system is organized using directories. Because there are many different Linux distributions, directories are standardized into the Filesystem Hierarchy Standard to allow compatibility for both users and applications. Linux users must understand their current location in the filesystem and how to interpret paths to other locations. These skills are directly related to file operations and management, which involves the creation and deletion of files and directories. Often, users will search the filesystem for resources needed.

Guidelines

These best practices and guidelines are provided for your use as revision tools or as quick references in your job role.

- Recognize file management commands

- Display all file contents by using `cat`

- Display the end of file contents by using `tail`

- Display file contents in a paginated format by using `less`

- Use redirectors to place command output into files.

- Use redirectors to send command output as the input for additional commands

Command Reference Table

This list of commands and their associated syntax can also be found in Appendix B.

Command	Syntax	Purpose	Covered in
`stat`	`stat {file-name}`	Display file metadata in a relatively user-friendly structure.	Lesson 4, Topic A
`file`	`file {file-name}`	Display file information based on the file type.	Lesson 4, Topic A
`ln`	`ln [options] {target-name} {link-name}`	Create links, either hard or symbolic.	Lesson 4, Topic A
`cd`	`cd {path}`	Move your present working directory to another directory.	Lesson 4, Topic B

Command	Syntax	Purpose	Covered in
`tree`	`tree {directory-name}`	Display the filesystem in a hierarchical structure, perhaps making it easier to understand a directory's location relative to other directories.	Lesson 4, Topic B
`mkdir`	`mkdir {new-directory-name}`	Create directories along the specified path.	Lesson 4, Topic B
`cp`	`cp {source-file} {new-file}`	Copy a file into a new location while retaining the source file in its original location.	Lesson 4, Topic B
`mv`	`mv {source-location} {destination-location}`	Place the file elsewhere in the filesystem.	Lesson 4, Topic B
`mv`	`mv {original-filename} {new-filename}`	The rename command in Bash.	Lesson 4, Topic B
`rmdir`	`rmdir {directory-name}`	Remove (delete) a directory with no files in it.	Lesson 4, Topic B
`rm`	`rm [options] {file-name}`	Remove (delete) a file or a non-empty directory.	Lesson 4, Topic B
`head`	`head {file-name}`	Display the first 10 lines of a file.	Lesson 4, Topic B
`tail`	`tail {file-name}`	Display the last 10 lines of a file.	Lesson 4, Topic B
`grep`	`grep {character-string]`	Search for strings of characters within a data stream. Grep is case-sensitive unless the -i option is used.	Lesson 4, Topic B
`xargs`	`command [options] [arguments] | xargs [options] {command}`	Read from standard input and executes a command for each argument provided.	Lesson 4, Topic B
`tee`	`command [options] [arguments] | tee [options] {file names}`	Read the standard input, sends the output to the default output device (the CLI), and also copies the output to each specified file.	Lesson 4, Topic B

Command	Syntax	Purpose	Covered in
find	find {where to search} {search criteria}	Search the filesystem for files that match the given parameters.	Lesson 4, Topic C
locate	locate [options] {string}	Search for files and directories along a specified path.	Lesson 4, Topic C
updatedb	updatedb	Build and update a database of files based on the /etc/updatedb. conf file.	Lesson 4, Topic C
which	which {command}	Display complete path of a specified command.	Lesson 4, Topic C

Lesson 5
Authoring Text Files

LESSON INTRODUCTION

Linux users edit text files in day-to-day activities and when making system configuration changes. Because a graphical user interface (GUI) is not always available, visual menus are not always possible; text editing in Linux is very different from text editing in other platforms. Text editors rely on various modes and metakeys to enable functions such as save and copy/paste. It's also essential to ensure that files are backed up, protected, and that their integrity is guaranteed. This Lesson focuses on Linux text editors such as Vim and archiving tools such as tar.

Lesson Objectives

In this lesson, you will:

- Edit text files.
- Manage text files.

Topic 5A

Edit Text Files

EXAM OBJECTIVES COVERED
1.2 Given a scenario, manage files and directories.

Text file editing is a basic but essential skill for Linux users. In Linux the graphical user interface is optional, making text editing unique in Linux compared to other operating systems. If the Linux system does not have a GUI, editors that rely on mouse-driven menu options cannot be used. Sysadmins must use the keyboard only to access all text editor program functions in this case. This Topic covers the common Linux text editors that all users should be familiar with. It is critical to be able to open, edit, save, and close files with any Linux editor.

Configuration File Concepts

Most Linux configurations are held in text files. Settings such as network addresses, video and display options, device initialization, and even user profiles are stored in text files. The role of sysadmins is to manage the Linux server's configuration. To change system settings, one must often edit these configuration files.

Recall that most Linux servers do not use a graphical user interface (GUI), and therefore word processing programs with mouse-clickable interfaces are not commonly available. Instead, **text editors** controlled entirely from a command-line interface are used to manipulate these configuration files. There are many text editors available for Linux, but two of the most common are Vim and Nano.

For example, the SSH (Secure shell) program is frequently used for remote administration with Linux systems. A text file at `/etc/ssh/sshd_config` must be edited to configure who is allowed to remotely connect to the server, what level of remote access they will have, and to present a warning or instructional message to the connecting user. The sysadmin must be proficient with text editors to ensure the server is properly configured for remote administration.

Common Text Editors

GUI-based text editors like gedit are usually self-explanatory and offer familiar functions. Tasks such as opening files and saving changes are handled via menus. Text editors that operate at the command-line, such as Vim and Nano, do not have mouse-driven menu options. Instead, these editors rely on keyboard keystrokes to manage the file. Nano accomplishes this by using the Ctrl metakey. Vim switches among different modes. Depending on the mode, the keyboard interacts differently with the program.

Text Editor Name	Description
vi	A visual text editor that was originally created for Unix® and was later cloned into FOSS versions.
Vim	The default text editor in most Linux distributions.

Text Editor Name	Description
Emacs	A flexible, powerful, and popular text editor used in Linux and Unix.
gVim	The graphical version of the Vim editor.
gedit	A simple yet powerful GUI-based text editor used in the GNOME desktop environment.
GNU nano	A small, user-friendly text editor.

Vim

The "Vi Improved," or Vim editor, is installed on most distributions. It is extremely powerful and a little complex, but the general functionality is straightforward. Vim has three modes. When switching modes, the keyboard will react differently. For example, pressing the `w` key in one mode inserts the "w" character in the text of the file. In a different mode, however, the `w` key writes or saves changes to the file.

The older version of Vim is named vi (pronounced "vee-eye"), and it is not often used on modern Linux systems. Frequently, when a user types `vi` to invoke the editor, the Vim editor is automatically invoked instead. The vi editor is more limited, but its basic functionality is the same as that of Vim.

```
            VIM - Vi IMproved


            version 8.2.2146
         by Bram Moolenaar et al.
      Modified by <bugzilla@redhat.com>
   Vim is open source and freely distributable


        Become a registered Vim user!
  type  :help register<Enter>     for information

  type  :q<Enter>               to exit
  type  :help<Enter>  or  <F1>  for on-line help
  type  :help version8<Enter>   for version info
```

The opening page of Vim.

To make working with Vim easier, begin by memorizing what the three primary modes do and how to switch among them.

Both Command Mode and Execute Mode manipulate the file by doing an action such as creating or saving a file, while Insert Mode actually manages the text in a file (writing or deleting words). The default mode you see upon opening Vim is the Command mode.

There is a fourth Vim mode named Visual, which allows the user to select or highlight text for copying, deleting, and other tasks. Visual mode is not covered in this course.

Users switch between modes by using the following keystrokes:

- `ESC` -- Enter Command mode.
- `:` -- Enter Execute mode.
- `i` -- Enter Insert mode (I, o, and O are also used).

Command Mode Keystrokes

Command mode provides several features for working with files. Options include jumping to the top or bottom of a file, jumping to a specific line number, and using keystrokes to make editing the files more efficient.

To move to the top, bottom, or specified line of the file:

- `gg` -- Move to the top of the file.
- `G` -- Move to the bottom of the file.
- `42G` -- Move to line 42 of the file.

To move the cursor around the text:

- `h` -- Move the cursor left.
- `j` -- Move the cursor down.
- `k` -- Move the cursor up.
- `l` -- Move the cursor right.

To delete a word, a line, or a specified number of lines of text:

- `d` -- Delete word at cursor's position.
- `dd` -- Delete line at cursor's position.
- `3dd` -- Delete three lines.

To copy and paste lines of text:

- `yy` -- Cut the line at the cursor's position (yank).
- `p` -- Put the yanked line at the cursor's new position (put).

To save and close the file:

- `ZZ` -- Write the file to disk and exit Vim.

 There are many additional commands in Command mode, but for the purpose of learning the editor, only some commands have been documented here.

Execute Mode Commands

Execute mode provides a command prompt. Several commands are available, but the most common are commands that save the file and exit the program.

Execute Mode Command	Purpose
`:w`	Write the file to disk (save).
`:w newfilename`	Write the file to disk with a new name.
`:q`	Quit Vim.
`:wq`	Write the file, then quit Vim.
`:q!`	Quit Vim without writing changes.

Observe that `ZZ` *in Command mode and* `:wq` *in Execute mode do the same thing.*

Insert Mode Commands

Insert mode is the common interface most users envision when thinking of a text editor. This is the mode where text is edited by adding or removing characters. Using the keyboard in this mode enables the traditional functionality of typing information into the file.

There are several ways of leaving Command mode and entering Insert mode. The primary difference in these methods is where the cursor appears for adding new text. The simplest way of entering Insert mode is by typing the lowercase `i` and then using arrow keys to position the cursor. However, other Insert mode commands may make editing more efficient.

Other ways of entering Insert mode:

- `i` -- Insert text before the cursor (standard entry method).
- `I` -- Insert text at the beginning of the selected line.
- `a` -- Insert text after the cursor.
- `A` -- Insert text at the end of the selected line.
- `o` -- Insert text on a new line below the selected line.
- `O` -- Insert text on a new line above the selected line.

Using these Command mode keystrokes switches Vim to Insert mode and adds text at the specified position.

Multiple Windows in Vim

Another powerful Vim feature is split-screen. Vim's interface can be split into windows vertically, horizontally, or both. Each window may focus on the same file, or different files can be open side by side. All split windows contain the full functionality of Vim.

Sysadmins might choose a horizontal split for a configuration file. Configuration files often contain examples and explanations at the top of the file, yet the actual lines to be configured may be much closer to the bottom of the file. One window may be open displaying the top of the file while another window displays a lower section of the file. The sysadmin can reference the top of the file while editing the bottom.

The key combination `Ctrl+w` provides the most split-screen functionality. To split Vim into two or more horizontal windows, type `Ctrl+w` and then type `s`.

```
74 #KerberosGetAFSToken no
75
76 # GSSAPI options
77 #GSSAPIAuthentication no
78 #GSSAPICleanupCredentials yes
79
80 # Set this to 'yes' to enable PAM authentication, account processing,
81 # and session processing. If this is enabled, PAM authentication will
82 # be allowed through the ChallengeResponseAuthentication and
83 # PasswordAuthentication.  Depending on your PAM configuration,
84 # PAM authentication via ChallengeResponseAuthentication may bypass
85 # the setting of "PermitRootLogin without-password".
private/etc/ssh/sshd_config
83 # PasswordAuthentication.  Depending on your PAM configuration,
84 # PAM authentication via ChallengeResponseAuthentication may bypass
85 # the setting of "PermitRootLogin without-password".
86 # If you just want the PAM account and session checks to run without
87 # PAM authentication, then enable this but set PasswordAuthentication
88 # and ChallengeResponseAuthentication to 'no'.
89 #UsePAM no
90
91 #AllowAgentForwarding yes
92 #AllowTcpForwarding yes
93 #GatewayPorts no
94 #X11Forwarding no
private/etc/ssh/sshd_config^^^^^^^^^^^^^^^^^^^^^^^^^^^^^^^^^^^^^^^^^^^^^
19
20 #Port 22
21 #AddressFamily any
22 #ListenAddress 0.0.0.0
23 #ListenAddress ::
private/etc/ssh/sshd_config
```

Vim screens split horizontally.

Users may find it useful to compare two files or may need to transfer content between the files. In this case, it's useful to have the files open side-by-side (vertical split). The user can glance back and forth between the two file versions, making whatever edits are desired.

Split Vim into two or more vertical windows by typing `Ctrl+w` and then `v`.

```
23 #ListenAddress ::                          1 #        $OpenBSD: sshd_config,v 1.103
24                                              018/04/09 20:41:22 tj Exp $
25 #HostKey /etc/ssh/ssh_host_rsa_key          2
26 #HostKey /etc/ssh/ssh_host_ecdsa_key        3 # This is the sshd server system-wide
27 #HostKey /etc/ssh/ssh_host_ed25519_key        onfiguration file.  See
28                                              4 # sshd_config(5) for more information.
29 # Ciphers and keying                         5
30 #RekeyLimit default none                     6 # This sshd was compiled with PATH=/us
31                                                /bin:/bin:/usr/sbin:/sbin
32 # Logging                                    7
33 #SyslogFacility AUTH                         8 # The strategy used for options in the
34 #LogLevel INFO                                 default sshd_config shipped with
35                                              9 # OpenSSH is to specify options with t
36 # Authentication:                              eir default value where
37                                             10 # possible, but leave them commented.
38 #LoginGraceTime 2m                             Uncommented options override the
39 #PermitRootLogin prohibit-password         11 # default value.
40 #StrictModes yes                           12
41 #MaxAuthTries 6                            13 # This Include directive is not part o
42 #MaxSessions 10                               the default sshd_config shipped with
43                                             14 # OpenSSH. Options set in the included
44 #PubkeyAuthentication yes                     configuration files generally override
45                                             15 # those that follow.  The defaults onl
46 # The default is to check both .ssh/aut       apply to options that have not been
   horized_keys and .ssh/authorized_keys2   16 # explicitly set.  Options that appear
47 # but this is overridden so installatio       multiple times keep the first value se
   ns will only check .ssh/authorized_keys    ,
48 AuthorizedKeysFile       .ssh/authorized  17 # unless they are a multivalue option
   _keys                                         uch as HostKey.
49                                             18 Include /etc/ssh/sshd_config.d/*
50 AuthorizedPrincipalsFile none              19
private/etc/ssh/sshd_config^^^^^^^^^^^^^^^^^^/private/etc/ssh/sshd_config
```

Vim screens split vertically.

To cycle from one window to the next, type `Ctrl+w` and then `w`. You can also use `Ctrl+w` with the four normal directional keys mapped in Vim.

nano

Nano is a simpler (but less powerful) text editor than Vim. As such, many users and administrators prefer nano for basic editing functions. Nano does not use the concept of modes. Instead, pressing the `Ctrl` key on the keyboard along with various character keys issues commands to the program.

The `nano` command invokes the editor. If an existing file is specified, the editor opens it. If no file is specified, nano creates a new file for editing.

Note that the name of the text editor is "nano," with no capitalization.

Shortcuts in nano

When nano opens a new or existing file, no further action is needed to begin editing. Simply pressing keys on the keyboard begins the process of entering text. You can move the cursor through the file using the arrow keys. Most commands are issued to nano by using the `Ctrl` key; however, other keys, such as `Alt` and `Tab`, may be used for some functions.

The `Ctrl` key is represented by the ^ ("caret") character in some documentation. Hence, ^X represents `Ctrl+X`.

Common nano Shortcut	Purpose
Ctrl + A	Move to the start of the line.
Ctrl + E	Move to the end of the line.
Ctrl + N	Move down one line.
Ctrl + P	Move up one line.
Alt + \	Move to the top of the file.
Alt + /	Move to the bottom of the file.
Ctrl + S	Save the file.
Ctrl + O	Write out the file (save as).
Ctrl + X	Exit Nano.

Menu showing the nano commands.

Nano is quite powerful and contains many keystroke shortcuts in addition to those mentioned here. Use the arrow keys, Page Up, Page Down, and Home keys to navigate within a document.

Copying parts of text on a line requires you to "mark" the text you want to copy with the `Ctrl+^` shortcut. You then navigate your cursor to highlight the text you want to copy. Pressing `Alt+^` copies the marked/highlighted text, and `Ctrl+U` pastes it. You can cut the current line by using `Ctrl+K`.

Gedit

The **gedit** text editor is the default text editor used in GNOME desktop environments and is a member of the GNU Project. Unlike Vim and nano, gedit has a GUI with a typical menu-based design that makes it easy to work with. It also has features such as syntax highlighting and spell checking and can be customized through plugins. While not as powerful as Vim, gedit may still be useful in systems that have a desktop environment installed.

Although you can launch gedit from the desktop, you can also use the CLI with the `gedit` command. The syntax is similar to `vim` and `nano`—typing the editor name with no argument opens a new file, whereas providing a file name as an argument either opens an existing file or creates a new one with that name.

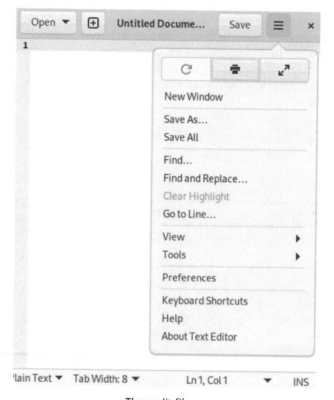

The gedit file menu.

Review Activity:

Text Files

Answer the following questions:

1. **A user contacts you and wants an easier text editor to use than Vim. There is no GUI installed on the system in question. What text editor do you suggest and why?**

2. **Explain how the keyboard responds depending on which mode Vim is currently in. How do modes add to Vim's functionality?**

3. **Why are text editors more important on Linux systems than on other systems?**

Topic 5B
Manage Text Files

EXAM OBJECTIVES COVERED
1.2 Given a scenario, manage files and directories.

Both user and system files must be protected. It is common to back up user files in case of hard disk failure. It is also common to back up system configuration files before making major changes. Doing so offers the ability to restore the original configuration file if something goes wrong with new changes. The `tar` utility is often used to back up or compress files. In addition, applications or other data files available on the web are commonly bundled with tar for ease of access. After downloading such files, verify their integrity to ensure the files are legitimate, complete, and uncorrupted.

Archive and Extract with tar

Users and sysadmins alike need to **backup**, bundle, and compress files and directories. Bundling and compressing files makes them easier to download, copy, or work with. While the primary tool for this work is `tar`, both `cpio` and `dd` may be used in some cases.

Downloading or copying many files simultaneously may be both inconvenient and inefficient. If the files are assembled into a single bundle, then only the bundle needs to be managed with download or copy functions. Many files can be handled as one, and they can be unbundled after the transfer is complete. In this way, tape archiver, or "tar," offers quite a lot of flexibility.

Helpdesk Ticket #01994

Submitted by: **Ali Selassi**	Department: **Marketing**	Assigned to: *you*	Date Opened: **2024-05-14**

Subject	Archiving contact files
Ticket Detail	I'm having a hard time archiving a whole bunch of files, can you assist? Thanks, Ali S
Date last updated	2024-05-14

When using `tar` to work with a group of files, the primary phases are:

1. Create a tarball (bundle).

2. Add files to the tarball.

3. Transfer the tarball to a different location (usually with the cp or mv commands).

4. Extract the files from the tarball.

The syntax for the `tar` command is `tar [options] {file1, file2, file3...}`

Some common options for `tar` are:

Option for the tar Command	Purpose
`-c`	Create a tarball.
`-x`	Extract files from a tarball.
`-t`	Test (or list) files in a tarball.
`-v`	Specify a verbose output.
`-r`	Append files to an existing archive.
`-f`	Specify the tarball filename.

Helpdesk Ticket #01994-r

Submitted by:	Department:	Assigned to:	Date Opened:
Ali Selassi	**Marketing**	*you*	**2024-05-14**

Subject	Archiving contact files
Ticket Detail	I'm having a hard time archiving a whole bunch of files, can you assist? Thanks, Ali S
Response	Sure thing, Ali. Please take a look at the attached walkthrough using the `-c` and `-x` options with `tar`
Date last updated	2024-05-15

Using the example in the helpdesk ticket, the following list is a demonstration of the tar utility. This series of commands will manage user Ali Selassi's proposed archive consisting of file1, file2, file3, and file4.

1. Create a new tarball:
   ```
   tar -cvf filearchive.tar file1 file2 file3
   ```

2. Display the files in the archive:
   ```
   tar -tf filearchive.tar
   ```

3. Add a file to the archive:
   ```
   tar -rf filearchive.tar file4
   ```

4. Extract the files from the archive (this is equivalent to a restore process in a backup/restore scenario).
   ```
   tar -xf filearchive.tar
   ```

```
[student@fedora projects]$ touch file1 file2 file3
[student@fedora projects]$ tar -cvf archive.tar file1 file2 file3
file1
file2
file3
[student@fedora projects]$ tar -tf archive.tar
file1
file2
file3
[student@fedora projects]$ touch file4
[student@fedora projects]$ tar -rf archive.tar file4
[student@fedora projects]$ tar -tf archive.tar
file1
file2
file3
file4
[student@fedora projects]$ rm -f f*
[student@fedora projects]$ ls
archive.tar
[student@fedora projects]$ tar -xf archive.tar
[student@fedora projects]$ ls
archive.tar    file1    file2    file3    file4
[student@fedora projects]$ ▮
```

The full CLI output of the different steps of the tar *utility.*

Keep in mind that as a user, you will frequently interact with tar archives as part of a download process. Experience with tar makes both file management and download processes easier.

Copy In and Copy Out with cpio

The cpio tool is found on most Linux distros and is similar to tar. The name describes its function: it will copy data in and out of an archive, hence cpio (copy in out).

When using cpio to back up files, the function is "copy out" of the filesystem into an archive by using the -o option. The related restore process is to "copy in" to the filesystem from the archive by using the -i option. The cpio tool typically relies on redirectors as part of these processes.

Option for the cpio Command	Purpose
-o	Copy out of the filesystem (backup).
-i	Copy in to the filesystem (restore).
-v	Specify the verbose mode.

To copy files out of the current directory and into an archive as part of a backup procedure, type:

```
ls | cpio -ov > /tmp/archive.cpio
```

To copy files in to the filesystem, thereby restoring the files, type:

```
cpio -iv /tmp/archive.cpio
```

There is quite a bit of cross-functionality possible, as cpio is capable of creating `tar` files.

Copy and Convert with dd

The `dd` command copies and converts files to enable them to be transferred from one type of media to another. The `dd` command has various operands, or actions, to perform.

The syntax of the `dd` command is `dd [options] [operands]`

You can use `dd` to perform a full backup of a storage partition. The following example copies data from /dev/sda1 to /dev/sdb2:

```
dd if=/dev/sda of=/dev/sdb
```

Using `dd`, you can also create an image of a drive and then clone a second drive with it:

```
dd if=/dev/sda of=drive_image.iso
dd if=drive_image.iso of=/dev/sdb
```

Operand for the dd Command	Purpose
`if={file name}`	Specify the file from which data will be read.
`of={file name}`	Specify the file to which data will be written.
`bs={bytes}`	Specify the total block size to read and write, in bytes. Bytes can also be formatted in a more human-friendly way, such as 50M to specify 50 megabytes and 10G to specify 10 gigabytes.
`count={count}`	Specify the number of blocks to be written to the output file from the input file.
`status={level}`	Specify the level of information to print to standard error: • `none` to suppress everything except error messages. • `noxfer` to suppress total transfer statistics. • `progress` to display transfer statistics periodically.

Compress Files

Compression is a procedure in which data is encoded to reduce the amount of bits that are used to represent that data. The compression process can significantly reduce the size of a file or collection of files in order to make the storage and transfer of data more efficient. Although the file takes up less space, it still contains the requisite information so that only redundant data is removed (lossless compression) or so that only noncritical data is lost (lossy compression).

Compression is commonly used to reduce the storage and transmission burden involved with creating, maintaining, and recovering from backups. Rather than backing up data one-to-one, you can compress that data and then store it.

Compressing with gzip

GNU zip (gzip) is a compression utility that reduces the size of selected files. Files compressed with `gzip` frequently have the .gz file extension. The `gzip` command has several options.

Option for the gzip Command	Purpose
-d	Reverse file compression (decompression).
-f	Force compression or decompression of a file even if it has multiple links or if the file exists.
-n	Omit saving the original file name and timestamp.
-N	Save the original file name and timestamp.
-q	Suppress all warnings.
-r	Enable directory recursion during compression or decompression.
-v	Display the name and percentage reduction of the compressed or decompressed file.
-t	Perform an integrity check on the compressed file.

The syntax of the `gzip` command is `gzip [options] [file names]`

The `gunzip` command is equivalent to issuing `gzip -d` at the command-line.

Compressing with xz

The `xz` command is a data compression utility, similar to `gzip`, that reduces the size of selected files and manages files in the .xz file format. The `xz` command has several options.

Option for the xz Command	Purpose
-d	Decompress a file.
-f	Force compression or decompression of a file even if it has multiple links or if the file exists.
-q	Suppress all warnings.
-v	Display the name and percentage reduction of the compressed or decompressed file.
-t	Perform an integrity check on the compressed file.

The syntax of the `xz` command is `xz [options] [file names]`

Compressing with bzip2

The `bzip2` command and its related commands manage file compression. Files compressed with `bzip2` frequently have the .bz2 file extension. The bzip2-related commands are described in the following table.

bzip2 Related Command	Purpose
`bzip2`	Compress a file.
`bunzip2`	Decompress a file.
`bzcat`	Decompress a file to standard output.
`bzip2recover`	Run the `diff` command on compressed files. Recover data from damaged .bz2 files.
`bzless`	Run the less command on compressed files.
`bzmore`	Run the more command on compressed files.

The syntax of the `bzip2` command is `bzip2 [options] {file names}`

For example, to compress files file1 and file2, type:

```
bzip2 file1 file2
```

Compressing with zip

The `zip` command is another compression utility that (unlike `gzip`, `xz`, and `bzip2`) also features file archiving functionality. In fact, `zip` is a combination of an older compression utility, called *compress,* and the `tar` archive command. Files compressed with `zip` frequently have the .zip file extension. The `zip` command has several options.

Option for the zip Command	Purpose
`-d`	Delete entries in a .zip archive.
`-e`	Encrypt the contents of an archive.
`-F`	Fix a corrupted .zip archive.
`-r`	Enable recursion.
`-T`	Perform an integrity check on the archive file.

The syntax of the `zip` command is `zip [options] [file names]`

Which Compression Method Should You Choose?

Which compression tool to use will often depend on your own particular needs, but some generalities can be made about each. The most important factors are the speed/time of compression and decompression, and the compression ratio, which is the size of the uncompressed file divided by the size of the compressed file (e.g., a 5 MB uncompressed file that becomes 1 MB when compressed has a ratio of 5:1).

For compression speed, tests tend to show that `gzip` is slightly faster than `bzip2`, and both are significantly faster than `xz` when the applied compression level increases. For decompression speed, `gzip` tends to be the fastest again, with `xz` and `bzip2` as second and third fastest, respectively. When it comes to compression ratio, `xz` tends to perform the best, followed by `bzip2`, with `gzip` having the worst ratio.

Ultimately, consider using:

- `gzip`—if you just care about compressing and decompressing files as fast as possible and are less concerned with storage space.

- `xz`—if storage space is at a premium, and time is not as much of a factor.

- `bzip2`—to strike a balance and for data that rarely needs to be decompressed.

Use Compression with tar

Frequently it's useful to bundle files with tar and compress them with a tool such as gzip. While this can be accomplished in two separate steps, it's easier to integrate the compression process into the `tar` process. The `tar` command recognizes compression utilities such as `gzip` and `bzip2`. Simply add `-z` to compress with `gzip`, or `-j` to compress with `bzip2`, to the regular `tar` command. Add the .gz or .bz2 file extension name to the bundle.

Helpdesk Ticket #01995-r

Submitted by: **Ali Selassi**	Department: **Marketing**	Assigned to: *you*	Date Opened: **2024-05-26**

Subject	Archiving contact files - follow up
Ticket Detail	Thanks for your help before, the tar command is really helpful. I'm trying to download files now and I need a way to make that process easier. Can you help? Thanks, Ali S
Response	Yes, you can combine the tar utility with a compression tool like gzip or bzip2. I've sent over a tutorial on how to use it.
Date last updated	2024-05-27

To combine `tar` and `gzip`, type:

```
tar -czvf myfiles.tar.gz *.txt
```

To combine `tar` and `bzip2`, type:

```
tar -cjvf myfiles..tar.bz2 *.txt
```

The same options are used with tar's file extraction option, `-x`. Place a `z` or `j` option in the command with `-x` to decompress and extract the files.

Confirm File Integrity

Integrity checking is the process of verifying that data has not been modified, whether intentionally or unintentionally, in any way. In other words, an integrity check can validate the security goal of integrity. It is good practice to perform integrity checking after you finish compressing and archiving a backup file to confirm that the data has not changed. This will help you avoid storing corrupted and inaccurate archives for future recovery, only to find out too late that the data was not properly backed up.

Several methods enable you to check data integrity, each of which may vary based on its security requirements or goals. One of the most common and secure methods of checking data integrity is hashing. By calculating the **hash** of a file like a backup archive, you can compare that hash to past values. If both are the same, you can be reasonably sure that the data has not changed in the meantime.

You'll use the md5sum *command to check file integrity in Lesson 12.*

Review Activity:

Text File Management

Answer the following questions:

1. **Why is it a good practice to back up a configuration file before making changes?**

2. **Why should the integrity of a file downloaded from the Internet be checked by tools such as SHA or MD5?**

Lesson 5

Summary

Linux users must be able to open, edit, save, and close text files using various text editors, especially Vim and Nano. Not only is user data held in text files, but system settings are also stored in these files and must be edited to make configuration changes. Furthermore, user data should be backed up or may need to be available for transfer to other systems. Archiving tools like tar play an important role in file management. The text editing skills covered in this Lesson are critical to all facets of Linux system use.

Guidelines

These best practices and guidelines are provided for your use as revision tools or as quick references in your job role.

- Make a copy of configuration files before making changes.

- Understand the text editors.

    - Know how to move between the three Vim modes.

    - Be able to use Vim to open, edit, save, and exit files.

    - Be able to use nano to open, edit, save, and exit files.

    - Be aware that various distributions may offer one or the other (or both) editors.

- Use `tar` to bundle files.

- Use compression to make files easier to manage.

- Combine `tar` and compression into a single command for efficiency.

- Recognize that `tar` is used with backup/restore processes and file downloads.

- Use hashing to verify file integrity.

Command Reference Table

This list of commands and their associated syntax can also be found in Appendix B.

Command	Syntax	Purpose	Covered in
`tar`	`tar [options] {file1, file2 ...}`	Bundle files for easier transfer.	Lesson 5, Topic B
`gzip`	`gzip [options] [file-names]`	Reduce size of files.	Lesson 5, Topic B
`xz`	`xz [options] [file-names]`	Reduce size of files.	Lesson 5, Topic B
`bzip2`	`bzip2 [options] {file-names}`	Manage file compression.	Lesson 5, Topic B
`zip`	`zip [options] [file-names]`	Reduce size of files with archiving functionality.	Lesson 5, Topic B

Lesson 6
Managing Software

LESSON INTRODUCTION

Maintaining software on Linux systems is usually accomplished with package managers. Package managers deploy, update, remove, and report on applications. However, due to the open-source nature of the Linux environment, software applications are often compiled from source code—something that is not common with other operating systems.

Because there are many different Linux distributions available, there are many package managers. As a general rule, most distributions either originated with Red Hat Linux (and therefore use the Red Hat package managers) or Debian Linux (and therefore use the Debian package managers).

This Lesson covers several common package managers, the process of acquiring and compiling software, and running software in a sandbox for security.

Lesson Objectives

In this lesson, you will:

- Understand software management.
- Manage Red Hat–derived software packages and repositories.
- Manage Debian-derived software packages and repositories.
- Compile from source code.
- Acquire software.
- Run software in a sandbox.

Topic 6A

Understand Software Management

 EXAM OBJECTIVES COVERED
1.6 Given a scenario, build and install software.

Linux software is usually distributed either as source code to be compiled or pre-compiled software packages. The packages are maintained using package managers, which are applications designed to manage packages throughout the software's lifecycle (install, update, remove). Several different package managers exist. Applications delivered as source code must first be compiled before installing. Compiling the software offers the opportunity to customize it.

This Topic covers the concepts of packages, package managers, and software compiling.

Red Hat, Debian, and Compiling Source Code

There are thousands of Linux distributions. With the open-source nature of Linux, anyone can create their own distribution, and many individuals and organizations do. Within the family of Linux distributions, however, there is a general split in how software applications are managed.

Broadly speaking, there are two common ways to manage software: Red Hat–based processes and Debian Linux-based processes. Most Linux distributions are derived from one or the other of these two major distributions, though there are also several other methods that are less widespread.

When downloading and using a particular Linux distribution, it is very likely it uses one of these two package-management suites. Red Hat and Debian package managers are both covered in this section, with a few references to other package managers.

Distinguish Package Management from Compiling Software

Software packages are precompiled. Compiling software converts the code from a human-readable programming language to a machine language. With closed-source software—such as proprietary, paid applications—the source code is not available to consumers or outside developers to view or alter. Open-source software, however, is available for both viewing and altering. If a developer alters an open-source application's source code, the updated code must be recompiled to run on a Linux system.

It is much more common for Linux users, especially developers and administrators, to compile software than it is for Windows or macOS users.

Compiling software offers several advantages:

- Software is optimized for your system's hardware, including special features.

- Software is optimized for your Linux distribution and kernel.

- You may be able to enable experimental or beta features.

- You can select specific options.

- You can learn how the software is constructed, discover bugs, and contribute improvements.

To effectively use Linux systems, users must be capable of both managing software packages and compiling software from source code.

Software Packages

Linux software is often distributed in packages that contain everything needed to run the software—executables, configuration files, supporting resources, and documentation. Therefore, the process of installing, maintaining, and removing software is referred to as package management, and the tools required to maintain software are **package managers**.

One critical component of package managers is the ability to report software information. Package managers track software installation information in a database that can be queried. Such queries might include a list of all installed software, a list of software versions, or specific information on a single software package. The ability to query the package manager's installation database provides sysadmins with essential information on the system and its applications.

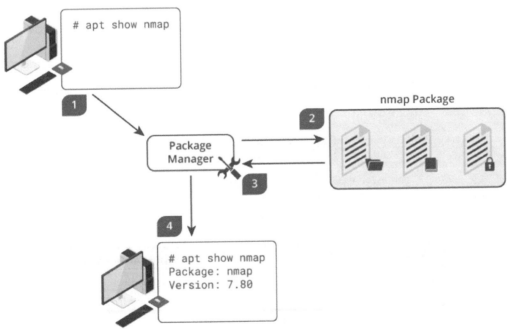

Querying a package manager. In step 1, a user at a terminal uses the `# apt show nmap` *command to find out more information about nmap. The package manager calls out to the nmap package (step 2), which provides information back (step 3). Finally, the package manager displays the nmap details at the terminal (step 4). (Images © 123RF.com.)*

A second critical part of package management is the source from which package managers pull the software. A storage location for software packages is referred to as a repository. Sysadmins control what repositories are available to package managers.

Repositories can be located in a few key areas:

- An internal server containing only authorized packages

- A distribution vendor, such as Red Hat or Ubuntu

- A public **package repository**

Sysadmins carefully control available repositories to ensure only authorized software and software versions are available for installation. Doing so helps ensure the security and stability of the system by allowing only legitimate software to be available.

Compare Red Hat and Debian Package Managers

The Red Hat and Debian package managers handle the software lifecycle in much the same way. Each approach has a method for installing, updating, removing, and reporting software on the system. Package managers track versions, the location of installed files, and place documentation files in standard locations.

 In an earlier lesson, the Filesystem Hierarchy Standard (FHS) was noted as being a consistent way of organizing Linux directories. Such organization allows package managers to exist. Package managers place configuration files in `/etc`, *log files in* `/var/log`, *documentation in* `/usr/share`, *and so on because those locations are standardized across distributions.*

Each package manager has its own related commands, and those commands cover the three major parts of the software lifecycle (installation, maintenance, and removal). Some basic examples are:

- `$ rpm -i {software-package}`

- `$ rpm -U {software-package}`

- `$ rpm -e {software-package}`

- `$ apt install {software-package}`

- `$ apt upgrade {software-package}`

- `$ apt remove {software-package}`

 The `-U` *option for* `rpm` *upgrades the specified software package.*

Red Hat Package Managers	Debian Package Managers
Red Hat Package Manager (RPM)	dpkg package manager
Yellow Dog Update Manager (YUM)	Advanced Packaging Tool (APT)
Dandified YUM (DNF) package manager	

 When discussing package managers, note that the name of the package manager is usually shown in uppercase letters as an acronym. The associated commands are displayed in lowercase letters because they would be typed at the command prompt. So the RPM package manager includes the `rpm` *command (to install .rpm files).*

The commands for these specific package managers are covered in detail later in this Lesson.

The SUSE ZYpp Package Manager

SUSE Linux uses its own package manager for software maintenance: ZYpp. The ZYpp package manager is the basis for the GUI tool YaST (Yet another Setup Tool) and the command-line zypper utility. The general concept for package management with `zypper` is the same as with the `rpm` and `apt` commands. Options exist for installing, updating, reporting, and removing software packages on the system.

Some examples of those options are:

- `$ zypper install {software-package}`

- `$ zypper update {software-package}`

- `$ zypper remove {software-package}`

Software Dependencies

Package managers make software maintenance much more straightforward. One challenging part of handling Linux software, however, is dependencies. Some software packages rely on other packages to function. If the software an application depends on is not installed, it will either fail entirely or not work as intended.

Early package managers required administrators to manually provide the dependent applications before installing the primary package. Modern package managers such as YUM, DNF, and APT install supporting applications automatically, ensuring that a single installation command provides the user with everything needed to run the program.

Periodically, package dependency issues still arise, so recognize the problem (failed dependency) and the solution (install the packages required for the primary application to run).

Review Activity:

Software Management

Answer the following questions:

---

1. **What are the software-management phases?**

2. **Why should administrators control software repository locations?**

3. **Why is compiling software more common with Linux systems than with other operating systems?**

Topic 6B

Manage RPM Software Packages and Repositories

EXAM OBJECTIVES COVERED
1.6 Given a scenario, build and install software.
1.7 Given a scenario, manage software configurations.

Many common Linux distributions are derived from Red Hat Linux. Common components of most of these distributions are package management and software package format. Packages for Red Hat–derived distributions use the .rpm file extension. There are three common package managers: RPM, YUM, and DNF.

Common examples of Red Hat–derived distributions include Red Hat Enterprise Linux and Fedora.

Red Hat Package Managers

The **Red Hat Package Manager (RPM)** is the oldest of the package managers discussed here. It provides good basic functionality with a simple syntax and a lot of flexibility. It maintains a software database for package queries. One of its main drawbacks is package management, which is not as robust as the following package managers: YUM and DNF.

Yellow Dog Update Manager (YUM) relies on .rpm packages and also tracks software in an RPM database. Like RPM, YUM alerts users to software dependencies. However, it also offers the ability to automatically install dependencies so that a single YUM command installs the specified software and all required software for it to function.

Both RPM and YUM are superseded by **Dandified Yum (DNF)**, which includes all the same functionality as both with additional plugins and features. Typically, any Linux system that uses .rpm software packages recognizes RPM, YUM, and DNF commands.

RPM Commands

The use of Red Hat package managers is primarily focused on installing, updating, upgrading, and uninstalling software packages. These packages have a .rpm file extension. RPM files are pre-compiled and usually include all supporting documentation and configuration files. The idea is that a single package contains the entire application.

Observe that in this Lesson, "Red Hat" usually refers to that Linux distribution in the context of a parent distro from which many other Linux distros are derived. RPM-oriented package managers are not necessarily developed or maintained by Red Hat itself.

Using RPM Commands

The syntax for the `rpm` command is `rpm [options] {package-name}`

Like many other Linux commands, the `-v` option provides verbose or detailed output, and it is common to include `-v` when manually running the command.

Options for the `rpm` command include:

Option for the rpm Command	Purpose
`-i`	Install a software package.
`-U`	Upgrade a package to a newer version and install it if it is not already present.
`-F`	Freshen a package to a newer version but do not install it if it is not already present.
`-e`	Erase or uninstall a software package.
`-h`	Display hash marks or progress bar.
`-v`	Specify a verbose or detailed output.

```
[student@fedora ~]$ rpm -qi vim-enhanced
Name         : vim-enhanced
Epoch        : 2
Version      : 8.2.4579
Release      : 1.fc35
Architecture : x86_64
Install Date : Sat 26 Mar 2022 10:00:23 AM EDT
Group        : Unspecified
Size         : 4443971
License      : Vim and MIT
Signature    : RSA/SHA256, Wed 16 Mar 2022 11:
8f
Source RPM   : vim-8.2.4579-1.fc35.src.rpm
Build Date   : Wed 16 Mar 2022 11:11:21 AM EDT
```

Querying the vim package with the `rpm` *command.*

Querying software is covered later in this section.

Here is an example of using RPM to manage a software package that installs the Z shell (assume the zsh.rpm package has been downloaded to the system, and the present working directory is the download location).

This command installs the software in verbose mode and provides a progress bar to track the installation process:

```
$ rpm -ivh zsh.rpm
```

This command does two things. It will update the package on a system that already has the package installed. It will also install the package on a system that does not currently have it. To accomplish either of these, type:

```
$ rpm -Uvh zsh.rpm
```

This command will update an existing package, if installed, but it will not install the package if it is not already present:

```
$ rpm -Fvh zsh.rpm
```

The importance of upgrade (-U) versus freshen (-F) may be difficult to visualize when thinking of a single system. On a single computer, you're likely to know whether the specific software package is present. However, the real importance of these two options is clear when the rpm command is used in scripts that maintain software on many systems. A single script may be used to manage software on 20 systems, some of which are supposed to have the software and some of which are not.

Removing the zsh.rpm package is just as simple. The progress bar and verbose options may be used to track the removal process as well:

```
$ rpm -evh zsh.rpm
```

```
[student@fedora ~]$ sudo rpm -ehv tree
Preparing...                    ############################### [100%]
Cleaning up / removing...
   1:tree-1.8.0-7.fc35           ############################### [100%]
[student@fedora ~]$
```

Removing the tree utility with the rpm *command.*

 The actual zsh.rpm package name will, in reality, be much longer and include information about the version and architecture for which the package is designed. The package name used here has been shortened for these examples.

RPM stores package information in a database. An important use of the RPM database is software verification. The database not only tracks what packages are installed, but it also tracks where all their components reside (configuration files, documentation, and so on). If a piece of software is not functioning correctly, package managers can check to confirm whether all the components exist in the proper places.

The syntax to verify software with the rpm command is:

```
$ rpm -V {package-name}
```

YUM Commands

The yum command works with .rpm packages and is the next evolution of the RPM package manager. It features a more intuitive syntax and the ability to handle software dependencies more elegantly.

The syntax for the yum command is yum [options] [subcommand] {package-name}

There are many common subcommands for the yum command, but the key examples are presented in the table below.

Subcommand for the yum Command	Purpose
`install`	Install the software package.
`remove`	Uninstall the software package.
`update`	Update the software package.

For example, to install the zsh.rpm package, type:

```
$ yum install zsh
```

Recall that some packages require other packages to be installed to function correctly. These dependencies are difficult to manage manually. However, the `yum` command can automatically install a package and any other software it depends on. The software simply has to be available in the repository along with the primary package.

By adding the `-y` option to `yum`, you automatically answer "yes" to any YUM questions about whether to also install required dependencies for the package. The addition of the `-y` option turns the command into "install the zsh.rpm package and any necessary packages for it to run."

The following command installs the zsh package and automatically installs any packages it depends on:

```
$ yum -y install zsh
```

Use the `deplist` option to display any dependencies for a given package without installing. This allows sysadmins to ensure any required packages are included in the software repository.

The YUM package manager allows sysadmins to discover what package contains a particular file, script, or command. The `provides` subcommand displays the contents of a given package. Here's an example:

```
$ yum provides {software-package}
```

```
[student@fedora ~]$ yum provides bash
Last metadata expiration check: 0:01:23 ago on Sat 26 Mar 2022 10:29:18 AM EDT.
bash-5.1.8-2.fc35.x86_64 : The GNU Bourne Again shell
Repo        : @System
Matched from:
Provide     : bash = 5.1.8-2.fc35

bash-5.1.8-2.fc35.x86_64 : The GNU Bourne Again shell
Repo        : fedora
Matched from:
Provide     : bash = 5.1.8-2.fc35

[student@fedora ~]$
```

Output from the `yum provides` *command for Bash.*

Update Packages with YUM

Both YUM and DNF can update installed packages. The process is much the same as for the rpm command.

An example with a YUM package:

```
$ yum update zsh.rpm
```

The YUM package manager can also display or report available updates without installing them. This is useful for seeing what is available without making any changes.

The command to check for updates for all installed packages is:

```
$ yum check-update
```

This may generate a lot of output. If there is a specific package that you want to check for updates, add the package name as an argument:

```
$ yum check-update {package-name}
```

To remove software by using YUM, type:

```
$ yum remove {package-name}
```

 The yum update *command, with no arguments, updates all software packages on the system.*

DNF Commands

The DNF package manager is the most advanced of the three software-management solutions and includes many practical features and updates. It is the assumed package manager on modern Red Hat–derived distributions, though YUM and RPM may also be available on those systems.

Subcommand for the dnf Command	Purpose
install	Install the software package.
remove	Uninstall the software package.
upgrade	Upgrade the software package.

To install the zsh package by using the `dnf` command, type:

```
$ dnf install zsh
```

Like `yum`, the `dnf` command recognizes the `-y` option as an "assume yes" for dependency queries, making the installation process far more streamlined. It also means that any script used to automate software installations can also install any necessary packages.

The `dnf list installed` command displays installed software on the system.

The `upgrade` subcommand checks the configured repositories for updated software and installs the newer versions. For example, to upgrade all software on the system, type:

```
$ dnf upgrade
```

Use the `remove` subcommand to uninstall a software package:

```
$ dnf remove zsh
```

The `autoremove` subcommand removes the software package but also uninstalls any dependencies that were installed with the package and are no longer necessary. By using `autoremove`, sysadmins can help keep systems from being cluttered with software that is no longer necessary.

 The autoremove *feature can also be configured with the YUM package manager.*

The DNF package manager recognizes package groups. Package groups are logical collections of related packages. If an administrator wanted to install all software for managing virtual machines, each individual package could be identified, downloaded, and installed. However, virtualization software is collected into a single package group to be installed as a unit:

```
$ dnf group install virtualization
```

 It is also possible to identify the group by using the @ symbol in the following command: `dnf install @virtualization`. *Note that this example uses the standard* `dnf install` *syntax.*

Which to Use?

When working with Red Hat–derived distributions, assume the use of the `dnf` command to manage packages. Sometimes the `rpm` command is useful for a single quick installation when no dependencies are involved. While DNF is the standard, YUM is still very common.

 It's a good idea to be able to administer basic package management by using all three commands.

To see a history of DNF package management, type:

```
$ dnf history
```

```
[student@fedora ~]$ dnf history
ID      | Command line              | Date and time        | Action(s)
-----------------------------------------------------------------------------
     6  | install -y tree           | 2022-03-26 10:34     | Install
     5  | remove tree               | 2022-03-26 10:32     | Removed
     4  | install -y tree           | 2022-03-26 10:31     | Install
     3  | -y install tree           | 2022-03-26 10:24     | Install
     2  | install -y vim            | 2022-03-26 10:00     | I, U
     1  |                           | 2021-10-26 01:40     | Install
[student@fedora ~]$
```

The `dnf history` *command displays recent package-management tasks.*

Query Packages on Red Hat Systems

Because RPM-based package managers track software in a database, sysadmins can query the database and discover important information about the packages. This information includes the installation date, release date, version, and a brief discussion of the package's function. Such information allows administrators to make informed choices about whether software should be installed, maintained, or even removed from the system.

The `rpm` command has two useful query options. The first provides information on all software on the system, and the second shows details about the specified package.

The syntax to display all installed software is:

```
$ rpm -qa > softwarelist.txt
```

The output from the `rpm -qa` command is likely to be immense, so it may be a good idea to redirect the results into a text file.

The syntax to display information about a specified package is:

```
$ rpm - qi {package-name}
```

```
[student@fedora ~]$ rpm -qi nano
Name        : nano
Version     : 5.8
Release     : 4.fc35
Architecture: x86_64
Install Date: Tue 26 Oct 2021 01:40:58 AM EDT
Group       : Unspecified
Size        : 2924434
License     : GPLv3+
Signature   : RSA/SHA256, Mon 26 Jul 2021 03:12:33
AM EDT, Key ID db4639719867c58f
Source RPM  : nano-5.8-4.fc35.src.rpm
Build Date  : Thu 22 Jul 2021 04:20:39 PM EDT
Build Host  : buildvm-x86-16.iad2.fedoraproject.org
Packager    : Fedora Project
Vendor      : Fedora Project
URL         : https://www.nano-editor.org
Bug URL     : https://bugz.fedoraproject.org/nano
Summary     : A small text editor
Description :
GNU nano is a small and friendly text editor.
[student@fedora ~]$
```

Results of the `rpm -qi` *command showing information about the nano package.*

The YUM and DNF package managers provide the same functionality.

There may be instances when a user, administrator, security auditor, or other individual needs to know exactly what software is installed on a specified Linux server.

Helpdesk Ticket #01996

Submitted by:	Department:	Assigned to:	Date Opened:
Kai Garcia	Engineering	*you*	2024-04-11

Subject	Security audit in progress
Ticket Detail	Hi, can you please provide a list of all the software installed on Server 02A. I appreciate your help, we need this as soon as possible.
	Thanks, KG
Date last updated	2024-04-11

The `yum` command to display installed software is:

```
$ yum list installed
```

The command to display information on a specified package using YUM is:

```
$ yum info {package-name}
```

 It's likely that the output of these commands will be redirected into a text file to be provided to the requesting user.

The related DNF commands to satisfy such a query are:

```
$ dnf list installed
$ dnf info {package-name}
```

```
[student@fedora ~]$ dnf info tree
Last metadata expiration check: 0:05:23 ago on Sat 26 Mar 2022 10:29:18 AM EDT.
Installed Packages
Name        : tree
Version     : 1.8.0
Release     : 7.fc35
Architecture : x86_64
Size        : 113 k
Source      : tree-1.8.0-7.fc35.src.rpm
Repository  : @System
From repo   : fedora
Summary     : File system tree viewer
URL         : http://mama.indstate.edu/users/ice/tree/
License     : GPLv2+
Description : The tree utility recursively displays the contents of directories
            : in a tree-like format.  Tree is basically a UNIX port of the DOS
            : tree utility.

[student@fedora ~]$ ▮
```

Output from the dnf info *command.*

 Observe that the syntax for YUM and DNF is very similar.

Why Repositories?

Repositories, often called "repos," are software storage locations that package managers can check when installing or updating software. Many repositories exist, and not all are trusted. In some cases, malware might be present, but there are other reasons that repositories may not be trusted.

Possible reasons for sysadmins to control available repositories include:

- **Software version control:** Some repositories may release beta or unapproved software that production servers should not use.

- **Application installation control:** Some repositories may contain unapproved software, such as games, that production systems should not have access to.

- **Vendor control:** Some repositories are oriented on specific vendors.

- **Bandwidth control:** Local repositories may be favored over Internet repositories for maintaining bandwidth efficiency.

Administrators use configuration files to inform package managers about what repositories are allowed and where they can be found on the local network or the Internet.

Manage Configuration Files for RPM repositories

When the `rpm`, `yum`, or `dnf` commands are issued to install a package, the commands must know where to look for the software. If a package has been downloaded to a specific file, the package manager can be directed to that file with the absolute path. However, locally downloaded and stored software is not recommended. Version control is difficult, as is enforcing standard applications. Therefore, administrators should define centralized repositories of packages and configure the YUM and DNF package managers to use those repositories when installing or updating software.

Sysadmins often prefer to maintain an internal repository on a local server that is referenced by all other Linux systems. This provides complete control over software availability and versions. Package manager configuration files define where these repositories can be found.

The three types of software repositories are categorized by their locations, and some are more commonly used than others.

- **Local repositories:** These repositories are stored on the system's local storage drive. Installation is easy, but version control is difficult because of the decentralized nature of local repositories. If you manage 20 Linux servers, each would have its own repository to be maintained.

- **Centralized internal repositories:** These repositories are stored on one or more systems within the internal LAN and managed by the Linux administrator. This centralized approach makes version control much simpler. If you manage 20 Linux servers, one could host the repository and the other 19 could download their packages from it.

- **Vendor repositories:** These repositories are maintained on the Internet, often by the distribution vendor. Version control is very difficult because the vendor decides what package versions are made available.

Use YUM and DNF to Configure Repositories

Administrators can designate a specific location as a YUM repository by using the `createrepo` command. The command updates the XML files that are used to reference the repository location. The repository might be on the local storage drive (a local repository), or available from an Apache webserver (centralized internal repository).

After running the `createrepo` command, the administrator must create a .repo configuration file that provides additional information about the repository. The .repo files are stored in the `/etc/yum.repos.d/` directory. Some of the components of the .repo file include:

- `[repo-name]` —The repository name.

- `name=Repository Name` —The human-friendly name of the repo.

- `baseurl=` —The path to the repo. May be a file (file:///) or http:// path.

- `enabled=1` —Enables the repo.

- `gpgcheck=0` —Disables GPG checking.

```
[student@fedora yum.repos.d]$ cat fedora.repo
[fedora]
name=Fedora $releasever - $basearch
#baseurl=http://download.example/pub/fedora/linux/releases/$releasever/Everythin
g/$basearch/os/
metalink=https://mirrors.fedoraproject.org/metalink?repo=fedora-$releasever&arch
=$basearch
enabled=1
countme=1
metadata_expire=7d
repo_gpgcheck=0
type=rpm
gpgcheck=1
gpgkey=file:///etc/pki/rpm-gpg/RPM-GPG-KEY-fedora-$releasever-$basearch
skip_if_unavailable=False
```

The fedora-repo configuration.

The `yum` command includes some additional subcommands for viewing and using repositories:

- `repolist` —Used to see all available repositories.

- `makecache` —Used to locally cache information about available repositories.

- `clean all` —Used to clear out-of-date cache information.

```
[student@fedora ~]$ yum repolist
repo id                     repo name
fedora                      Fedora 35 - x86_64
fedora-cisco-openh264       Fedora 35 openh264 (From Cisco) - x86_64
fedora-modular              Fedora Modular 35 - x86_64
updates                     Fedora 35 - x86_64 - Updates
updates-modular             Fedora Modular 35 - x86_64 - Updates
[student@fedora ~]$ ▌
```

`yum` *lists the configured repositories.*

Global settings, such as where to find repository configuration files, log file locations, and cache information, are stored in the `/etc/yum.conf` file. The difference between this file and the repository configuration files is that this file defines how the YUM package manager works, while the repository files define where the package manager searches for packages.

The DNF package manager uses a configuration file stored at `/etc/dnf/dnf.conf` to define its global settings. These are the same types of global settings as defined for YUM. DNF also looks to the `/etc/yum.repos.d` directory for repository reference files.

Updating Configuration Files

One serious concern for sysadmins is managing configuration files when updating software via package managers. Many service configuration files are highly modified by administrators to ensure the software meets the organization's needs, and sysadmins need to ensure these files are not overwritten.

Two options help manage this situation: RPMNEW and RPMSAVE.

The RPMNEW file is created when an .rpm file is installed and a customized configuration file is found. The .rpmnew file contains the new configuration settings suggested by the vendor. The administrator can then compare the new configuration file to the modified file and adjust the settings as desired.

The RPMSAVE file takes the opposite approach. It saves a copy of the administrator's modified configuration file with a .rpmsave file extension and implements the new configuration file with the vendor-suggested settings. The administrator still has the opportunity to compare the two files and define any settings needed.

Typically, sysadmins use the RPMNEW file because it maintains the customized settings and therefore does not change the configuration of production services. The two files can be compared using the diff command.

 Services are covered later, but recall that for configuration file changes to be implemented, the sysadmin must restart services.

Review Activity:

RPM Software Packages and Repositories

Answer the following questions:

1. **What information might sysadmins query the RPM database to retrieve?**

2. **Why might sysadmins restrict certain software repositories?**

3. **Why are .rpmnew files important during an upgrade?**

Topic 6C

Manage Debian-based Software Packages and Repositories

EXAM OBJECTIVES COVERED
1.6 Given a scenario, build and install software.
1.7 Given a scenario, manage software configurations.

While the previous section covered the Red Hat approach to package management and this section covers the Debian package-management system, it's worth noting that package management concepts remain constant. Both approaches manage the software through its entire lifecycle, from installation, to update, to removal.

Many Linux distributions trace their lineage back to Debian, one of the oldest distros. The most widely used distros include Debian, Ubuntu, Linux Mint, and Kali Linux, though there are many other examples. Debian's common dpkg package-management system has been replaced by the `apt` command.

Debian Package Managers

Debian package managers store software inventory information in a database. The database can be queried to display information on software version, installation date, source, description, and more. The `apt` command is the more robust, and preferred, of the two package managers.

Using apt Commands

Although dpkg is the original installer for Debian-derived distributions, today .deb packages are more commonly managed using **Advanced Package Tool (APT)**. APT is a front-end manager to the **dpkg** system, much like YUM is a front-end manager to the RPM system.

Until recently, the common software-management tools were implemented as a mix of the `apt-get` and the `apt-cache` commands, along with several other variations on the `apt-*` format. Many Debian-derived distributions now use the more streamlined package manager simply named APT.

The syntax for the `apt` command is `apt [subcommands] {package-name}`

Common `apt` options include:

Option for the apt Command	Purpose
`install`	Install the package.
`remove`	Uninstall the package.
`purge`	Uninstall the package, and remove its configuration files.

Option for the apt Command	Purpose
`show`	Display package information.
`version`	Display package version.
`upgrade`	Upgrade the specified package (or all packages).

The apt commands for installing and removing software are:

```
$ apt install {software-package}
$ apt remove {software-package}
```

Subcommands such as `show` and `version` display specific information about the package, allowing administrators to see version, installation information, and source for the package.

```
$ apt show {software-package}
$ apt version {software package}
```

Sometimes security auditors or sysadmins need to create a comprehensive list of installed software. The `apt list` command displays such results. For example, to see all installed software on a system, type:

```
$ apt list --installed
```

One interesting package for Debian-based distributions is `build-essential`. This package contains the packages required for building deb packages. It's particularly important to those developers distributing software in the .deb file format.

```
$ apt install build-essential
```

Manage Dependencies with APT

Like the RPM package managers, APT can automatically install all necessary dependencies for a given package. This option is `-f` (force), and the syntax is:

```
$ apt -f install {software-package}
```

Update Packages

As part of software life-cycle management, APT can update installed software. Software updates are usually a two-step process with APT. The first step is for APT to discover updated packages in the configured repositories. The second step is to actually install the updates.

 APT repositories are discussed more in the next section.

First, update APT with information about newer versions of available software as compared to the packages already installed. This does not update the actual software. The command is:

```
$ apt update
```

Once APT is aware of available software, it checks that software against the current installations. By using the `upgrade` subcommand, administrators can upgrade any or all packages to current versions. The `apt` command for upgrading is:

```
$ apt upgrade {package-name}
```

If no argument is specified with `apt upgrade`, then all packages are upgraded to the latest version.

Use dpkg Commands

The `dpkg` command is sometimes used to manage software, especially on older systems. The command includes the options to install and remove software, as well as update the application query for software information.

Some common `dpkg` options include:

Option for the dpkg Command	Purpose
`-i`	Install the package.
`-r`	Remove the package.
`-l`	List package information.
`-s`	Report the package's installation status.

The syntax of the `dpkg` command is `dpkg [options] {package-name}`

Installing software with `dpkg` uses a syntax similar to other package manager commands:

```
$ dpkg -i {package-name}
```

Removing the software likewise has a similar look:

```
$ dpkg -r {package-name}
```

The dpkg package manager has mostly been replaced by APT in much the same way that the RPM manager has been replaced by YUM and DNF.

Query Packages on Debian Systems

Users and sysadmins alike need to understand what versions of certain software are installed on the system. Unauthorized software should not be installed. The `apt` command provides a mechanism for displaying and understanding information about the software, including version numbers. The `show` subcommand is particularly useful:

```
$ sudo apt show {package-name}
```

```
student@ubuntu20:~$ sudo apt show nmap
Package: nmap
Version: 7.80+dfsg1-2build1
```

Output of the `sudo apt show` command displaying details of the nmap package.

Sometimes a piece of software is unfamiliar to the user, and the ability to see the vendor, the install date, and the description of the software makes it easier to understand why the software is installed (and potentially whether it can be removed).

Manage APT Repository Configuration Files

Like other package managers, APT recognizes software storage repositories from which it can install or upgrade software. Sysadmins customize which repositories APT accesses. Repositories are exposed to APT in the `/etc/apt/sources.list` file and in the `/etc/apt/sources.list.d/` directory. Like YUM repositories, APT repositories may also be on the local system, on the local network, or hosted on the Internet.

Entries in the `/etc/apt/sources.list` include the following fields, separated by a space:

```
deb URL distro-name components
```

Be sure to let APT know about new repositories after editing the `/etc/apt/sources.list` file by running the `apt update` command.

Understanding /etc/apt.conf

The apt.conf configuration file is a method for managing the configuration of the APT suite of tools. The file contains settings that are loaded when APT starts and controls installation priorities, proxies, and other settings. Depending on the distribution, the configuration file may be found at `/etc/apt.conf`, `/etc/apt/apt.conf`, or along other paths.

Review Activity:

Debian Software Packages and Repositories

Answer the following questions:

1. What are the two steps for upgrading software with apt?

2. Explain the difference between the two steps in upgrading software with apt.

Topic 6D

Compile from Source Code

EXAM OBJECTIVES COVERED
1.1 Summarize Linux fundamentals.

Package managers are efficient and convenient forms of acquiring and installing software. However, there may be times when you want to build software from source code—after all, most Linux software is open source.

Why Compile Software?

Software that is packaged as an .rpm or a .deb is pre-compiled by the vendor. Usually, this packaged software is configured with generic settings and options. A Linux user may want to modify the software, for example, to optimize it for their specific hardware. This may result in maximum performance. Packaged software is most common in Linux, but compiling your own software is a normal Linux task. The same is not true for Windows and macOS, where nearly all software is pre-compiled (because you don't typically have access to the open-source code).

What Is the GCC?

Compiling software manually does not use a management tool as packaged software does. To compile software, there must be a compiler installed. Compilers translate source code written in a human-friendly programming language, such as C or C++, into machine-readable binaries.

A common compiler for Linux is the GNU Compiler Collection (GCC), implemented as the gcc utility. There are often other supporting libraries that must also be in place.

The required libraries vary by the software being compiled. Typically, software developers will provide a list of these necessary libraries with the application source code. These may be header files (.h file extension) or library files (.a file extension).

The Compile Software Commands

Compiling software is a three-step process. First, the system must be checked, and compile instructions must be created. Second, the source code is compiled into machine language. Finally, the new software is installed.

The first step uses a configure script to ensure the necessary dependencies and compilers are available. The `configure` script creates a makefile containing the instructions for compiling the software.

The command is:

```
$ ./configure
```

The Bash shell only checks for executable files such as programs and scripts in specific locations. Usually, a user's home directory is not one of these locations (nor should it be, for security reasons). However, it's as if the software the user is compiling has been downloaded to the home directory. The . / *instruction tells Bash to "check here" at the present location for the specified executable file.*

The second step is the actual compile process. In most cases, once the makefile is created, simply issuing the `make` command without arguments will compile the application. The `make` command automatically looks for the makefile in the current directory. You can, however, issue `make` with various options.

A makefile is a file that contains instructions used by a compiler to build a program from source code. These instructions typically define the resources that the program depends on in order to function properly, as well as any additional directives as defined by the developer.

Once the compile process completes, it's time to install the software. This is the final step in the process. The `make install` command installs the program, placing the appropriate files in the appropriate locations (configuration files, log files, and so on). The software is now available and ready to run.

Compile Software

When an administrator downloads software, there is a common process to build the executable file called **software compilation**.

1. Unpack the download, typically using `tar` and/or `gzip` commands.

2. Change into the directory that gets created as part of the unpacking process.

3. Run the `./configure` command to gather system information needed by the application. This information is stored in the makefile, which is referenced during the next step.

4. Use the `make` command to compile the application using the information stored in the makefile. Note that this usually requires root privileges.

5. Use the `make install` command to install the resulting binaries (the application).

Many developers will provide instructions and options that may modify this process somewhat. Specifically, there may be options or modifications that can be made to the makefile before the `make` command is run to optimize the software for the system or the user's needs. It is important to review any README or other instruction files that are downloaded as part of the software.

Remove Compiled Software

If you need to remove the software you compiled, the process can be a bit tricky. The makefile includes all directories and files created during the installation process. Examine this file, and remove each file and directory specified in the makefile. While this may be time-consuming, it ensures all traces of the application are gone.

To be able to remove the software components, you must save the makefile so that you can use it as a reference.

Review Activity:

Source Code

Answer the following questions:

1. **What is the effect of using ./ before an executable file?**

2. **Why is it more common to compile software with Linux than with other operating systems?**

Topic 6E

Acquire Software

EXAM OBJECTIVES COVERED
1.5 Given a scenario, use the appropriate networking tools or configuration files.

Repositories are not the only way to download and install software. Several other tools are used in this topic to enable you to acquire the files necessary to use software. These tools provide alternate ways of downloading files from web servers and managing compression.

Review Download Sites

Because of the open-source nature of Linux software, it is very common to be able to freely download applications directly from the application vendor. There are also many websites that centralize information about available software and about Linux distributions.

You can search the Internet for Linux software. Here are a few examples of Linux applications that are available for download:

- Audacity®, a music production application

- Atom, a powerful text editor

- GIMP, a powerful image editorNmap, a very useful network mapping utility

You can also search open-source hosting sites, such as GitHub®, for software.

wget And curl Commands

Most of us are familiar with accessing websites using a web browser such as Firefox. It is also possible to access websites from the command line. This is especially useful when downloading a file for which you already know the URL. The `wget` and `curl` commands can be written into scripts, automating the process of downloading package files.

The following is an example of using `wget` to download a file from the Samba website:

```
$ wget http://download.samba.org/pub/samba/samba-latest.tar.gz
```

Here is an example of using `curl` to download a file from the Nmap website:

```
$ curl -o nmap-7.70.tar.bz2 https://nmap.org/dist/nmap-7.70.tar.bz2
```

The syntax of the `wget` command is `wget [options] {URL}`

The `curl` command uses the same syntax.

The common options for `wget` include:

Option for the wget Command	Purpose
`-P`	Download to a different directory from the current one.
`-b`	Download in the background.

While there are many options for the `curl` command, common examples include:

Option for the curl Command	Purpose
`--progress-bar`	Display a progress bar during the download.
`--verbose`	Display additional download information.

For example, to download a file to the `~/projects` directory instead of the current directory, type:

```
wget -P /home/USER/projects {URL}
```

Comparing wget and curl

While `wget` and `curl` perform the same basic function, there are some key differences:

- `wget` is a command line utility only, whereas `curl` is implemented using the cross-platform `libcurl` library and is therefore more easily ported to other systems.

- `wget` can download files recursively, whereas `curl` cannot.

- `curl` supports many more network protocols than does `wget`, which only supports HTTP/S and FTP.

- `wget` is better suited for straightforward downloading of files from a web server, whereas `curl` is better suited to building and managing more complex requests and responses from webservers.

Use tar to Manage Source Code

Linux often uses two particular utilities to help manage files. The first utility is tape archiver or tar. The second is a compression utility, such as gzip. The purpose of `tar` is to bundle together multiple files into a single tarball with a .tar extension. This makes downloads much easier since there is only one download necessary to acquire multiple files. The server administrator creates the bundle of files, and whoever downloads the bundle extracts the files from it.

To extract the files bundled with `tar`, use the `-x` option with tar:

```
$ tar -xf archive.tar
```

If the tarball archive is compressed, use the `-z` option along with the `-x` extract option to uncompress the file.

Recall that `tar` was covered in an earlier lesson. It is covered here only in the context of downloading software or source code from the Internet.

Review Activity:

Software Acquisition

Answer the following questions:

1. **How can wget or curl be used to download files from the Internet in a way that a web browser can not be used?**

2. **How might tar be used to distribute an application?**

Topic 6F

Run Software in a Sandbox

EXAM OBJECTIVES COVERED
1.6 Given a scenario, build and install software.

Typically, software and the operating system share resources and can affect each other. This design creates potential security threats where one piece of software can impact the entire system. Isolating software with sandboxing helps mitigate this potential vulnerability.

Why Sandbox?

One of today's greatest **cybersecurity** threats is ransomware. Malware may enter a network environment via poorly tested or poorly written software, which then gains access to user data. One way of mitigating this threat is for end-users to run software in a sandbox environment.

Sandboxing is also known as "jailing" an application.

A **sandbox** is a virtual machine or container that isolates the application from the rest of the system and mediates communication between hardware resources and the program. Such a design is often more secure than an operating system and many applications sharing unmediated access to system resources. Developers testing new software and cybersecurity professionals examining malware code are among those who benefit from sandbox solutions.

Sandboxing differs from an older practice known as chroot. By using `chroot`, administrators told the application that a given directory was the "root" or highest point in the filesystem. Since the application was unaware of any directories above this root, it couldn't access the rest of the system. In some cases, this practice is still appropriate today.

Sandboxing relies on applications to enforce boundaries, while chroot uses the filesystem.

Sandbox Software

The following three package managers distribute and run software in a sandboxed environment: Snaps, Flatpak, and AppImage.

Snaps

Canonical, the group responsible for Ubuntu Linux, uses the Snap package manager to deploy and maintain software. The software is distributed as "Snaps" and managed by the snapd daemon and the `snap` command. Each Snap is self-contained with everything necessary to run included in the package. The packages run in an isolated sandbox environment.

Once Snap is installed, packages can be downloaded from the Snap Store. After that, application management is similar to that of other package managers:

```
$ snap install {software-package}
$ snap info {software-package}
$ snap list
$ snap remove {software-package}
```

Flatpak

Another package manager that runs applications in a sandbox is Flatpak. Using the `flatpak` command, users can manage software on a system-wide or per-user basis. Repositories—called "remotes"—store software distributed as flatpaks.

To install `{software-package}` from a remote named org.demo.sample, type:

```
$ flatpak install {software-package} org.demo.
sample
```

AppImage

AppImage offers self-contained applications that run consistently on Linux systems in a sandboxed environment. AppImage applications are distributed and managed as a single file containing everything needed to run the application. Application developers decide what distributions to support and then ensure that all needed dependencies and libraries are included with the AppImage file.

AppImage applications are standalone components, and while they can be installed in the traditional manner, they do not have to be. They can be accessed and run as mounted drives.

Drive mounting and access is covered in a later section.

Review Activity:

Software in Sandbox

Answer the following questions:

1. **What is the advantage of sandboxing?**

2. **True or False? The original practice, known as chroot, that predates the current method of sandboxing, is deprecated and no longer used.**

Lesson 6

Summary

Red Hat and Debian package managers handle software maintenance for most Linux distributions. There are also package managers that run applications in isolated sandbox environments for ease of maintenance and security. Some software is acquired in the form of source code, which allows users to customize the application for specific features or hardware before compiling it. This process is uncommon on platforms that use proprietary software but is more prevalent with open-source code.

Guidelines

These best practices and guidelines are provided for your use as revision tools or as quick references in your job role.

- Recognize which package managers are used by which distributions:

    - rpm, yum, and dnf commands are usually used by Red Hat–derived distributions.

    - apt command is usually used by Debian-derived distributions.

    - ZYpper is used by SUSE Linux.

- Be able to conduct basic package management with any package manager, including installing, updating, removing, and inventorying software packages.

- Be prepared to recognize and manage dependencies.

- Be able to install, update, and remove software by using the `rpm`, `yum`, `dnf`, and `apt` commands.

- Be able to query packages by using the `rpm`, `yum`, `dnf`, and `apt` commands.

- Be able to configure software repositories for the RPM, YUM, DNF, and APT package managers.

Command Reference Table

This list of commands and their associated syntax can also be found in Appendix B.

Command	Syntax	Purpose	Covered in
rpm	rpm [options] {package-name}	Package management in Red Hat distros.	Lesson 6, Topic B
yum	yum [options] [subcommand] {package-name}	Software package management in Red Hat distros.	Lesson 6, Topic B
apt	apt [subcommands] {package-name}	Package management in Debian-based distros.	Lesson 6, Topic C
dpkg	dpkg [options] {package-name}	Manage software packages in older Debian-based distros.	Lesson 6, Topic C
wget	wget [options] {URL}	Download package files housed on websites from the command line.	Lesson 6, Topic E
curl	curl [options] {URL}	Download package files housed on websites from the command line.	Lesson 6, Topic E

Lesson 7

Administering Storage

LESSON INTRODUCTION

Storage management involves planning, understanding hardware, and using many tools to accomplish storage goals. Sysadmins must know what types of hardware are available and what type will work with the Linux system in question. They must also know the performance requirements for data stored on any drives. Direct-attached storage disks are managed as single entities with traditional partitions or can be combined into logical volumes for more flexible storage space. Network-based storage, such as NAS, SAN, and cloud technologies, may also be used. Finally, sysadmins must understand the available Linux tools for troubleshooting and performance monitoring.

Lesson Objectives

In this lesson, you will:

- Understand storage.
- Deploy storage.
- Manage storage options.
- Troubleshoot storage.

Topic 7A

Understand Storage

EXAM OBJECTIVES COVERED
1.1 Summarize Linux fundamentals.

Managing a Linux server that stores a significant amount of data requires an understanding of storage technologies. Various storage formats are better suited to storing specific types of data. In addition, the balance between cost and performance must be maintained, leading administrators to make particular choices when it comes to interfaces such as SATA, SCSI, and SAS.

Storage Concepts

Storage capacity for user data, databases, logs, configuration files, operating system and application executables, and other resources are of major concern to sysadmins. Capacity is only one part of the issue, however. Related is the ability to maintain cost-effective, reliable, and secure storage media that is accessible to users and services.

The storage concepts in this section compare various storage technologies and configuration options that inform the choices that Linux administrators make for storage.

Cloud-based storage is a growing online service and has become a critical part of much storage management. General cloud concepts are covered in a later Lesson.

Some examples of storage media types include:

- **Hard disk drive (HDD):** Spinning magnetic disks, usually inexpensive, large, and relatively slow

- **Solid-state disk (SSD):** Flash memory storage, usually expensive, fast, small, and shorter -lived

- **Universal Serial Bus (USB):** Connection protocol for various external devices, including storage drives

- **Thumb drive:** Removable storage media, usually connects via USB

- **External:** Removable storage disk, usually connects via USB

Types of Storage Design

Stored data is usually managed via one of three different designs: file, block, and object storage. While these don't tend to impact Linux on a day-to-day basis, it is important to recognize some basic differences.

File storage is the common approach to storing data on local drives, with data organized into discrete files stored in directories. These directories are organized in a hierarchical structure. Data is easy to retrieve and change, but file storage does not scale well: it must be scaled out rather than scaled up.

Block storage is a good choice for large quantities of unstructured data stored across multiple platforms and storage types. Commonly used with SAN technologies, it is quick, reliable, and efficient.

Object storage is cost-effective and very scalable but best for static data because it's difficult to modify data once written. This makes it particularly unsuited for databases.

A typical Linux server will rely on file storage by using one or more internal drives that use a standard filesystem to organize and retrieve data.

Traditional Hard Disk Partitioning versus LVM Deployment

The basic process for adding storage to a system is to install the drive, partition it, add a filesystem, and then mount it. In addition to traditional partitioning, technologies such as a **Logical Volume Manager (LVM)** permit the aggregation of storage space from multiple disks, providing flexibility and scalability options.

Both traditional partitions and LVM are covered in Topic 7B.

Storage Interfaces

Internal storage devices use different protocols and interfaces to communicate with the rest of the system. These designs vary by speed, communication type, and scalability. Various solid-state drives, hard disk drives, and flash storage use these interfaces.

Serial Advanced Technology Attachment (SATA) is a common inexpensive storage media that uses a serial connection to communicate with the motherboard. This is the slowest of the three options discussed here but the least expensive. It is a good all-around solution for most systems.

Small Computer Systems Interface (SCSI) tends to be expensive with less capacity than most SATA drives but makes up for this by being very fast. For servers, RPMs of 10,000 and 15,000 are common, while desktop and laptop drives might spin at 7,200 or 5,400 RPMs. Multiple SCSI drives can be attached to the same chain, making their scalability far more flexible than SATA.

Serial Attached SCSI (SAS) is an upgraded SCSI design with larger capacities, faster transfer speeds, and greater flexibility. However, these benefits come with a higher cost. The cost may be well worth it for mission-critical servers.

Linux administrators must balance speed, capacity, and cost when deciding which of the standards is appropriate for a new Linux workstation or server.

Types of Partitions

Storage drives are divided into **partitions** for more efficient and organized use. On a Linux server, these partitions may store different types of operating systems, applications, or data files. There are two ways of tracking these divisions of the drive: a Master Boot Record (MBR) or a GUID Partition Table (GPT). These two entries identify where on the physical drive the partition divisions are located.

The MBR is the traditional choice, but it is limited. Many server administrators use the GPT because it recognizes more partitions (divisions) of the drive, which is important for larger-capacity storage devices.

Creating partitions is covered in a later section.

The **master boot record (MBR)** is the first physical sector on a storage drive and a type of partition structure. The MBR boot sector contains the boot loader that loads the operating system into memory. It also contains the partition table of the storage drive. MBR determines what sectors are available to each partition, as well as which partitions are bootable and which are not.

For many years, MBR was the dominant partition structure used in Linux and other operating systems. However, it has three major disadvantages:

- The maximum storage space of an MBR-partitioned drive is two terabytes.

- MBR-partitioned drives can have a maximum of four primary partitions.

- The boot data is stored all in one sector, which increases the risk of corruption.

The **GUID Partition Table (GPT)** is a successor to MBR that makes up for the latter's shortcomings. Like MBR, it is a partition structure, but it employs a more modern design and is part of the UEFI standard. Every partition on a drive is assigned a globally unique identifier—a GUID—to distinguish it from every other partition on (theoretically) every drive.

The storage space and partition number maximums are so large that they are not currently achievable, and any limitations are going to be imposed by the file system type or operating system kernel, rather than GPT itself. GPT also has the advantage of storing its boot data in multiple locations on a drive to enhance redundancy. If the primary location is corrupted, GPT can leverage one of the other copies to restore the boot data.

Whenever possible, partitioning a drive with GPT is preferable to MBR.

Filesystem in Userspace (FUSE)

Linux is one of several common operating systems that supports the **Filesystem in Userspace (FUSE)** kernel module. This feature provides support for many virtual filesystems. Filesystems are created in userspace by non-privileged users, without kernel modifications, and FUSE provides a kernel connection.

The use of FUSE is not inherent in Linux administration. The key factor here is that Linux is capable of this feature, which provides a great deal of flexibility.

RAID Arrays

A standalone storage disk is a single point of failure. When the disk fails, the data on it is likely to become inaccessible. In addition, individual disks have limited transfer speeds and storage capacity.

Storage disks may be organized into RAID arrays to mitigate the limitations of standalone drives. A **Redundant Array of Inexpensive Disks (RAID)** combines storage disks together. Depending on the configuration, the result may be greater capacity, greater fault tolerance, and increased speed.

Two different designs manage RAID arrays: hardware and software. Hardware RAID uses a dedicated controller attached to the motherboard. This is usually faster, more flexible, and more expensive. Software RAID relies on the operating system to manage the storage, which is usually slower, less flexible, and less expensive (because no special hardware is required).

In a server, hardware RAID is almost always preferred.

Various RAID standards exist and are primarily identified by number, but three of the most common are RAID 0, RAID 1, and RAID 5. Each has advantages and disadvantages to consider.

RAID details are covered in Topic 7C.

Set Disk Quotas

A **storage quota** is the storage space allotted to a user for file storage on a computer. Storage quotas are configured on a per-user basis. File systems that implement storage quotas can have a soft limit, a grace period, and a hard limit. Once a user exceeds the soft limit, they will be placed in the grace period, the default setting for which is seven days. The user is allowed to exceed this soft limit within this grace period but cannot exceed the hard limit maximum. If the user returns below the soft limit, the timer resets. If the user still exceeds the soft limit when the timer expires, the soft limit becomes a hard limit, and the user will be unable to use any additional storage.

Storage quotas are a good measure to prevent or respond to issues that arise due to excessive storage use. You can use these quotas to ensure that users are not consuming all of a drive's space and leaving none for other users or the system.

Quota management is the effective allotment and monitoring of quotas for all users. Linux has various commands that help ease the job of quota management for the system administrator.

Before you can use these commands, you must activate user and/or group quotas on the file system. You can do this by editing the `/etc/fstab` file to add the options `usrquota` and `grpquota` to the relevant file system.

Quota reports are created by the system so you can view storage space usage by each user. These reports enable you to check which user is taking up maximum disk space. They can also help you troubleshoot issues with quotas themselves—for example, quotas that are either too restrictive or too permissive.

A quota report contains the following details:

- The name of the user/group.
- The total number of blocks (in kilobytes) that are being used by the user/group on a file system.
- The user's/group's storage soft limit.
- The user's/group's storage hard limit.
- The grace period.
- The total number of inodes that have been used on a file system by the user/group.
- The soft limit on inodes.
- The hard limit on inodes.

Review Activity:

Storage Concepts

Answer the following questions:

1. Explain the key differences between MBR and GPT partition tables.

2. How might quotas help sysadmins manage storage capacity on a server?

3. Do all RAID array designs provide fault tolerance?

Topic 7B

Deploy Storage

EXAM OBJECTIVES COVERED
1.3 Given a scenario, manage files and directories.

Consider a scenario requiring an administrator to deploy additional storage on an existing Linux server. The drive must be installed, detected, partitioned, formatted, and mounted to be available to users. There are many tools and commands to display drive information and manipulate storage space. This section steps through such a scenario and explains the utilities needed to manage server storage.

Deploy a Traditional Hard Disk Drive

As a Linux administrator you'll commonly be asked to manage storage, which almost always translates into making more storage capacity available. Assume that you've selected the appropriate drive based on interface requirements (SATA, SCSI, or SAS) and that performance requirements such as speed and capacity have been satisfied.

Once the drive is physically installed, confirm that Linux is aware of the new device. Depending on the type of drive and the information needed, several commands are available that display device information. Use these commands to view device information.

The hwinfo Command

The `hwinfo` command displays details about system components. The command can provide information on any or all components. In the case of storage, the `--storage` flag is added to display storage controllers, while the `--block` flag displays information on storage disks and partitions. Because at this point in the installation no partitions have been created yet, confirm controllers by typing:

```
hwinfo --short --storage
```

Note that these flags are preceded by two dash characters: (--).

To confirm the proper disk type is installed and compatibility with the storage controllers, type:

```
# hwinfo --short --storage
```

Add the - - short option to focus on general information about the specified device.

The `hwinfo` *tool is also used to gather CPU, memory, Bluetooth, and network device data. It is covered in more detail in the next Lesson.*

The lsblk Command

The `lsblk` command displays information on storage devices the system is aware of. This information includes the device name, capacity, and mount point (if configured). Mount points are covered in a later section.

The `lsblk` command displays more information than most sysadmins require for this scenario. The specific data to look for is `/dev/sd*` content, which shows the recognized drives and partitions (if any).

Confirm that the new hard disk drive has been recognized. The syntax for the `lsblk` command is `lsblk {drive-path}`

For example, to see all devices recognized, type `lsblk` with no arguments. To see information on a specific storage device (such as storage device a), type the command with the device path:

```
# lsblk /dev/sda
```

```
[student@fedora home]$ lsblk /dev/sda
NAME      MAJ:MIN RM SIZE RO TYPE MOUNTPOINTS
sda        8:0     0   80G  0 disk
├─sda1     8:1     0    1G  0 part /boot
└─sda2     8:2     0   79G  0 part /home
                                   /
[student@fedora home]$ ▉
```

Output from the `lsblk /dev/sda` *command displaying capacity and partition information.*

The lsscsi Command

If the system uses SCSI devices, the `lsscsi` command displays information about each device. Data for each device is displayed on a separate line and includes the device name, manufacturer, model, etc. If you add the `-s` option, device size information is shown.

For example, if the new device is an SCSI disk, type `lsscsi -s` to see device details and size output.

The `lsscsi` *command also displays NVMe storage device information.*

Disk and Partition References

Storage disk information such as manufacturer, model, and capacity may be reported by some tools. Most references to the storage media include a path. All hardware devices are mapped to the `/dev` directory. Storage disks are displayed there using the `sd` string.

The `sd` string (which used to stand for "SCSI disk" but now means "storage disk") is followed by a letter defining the drive's location. Any numbers that follow reference a partition, if any have been created.

So, the first storage disk in the system is displayed as `/dev/sda`. In this example, a second disk is added to the system, so it is labeled as `/dev/sdb`.

```
sda        8:0    0   80G   0 disk
├─sda1     8:1    0  512M   0 part /boot/efi
├─sda2     8:2    0    1K   0 part
└─sda5     8:5    0 79.5G   0 part /
sr0       11:0    1 1024M   0 rom
```

Partition information for the first disk (sda).

Partition the Drive

Once you've installed the drive and it's been recognized by Linux, you must divide the storage capacity into usable space. Creating partitions is the first step in organizing the storage space. Considerations such as MBR vs. GPT must be taken into account, and then you'll partition the space using `fdisk` or `parted`. After creating the partitions, update the system with `partprobe` and confirm the partitions in the `/proc/partitions` directory.

Recall that the Master Boot Record (MBR) or GUID Partition Table (GPT) is used to define the location of partitions on the disk. The MBR is limited by drive size (2 TB maximum) and the number of partitions (four). These limitations must be taken into account when deciding on a partition method.

Partition Design

It is common to dedicate specific partitions to certain FHS directories. For example, it may be useful to place the `/boot` directory on its own partition. In addition, the `/home` and `/var` directories may also be mounted to dedicated partitions. The reason these two directories are often attached to dedicated partitions is that they are particularly at risk for filling up. Users may create or download a great many files to their home directories, or log files stored at `/var/log` may suddenly increase in size due to failing applications or services. If the partition where the root of the filesystem (/) resides fills, the system will crash. To prevent this, directories such as `/home` and `/var`, which are at risk for filling, are placed on separate partitions from `/`.

Linux also commonly dedicates a partition to virtual memory. Using a process called "swapping," Linux moves data between memory and the hard drive if the memory is in danger of being fully consumed. A dedicated swap partition is often set aside that is 1.5 times the quantity of the total RAM.

 Memory management and swapping are discussed in detail in Topic 8D.

The fdisk Utility

The fdisk utility is a menu-driven program that is used to create, modify, or delete partitions on a storage drive. Using `fdisk`, you can create a new partition table or modify existing entries on the partition table. The fdisk tool understands the DOS and Linux type partition tables. The fdisk utility also enables you to specify the size of partitions.

```
Generic
   d   delete a partition
   F   list free unpartitioned space
   l   list known partition types
   n   add a new partition
   p   print the partition table
   t   change a partition type
   v   verify the partition table
   i   print information about a partition
```

The `fdisk` *command menu.*

The syntax of the `fdisk` utility is `fdisk [options] {device name}`

Option for fdisk	Purpose
n	Create a new partition. The sub-options enable you to specify the partition type and partition size.
d	Remove a partition.
p	Print (list) the existing partitions.
w	Write the changes to the drive, and exit the utility.
q	Quit the changes to the drive, and exit the utility.

To create partitions on the newly installed storage disk by using `fdisk`, use the following steps:

1. Type `fdisk /dev/sdb` to edit the partition table for the second (new) disk.

2. Type m to display the menu of `fdisk` features.

3. Type n to create a new partition.

4. Type p to create a new primary partition, or type l to create a logical partition.

5. Select `Enter` to start the partition at the first available sector.

6. Type a value such as +10G to create a 10 GB partition.

7. Type p to display the new partition information (note that no changes have been made at this point).

8. Type w to write (save) the changes to the partition table and exit `fdisk`.

9. Type `fdisk -l /dev/sdb` to confirm the partition information.

Once one or more partitions are created, use `fdisk -l /dev/sdb2` to display the partition information.

```
student@ubuntu20:~$ sudo fdisk -l /dev/sda
[sudo] password for student:
Disk /dev/sda: 80 GiB, 85899345920 bytes, 167772160 sectors
Disk model: Virtual Disk
Units: sectors of 1 * 512 = 512 bytes
Sector size (logical/physical): 512 bytes / 4096 bytes
I/O size (minimum/optimal): 4096 bytes / 4096 bytes
Disklabel type: dos
Disk identifier: 0x2bcda5b9

Device     Boot   Start      End      Sectors   Size Id Type
/dev/sda1  *       2048  1050623    1048576   512M  b W95 FAT32
/dev/sda2       1052670 167770111 166717442 79.5G  5 Extended
/dev/sda5       1052672 167770111 166717440 79.5G 83 Linux

Partition 2 does not start on physical sector boundary.
```

Output from the `fdisk -l /dev/sda` command displaying partition information.

The Parted Utility

The **GNU Parted** utility is also used to manage partitions. It is particularly useful when creating partitions on new storage drives. It can be used to create, destroy, and resize partitions. The `parted` command runs the GNU Parted utility. Like fdisk, Parted includes a menu-driven interactive mode where you can input various options.

The syntax of the `parted` command is `parted [options] {device name}`

Option for parted	Purpose
`select`	Choose which device or partition to modify.
`mkpart`	Create a partition with a specified file system type.
`print`	List the partition table.
`resizepart`	Modify the end position of a partition.
`rm`	Delete a partition.
`quit`	Write changes and exit the GNU Parted utility.

To create partitions on the newly installed storage disk by using `parted` (and only if you haven't done so via `fdisk`), follow this process:

1. Type `parted /dev/sdb` to edit the partition table for the second (new) disk.

2. Type `mklabel gpt` to create a GPT table.

3.   Type `mkpart primary ext4 1MB 2000MB` to create a new primary partition of the specified size.

4.   Type `print` to display the new partition information.

5.   Type `quit` to write changes to the partition table and exit parted.

GNU Parted is a critical tool for any sysadmin. The utility recognizes and can resize **New Technology Filing System (NTFS)** partitions, which are commonly found on Windows Servers.

The partprobe Command and the /proc/partitions Directory

Whether you used `fdisk` or `parted` to create partitions on the new disk, the next step is to update Linux with the new information. The `partprobe` command causes the system to redetect the storage disks and any partition changes. Run this command to confirm the new partitions exist as expected.

Partition information is stored in a file named `/proc/partitions`, which is recreated each time the system boots or the `partprobe` command is run. The dynamic nature of this file means that it reflects changes to the system's configuration (changes that are detected during system startup or via the `partprobe` command).

Because Linux treats `/proc/partitions` as a file, display its contents by using the `cat` command:

```
# cat /proc/partitions
```

When viewing the output from `/proc/partitions`, recall that `sd` stands for storage disk and that letter designations such as `a` and `b` represent specific drives. Any numbers in the output represent partitions on that drive. Therefore, `/dev/sdb3` is the third partition storage device b.

```
[student@fedora home]$ cat /proc/partitions
major minor  #blocks  name

  11        0   1048575 sr0
   8        0  83886080 sda
   8        1   1048576 sda1
   8        2  82836480 sda2
 252        0   3991552 zram0
[student@fedora home]$
```

The output of the `cat /proc/partitions` *command displaying partitions recognized by the system.*

The blkid Command

Another useful utility for displaying partition information is the `blkid` command. The command displays known information on the partitions. One particularly useful piece of information is the UUID of the partition. The Universally Unique ID value is a more reliable identifier for the partition than the path `/dev/sdb2` since the path is possibly changeable.

```
[student@fedora home]$ blkid /dev/sda1
/dev/sda1: UUID="e5b48c5b-0898-4fb2-ae82-6c9876ce0057"
 BLOCK_SIZE="4096" TYPE="ext4" PARTUUID="e858290d-01"
[student@fedora home]$ ▊
```

The output of the `blkid` *command displaying the UUID for the /dev/sda1 partition.*

Add a Filesystem to a Partition

After creating the partitions on a new drive, you must add a filesystem to organize the storage of the actual data. Different filesystems have different benefits, and there are many of them. In general, most Linux distributions use either the ext4 or XFS filesystems. Many maintenance tools exist for these filesystems that allow for repair, resizing, and identifying filesystem information.

The ext4 Filesystem

The ext4 filesystem is the older of the two options. It provides journaling and is recognized by most distributions.

 The ext toolset enables a variety of administrative tasks to manage the filesystem. These tasks are covered in a later section.

To format the new partitions, use the `mkfs` command. The command expects to know the desired filesystem and a target partition.

To place the ext4 filesystem on the second partition on the new disk, type:

```
# mkfs.ext4 /dev/sdb2
```

The `mkfs` also recognizes a slightly different syntax. The following command achieves the same result as the example command above:

```
mkfs -t ext4 /dev/sdb2
```

 The `mkfs` *command overwrites existing data on the partition, making that data difficult or impossible to recover. Use it carefully!*

The XFS Filesystem

While the ext4 filesystem has been the default for many Linux distributions, it is very common to find newer systems relying on XFS instead. XFS has many modern advantages over ext4 and relatively few disadvantages.

- XFS recognizes a larger partition size.
- XFS recognizes a larger file size.
- XFS avoids inode exhaustion.

To format the second partition on the new disk with the XFS filesystem, use the `mkfs` command but with a different option:

```
# mkfs.xfs /dev/sdb2
```

XFS Tools are available to help manage the filesystem. Management tasks include resizing the filesystem and gathering information. The tools are covered in a later section.

The Btrfs Filesystem

An additional filesystem choice is Btrfs. This filesystem is very scalable, provides easy management features, and is reliable. It is the default for modern Linux distributions such as SUSE Linux Enterprise Server 15 and Fedora 35, though it has been removed from RHEL 8 support, which prefers XFS.

The syntax to add the Btrfs to a partition is the same as for XFS and ext4. To add this filesystem to the second partition on the second drive, type:

```
# mkfs.btrfs /dev/sdb2
```

Like XFS and ext4, Btrfs has a toolset to provide detailed information and troubleshooting utilities. The toolset may already be installed on the system, or it may need to be downloaded. In some cases, you will be required to compile the toolset. The package is named btrfs-tools.

Information about a Btrfs-formatted partition is displayed with the following command:

```
# btrfs filesystem show
```

The btrfs-tools package can also resize filesystems, much like XFS and ext4.

Whichever filesystem is selected for the new partition, the `mkfs` command is used to install it. Each filesystem also has its own management and troubleshooting tools.

Manually Test Mount

Now that you have installed the drive, created the partitions, and placed the filesystem, the storage capacity is ready for use. Plan to test the storage space to ensure it's accessible to users. Storage capacity is added to the FHS by a process called mounting. Capacity can be manually attached by using the `mount` command and detached by using the `umount` command.

The mount and umount Commands

A new disk has been installed, partitioned, and provided with a filesystem. It is now ready to be attached to a directory in the FHS. Attaching the storage area to a directory makes the storage area accessible to users.

The term for attaching storage to the FHS is referred to as "mounting," and the command is `mount`. The logical reverse of this is to detach or unmount the storage area, and the related command is `umount`.

 Observe that `umount` *is a slightly confusing way of unmounting. The command and the concept are not spelled the same.*

To mount the partition, first create a directory. The directory is referred to as a **mount point**. Suppose the new storage capacity will be used to manage project data. At the root of the filesystem, create a new directory named `projects`, and then `issue` the mount command:

```
# mkdir /projects
# mount /dev/sdb2 /projects
```

Note that the syntax is similar to the `mv` or `cp` commands—from here to there. The command could be interpreted as "attach the partition found at /dev/sdb2 to the directory found at /projects."

To test that the storage area is attached and usable, use the `du` and `df` commands.

External storage devices such as USB drives are mounted similarly. The path to the device is specified along with the desired mount point. For removable drives, this mount point is often a subdirectory of the `/mount` directory.

Assuming the USB drive is identified as sdc, use the following command to mount the USB storage device:

```
$ mount /dev/sdc /media/usb
```

 Sometimes there is confusion with the use of the word "filesystem." One use involves the format of a partition used to store data, such as ext4 or XFS. Another use involves the organization of directories in a logical tree, such as the Linux Filesystem Hierarchy Standard.

Test the Storage

You have partitioned the storage disk and formatted it with a filesystem. It's identified as `/dev/sdb2`, and it has been manually mounted to a directory named `/projects`. The next step is to test whether the storage space is available.

There are two approaches to testing: use reporting tools and actually storing data in the new space. The `df` and `du` commands report storage information about specified partitions or directories. Commands such as `touch`, `mv`, and `cp` place data in the new storage location.

The du and df Commands

The `df` and `du` commands facilitate storage-space tracking. The `df` command ("disk free") enables you to view the device's free space, file system, total size, space used, percentage value of space used, and mount point. The `du` command ("disk usage") displays how a device is used, including the size of directory trees and files within it. It also enables you to track space hogs, which are directories and files that consume large amounts of space on the storage drive. These are go-to commands to confirm excessive storage-space consumption that might be causing system issues.

First, verify the disk usage of `/projects`. The command is: `du -h /projects`

```
student@ubuntu20:/projects$ sudo du -h /boot
4.0K    /boot/efi
2.3M    /boot/grub/fonts
2.5M    /boot/grub/i386-pc
7.1M    /boot/grub
73M     /boot
```

Output from the `du -h /boot` *command displaying the size of each file in the directory.*

The result shows files and directories consuming space in the `/projects` directory. Add the `-h` option to display the capacity in a human-friendly format; otherwise, the output will display in bytes, which may be difficult to translate.

Next, check the storage space in use by using the `df` command. The syntax is the same as for `du`, with the command being: `df -h /projects`

```
student@ubuntu20:~$ df -h /dev/sda1
Filesystem      Size  Used Avail Use% Mounted on
/dev/sda1       511M  4.0K  511M   1% /boot/efi
```

Output from the `df -h /dev/sda1` *command displaying the size of the partition.*

To see a summary of space in use on all disks, type `df` without any arguments.

Both utilities are important to troubleshooting, testing, and capacity planning.

Move Data to the New Storage

Finally, to prove that storage space is available, copy an existing file to the `/projects` directory (or use the `touch` command to create an empty file in `/projects`). The command `ls /projects` should show the file.

Automatically Mount New Storage

Manually mounting the partition is effective for testing purposes, but it's not realistic to ask end-users to mount and unmount storage space regularly. Instead, you need to automate the process to occur during the system's boot phase so that the space is immediately available to users.

Use a systemd.mount File

Many modern Linux distributions rely on the systemd system and service management software suite to configure operating system settings and options. One aspect of the systemd init process is to manage the automatic mounting of partitions to the filesystem.

The `systemctl` command is used to display and change settings within systemd. To display mounted partition information, type: `systemctl -t mount`

The following steps configure the system to mount the partition automatically:

1. Get UUID by using the `blkid` command (covered earlier): `blkid /dev/sdb2`

2. Create a systemd unit file by using a text editor.

3. Restart the systemd service daemon: `systemctl daemon-reload`

4. Start the filesystem: `systemctl start projects.mount`

5. Enable the filesystem: `systemctl enable projects.mount`

The following is a sample of a systemd unit file that mounts the `/projects` directory to the partition with the specified UUID. Assume the unit file is named `projects.mount`.

```
# This file mounts the /projects directory via
systemd
[Unit]
```

```
Description=Project Directory (/projects)
DefaultDependencies=no
Conflicts=umount.target
Before=local-fs.target umount.target
After=swap.target
[Mount]
What=/dev/disk/by-uuid/eca1646e-3245-5bf5-faab-
31f6c424c09f
Where=/projects
Type=ext4
Options=defaults
[Install]
WantedBy=multi-user.target
```

 The systemd suite is covered in detail later in the course.

The /etc/fstab File

Some distributions, especially older ones, rely on the `/etc/fstab` file to mount partitions. Systems that use systemd still have and reference `/etc/fstab`, but they supplement its settings.

The system reads `/etc/fstab` during startup. Partitions defined are identified and mounted to the filesystem at the specified locations. The file is edited with a standard text editor, but you must be careful not to make typographical errors.

The `/etc/fstab` file is divided into six fields.

/etc/fstab Field	Value
Block device	Drive and partition
Mount point	Where the partition is mounted
Filesystem type	The filesystem on the partition (XFS or ext4)
Mount options	Read-write or read-only options, others
Dump	Whether dump program backs up partition (1 or 0)
FSCK order	Order fsck checks partitions (1 for root, 2 for all others)

A sample entry in the `/etc/fstab` file for the `/projects` directory might look like this:

```
/dev/sdb2    /projects        xfs        rw        0        2
```

During system startup, the kernel reads `/etc/fstab` and mounts the specified partitions to the listed mount points.

Storage Deployment Summary

Because there are many steps necessary to add storage capacity to a Linux system, it's useful to see a summary of the process:

1. Physically install the storage device.

2. Confirm that Linux sees the storage device by using tools such as `hwinfo`, `lsblk`, and `lsscsi`.

3. Partition the drive with `fdisk` or `parted`.

4. Add a filesystem such as ext4 or XFS by using the `mkfs` command.

5. Manually test mount the storage capacity to a mount point by using the `mount` command.

6. Ensure the storage space is usable by copying actual data to the location using `cp`.

7. Configure automatic mounting so that the capacity is available when the system boots.

Manage Filesystems

Filesystems such as ext4 and XFS may require periodic maintenance. You may wish to relabel the filesystem to something more descriptive or configure tunable performance parameters. The filesystem may need to be expanded or shrunk when using tools like parted to resize partitions. Here are several ext4 filesystem management tools.

The fsck Command

A file system's superblock contains metadata about that file system, including its size, type, and status. The superblock is critical to the function of the file system, and if it becomes corrupt, you may be unable to mount and work with the file system. You can use a tool like fsck to repair the superblock, if necessary.

The e2label Command

File system labels are assigned to file systems for easy identification. The labels may be up to 16 characters long and can be displayed or changed using the `e2label` command for ext# file systems and the `xfs_admin` command for XFS file systems.

The syntax for setting ext# file system labels is `e2label /dev/{device name}{partition number} {label name}`

The resize2fs Command

The `resize2fs` command is used to enlarge or shrink an ext2/3/4 file system on a device. You can enlarge a mounted file system, but you must unmount the file system before you can shrink it. You can specify the desired size of the file system in order to either enlarge or shrink it. If you don't specify a size, the file system will be resized to the same size as the partition.

It's important to note that `resize2fs` does not resize partitions, only the file system. You must use a command such as `fdisk` or an LVM tool to first expand the size of the partition/volume and to then enlarge the file system.

The syntax of the `resize2fs` command is `resize2fs [options] {device/file system name} [desired size]`

The tune2fs Command

The `tune2fs` command helps you configure various "tunable" parameters associated with an ext2/3/4 file system. Tunable parameters enable you to remove reserved blocks, alter reserved block count, specify the number of mounts between checks, specify the time interval between checks, and more.

You can also use `tune2fs` to add a journal to an existing ext2 or ext3 file system (neither of which includes journaling by default). If the file system is already mounted, the journal will be visible in the root directory of the file system. If the file system is not mounted, the journal will be hidden.

The syntax of the `tune2fs` command is `tune2fs [options] {device/ file system name}`

The dumpe2fs Command

The `dumpe2fs` command is used to dump ext2, ext3, and ext4 file system information. It prints the superblock and block group information for the selected device. This can be useful when troubleshooting a faulty file system.

The syntax of the `dumpe2fs` command is `dumpe2fs [options] {device/ file system name}`

Option for the dumpe2fs Command	Purpose
`-x`	Print a detailed report about block numbers in the file system.
`-b`	Print the bad blocks in the file system.
`-f`	Force the utility to display the file system status irrespective of the file system flags.
`-i`	Display file system data from an image file created using the `e2image` command.

XFS Tools

There are many tools that enable you to work with the XFS file system.

XFS Tool	Purpose
`xfs_info`	Display details about the XFS file system, including its block information.
`xfs_admin`	Change the parameters of an XFS file system, including its label and UUID.
`xfs_metadump`	Copy the superblock metadata of the XFS file system to a file.
`xfs_growfs`	Expand the XFS file system to fill the drive size.
`xfs_copy`	Copy the contents of the XFS file system to another location.
`xfs_repair`	Repair and recover a corrupt XFS file system.
`xfs_debug`	Debug the XFS filesystem.

Logical Volume Manager Storage

It's common to add a single storage disk to a system to provide additional capacity. The disk is then partitioned and its capacity used. The Logical Volume Manager configuration is an alternative to this traditional partitioning scheme. The LVM configuration is flexible and very scalable, often providing a better storage option than single storage disks.

In the next section the discussion of LVM replaces the partitioning stage of adding a disk. Other steps, such as detecting the storage disks and applying a filesystem, remain the same.

The section begins with LVM concepts and then continues with LVM configurations.

Configure Logical Volume Manager

Logical Volume Manager functions based on three configuration layers for storage. The first layer is one or more **Physical Volumes (PV)**. PVs are drives or partitions allocated to LVM. The next layer represents the aggregated storage capacity of any designated PVs that are added to the **Volume Group (VG)**. The top layer consists of one or more **Logical Volumes (LV)**, which are treated by the system as if they were standard partitions. In reality, they are carved space from VGs that may store data on multiple PVs.

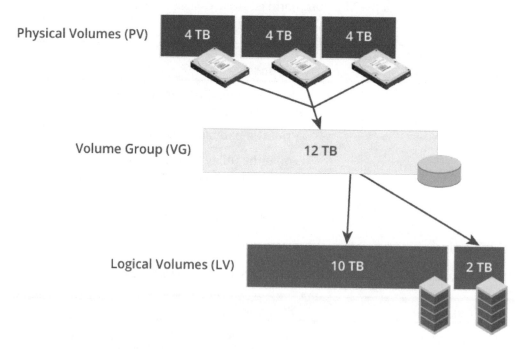

The three levels of the Logical Volume Manager. Physical volumes combine to form the volume group, which is then divided out in logical volumes to meet storage needs. (Images © 123RF.com.)

LVM provides a great deal of flexibility. Additional storage capacity can be added to the VG and granted to the LV to provide storage space without interrupting or reconfiguring user resources.

LVM maps whole physical devices and partitions (e.g., `/dev/sda1`, `/dev/sdb2`, and so on) into one or more virtual structures called volume groups. Within these volume groups are one or more logical volumes. Ultimately, the logical volumes become the storage devices that the system, user, and applications work with.

The `/dev/mapper/` directory contains all of the logical volumes on the system that are managed by LVM. Devices in this directory are typically formatted as:

```
/dev/mapper/<volume group name>-<logical volume
name>
```

In some cases, this directory may just include links to the actual logical volume location.

Many distributions support LVM, and several actually place the root file system on logical volumes during installation.

Compared to traditional physical partition management, LVM provides the following benefits:

- Dynamically create, delete, and resize volumes without having to reboot the system.

- Day-to-day management of volumes is easier once everything is set up.

- Map multiple logical volumes across multiple physical devices.

- A logical volume can exceed the size of any one physical device (as long as it doesn't exceed the total size of devices in the volume group).

- Create virtual snapshots of each logical volume so you can quickly and easily revert a volume to a specific state.

One potential downside to LVM is that the initial setup can be somewhat complex.

LVM Management Tools

LVM divides its volume management tools into three categories based on the three different components that make up LVM: the physical volume (PV), the volume group (VG), and logical volume (LV) tools.

Physical Volume Tool	Purpose
pvscan	Scan for all physical devices that are being used as physical volumes.
pvcreate	Initialize a drive or partition to use as a physical volume.
pvdisplay	List attributes of physical volumes.
pvchange	Change attributes of a physical volume.
pvs	Display information about physical volumes.
pvck	Check the metadata of physical volumes.
pvremove	Remove physical volumes.

Volume Group Tool	Purpose
vgscan	Scan all physical devices for volume groups.
vgcreate	Create volume groups.
vgdisplay	List attributes of volume groups.
vgchange	Change attributes of volume groups.

Volume Group Tool	Purpose
vgs	Display information about volume groups.
vgck	Check the metadata of volume groups.
vgrename	Rename a volume group.
vgreduce	Remove physical volumes from a volume group to reduce its size.
vgextend	Add physical volumes to volume groups.
vgmerge	Merge two volume groups.
vgsplit	Split a volume group into two.
vgremove	Remove volume groups.

Logical Volume Tool	Purpose
lvscan	Scan all physical devices for logical volumes.
lvcreate	Create logical volumes in a volume group.
lvdisplay	List attributes of logical volumes.
lvchange	Change attributes of logical volumes.
lvs	Display information about logical volumes.
lvrename	Rename logical volumes.
lvreduce	Reduce the size of logical volumes.
lvextend	Extend the size of logical volumes.
lvresize	Resize logical volumes.
lvremove	Remove logical volumes.

Deploy a Logical Volume Manager

The previous section covered the deployment of a single storage disk and partition. However, if the production file server is expected to see significant traffic and unknown storage requirements, you may decide that using LVM would provide a more robust storage solution.

Once the disks are partitioned, it's time to create the LVM structure. First, you'll designate the drives as LVM Physical Volumes (PV), then you'll aggregate them into a Volume Group (VG), and finally, you'll allocate Logical Volumes (LV). The Logical Volumes will be configured with filesystems, just like standard partitions were in the earlier section.

You've installed two disks in the server that will become part of the LVM configuration. Use the following steps to deploy a new Logical Volume. Display the results of each command.

Deploying the LVM

First, designate the two drives as LVM physical volumes by using the `pvcreate` command followed by the path to the partitions:

```
# pvcreate /dev/sdb
# pvcreate /dev/sdc
# pvdisplay
```

The `pvdisplay` command allows you to confirm the configuration by displaying the current settings.

Next, create a volume group named `vg_projects` containing the two physical volumes designated above (`/dev/sdb` and `/dev/sdc`):

```
# vgcreate vg_projects /dev/sdb /dev/sdbc
# vgdisplay
```

Creating a volume group aggregates the storage capacity of one or more physical volumes. The total capacity can then be managed as a single unit. The syntax for the `vgcreate` command is `vgcreate [options] new_vg_name PVs_to_add`

Options include the ability to set a maximum number of PVs or LVs associated with the VG. Use the `vgdisplay` command to see the VG's information.

Logical volumes are storage space carved from some or all of the capacity of a VG. These logical volumes are treated by administrators as if they were standard storage disks.

The syntax for the `lvcreate` command is `lvcreate [options] new_lv_name`

Create a logical volume named `projects` consisting of 500G of storage capacity within the `vg_projects` volume group:

```
# lvcreate --name projects --size 500G vg_projects
# lvdisplay
```

The `lvdisplay` command shows the current configuration of the logical volumes.

The remaining deployment steps are the same as with traditional partitioning. You will add a filesystem to the Logical Volume by using the `mkfs` command. Then you'll create a mount point, and the LVM storage space is mounted. The storage capacity is now ready for users.

Resize LVM Storage

Using the `pvcreate` command enables you to add more storage space to an LVM configuration by designating the new space as a physical volume and then adding the physical volume to an existing volume group. This automatically increases the capacity of the volume group. The logical volume is then extended with the additional capacity.

Note that once the space is added to the logical volume, the filesystem must be resized to format and take advantage of the increased capacity. The XFS tools or ext4 utilities are used to resize the filesystem.

Review Activity:

Storage Deployment

Answer the following questions:

1. **What does /dev/sdc3 specify?**

2. **What role does the partprobe command play in the process of adding storage?**

3. **What command adds the XFS filesystem to /dev/sdb2?**

4. **What is a mount point?**

5. **What are the three layers of an LVM deployment?**

Topic 7C

Manage Other Storage Options

EXAM OBJECTIVES COVERED
1.3 Given a scenario, manage files and directories

In some cases, direct-attached storage, such as internal drives, will not be sufficient for the reliability, performance, or scalability requirements of a project. In such cases, larger storage solutions, such as RAID, NAS, and SAN storage, may be required. For security reasons, disk contents may need encryption.

Linux Unified Key Setup

Data stored on a disk is vulnerable to security breaches. One way of mitigating this risk is to encrypt the data before it is written onto the disk. **Linux Unified Key Setup (LUKS)** is a platform-independent full-drive encryption solution that is commonly used to encrypt storage devices in a Linux environment. On Linux, LUKS uses the dm-crypt subsystem incorporated in the Linux kernel around version 2.6. This subsystem creates a mapping between an encrypted device and a virtual device name that the user space software can use. LUKS offers a high degree of compatibility with various software because it standardizes the format of encrypted devices.

The `cryptsetup` command is used as the front-end to LUKS and dm-crypt. The LUKS extensions to `cryptsetup` support various actions, including those listed in the table below.

The syntax of the `cryptsetup` command is `cryptsetup [options] {action} [action arguments]`

In this syntax, various LUKS commands are substituted for the `{action}` field.

LUKS Action	Purpose
`luksFormat`	Format a storage device using the LUKS encryption standard.
`isLuks`	Identify whether a given device is a LUKS device.
`luksOpen`	Open a LUKS storage device and set it up for mapping, assuming the provided key material is accurate.
`luksClose`	Remove a LUKS storage device from mapping.
`luksAddKey`	Associate new key material with a LUKS device.
`luksDelKey`	Remove key material from a LUKS device.

Before encrypting a device, it's a good idea to overwrite its contents with random data or all zeros. This ensures that no sensitive data from past use remains on the device. The shred *command can be used to securely wipe a storage device in this manner. The syntax is* shred [options] {file-name}

Redundant Array of Independent Disks

As identified earlier, individual storage disks are a single point of failure, putting data at risk of being lost or unavailable. One way of mitigating this risk is to use redundant arrays of independent disks (RAID) or combinations of two or more disks to store data. However, not all RAID standards mitigate the risk of lost data; some forms only provide performance benefits.

RAID Standards

Three common RAID standards are RAID 0 (disk striping), RAID 1 (disk mirroring), and RAID 5 (disk striping with parity).

Disk striping (RAID 0) relies on at least two disks. The disk partitions are divided into sections called stripes and data is written sequentially through the stripes. Because RAID 0 provides no fault tolerance, it is mainly used for performance benefits with application data that does not need to be preserved (such as caching).

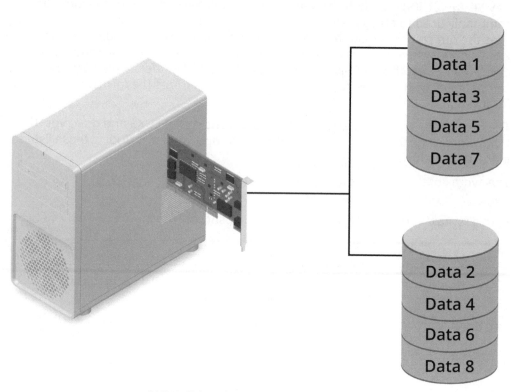

RAID 0 disk striping. (Images © 123RF.com)

Disk mirroring (RAID 1) duplicates data on two storage disks. This provides complete redundancy (100% of the data resides on each disk) but is a relatively inefficient use of storage capacity. RAID 1 usually results in faster reads than a single standalone disk.

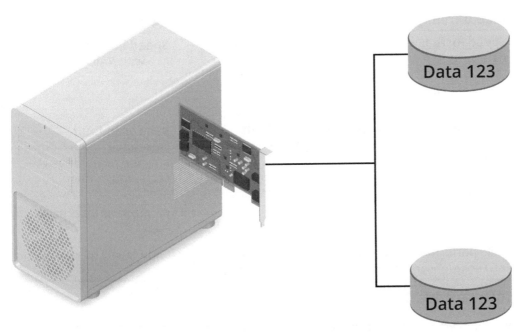

RAID 1 disk mirroring. (Images © 123RF.com)

Disk striping with parity (RAID 5) is a modification of RAID 0 that provides fault tolerance. Like RAID 0, stripes are created on the storage media, and data is distributed across the stripes. In addition to regular data, parity information is added to each disk. This parity information is used to recreate the missing data from any one failed storage drive. RAID 5 is particularly useful for file servers.

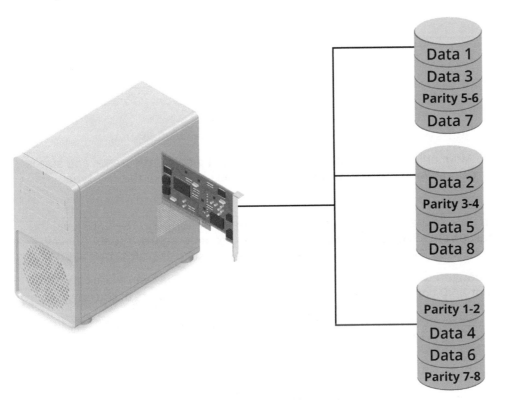

RAID 5 Disk striping with parity. (Images © 123RF.com)

RAID 0 Traits	RAID 1 Traits	RAID 5 Traits
Speed increase - less data written to each drive, and data written simultaneously to each drive	**Speed increase for reads** - either disk services the read call	**Speed increase** - much like with RAID 0
Reduced fault tolerance - the failure of any one drive results in all the data being unusable	**Increased fault tolerance** - even if one disk fails, the other disk contains everything needed to continue	**Increased fault tolerance** - data from any one failed drive is recreated in memory
Requires at least two disks	Requires two disks	Requires at least three disks

While performance benefits are always appreciated, most administrators will select RAID solutions in an effort to gain fault tolerance.

Software RAID

Most servers contain hardware RAID controller cards. These cards provide a performance benefit and allow flexible configurations. However, operating systems such as Linux can configure and manage storage devices like RAID arrays. In Linux, the `mdadm` command manages RAID. Think of the `mdadm` command as "multiple device administration."

To display information on a RAID array, use the `mdadm` command with a series of flags. The flags set `mdadm` into different modes, such as Assemble, Monitor, and Build.

mdadm Flag	Purpose
`--monitor`	Monitor changes to the array, such as a failed drive.
`--manage`	Add or remove storage, designate spares.
`--verbose`	Provide detailed output.

The mdadm utility also provides a dynamic file that displays messages and status information related to RAID arrays. To display the contents of this file, type:

```
cat /proc/mdstat
```

The output of the `cat /proc/mdstat` command displays the RAID level the kernel currently supports and any current RAID configurations. The RAID levels are referred to as "Personalities" and will exhibit values such as [raid1] or [raid5].

Any configured RAID arrays are identified on an md_d0 line, which consists of the current RAID configuration and a list of disks that are members of the array. For example, the output might look like the following:

```
Personalities : [raid0] [raid1] [raid5]
md_d0 : active raid1 sde1 sdf1
```

Network-Attached Storage

A **network-attached storage (NAS)** device is a dedicated network node that provides inexpensive, scalable, and easy-to-configure storage. The device is essentially an enclosure of storage drives managed by a minimal open-source operating system.

The NAS has a network configuration (usually an IP address) that makes it accessible from any client able to reach that address.

Distinguish Network File Systems for NAS

Files stored on the NAS are made available on the network by using one of two common network file systems: either **Network File System (NFS)** or **Server Message Blocks (SMB)**. SMB is commonly associated with Microsoft Windows systems, but it is not exclusive to them.

 SMB is sometimes referred to as Common Internet File System (CIFS).

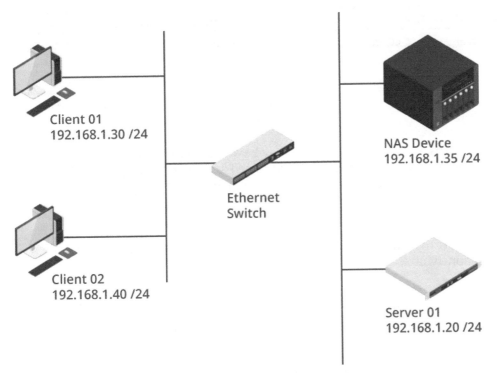

A small network segment containing a Network-Attached Storage device. (Images © 123RF.com.)

The SMB protocol provides users with shared access to files and other resources across a **local area network (LAN)**. SMB clients make requests for resources to SMB servers, which respond and provide the appropriate level of access. This protocol is primarily used with Windows computers. However, SMB-compatible software called Samba helps interface Linux and Windows hosts running network shares.

Common Internet File System (CIFS) is a specific implementation of SMB. Microsoft designed it as a successor to SMB version 1, but SMB versions 2 and 3 superseded it. However, Linux still uses the CIFS name in some of its tools, though these tools support newer versions of SMB.

Network File System offers similar functionality to SMB, but the protocols are not compatible. NFS is preferred in situations where Linux clients access Linux servers. In environments that are a mix of Windows and Linux, the SMB protocol is the better choice.

NFS configurations are covered in a future section.

Storage-Area Network

A **storage-area network (SAN)** is a significantly more expensive and complex option. However, it is usually faster and more scalable. Dedicated storage devices are managed as a single unit and are controlled by one or more Linux servers.

Network protocols communicate between the management nodes and the storage devices. Two common protocols are **Fibre Channel (FC)** and **Internet Small Computers Systems Interface (iSCSI)**.

iSCSI Attributes	Fibre Channel Attributes
Relatively easy to configure	More difficult to configure
Standard and common to most IP networks and servers	Performance increase over iSCSI
SCSI commands over a standard IP network	SCSI commands over a Fibre Channel network

In some cases, Fibre Channel devices may be attached to the server. The `fcstat` command displays information about existing Fibre Channel adapters. These adapters are typically found in conjunction with SAN solutions.

The syntax for the `fcstat` command is `fcstat [options] {driver-name}`

For example, to display driver-collected information for the Fibre Channel connection, type:

```
fcstat fcs0
```

The fcstat command also contains subcommands that provide additional detail, such as link statistics. The syntax for displaying link statistics is:

```
fcstat link_stats {link-number}
```

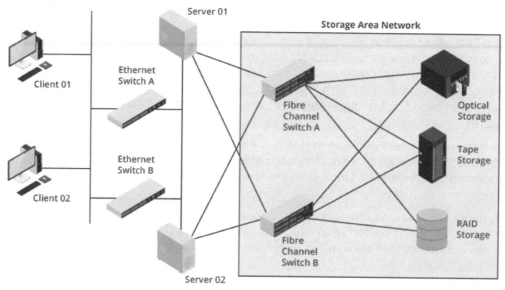

A network segment featuring a SAN using Fibre Channel protocols. (Images © 123RF.com.)

Identify multipathd

One common attribute of SAN implementation is multipathing. This concept refers to providing multiple connections between a server and its SAN storage devices. The benefit is fault tolerance (in the event one path becomes unavailable) and performance (**load balancing** across paths). In Linux, `multipathd` is responsible for checking and displaying information about paths.

The multipathd daemon manages the paths and reconfigures the network map as needed to react to changes in paths (such as failures).

The `multipathd` command displays information about the state of paths. For example, to display the current configuration, type `multipathd show config`.

Network File Systems for SAN

Like standard file servers and NAS devices, SAN storage solutions may be configured with NFS or SMB network filesystems. Users can connect to these shared resources to access files and directories.

Note that the NFS and SMB protocols provide communication between network clients and the filesystem. These operate on a higher level than iSCSI and Fibre Channel, which govern the communication between the hosting server and connected SAN storage.

Review Activity:

Storage Options

Answer the following questions:

1. **Why is RAID 5 fault tolerant and RAID 0 not?**

2. **You purchase two 100 GB storage disks to use in a RAID 1 mirror. Assuming the entire storage capacity of both disks is at your disposal, what is the maximum amount of data your RAID 1 array can store?**

3. **What do the Fibre Channel and iSCSI standards provide?**

Topic 7D

Troubleshoot Storage

EXAM OBJECTIVES COVERED
4.1 Given a scenario, analyze and troubleshoot storage issues.

Storage media performance is based on capacity and read/write capabilities. Read/write tasks are measured based on input and output performance values and sysadmins want these tasks to be as efficient as possible. Slow disk performance can significantly impact the overall server performance. Measuring and addressing I/O issues requires the use of several tools, as noted in this Topic.

Disk Performance

Storage devices read and write data, an action referred to as input/output (IO). Even with solid-state storage, drive actions may be one of the slowest tasks the server performs. Factor in many users reading and writing simultaneously, and it's easy to see why disk performance is a concern for sysadmins.

NVMe storage disk detection may fail during the initial installation of the drive or during later boot sequences. Ensure the BIOS settings are correct for the storage disk type and that the GRUB2 configuration file does not contain typos when referencing the NVMe drive.

NVMe disks are also prone to failure from heat, so proper cooling is essential, and frequent backups are recommended.

GRUB2 is discussed in a later section.

High Latency

Latency refers to the time it takes for data to travel across the communications media. In the case of direct-attached storage (such as local storage disks), the media is the motherboard, disk controllers, and connecting cables. Latency is any delay as the data travels the path. Some latency is inevitable; the goal is to ensure the latency is acceptable within the server's performance requirements. The goal is for this number to be as low as possible.

The organization's individual needs define storage performance. Often these needs will vary by service. For example, web services have different performance requirements than database services. Hardware specifications, software, and specific configurations impact disk IO performance and wait times. These variables make it difficult to identify ways to decrease latency and improve throughput.

Low Throughput

Throughput is a measure of the storage device's effective bandwidth, or ability to move data to or from the drive. The goal is for this number to be as high as possible.

Managing disk performance begins with purchasing a server with the appropriate storage specifications. These specifications impact the drive's throughput. Often, this means SCSI or SAS storage, as SATA may not perform well enough for servers with many storage devices. The drives themselves are important, too, not just the control interface. For physical disks, the RPM value should be as high as possible—often 15,000 RPMs.

Organizing storage into RAID arrays may also provide a performance benefit in addition to fault tolerance. Hardware RAID controllers are typically preferred.

Measuring IOPS

You can check performance by keeping track of the **Input/Output Operations per Second (IOPS)**. Identifying throughput to ensure that disk performance is acceptable on a Linux server involves the `iostat` and `ioping` commands.

The iostat utility generates reports on CPU and device usage. For storage, it provides input and output statistics for block devices and partitions. Using the `-d` option to specify device information only, the `iostat` command lists the following statistics for each storage device:

- Transfers (I/O requests) per second (tps).

- Number of blocks read per second (kB_read/s).

- Number of blocks written per second (kB_wrtn/s).

- The total number of blocks read (kB_read).

- The total number of blocks written (kB_wrtn).

You can use this report to monitor how a storage drive is being used and to identify any potential bottlenecks. For example, a faulty drive might have lower reads and/or writes per second than expected. You can also use the report to help you decide how to best distribute the I/O load between the available devices.

The syntax of the `iostat` command is `iostat [options] [device names]`

The `ioping` command generates a report of device I/O latency in real time. It will continuously "ping" the specified device with requests and print information about each request at the command line. By default, this information tracks how long it took an I/O request to finish. Aside from specifying a device to test, you can also specify a path name to test whatever device is associated with that path.

Consider using `ioping` to troubleshoot latency issues with storage devices, especially if you believe your read and/or write speeds are slower than they should be.

The syntax of the `ioping` command is `ioping [options] {file/directory/device name}`. Some of the associated options are listed here:

Options for the ioping Command	Purpose
`-c {count}`	Specify the number of I/O requests to perform before stopping.
`-i {time}`	Set the time (interval) between I/O requests.
`-t {time}`	Set the minimum valid request time. Requests faster than this are ignored.
`-T {time}`	Set the maximum valid request time. Requests slower than this are ignored.
`-s {size}`	Set the size of requests.

Both `iostat` and `ioping` are useful for troubleshooting I/O errors that may occur due to failing drives, performance issues, or storage disk driver problems.

Using I/O Schedulers

I/O scheduling is the process by which the operating system determines the order of input and output operations of block storage devices. Scheduling is important because, compared to CPU and memory operations, block storage operations are relatively slow—especially in disk-based technology like hard disk drives. The Linux kernel, therefore, doesn't write or read to a drive in the order that requests are submitted; instead, it prioritizes certain requests over others to minimize performance issues that can come with I/O tasks.

Although the kernel handles scheduling automatically, you can configure the scheduler with different behavior types. Some behaviors are more appropriate than others in certain situations, and setting a new type may increase read/write speeds. Sysadmins typically change the scheduler during the troubleshooting process to finely tune storage performance when every bit of performance matters.

There are a number of different schedulers available to modern Linux kernel versions. Three of the most commonly used are Deadline, cfq, and noop.

Deadline

The Deadline scheduler performs sorting of I/O operations using three queues: a standard pending request queue, a read first in first out (FIFO) queue, and a write FIFO queue; the latter two are sorted by submission time and have expiration values.

When a request is submitted, it is sorted into the standard queue and placed at the end of its appropriate FIFO queue. When the top request of the FIFO queue becomes older than the queue's expiration, the scheduler stops working with the standard queue and starts servicing requests from the top of the FIFO queue—in other words, it switches to the oldest requests. This ensures that the scheduler doesn't "starve" a request for too long. This makes it ideal for certain workloads like multi-threaded workloads.

CFQ

This refers to the Complete Fair Queuing (CFQ) scheduler. It is the default scheduler for modern versions of the Linux kernel. In this scheduler, each process is given its own queue, and each queue has an interval by which it is accessed (its time slice). The scheduler uses a round-robin system to access each queue and services requests from these queues until either their time slices or requests are exhausted.

When the queue is empty, the CFQ waits 10 milliseconds for any new requests in the queue, and if it doesn't see any, it moves on to another queue. Like the deadline scheduler, this helps to minimize request starvation. Its advantage is that it services processes fairly and provides good performance in most workload situations.

Noop

Noop is the simplest scheduler and does not sort I/O requests, but merely merges them. This can be ideal in situations where the device or its storage controller performs its sorting operations. It can also benefit devices that don't have mechanical components requiring seek time, like SSDs and USB flash drives, because this scheduler doesn't expend much effort in reducing seek time. However, the previous two schedulers are preferred in most other situations.

Set the scheduler on a particular device by modifying the scheduler file located at `/sys/block/<device name>/queue/scheduler`.

Setting the scheduler is as simple as echoing the desired option to this file, as in:

```
echo noop > /sys/block/sda/queue/scheduler
```

Note that this sets the scheduler for runtime only; the setting will revert upon reboot. To ensure your changes persist, you must modify the system's boot loader configuration.

Capacity Issues

One of the great challenges for sysadmins is managing storage capacity. Storage space is relatively inexpensive, and there are many storage options, from direct-attached storage to network storage to cloud storage. Users often see no need to delete data, and many files are kept just in case they're needed.

Display Storage

To manage storage, begin by understanding what storage devices exist. Tools such as blkid and lsblk display information about recognized storage devices. Another resource is the `/proc/partitions` file, which delineates the partitions that Linux is aware of. Display this information with the `cat /proc/partitions` command. Finally, both `fdisk` and `parted` display drive and partition information.

If the storage devices are organized using LVM, commands such as `pvdisplay`, `vgdisplay`, and `lvdisplay` provide information about the configured volumes.

The `mount` command displays all attached storage and may be useful for understanding exactly where particular storage devices reside (they won't always be local).

Find Issues

The `du` and `df` commands are commonly used to gather specific storage utilization information. Both tools are flexible and have many options.

Use `df` to get general information on the mounted storage capacity. Use `df` with a specific device path to gather more information about a given partition. For example:

```
# df
# df /dev/sda2
```

```
[student@fedora ~]$ df -h /dev/sda2
Filesystem      Size  Used Avail Use% Mounted on
/dev/sda2       79G   4.7G   73G    7% /
[student@fedora ~]$ █
```

Output from the df *command.*

The du command provides utilization information and usually targets a specific directory. Most sysadmins will immediately use du to target the /home directory (within which are the home directories of all standard users). Users often consume a great deal of storage capacity. You might use du in the following ways:

```
# du /home
# du /var/log
```

```
[student@fedora ~]$ du -hs test
4.0K    test
[student@fedora ~]$ █
```

Output from the du *command.*

Resolve Capacity Issues

What should administrators suggest when the above tools identify storage capacity challenges? One obvious approach is scaling up (larger capacity drives) or scaling out (more drives). These suggestions are not free, however. Another option is to move the data to a different storage location, such as a NAS or SAN. Some data can also be archived and compressed by using the tar command.

Cloud storage is a viable option for many organizations. Cloud storage may provide cost-effective, secure, and scalable storage for user data, backups, and company information. Consider recommending cloud-based **Storage as a Service (STaaS)**.

Whether dealing with direct-attached storage, NAS, SAN, or STaaS, disk quotas help sysadmins manage storage capacity by forcing users to remove or archive unused data. Many users do not realize the impact that storing large amounts of data on a server can have on the server's cost, maintenance, and performance.

Inode Exhaustion

Each file created on a Linux partition is given an identifier by the filesystem. This identifier—called an inode—uniquely identifies the file. Filesystems such as ext4 have a limited number of inodes available to allocate. While the available number is very high, filesystems that store many small files may eventually run out of inodes to assign. This is referred to as inode exhaustion.

If you receive an error message such as "No space left on drive" or "Cannot create directory" but there is still storage capacity available on the drive, you've likely encountered an inode exhaustion issue.

You can use the df and du commands again in this case to troubleshoot this issue.

The df -i command displays the percentage of inodes consumed and available in the IUse% column of the output. If you have available storage space but are receiving an error message when creating files, check this value.

The `--inodes` and `-d` options for `du` also display information on which directories are consuming the most inodes. Try the following command:

```
# du --inodes -d /
```

Be aware that this command may take some time to complete depending on the size of the filesystem.

XFS and BtrFS dynamically allocate inodes and are far less likely to run into this issue. Their available inodes are based on a percentage of the filesystem size.

Filesystem Issues

Filesystem corruption often occurs when Linux servers are not shut down gracefully. This is more prevalent with non-journaled filesystems (most modern filesystems, such as XFS and ext4, are journaled).

The fsck utility can be run on disks to detect and attempt to correct issues. Note that the volume must be unmounted for `fsck` to be run against it. The `fsck` command was discussed in Topic 7B.

Filesystem mismatch errors may be reported, especially after changes to the filesystem or partition size. This issue may occur when an application (or the system) attempts to write to the storage disk location where the filesystem superblock resides. It may also happen if the storage disk itself is damaged or if there is a misconfiguration of the filesystem or partition table.

You may be able to recover and access data by unmounting the filesystem (in rescue mode) and using a repair utility such as fsck.

Mount Options Issues

Errors in the `/etc/fstab` file or in `systemd.mount` unit files may cause filesystems not to mount when the system boots. One of the most common issues is references in the file that point to nonexistent drives or nonexistent mount points. Another common issue is typographical errors of any sort that direct the system to mount a filesystem in an invalid manner.

Care must be taken when working with `/etc/fstab` and `systemd.mount` files to not make any errors. If necessary, boot into `rescue.target` to correct these files.

Device Issues

There are common troubleshooting steps for storage devices. Begin by ensuring Linux is aware of the device. Commands such as `blkid` and `lsblk` display storage device information. The `hwinfo` command can be filtered to show storage disks, too. If the disk is not detected by Linux, confirm its physical connectivity by checking the interface and power cable for a tight connection. If the drive is installed in a motherboard slot, confirm the connection is good.

Once physical connectivity is established, Linux should be able to detect the drive.

 The CompTIA troubleshooting methodology was covered in Topic 1D.

Use `fdisk` or `parted` to display details on partition information. The `/proc/partitions` file displays general partition information that the system is aware of. Use the `partprobe` command to refresh this information.

If issues with the filesystem are suspected, use the various ext4 or XFS tools to confirm the status of the filesystem.

Verify the drive can be mounted by using the `mount` command. First, create a directory that acts as a mount point, and then attach the storage capacity to the directory. If the partition is not automatically mounted at boot, check for typographical errors in `/etc/fstab` or the `systemd.mount` file.

Network file servers share directories by using NFS or SMB to make storage capacity available from across the network. These remote filesystems may also be mounted. When troubleshooting mount issues with remote filesystems, first ensure network connectivity is established by using tools such as `ping` and `ip addr`. Next, verify the network file server has made the directories available on the network and that the user has permission to mount and read/write to the directories.

Network tools such as `ping` and `ip addr` are covered in a later Lesson.

Display LVM Settings

Use the various display commands associated with LVM to detect issues. By thinking of LVM deployments as three layers, it is easier to anticipate where problems may arise. The `lvdisplay` command shows Logical Volume settings, including which Volume Group the storage space is pulled from.

The `vgdisplay` command shows Volume Group configurations, including which Physical Volumes are associated with the VG.

Use the `pvdisplay` command to view Physical Volume information. This information can be supplemented by using commands such as `blkid`, `lsblk`, and `cat /proc/partitions`.

Display RAID Settings

Many hardware RAID controllers provide their own software-management suites. For software RAID implementations, use the `mdadm` command to display and manage RAID configuration settings. In addition, the `/proc/mdstat` file provides status information.

Both `mdadm` and `/proc/mdstat` were covered in an earlier section.

The fstrim Command

Based on how solid-state drives manage data, when users delete files, the files do not actually get erased. Instead, the space is marked as available, but the content remains. From the user's perspective, the data is gone and unavailable. SSD trimming actually removes the data and frees the space. SSD trimming is an optional feature that proactively removes data so that the space is ready for new information to be written.

Linux supports the `fstrim` command. Both the drive and filesystem must be compatible with the trim function.

Review Activity:

Storage Troubleshooting

Answer the following questions:

1. **What command reports real-time disk latency information?**

2. **List the commands necessary to show configuration information for each of the three layers of LVM.**

3. **When trying to save a file to a storage disk, you receive a message stating the drive is out of space. The df command indicates there is plenty of free space. What might be the issue?**

4. **You have added a partition to an existing disk by using fdisk. The partition is not displayed by the cat /proc/partitions command. What other command do you need to run?**

Lesson 7

Summary

Proper administration of storage directly impacts the server's performance and the ability of users to access critical data. System specifications, such as SATA, SCSI, and SAS play an important role, as do design decisions such as traditional partitioning versus LVM-based storage. In fact, it may be more efficient to store data on NAS, SAN, or cloud-based devices rather than on internal storage disks. Monitoring performance and troubleshooting storage disk issues are common sysadmin tasks.

Guidelines

These best practices and guidelines are provided for your use as revision tools or as quick references in your job role.

- Understand the process of configuring storage with traditional partitions.

- Understand the process of configuring storage with LVM.

- Compare the benefits of LVM.

Command Reference Table

This list of commands and their associated syntax can also be found in Appendix B.

Command	Syntax	Purpose	Covered in
lsblk	lsblk {drive-path}	Display information about storage devices recognized by the system.	Lesson 7, Topic B
lsscsi	lsscsi [options]	Display information about SCSI devices.	Lesson 7, Topic B
fdisk	fdisk [options] {device-name}	Create, modify, or delete partitions on a storage drive.	Lesson 7, Topic B
parted	parted [options] {device-name}	Create, destroy, and resize partitions.	Lesson 7, Topic B
mkfs	mkfs [options] {filesystem-name} {partition-name}	Format new partitions.	Lesson 7, Topic B
mount	mount {filesystem-name} {directory-name}	Attach storage to the FHS.	Lesson 7, Topic B

Command	Syntax	Purpose	Covered in
umount	umount {filesystem-name} {directory-name}	Detach storage from the FHS.	Lesson 7, Topic B
df	df [options] {directory-name}	Display device storage information.	Lesson 7, Topic B
du	du [options] {directory-name}	Display device usage information.	Lesson 7, Topic B
e2label	e2label /dev/ {device name} {partition number} {label name}	Display or modify file system labels.	Lesson 7, Topic B
resize2fs	resize2fs [options] {device/file system name} [desired size]	Change the size of an ext2/3/4 file system on a device.	Lesson 7, Topic B
tune2fs	tune2fs [options] {device/ file system name}	Configure parameters associated with an ext2/3/4 file system.	Lesson 7, Topic B
dumpe2fs	dumpe2fs [options] {device/ file system name}	Dump ext2, ext3, and ext4 file system information.	Lesson 7, Topic B
cryptsetup	cryptsetup [options] {action} [action arguments]	Encrypt data before it is written to disk.	Lesson 7, Topic C
shred	shred [options] {file-name}	Securely wipe a storage device by overwriting contents with random data or all zeros.	Lesson 7, Topic C
iostat	iostat [options] [device names]	Display reports on CPU and device storage.	Lesson 7, Topic D
ioping	ioping [options] {file/ directory/ device name}	Generate a report of device I/O latency in real time.	Lesson 7, Topic D

Lesson 8

Managing Devices, Processes, Memory, and the Kernel

LESSON INTRODUCTION

Linux sysadmins must identify and configure hardware resources. First, administrators must be able to find hardware information using a series of commands to identify CPU, memory, bus, and other hardware devices. Next, sysadmins manipulate processes consuming hardware resources to optimize and troubleshoot the system. Often the focus of this optimization is the CPU and memory. Finally, the Linux kernel—the core of the operating system—may be managed to maintain performance, enable modern features, and provide compatibility with current hardware.

Lesson Objectives

In this lesson, you will:

- Gather hardware information.
- Manage processes.
- Manage memory.
- Manage the Linux kernel.

Topic 8A

Gather Hardware Information

EXAM OBJECTIVES COVERED
1.1 Summarize Linux fundamentals.
4.3 Given a scenario, analyze and troubleshoot central processing unit (CPU) and memory issues.

Identifying recognized hardware on the Linux system is a critical part of device management. Various commands provide details on the CPU, memory, graphics cards, network cards, and storage controllers. Linux also recognizes newly installed devices by using a device manager called udev. Often, device information is dynamically gathered by Linux during the boot process to ensure that the displayed information accurately reports recognized hardware.

Use Hardware Information Tools

Several tools exist to report hardware details. These commands may display manufacturer, model information, and Linux configuration settings. General tools, such as the `hwinfo` command, often contain useful options to narrow report results, allowing you to focus on just the hardware you need.

Hardware information can be used for many sysadmin tasks, including system upgrades, performance monitoring, troubleshooting, and inventory management. For example, if you submit a support ticket to a software vendor, you will likely need to provide details about the system the software runs on.

Use the hwinfo Tool

The `hwinfo` command displays detailed information on hardware resources Linux is aware of. These resources include:

- Central processing unit (CPU)

- Storage disk controllers

- USB controllers

- Graphics cards

- Network interface cards (NIC)

- Print devices

One common option used with `hwinfo` is `--short`, which returns abbreviated information on the resources. Using either `hwinfo` or `hwinfo --short` displays information on all detected hardware. However, it's more likely you'll want details for specific devices.

Option for the hwinfo Command	Purpose
`--cpu`	CPU information
`--netcard`	NIC information
`--storage`	Storage disk controllers information
`--block`	Storage disk information
`--usb`	USB controller information

For example, to display CPU information, type `hwinfo --short --cpu`

```
student@ubuntu20:~$ hwinfo --short --cpu
cpu:
                      Intel(R) Xeon(R) Gold 6230 CPU @ 2.10GHz
, 2095 MHz
```

The output of the `hwinfo` *command.*

Use the dmidecode Tool

Similar to `hwinfo`, `dmidecode` displays system information for current devices. It also indicates upgrade possibilities by showing maximum processor and memory upgrades.

Display information for specific devices by using the `-t` option along with the device type. For example, type `dmidecode -t cpu` to display CPU information.

The output from `dmidecode` *may be very long. Use the pipe redirector to display the information in a pagination utility such as* `less` *or* `more`*.*

Display Bus Information

You can display additional information about devices attached to specific busses with commands such as `lspci` and `lsusb`. Both commands offer various levels of detail (or verbosity) to display just the information you need.

With either command, try the `-tv` option to display verbose information in a tree structure, allowing you to see devices connected to specific controllers.

```
student@ubuntu20:~$ lspci -tv
-[0000:00]-+-00.0  Intel Corporation 440BX/ZX/DX - 82443BX/ZX/D
X Host bridge (AGP disabled)
           +-07.0  Intel Corporation 82371AB/EB/MB PIIX4 ISA
           +-07.1  Intel Corporation 82371AB/EB/MB PIIX4 IDE
           +-07.3  Intel Corporation 82371AB/EB/MB PIIX4 ACPI
           \-08.0  Microsoft Corporation Hyper-V virtual VGA
```

Output of the `lspci` *command along with the* `-tv` *option.*

Devices in the /dev Directory

The udev device manager provides plug-and-play functionality by generating device files when the system boots for whatever hardware devices it detects. These device files provide an interface for Linux (and users) to interface with the devices.

Note that the device files are not the same thing as the device drivers. Device drivers reside between the device files and the hardware devices, allowing communication between the two (and therefore between the OS and hardware).

Use the udev Device Manager

The **udev** device manager detects hardware changes, such as the addition or removal of a hardware device, on the system. The devices are represented as files in the /dev directory.

 Recall that in the previous section, you displayed storage device information from the /dev/sda file.

It's possible to test the udev device manager by using the monitor subcommand. Run udevadm monitor and then attach a new USB device to the system. You should see the device is detected and the output shows device details.

Information can be displayed for specific attached devices by using the udevadm command. For example, type udevadm info /dev/sda to see storage device information.

 The term "storage device" represents traditional magnetic hard disk drives, modern solid-state drives, USB flash drives, and any other media used to store data.

Identify Block, Character, and Special Devices

If you execute the ls -l command on the /dev directory, the device files are displayed. You might notice the leftmost field in the permissions string is either the letter b or c. These characters identify the device as either a block or character device.

```
[student@fedora ~]$ ls -l /dev
total 0
crw-r--r--. 1 root     root      10, 235 Mar 26 09:55 autofs
drwxr-xr-x. 2 root     root          140 Mar 26 09:55 block
drwxr-xr-x. 2 root     root           80 Mar 26 02:55 bsg
crw-rw----. 1 root     disk      10, 234 Mar 26 09:55 btrfs-control
lrwxrwxrwx. 1 root     root            3 Mar 26 09:55 cdrom -> sr0
```

Partial output of the /dev directory.

Character devices, such as keyboards, deal with data on a per-byte or character level. Hard disk drives, however, are examples of block devices. Data is moved in blocks, and the device can be mounted as a storage area. Information may be cached, too. Device drivers are developed differently for each of the two device types.

Device Type	I/O Process Method	Example
Block device	Processes I/O in blocks and can be mounted	Storage devices
Character device	Processes I/O on a per-character basis	Keyboard, mouse

Three other device files are listed: `null`, `zero`, and `urandom`. These are known as the special device files.

The `/dev/null` special file is a writeable location that is used as a target for generated data that should be discarded. This data may be error messages that are redirected to `/dev/null` by using the `2>` redirector.

The `/dev/zero` file is a way of filling storage capacity. For example, using the `dd` command, a sysadmin can create a file of a specified size as part of testing. For example, to create a one MiB file named `foo.txt`, run the following command:

```
# dd if=/dev/zero of=foo.txt count=1024 bs=1024
```

This command uses `/dev/zero` as the source of data that fills the file to its specified size.

The `/dev/urandom` file can create is a source of random characters for tasks such as creating completely randomized passwords. Take care of how this command runs on low-performing systems at the risk of consuming all available resources.

Display CPU Information

The utilities `hwinfo` and `dmidecode` are not the only commands that can display processor information. Two other CPU-specific display commands are `lscpu` and `cat /proc/cpuinfo`.

Sysadmins may need details on the CPU(s) as part of performance monitoring, hardware inventory, when considering processor upgrades, and when building a virtualization host.

The `lscpu` command gathers information on the CPU. The entire output can be displayed or specific columns selected. Information on each CPU includes cores, sockets, caches, family, and model. The output isn't well-formatted by default, so add the `-e` option to display the results in columns:

```
$ lscpu -e
```

The `/proc/cpuinfo` file is dynamically created when the system boots, providing current configuration information about the CPU. This information includes the processor's specifications but also details on a per-core basis. You can read the file by using commands such as `cat`.

```
student@ubuntu20:~$ head /proc/cpuinfo
processor       : 0
vendor_id       : GenuineIntel
cpu family      : 6
model           : 85
model name      : Intel(R) Xeon(R) Gold 6230 CPU @ 2.10GHz
stepping        : 7
microcode       : 0xffffffff
cpu MHz         : 2095.077
cache size      : 28160 KB
physical id     : 0
```

A portion of the output from the head `/proc/cpuinfo` *command.*

Display Memory Information

Troubleshooting and managing system memory is just as important as monitoring the CPU. Linux reports the memory configuration of the system in several places.

 This section covers installed memory, not how that memory is being utilized. Memory utilization is covered in a future section.

Memory Tools

Use the `lsmem` command to display memory blocks, including their size and state (online, offline).

```
student@ubuntu20:~$ lsmem
RANGE                                           SIZE   STATE  REMOVABLE BLOCK
0x0000000000000000-0x00000000f7ffffff           3.9G online            yes  0-30
0x0000000100000000-0x0000000187ffffff           2.1G online            yes 32-48

Memory block size:          128M
Total online memory:          6G
Total offline memory:         0B
```

The output of the `lsmem` *command.*

Much like the `/proc/cpuinfo` file, the `/proc/meminfo` file displays statistics and details about currently recognized memory on the system. The file can be read using the `cat` command.

```
student@ubuntu20:~$ head /proc/meminfo
MemTotal:        6073980 kB
MemFree:         2770164 kB
MemAvailable:    4868040 kB
Buffers:           57136 kB
Cached:          2189920 kB
SwapCached:            0 kB
Active:          1839512 kB
Inactive:        1143340 kB
Active(anon):     720940 kB
Inactive(anon):    11060 kB
```

A portion of the output from the `head /proc/meminfo` *command.*

File contents might be useful when troubleshooting memory. For example, if you believe the system has 64 GB of RAM installed, but only 32 GB are reported, you can use this file to see what memory Linux recognizes. Doing so may help identify which sticks of RAM are not recognized (and therefore, may not be seated in the motherboard correctly).

Review Activity:

Hardware Information

Answer the following questions:

1. **What two commands display information on motherboard busses?**

2. **When is the /dev directory populated?**

3. **How might /dev/zero be used to help create a file of a given size?**

4. **What file has the make, model, number of cores, and other details about the CPU?**

Topic 8B

Manage Processes

EXAM OBJECTIVES COVERED
1.4 Given a scenario, configure and use the appropriate processes and services.
4.3 Given a scenario, analyze and troubleshoot central processing unit (CPU) and memory issues.

Processes are instances of running code. These may be parts of the OS, services, applications, or scripts. Some processes are executed as part of the system, while others are initiated and managed by users. Each process is assigned a unique process identification number (called a PID), and this number is used to manage the process throughout its life cycle. This section covers process management, troubleshooting, and optimization.

Processes Concepts

Process management is an essential part of performance monitoring and troubleshooting on Linux systems. Sysadmins manage processes with tools that indicate their resource consumption, status, and priority levels.

What Is a Process?

A **process** is an instance of running code. Applications reside dormant on the storage disk until executed by a command or initiated by the system. When executed, the processor loads an instance of the application into memory and manages it . At that point, it is a running program.

As with other system functions, processes are managed by number rather than name. These numbers are called **process identifiers (PID)**, and a PID is almost always used to manipulate the process. Most processes start and stop without issue, but periodically administrators may need to see what processes are running or discover which processes are consuming large amounts of system resources.

Manipulate Processes

Sysadmins view and manipulate processes as part of system management. Many basic commands display specific process information. The most important basic information to acquire is the PID.

Display the Process ID

Use commands such as `pgrep`, `pidof`, and `grep` to display process ID numbers. Whether `pgrep` or `pidof` are installed depends on the Linux distribution.

The `pgrep` command functions similarly to the `grep` command for which it is named. It searches for process information based on a string that completely or partially identifies the process. For example, to search for the PID of the `sshd` and any active SSH connections, type the following command:

```
# pgrep ssh
```

One or more process IDs are displayed. The `-l` option is useful with `pgrep` because it displays the actual process name along with the PID.

```
student@ubuntu20:~$ pgrep -l ssh
2298 ssh-agent
```

Output of the `pgrep -l ssh` command displaying the PID.

Much like `pgrep`, the `pidof` command also displays process ID information. The primary difference between the two commands is that `pidof` requires accurate knowledge of the process name, whereas `pgrep` searches for a string that may be contained within the name. For example, when searching for SSH processes, `pgrep ssh` will display any process containing the "ssh" string, while `pidof ssh` will likely return nothing because no process name exactly matches the "ssh" string.

```
student@ubuntu20:~$ pidof ssh-agent
2298
```

Output of the `pidof ssh-agent` command. Note the use of the full process name.

 It is possible to combine the `grep` command with the `ps` command to display process information, including the PID. For example, the `ps ef | grep sshd` command displays process information for the `sshd` process, including its PID. The `ps` command is covered in a later section.

Process Signals

Sysadmins directly impact processes by using the PID, as displayed by `pgrep` or `pidof`. So what activities do administrators undertake? Often, the process needs to be ended. This usually occurs when the application is closed, such as when quitting Vim. However, sometimes a process does not end gracefully, and the administrator must directly manage it using signals.

Three ways of ending processes are SIGTERM (signal -15), SIGKILL (signal -9), and SIGHUP.

Before covering these signals it's important to understand how applications shut down, or exit. A graceful exit uses SIGTERM. It is performed to avoid data loss or corruption and ensures the program shuts down according to its design. This means the program completes its regular shutdown procedure and no longer resides in memory or has a process ID associated with it. For example, when using Vim, the `:q` command initiates a graceful exit.

Sometimes, however, the graceful exit fails or is unavailable. In that circumstance, a non-graceful exit is required. This is referred to as "killing" the program. The SIGKILL signal is usually a last resort.

The SIGHUP signal requests that a process exit when the terminal running the process closes. It's assumed that if the terminal closes, the user is no longer interested in the results of the command.

The `kill` command is used to pass these signals to processes. For example, to initiate a graceful exit, type:

```
$ sudo kill -15 {PID}
```

Likewise, `kill -9 {PID}` sends a SIGKILL message to the process.

SIGTERM is the normal kill signal sent to applications. SIGKILL is used when an application refuses to exit via SIGTERM. SIGHUP tells the application to exit when the shell closes.

An alternative command to `kill` is the `pkill` command, which also references the process by PID. Additionally, `pkill` can also terminate processes based on name, users, and other criteria.

For example, `pkill` can kill all processes associated with the Firefox application (which may have many spawned processes):

```
$ sudo pkill -15 firefox
```

List Running Processes and Open Files

Commands such as `pgrep` display individual processes. Sysadmins often wish to see a more comprehensive list of the processes running on the system. Various utilities display this information, including `top`, `htop`, `ps`, and `lsof`.

The top Command

The `top` command dynamically displays the processes consuming the most system resources. By default, `top` updates this information every three seconds. The `top` command is an interactive utility. Press `Shift+P` to display resources based on CPU consumption or `Shift+M` to display based on memory consumption.

```
top - 07:29:23 up 24 min,  1 user,  load average: 0.00, 0.04, 0.12
Tasks: 221 total,   1 running, 220 sleeping,   0 stopped,   0 zombie
%Cpu(s):  5.0 us,  0.7 sy,  0.0 ni, 94.3 id,  0.0 wa,  0.0 hi,  0.0 si,  0.0 st
MiB Mem :   5931.6 total,   2700.1 free,    925.4 used,   2306.1 buff/cache
MiB Swap:   2048.0 total,   2048.0 free,      0.0 used.   4749.3 avail Mem

   PID USER      PR  NI    VIRT    RES    SHR S  %CPU  %MEM     TIME+ COMMAND
  2362 student   20   0 3716096 337452 123376 S   4.3   5.6   0:20.06 gnome-+
  2183 root      20   0  240576  73140  44312 S   1.3   1.2   0:07.13 Xorg
     5 root      20   0       0      0      0 I   0.3   0.0   0:01.32 kworke+
  2670 student   20   0  823596  51820  38968 S   0.3   0.9   0:03.11 gnome-+
```

Partial output of the `top` *command.*

The upper portion of `top`'s output displays useful information including system uptime, memory consumption (both physical and virtual memory), and process statistics. Sysadmins rely heavily on `top` because it is one of the most useful monitoring programs.

Understand CPU Time

Managing CPU utilization time combines several metrics. These metrics, most of which can be displayed in the CPU line of the `top` command's output, indicate how busy the processor is (and therefore, whether the processor is the bottleneck).

Value	Purpose
%us	Displays CPU time spent running user processes.
%s	Displays CPU time spent running the Linux kernel.
%id	Displays CPU idle time. (If this is high, the CPU is working hard.)
%wa	Displays I/O wait time. (If this is high, the CPU is ready to work but waiting for I/O access.)
%st	Displays Steal. (If this is high, a virtual CPU is waiting for access to the physical CPU.)

Processor utilization metrics.

Note that with %st, you are working with a virtual CPU (vCPU) in a virtualized environment. For example, if a physical Linux server hosts two Linux virtual machines, then the vCPUs of the VMs may be awaiting access to the physical CPU in the host server. If this value is high, the VMs may put too much strain on the physical processor resources of the host server.

```
top - 07:31:17 up 26 min,  1 user,  load average: 0.00, 0.02, 0.10
Tasks: 221 total,   1 running, 220 sleeping,   0 stopped,   0 zombie
%Cpu(s):  0.7 us,  0.0 sy,  0.0 ni, 99.3 id,  0.0 wa,  0.0 hi,  0.0 si,  0.0 st
```

Processor information from the `top` command.

The htop Command

The `htop` command is a user-friendly supplement to top. It color-codes output and provides a great deal of interactivity. Like `top`, `htop` is used for monitoring and process management. The interface includes bar graphs to display CPU and memory utilization. The output is also customizable.

```
CPU[|||                                5.8%] Tasks: 124, 243 thr, 88 kthr; 1 runnin
Mem[||||||||||||||||||||||||||||1.15G/3.81G] Load average: 0.03 0.04 0.07
Swp[||                        6.91M/3.81G] Uptime: 01:01:32
```

PID	USER	PRI	NI	VIRT	RES	SHR	S	CPU%▽	MEM%	TIME+	Command
1434	student	20	0	3933M	276M	115M	S	1.9	7.1	1:46.35	/usr/bin/gnom
31240	student	20	0	218M	4248	3284	R	1.9	0.1	0:01.48	htop
1601	root	20	0	253M	29528	7956	S	0.6	0.7	0:04.39	/usr/libexec/

Output of the `htop` command.

The ps Command

The standard command to display process status is `ps`. This command has many options to filter and display the exact process information you need.

Option for the ps Command	Purpose
`-e`	Display all processes.
`-a`	Display all processes with a controlling terminal but not status or full command.
`u`	Display the username that started the process.
`-f`	Display supplementary information.
`p- {PID}`	Display processes associated with a given PID.

The `ps` command supports three different styles of command option syntax: Unix-style (preceded by a hyphen), GNU-style (preceded by two hyphens), and BSD-style (no hyphen). Mixing these styles will produce unique results. For example, the `ps a` command (BSD-style) will print all processes with a controlling terminal, including session leaders (the first member of a group of processes). It will also print the status of each process as well as the full command (including options) of each process.

The `ps -a` command (Unix-style) also prints all processes with a controlling terminal but does not include session leaders, the status of each process, nor the full command of each process.

 The `ps` command is a perfect example of why `man` pages are so helpful. The command has many possible combinations, and it may be difficult to remember them all.

```
student@ubuntu20:~$ ps -ef
UID          PID     PPID  C STIME TTY          TIME CMD
root           1        0  0 07:04 ?        00:00:05 /sbin/init splash
root           2        0  0 07:04 ?        00:00:00 [kthreadd]
root           3        2  0 07:04 ?        00:00:00 [rcu_gp]
```

Partial output of the `ps -ef` command.

The lsof Command

The `lsof` command displays open files as well as what process opened them. Such information is useful for troubleshooting or monitoring purposes whether configuration files or device files are open. If no options are added, the command lists all open files. Chances are this output will be very large.

Perhaps you need to see files opened by a specific user. In that case, the `-u {username}` option filters the output for the specified user. Another option is to display files opened by a specific process, such as a database or webserver. The `-c {process}` option displays this information.

```
sudo lsof | grep ssh
[sudo] password for student:
lsof: WARNING: can't stat() fuse.gvfsd-fuse file system /run/user/125/gvfs
      Output information may be incomplete.
lsof: WARNING: can't stat() fuse.gvfsd-fuse file system /run/user/1000/gvfs
      Output information may be incomplete.
NetworkMa  458                              root  mem        REG
  8,5   445976    4334047 /usr/lib/x86_64-linux-gnu/libssh.so.4.8.4
NetworkMa  458  498 gmain                   root  mem        REG
  8,5   445976    4334047 /usr/lib/x86_64-linux-gnu/libssh.so.4.8.4
NetworkMa  458  535 gdbus                   root  mem        REG
  8,5   445976    4334047 /usr/lib/x86_64-linux-gnu/libssh.so.4.8.4
```

Partial output of the `lsof | grep ssh` *command.*

Use the `| grep {string}` *command to search for specific information.*

The systemd-analyze blame Command

Many processes launch during the boot process. In the event of slow boot times, it may be useful to analyze exactly what processes are consuming the most time during startup. It may be that some processes are not necessary to the system. Most modern Linux systems use a configuration manager named `systemd`.

The `systemd-analyze blame` command displays the processes that take the most time to start during boot operations.

The `systemd` *manager was discussed in an earlier section.*

```
student@ubuntu20:~$ systemd-analyze blame
30.066s NetworkManager-wait-online.service
11.547s plymouth-quit-wait.service
10.054s gdm.service
 7.225s snapd.service
 6.084s dev-loop5.device
 4.575s dev-loop6.device
 3.946s dev-sda5.device
 1.765s man-db.service
```

Partial output of the `systemd-analyze blame` *command.*

The sar Command

The `sar` command displays system usage reports based on data collected from system activity. These reports consist of various sections, each of which include the type of data and the time of data collection. The default mode of the `sar` command displays CPU usage in various time increments for each category of resource that accessed the CPU, such as the users, the system, the I/O scheduling, etc. It also displays the percentage of the CPU that was idle at a given time. At the bottom of the report is an average of each data point across listed time periods. By default, `sar` reports the data collected every 10 minutes, though you can use various options to filter and shape these reports.

You can use `sar` to identify excessive load on the CPU. You're given details about when excessive usage occurs as well as what might be causing that excessive usage.

The syntax of the `sar` command is `sar [options]`

Display System Uptime

The `uptime` command displays how long the system has been up. This troubleshooting tool allows sysadmins to determine whether a server recently restarted—an indication of its stability. This tool also displays the CPU workload over the last one, five, and 15 minutes.

```
[student@fedora home]$ uptime
 18:42:54 up 35 min,  1 user,   load average: 0.00, 0.00, 0.07
[student@fedora home]$
```

Output of the `uptime` *command.*

The results of `uptime` are also displayed at the beginning of the output of the `top` command.

Understand Process States

Processes exist in one of several states. Identifying and understanding these states help with both troubleshooting and performance monitoring. The process state indicates resource consumption.

The `top` command displays the total number of processes existing in each of the possible states. The `ps` command can also be filtered to display the state of processes.

```
student@ubuntu20:~$ ps -o pid,state,command
  PID S COMMAND
 5598 S bash
 7309 R ps -o pid,state,command
```

Output of the `ps -o pid,state,command` *command.*

Some applications are complex enough to require multiple processes to function. If this is the case, a parent process launches one or more child processes, depending on what's needed by the program. The child processes are linked to their parent process. When a parent process terminates, its child processes should terminate as well. When a child process terminates, it notifies its parent process and awaits acknowledgment before exiting.

One way of displaying parent and child processes is by using the `pstree` command.

```
student@ubuntu20:~$ pstree
systemd─┬─ModemManager───2*[{ModemManager}]
        ├─NetworkManager───2*[{NetworkManager}]
        ├─accounts-daemon───2*[{accounts-daemon}]
        ├─acpid
        ├─at-spi-bus-laun─┬─dbus-daemon
                          └─3*[{at-spi-bus-laun}]
```

Output of the `pstree` command displaying parent and child processes.

Identify Process States

There are four process states, though one of them is divided into two substates. Recognize these process states to make troubleshooting and application management easier.

Process State	Description
Running	The process functioning normally and receiving the resources it needs.
Sleeping	The process is awaiting access to resources to be able to run.
Stopped	The process is exiting or terminating and releasing resources.
Zombie	Child processes send their exit status to parent processes to be released for exiting.

The sleeping state indicates a process awaiting access to resources. The state is a normal consequence of resource sharing. The sleep state has two substates: interruptible and uninterruptible.

- **Interruptible:** The process waits for a specific time slot or event before attempting to enter the running state.

- **Uninterruptible:** The process waits for a specific time-out value before attempting to enter the running state.

Exiting processes can get stuck in the zombie state if their parent process exits before releasing the child process. These processes must be manually killed by the sysadmin.

Runaway Processes

Bugs or misconfigurations may lead some applications to steadily consume more resources, eventually congesting the system and impacting its performance. These processes may not always terminate correctly.

It's best to attempt to terminate the process gracefully by using a command such as `sudo kill -15 {PID}`. Because the process is already misbehaving, a more forceful attempt such as `sudo kill -9 {PID}` or `pkill` may be necessary.

High Utilization

Linux systems that display high CPU utilization and load averages may be suffering from a number of issues. High utilization may be due to software bugs, misconfigurations, untuned default settings, or properly functioning but high-demand applications (such as rendering, databases, or dev programs).

Since Linux itself is relatively well-tuned, the problem is likely with a user application. Use commands such as `ps` or `top` to identify processes consuming resources and why those processes were launched.

```
student@ubuntu20:~$ ps -u
USER        PID %CPU %MEM    VSZ   RSS TTY      STAT START   TIME COMMAND
student    2177  0.0  0.1 172652  6560 tty2     Ssl+ 07:07   0:00 /usr/lib
student    2220  0.0  0.2 199560 15412 tty2     Sl+  07:08   0:00 /usr/lib
student    5598  0.0  0.0  19248  4756 pts/0    Ss   07:34   0:00 bash
student    8314  0.0  0.0  20132  3228 pts/0    R+   07:47   0:00 ps -u
```

Output of the `ps -u` *command showing processes started by the current user.*

Utilization at or near 100% indicates the processor's demand is too high. The lower this percentage is, the more CPU capacity is available to additional workloads.

Set Priorities for CPU Processes

For systems experiencing high utilization, if the workload cannot be reduced, then other settings may be used to better manage necessary processes. Processes are launched with a priority level, and this level can be adjusted using the `nice` and `renice` commands.

Manage Process Priorities

Processes are launched with priority levels ranging from -20 to 19. Most processes start with a priority of 0. Processes with a priority nearer to -20 are higher priority than those nearer to 19.

The `nice` command allows users to start new processes at a specified priority level. This level overrides the normal priority of that process.

```
$ sudo nice -priority ./backup.sh
```

Running processes can be assigned a different priority level without restarting the application by using the `renice` command.

```
$ sudo renice -priority ./backup.sh
```

The difference between `nice` *and* `renice` *is that* `nice` *is used when starting a new application, and* `renice` *is used when changing the priority of a running process.*

Job Control

Process management is usually considered from a system-wide perspective and handled by the root user (system administrator). Processes represent all running code on the system. Individual users, however, can manage scripts or applications that they have started.

Manage Jobs

Jobs are a subset of processes and refer specifically to any process the current user has started. Users can display processes they are running by using the `jobs` command. The resulting output shows a numbered list of all existing jobs. These job numbers are used to identify and manipulate the processes.

Normally, when a command is executed, it processes in the foreground, consuming the shell until the command completes. Upon completion, the command exits and the shell prompt is available to the user to run another command.

For example, imagine a backup script that takes 10 minutes to complete. Until the script completes, the command prompt is unavailable to the user. In this case, the script is running in the foreground as a job associated with the user. The system sees the script as a process.

However, scripts and other commands can be executed in the background. The process or script runs, but the shell is returned to the user rather than consumed until termination. To background a job, such as the backup.sh script, append the ampersand `&` to the command:

```
$ backup.sh &
```

You can display the status of the jobs by using the `jobs` command. When a job is executing in the background, you cannot see its status. The `jobs` command displays current jobs and identifies each with a number enclosed by square brackets.

Remember, a job is simply a process or command.

What if you need to see the actual process running (for example, to check the status of a progress bar or to ensure the program hasn't unexpectedly halted)? You can move a backgrounded job to the foreground by using the `fg` command, `%` symbol, and the job number. For example, to foreground the script with a job number of 1, type:

```
$ fg %1
```

The job is now running in the foreground for you to observe.

Pause the job with `Ctrl+Z`, and then background it with `bg %[1]`. This command returns the job to the backgrounded status to remove it from the shell.

```
$ bg %1
```

Check the status again by using the `jobs` command.

Jobs can also be managed by using the `Ctrl` meta key. The following key combinations are useful for managing jobs:

- `Ctrl+Z` - Pauses a job temporarily, often so it can be moved to the background.

- `Ctrl+D` - Exits the program and logs the user out of the current session.

- `Ctrl+C` - Stops a running process.

The `nohup` ("no hangup") command prevents a process from ending when the user logs off. For example, if an administrator launches a backup script and then logs off the system, the script would stop running. By placing the `nohup` command in front of the normal command, the script would continue even after the administrator logged off.

The syntax of the `nohup` command is `nohup {command/script}`

Review Activity:

Processes

Answer the following questions:

1. **Differentiate between stopped processes and zombie processes.**

2. **Differentiate between -15 and -9 kill signals.**

3. **What keys are used to cause** `top` **to display resources by memory consumption or by CPU consumption?**

4. **Differentiate between the nice and renice commands.**

Topic 8C

Manage Memory

EXAM OBJECTIVES COVERED
4.3 Given a scenario, analyze and troubleshoot central processing unit (CPU) and memory issues.

Random Access Memory (RAM) provides a temporary, volatile, and fast storage area for the processor. Without sufficient RAM, users cannot open applications, and the system would be unable to provide services. Memory is a finite resource on computer systems and sometimes there is not enough storage capacity in RAM to support the system's services. In this case, additional storage capacity can be borrowed from storage drives, such as solid-state drives or hard disk drives. This borrowing is referred to as virtual memory. While these devices provide additional capacity, they often result in a slower system than RAM.

This section identifies system memory issues and covers the use of virtual memory.

Virtual Memory

Both **Random Access Memory (RAM)** and storage devices are storage locations. While disks are nonvolatile storage locations that maintain data even when power is removed, RAM is a temporary storage location. However, both locations are used to store data. RAM is a much more finite and limited system resource than storage disks. In addition, there is usually far less storage capacity in memory than on a drive.

Each process that runs is assigned a quantity of RAM, and because this memory is finite, a system's entire memory can be consumed. On old systems, this resulted in an "out of memory" error that required users to close some applications before launching others. Modern operating systems, however, swap or trade information between RAM and the storage disk. Additional storage space is borrowed from the storage disk and used as RAM. This concept is referred to as "virtual memory," and the data is "swapped" between the two storage locations.

However, storage devices are substantially slower than RAM, so swapping places a significant performance hit on the system.

Swap Space

Swap space is a partition on the storage device that is used when the system runs out of physical memory. Linux pushes some of the unused files from RAM to the swap space to free up memory. Usually, the swap space equals 1.5 x the quantity of RAM.

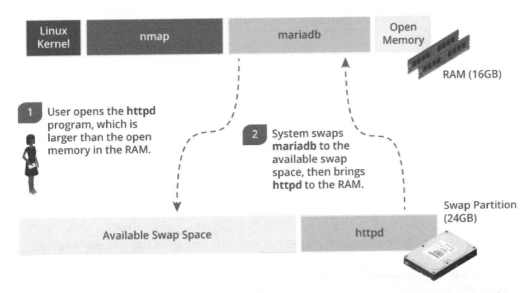

An example of swap space operations. Here a user attempts to open the httpd program (1) that exceeds the available space in the RAM. The system moves the mariadb file into the swap partition (2) to make space for httpd in the RAM. (Images © 123RF.com.)

The configuration of swap space can alleviate memory-related issues, especially when the system and applications request more memory than the system has. Systems with a low amount of RAM are particularly vulnerable to these issues. Swap space is not a replacement for adding more memory, but it can help minimize system and application sluggishness, unresponsiveness, and crashes. There are three different swap types or configurations:

- **Device swap:** configured when you partition the storage device and used by the OS to run large applications.

- **File system swap:** configured primarily upon installing Linux and used by the OS as an emergency resource when the available swap space runs out.

- **Pseudo-swap:** enables large applications to run on computers with limited RAM.

Swap files are created for storing data that is to be transferred from a system's memory to a storage device. They are dynamic and change in size when data is moved in and out of memory.

A swap partition is an area of virtual memory on a storage device to complement the physical RAM in the computer. Linux systems use swap partitions because they perform better than swap file systems.

Swap Management Commands

Sysadmins use the `mkswap` command to create swap space on a storage partition. You'll typically use it when you wish to move swap space to a different partition. For example, you might want to save space on a low-capacity boot drive. The `mkswap` command provides options to perform various tasks.

Option for the mkswap Command	Purpose
-c	Verify that the device is free from bad sectors before mounting the swap space.
-p	Set the page size to be used by the mkswap command. A page is a chunk of memory that is copied to the storage device during the swap process.
-L {label}	Activate the swap space using labels applied to partitions or file systems.

After creating swap space, you won't need it active all the time. Use the swapon and swapoff commands to activate or deactivate the swap partition on a specified device. Some frequently used options are shown in the following table.

Option for the swapon and swapoff Commands	Purpose
swapon -e	Skip devices that do not exist.
swapon -a	Activate all of the swap space.
swapoff -a	Deactivate all of the swap space.

Memory Exhaustion

It is critical, particularly on Linux servers, to ensure the system has plenty of free memory. Too little RAM greatly reduces system performance. On Linux systems hosting major business applications such as databases or webservers, such performance issues can impact the entire organization.

The server's specifications should include more memory than the system is anticipated to need.

The free and vmstat Commands

In addition to commands such as top, the free and vmstat commands are useful for monitoring memory utilization.

The free command displays the quantity of free or unused memory. If the system is running a number of applications, this information indicates how much memory is still available to run additional processes.

Much like the du and df disk management tools, the free command uses the -h option to display results in a human-readable format. The quantities of memory are displayed in logical units, such as GB.

Because you want the server to have plenty of memory to support its functions, you want the available free memory value to be high.

```
student@ubuntu20:~$ free -h
              total        used        free      shared  buff/cache   available
Mem:          5.8Gi       978Mi       2.5Gi        12Mi       2.3Gi       4.6Gi
Swap:         2.0Gi          0B       2.0Gi
```

Output of the free -h *command. Observe the used and free columns.*

The `vmstat` command displays the use of virtual memory. Recall that virtual memory involves swapping data between two storage locations: physical memory and storage disk(s). Such swapping is time-consuming and reduces the performance of the system. Significant use of virtual memory indicates that the system needs more memory or a reduced workload.

Because the use of virtual memory indicates the system is overwhelmed, you want the utilization number from `vmstat` to be low.

```
student@ubuntu20:~$ vmstat
procs -----------memory---------- ---swap-- -----io---- -system-- ------cpu-----
 r  b   swpd   free   buff  cache   si   so    bi    bo   in   cs us sy id wa st
 4  0      0 2667424  60248 2343972    0    0   354   601    1  561  8  2 90  0  0
```

Output of the `vmstat` *command.*

Out of Memory (OOM) Scenarios

Memory leaks occur when programs request memory space but never return it. This could be due to software bugs or misconfigurations and could lead to a system crash if all of its memory is consumed. Tools that measure memory utilization, such as `top`, `htop`, and `sar`, can be used to detect memory leaks.

The Linux kernel may over-allocate memory resources. It relies on **out-of-memory killer (OOM Killer)** to recover over-allocated memory space. In some cases, this may cause applications to quit unexpectedly. OOM Killer logs applications it kills, usually in `/var/log/messages`.

Free Memory versus Cache

Don't confuse free system memory with the CPU cache. The CPU cache provides very quick access to small amounts of information. The cache is a component of the CPU, and its size varies by model.

Use the `cat /proc/cpuinfo` command to display cache information. The larger the cache, the greater the benefit for running processes. Traditional RAM is relatively large and less quickly accessed than cache memory.

Review Activity:

Memory

Answer the following questions:

1. **Explain the concept of virtual memory.**

2. **What is a swap partition?**

3. **Differentiate between the free and vmstat commands.**

Topic 8D

Manage the Linux Kernel

EXAM OBJECTIVES COVERED
1.6 Given a scenario, build and install software.
1.7 Given a scenario, manage software configurations.
2.1 Summarize the purpose and use of security best practices in a Linux environment.
4.5 Given a scenario, use systemd to diagnose and resolve common problems with a Linux system.

One of the defining features of Linux is that it is modular, enabling you to adjust low-level system configurations at boot and during operation. This provides you with a great deal of flexibility in adjusting how your system runs and what types of devices it can leverage. In this section, you'll explore more about the Linux kernel and some of its features, and then you'll customize the kernel to meet your unique business needs.

You'll begin by identifying some of the key concepts and components that make up the Linux kernel. This will give you a better sense of what services the kernel provides and how you might go about customizing those services.

What is the Linux Kernel?

The **kernel** is the core of an operating system. All other components rely on it. The kernel manages file system access, memory, processes, devices, and resource allocation on a system. The kernel also controls all the hardware devices plugged into the system. It is one of the first elements to be loaded on startup and remains in the main memory during the computer's operation. The kernel also contains system-level commands and other functions that are normally hidden from users.

Kernel Space and User Space

Kernels tend to divide software running into two spaces: kernel space and user space. The **kernel space** is simply where the kernel executes the services that it provides. The **user space** is the area of memory that includes everything outside of kernel space. This can include everything from high-level applications that the user interacts with to processes that run in the background to various low-level system libraries.

Software running in user space can access resources provided by kernel space through the use of system calls. These calls provide the resources a user space application needs to perform a task. For example, an application might issue a system call to the kernel so that it can leverage input/output (I/O) services that write data to a storage device.

The split between these two memory regions is useful because it promotes greater stability and security. Software in one space cannot interfere with software in the other.

Device Drivers

A device driver is a software program that enables a computer's operating system to identify the characteristics and functions of a hardware device, communicate with it, and control its operations. It acts as an interface between the operating system and hardware devices such as storage drives, printers, scanners, monitors, and keyboards. Device drivers can be included in the operating system or installed on-demand.

When the system boots, drivers are loaded with the kernel, enabling Linux to work with various devices. While the kernel and drivers are separate pieces, they work together to allow Linux to use the device's features. For example, printer drives let Linux know what features the printer has (color, duplexing, and collation) and how to expose those features to the user. The drivers are not part of the kernel and can therefore be updated without making changes to the kernel.

Display Kernel Version Information

The Linux kernel is continually updated by creator Linus Torvalds and many other volunteers. Each new version of the kernel is given a kernel version number to distinguish it from past and future versions. The current naming convention for kernel versions is **major.minor**, where major is the major version number and minor is the minor version number. For example, version 5.16 was released in February 2022.

The latest Linux kernel and stable releases can be found at www.kernel.org.

By default, `uname` prints the name of the kernel—Linux. You can view the kernel version number of your current system by using the `uname -r` command. You can also enter `uname -i` to view the hardware platform. To print all information, enter the `uname -a` command.

```
[student@fedora home]$ uname -a
Linux fedora 5.14.10-300.fc35.x86_64 #1 SMP Thu Oct 7 20:48:44
 UTC 2021 x86_64 x86_64 x86_64 GNU/Linux
[student@fedora home]$
```

Output of the `uname -a` command. Observe the kernel version is 5.14.

Manage Kernel Modules

Now that you've explored the Linux kernel, you're ready to install and configure some kernel modules. This will enable you to extend the kernel's functionality for specific purposes.

What Are Kernel Modules?

A **kernel module** is a system-level object that extends the functionality of the kernel. It can be dynamically loaded or unloaded into the kernel when required. It enables the kernel to update or recompile itself without requiring the system to reboot.

Using kernel modules has several advantages:

- They reduce the burden on the kernel because otherwise all of the modules' functionality would have to be added directly to the kernel.

- They lower memory consumption due to dynamic loading of the kernel.

- They extend the functionality of the system and avoids rebuilding and rebooting.

A kernel module file consists of a .ko extension. Modules built for a specific kernel version may not be compatible with another version of the kernel.

Kernel Module Commands

Kernel module management commands enable you to view, load, unload, or modify kernel modules.

Kernel Module Command	Purpose
`lsmod`	Display the currently loaded kernel modules, their sizes, usage details, and their dependent modules.
`modinfo`	Display information about a particular kernel module, such as the file name of the module, license, description, author's name, module version number, dependent modules, and other parameters or attributes. The syntax of this command is `modinfo [options] {module name}`
`insmod`	Install a module into the currently running kernel. This command inserts only the specified module and does not insert any dependent modules. The syntax of this command is `insmod {module name}`
`rmmod`	Remove a module from the currently running kernel. The syntax of this command is `rmmod {module name}`

The modprobe Command

The `modprobe` command is used to add or remove modules from a kernel. This command is capable of loading all the dependent modules before inserting the specified module. It is therefore preferred over using the `insmod` and `rmmod` commands.

To add modules using `modprobe`, use the `-a` option and specify the modules you want to add. To unload a module, use the `-r` option and specify the modules you want to remove.

The syntax of the `modprobe` command is `modprobe [options] {module names}`

Additional options for the `modprobe` command include those in the following table.

Option for the modprobe Command	Purpose
`-f`	Force the module to be inserted or removed.
`-n`	View the output results without actually executing operations.
`-s`	Print errors to the system log (syslog) rather than stderr.
`-v`	Enable verbose mode.

The depmod Command

For `modprobe` to accurately install dependent modules, it reads the modules.dep file to identify how modules are linked to one another. The `depmod` command is used to update this database of dependencies so that `modprobe` can function properly.

The `depmod` command searches the contents of `/lib/modules/<kernel version>/` for each module. A module may export a "symbol," indicating that it can provide a service to other modules. Other modules may call these exported symbols into their own code to leverage their capabilities. So, `depmod` builds the modules.dep file by aggregating all instances of symbols being exported and used.

The syntax of the `depmod` command is `depmod [options]`

Symbols provide a way for modules to call upon the functions or other programming objects of other modules. For example, module1 has a C function named `foo()` that performs some useful task. Another module, module2, wants to use `foo()` when it is linked to the kernel, rather than incorporate that routine in its own code. This is only possible if module1 explicitly exports `foo()` for external use. It does this by using `EXPORT_SYMBOL()` or one of its variants on the function. The `foo()` function then becomes available as a symbol for any other module in the kernel to leverage.

Module Directories

The `/usr/lib/` directory contains shared libraries and binaries for general programs and software packages. The files in this directory are not meant to be executed by the user or custom shell scripts. More specifically, the `/usr/lib/modules/` directory contains the modules of different kernel versions installed. It holds a directory named after the kernel's version number. Inside this directory, modules are stored across various subdirectories based on their categories. For example, a Bluetooth driver may be stored in:

```
/usr/lib/modules/<kernel version>/kernel/drivers/
bluetooth/
```

Inside `/usr/lib/modules/<kernel version>/kernel/` are several subdirectories, some of which are described in the following table.

Module Subdirectory	Purpose
arch	Contains modules for architecture-specific support.
crypto	Contains modules for encryption and other cryptographic functions.
drivers	Holds modules for various types of hardware.
fs	Contains modules for various types of file systems.
net	Holds modules for networking components such as firewalls and protocols.

The `/etc/modprobe.conf` file is a configuration file that contains settings that apply persistently to all the modules loaded on the system. It is used to configure modules and their dependencies and to specify module aliases. An alias is just an alternative name to use for a module.

In newer Linux distros, this file is deprecated. The `/etc/modprobe.d/` directory is used instead and contains various .conf files. Other than creating aliases, these files can tell `modprobe` to run additional modules with specific options when your chosen module is loaded into the kernel. This enables the chosen module to leverage another module's functionality without actually loading it into the kernel.

You might do this when your module doesn't directly depend on a second module but does run better if that second module is installed.

Files ending in .conf in the `/etc/modprobe.d/` directory can use one of several commands.

.conf File Command	Purpose
`alias {alternative name} {module name}`	Specify an alternative name for a module with a long name.
`blacklist {module name}`	Ignore internal aliases, which occur when modules define their own aliases.
`install {module name} {command}`	Run the specified command without inserting the module into the kernel.

Kernel Updates and Parameters

In addition to loading modules into the kernel at runtime, you can also change some of the kernel's parameters while it is running. You can use these parameters to improve system performance, harden security, configure networking limitations, change virtual memory settings, and more.

The `/proc/sys/` directory lists the parameters that you can configure on your system. Like the directories containing kernel modules, this `/proc/sys/` directory is divided into several categories, including those in the following table.

/proc/sys Subdirectory	Related Parameters
`crypto`	Encryption and other cryptographic services.
`debug`	Debugging the kernel.
`dev`	Specific hardware devices.
`fs`	File system data.
`kernel`	Miscellaneous kernel functionality.
`net`	Networking functionality.
`user`	User space limitations.
`vm`	Virtual memory management.

Manage Kernel Parameters

The `sysctl` command displays or sets kernel parameters at runtime. It has various options, as defined in the following table.

Option for the sysctl Command	Purpose
`-a`	Display all parameters and their current values.
`-w {parameter}={value}`	Set a parameter value.
`-p[file-name]`	Load `sysctl` settings from the specified file or `/etc/sysctl.conf` if no file name is provided.
`-e`	Ignore errors about unknown keys.
`-r {pattern}`	Apply a command to parameters matching a given pattern, using extended regular expressions.

The syntax of the `sysctl` command is `sysctl [options]`

The `/etc/sysctl.conf` file enables configuration changes to a running Linux kernel. These changes might include improvements to networking, security configurations, or logging of information.

Kernel Panic

A **kernel panic** is a mechanism by which the system detects a fatal system error and responds to it. A fatal error typically results in the system becoming unstable or totally unusable. Software that handles kernel panics will display an error message to the user and dump the current state of kernel memory to a storage device for later debugging. Depending on how the system is configured, the panic handler will either reboot the system automatically or wait for the user to do so.

In Linux, kernel panic can happen for many reasons and at any point during operation, but it is usually experienced during the boot process. Common causes include the following:

- The kernel itself is corrupted or otherwise improperly configured.

- The `systemd` program is not executed during boot, leaving the system unusable.

- The kernel cannot find or otherwise cannot mount the main root file system.

- Malfunctioning or incompatible hardware is loaded into the kernel on boot.

The equivalent of a kernel panic in Microsoft Windows is the well-known Blue Screen of Death (BSoD).

The dmesg Command and dmesg Log File

The dmesg ("display message" or "driver message") command is used to print any messages that have been sent to the kernel's message buffer during and after system boot. Device drivers send messages to the kernel indicating the status of modules and parameters that the drivers use. These drivers can also send diagnostic messages to the kernel when they encounter errors. Other kernel components can also send messages to the buffer.

In addition to using the dmesg command, you can also access the message buffer from the /var/log/dmesg file. In either case, you can leverage dmesg to look for potential issues with kernel components or to validate that certain modules are being loaded.

The syntax of the dmesg command is dmesg [options]

The dmesg command includes several common options:

Option for the dmesg Command	Purpose
-c	Clear the kernel buffer after printing its contents.
-f {facility list}	Restrict output to the specified comma-separated list of facilities. A facility is a component category that is producing messages, such as user for user-level messages.
-l {level list}	Restrict output to the specified comma-separated list of levels. A level defines a message's nature and priority, such as notice for messages that aren't considered critical.
-e	Display a human-readable version of the time of each message as well as its delta, or the difference in time between subsequent messages.
-L	Color-code messages for easier readability.
-H	Output in a human-friendly format, combining both -e and -L options and using a text pager.
-h	List the available options as well as the available facilities and levels.

```
[    0.000000] Linux version 5.8.0-43-generic (buildd@lcy01-amd64-018)
 (gcc (Ubuntu 9.3.0-17ubuntu1~20.04) 9.3.0, GNU ld (GNU Binutils for U
buntu) 2.34) #49~20.04.1-Ubuntu SMP Fri Feb 5 09:57:56 UTC 2021 (Ubunt
u 5.8.0-43.49~20.04.1-generic 5.8.18)
[    0.000000] Command line: BOOT_IMAGE=/boot/vmlinuz-5.8.0-43-generic
 root=UUID=f143a8ab-8c16-4cdb-b4f8-393a61c1bfd6 ro quiet splash vt.han
doff=7
[    0.000000] KERNEL supported cpus:
```

Partial output of the dmesg *command.*

Manage Application Crashes

Application crashes may occur due to software bugs or system access issues. For example, incorrect pointers to memory spaces may cause an application to quit unexpectedly. If this occurs frequently, consider enabling a core dump—an operation usually disabled by default on most distributions. The core dump serves as a crash report and can be sent to the developer for further analysis. The dump includes the running state of the application at the time of the crash along with any virtual memory information associated with it.

Address application issues by considering some of the following questions:

- Did the application compile correctly?

- Did you modify any parameters before compiling?

- Did you configure any nonstandard settings during or after the installation?

- Is the application fully up-to-date and patched?

- Have you examined the application's log file (if it exists)?

The systemd management system includes a very robust journaling and logging component that can be useful for understanding system and application crashes. Note that systemd journal is a different and independent service from rsyslog, the traditional Linux log file service. The journal is maintained by the journald daemon and draws information from more sources than rsyslog. It also displays the log files more easily by using the `journalctl` command and a series of options.

For example, to display journal entries for SSH, type:

```
$ sudo journalctl -u ssh
```

The journal can be helpful when troubleshooting system and application crashes that occur frequently due to the level of detail provided and the robust filtering options.

 The rsyslog service is discussed in a future section.

Review Activity:

The Linux Kernel

Answer the following questions:

1. **What is a kernel module?**

2. **What does the output of the dmesg command display?**

3. **Where else is dmesg output found?**

Lesson 8

Summary

Linux provides many commands to display and manage system hardware. These commands allow sysadmins to understand the system's current configuration, including drivers, OS kernel (and its related modules), and recognized hardware. In addition, the processes consuming hardware resources must be optimized and managed. Finally, for both stability and security, the OS kernel must be kept up-to-date.

Guidelines

These best practices and guidelines are provided for your use as revision tools or as quick references in your job role.

- Consider whether what's reported in the `/proc` and `/dev` directories is hardware Linux recognizes, not necessarily the hardware installed. Hardware that is not properly connected may not be displayed.

- Use `/dev/null` as a target to data to be discarded.

- Use `/dev/zero` as a source of data to be written.

- Use `/dev/urandom` as a source of random data to be written.

- Processes are instances of running code and identified by a PID.

- Processes are displayed by using commands such as `ps`, `top`, and `htop`.

- Performance information related to processes is displayed by using commands such as `top`, `htop`, and `sar`.

- Processes exist in various states, including running, sleeping, stopped, and zombie.

- Jobs are processes started and managed by users.

Command Reference Table

This list of commands and their associated syntax can also be found in Appendix B.

Command	Syntax	Purpose	Covered in
hwinfo	hwinfo [options] {device}	Display detailed information about hardware resources.	Lesson 8, Topic A
dmidecode	dmidecode [options] {device}	Display system information for current devices.	Lesson 8, Topic A
lspci	lspci [options]	Display information about devices attached to specific busses.	Lesson 8, Topic A

Command	Syntax	Purpose	Covered in
lsusb	lsusb [options]	Display information about devices attached to specific busses.	Lesson 8, Topic A
lscpu	lscpu [options]	Display CPU information.	Lesson 8, Topic A
lsmem	lsmem [options]	Display information about memory blocks.	Lesson 8, Topic A
ps	*The ps command supports multiple command syntax formats.*	Display process status.	Lesson 8, Topic B
sar	sar [options]	Display system usage reports.	Lesson 8, Topic B
nohup	nohup {command/ script}	Prevent a process from ending when the user logs off.	Lesson 8, Topic B
mkswap	mkswap [options]	Create swap space on a storage partition.	Lesson 8, Topic C
swapon	swapon [options]	Activate the swap partition ona specific device.	Lesson 8, Topic C
swapoff	swapoff [options]	Deactivate the swap partition on a specific device.	Lesson 8, Topic C
free	free [options]	Display the quantity of free or unused memory.	Lesson 8, Topic C
vmstat	vmstat [options]	Display the virtual memory usage.	Lesson 8, Topic C
modinfo	modinfo [options] {module-name}	Display information about a particular kernel module.	Lesson 8, Topic D
insmod	insmod {module-name}	Install a module into the currently running kernel.	Lesson 8, Topic D
rmmod	rmmod {module-name}	Remove a module from the currently running kernel.	Lesson 8, Topic D
modprobe	modprobe [options] {module-names}	Add or remove modules from a kernel.	Lesson 8, Topic D
depmod	depmod [options]	Build the modules. dep file by aggregating all instances of symbols being exported and used.	Lesson 8, Topic D

Command	Syntax	Purpose	Covered in
sysctl	sysctl [options]	View or set kernel parameters at runtime.	Lesson 8, Topic D
dmesg	dmesg [options]	Print any messages that have been sent to the kernel's message buffer during and after system boot.	Lesson 8, Topic D

Lesson 9

Managing Services

LESSON INTRODUCTION

Linux servers (and Linux workstations, too) enable users and applications to complete tasks that drive business. This function begins with the initialization of the Linux kernel by systemd and SysVinit. These utilities start any configured services, such as SSH for remote administration or make websites available via Apache. Finally, sysadmins must configure the system for the comfort and practicality of the users and their preferred locale settings.

Lesson Objectives

In this lesson, you will:

- Manage system services.

- Configure common system services.

- Configure localization settings.

Topic 9A

Manage System Services

EXAM OBJECTIVES COVERED
1.4 Given a scenario, configure and use the appropriate processes and services.
4.5 Given a scenario, use systemd to diagnose and resolve common problems with a Linux system.

Most Linux systems initialize using either the newer systemd or older SysVinit processes. Both initialization programs start and manage services and daemons that make the server useful. Each program also has a separate group of management commands. Systemd is very robust and includes the ability to manage boot options, service startups, and even scheduled tasks by using unit files and directives. This Topic covers the use of both management systems.

What Are Services and Daemons?

While the terms *service* and *daemon* are sometimes used interchangeably, there are specific differences between the two.

Daemons are noninteractive programs running on the system. They do not provide direct communication with users and operate in the background.

Services are interactive, though they too operate in the background. Users may interact with services. Services are the purpose behind server computers.

Note that services are usually implemented as daemons and also contain an interactive component. Hence, services such as SSH will have a related daemon, such as sshd.

Service and daemon management is an essential part of the sysadmin role. Here are a few critical services that users rely on throughout the business day:

- **Web service**: Makes web pages available across the network and relies on `httpd`.

- **SSH service**: Allows secure remote administration and relies on `sshd`.

- **NFS service**: Allows remote access to exported directories and relies on several daemons, including nfsd and mountd.

- **NTP service**: Synchronizes time among network servers and relies on `ntpd`.

System Initialization

System initialization is the process that begins when the kernel first loads. It involves the loading of the operating system and its various components, including the boot process. System initialization is carried out by an init daemon in Linux—the "parent of all processes." The **init daemon** refers to a configuration file and initiates the processes listed in it. This prepares the system to run the required software. The init daemon runs continuously until the system is powered off, and programs on the system will not run without it.

On Linux, there are two main methods that initialize a system: systemd and SysVinit. Which method is active on your Linux system will affect how you manage services on that system.

Most modern Linux distributions use systemd to manage initialization. However, some distributions, especially older ones, rely on a different initialization mechanism named System V. The exam focuses on systemd, but some knowledge of System V is still important.

 System V initialization is covered later in this Topic.

systemd

The **systemd** software suite provides an init method for initializing a system. It also provides tools for managing services on the system that derive from the init daemon. The systemd suite is now the dominant init method in modern Linux distributions, and was designed as a replacement for other methods like SysVinit.

The systemd suite offers several improvements over older methods. For example, it supports parallelization (starting programs at the same time for quicker boot) and reduces shell overhead. In systemd, Control Groups (cgroups) are used to track processes instead of process IDs (PIDs), which provides better isolation and categorization for processes.

Use systemctl Commands

One of the most frequent tasks for administrators is managing services and daemons. Management includes starting, stopping, and checking the status of these applications.

It's critical to remember that Linux services and daemons acquire their settings from configuration files that are read when the system or the applications start. Any changes to these settings occur by editing the files, which must then be reread to discover the new configurations. In addition, administrators may choose whether a given service starts when the system boots.

Managing Services with systemctl

The systemd command to manage startup options is systemctl. This command relies on the command subcommand argument syntax. There are many subcommands, but several of the most common are listed here.

systemctl Subcommand	Purpose
`start`	Start the service or daemon (not persistent).
`stop`	Stop the service or daemon (not persistent).
`restart`	Restart the service or daemon.
`enable`	Set the service or daemon to start at boot (persistent).
`disable`	Set the service or daemon not to start at boot (persistent).
`status`	Display the current status of the service or daemon.
`mask`	Prevent a service from being started by any other service.

Note that *enabling* a service and *starting* a service are two different things. Enabling a service configures the service to start the next time the server starts. This merely sets the default status in the configuration file, and it does not start the service in the current runtime. Starting a service turns on the service in the current runtime but does not set its default startup status in the configuration file. Usually, when a new service is installed, the sysadmin will both start the new service and enable it.

```
[student@fedora ~]$ sudo systemctl status sshd
● sshd.service - OpenSSH server daemon
     Loaded: loaded (/usr/lib/systemd/system/sshd.service; disabled; vendor pre▶
     Active: active (running) since Sat 2022-02-19 12:53:08 EST; 49s ago
       Docs: man:sshd(8)
             man:sshd_config(5)
   Main PID: 2639 (sshd)
      Tasks: 1 (limit: 4630)
     Memory: 1.0M
        CPU: 11ms
     CGroup: /system.slice/sshd.service
             └─2639 "sshd: /usr/sbin/sshd -D [listener] 0 of 10-100 startups"

Feb 19 12:53:08 fedora systemd[1]: sshd.service: Deactivated successfully.
Feb 19 12:53:08 fedora systemd[1]: Stopped OpenSSH server daemon.
Feb 19 12:53:08 fedora systemd[1]: Starting OpenSSH server daemon...
Feb 19 12:53:08 fedora sshd[2639]: Server listening on 0.0.0.0 port 22.
Feb 19 12:53:08 fedora sshd[2639]: Server listening on :: port 22.
Feb 19 12:53:08 fedora systemd[1]: Started OpenSSH server daemon.
[student@fedora ~]$ sudo systemctl restart sshd
[student@fedora ~]$
```

Using the systemctl commands.

The term "persistent" describes a setting that remains in place even after a reboot. Enabling a service means it will start each time the system boots, whereas starting a service means it will run for the current system's runtime but will revert back to its default status upon reboot.

The difference between disabling/stopping a service and masking a service is that with masking, a symlink (symbolic link) is created to `/dev/null`, preventing the service from being started by any other service. Disabling a service merely deletes the symlink to the service's unit file. Another service might still call and start this disabled service. Masking a service is a much stronger way of preventing it from running.

Systemd unit files are discussed in a later section.

Understand systemd Unit Files

Under the systemd initialization process, the term *unit* refers to a resource that systemd knows how to manage via daemons and configuration files. This system is much more flexible than earlier initialization methods.

Unit files define how systemd manages the unit. The default unit files are stored at `/lib/systemd/system`, but the configurations are managed by sysadmins at `/etc/systemd/system` (the unit files in this location override any setting from the `/lib/systemd/system` directory).

There are many systemd unit file types, with .service, .timer, .mount, and .target as the primary examples.

Unit files include **[sections]** followed by **directive=value** statements. Two common sections are **[Unit]** and **[Install]**. The **[Unit]** section typically manages the unit's relationship to other units, including **Wants=** and **Requires=** directives. The **[Install]** section specifies the results of enable and disable actions by the administrator. This includes **WantedBy=** and **RequiredBy=** directives.

Note the **[Unit]** section and four directives in the example image below.

```
[student@fedora system]$ cat emergency.target
#  SPDX-License-Identifier: LGPL-2.1-or-later
#
#  This file is part of systemd.
#
#  systemd is free software; you can redistribute it and/or modify it
#  under the terms of the GNU Lesser General Public License as published by
#  the Free Software Foundation; either version 2.1 of the License, or
#  (at your option) any later version.

[Unit]
Description=Emergency Mode
Documentation=man:systemd.special(7)
Requires=emergency.service
After=emergency.service
AllowIsolate=yes
```

The emergency.target file.

Service Unit Files

Unit files that end with the .service suffix represent processes systemd manages. These files typically include dependency directives such as **Requires=** and **After=** that describe any other components this service depends on and when it should run to ensure those dependent components are loaded. These directives ensure that services start on time so that all prerequisites are complete before the next service to starts. Mistakes in the **Requires=** and **After=** lines may prevent services from starting on time.

Directives for .service Unit Files	Purpose
Before=	When multiple units are specified, this unit will start before any unit listed in this field.
After=	When multiple units are specified, this unit will start after any unit listed in this field.
Requires=	Units listed will be started if possible, and the primary unit will fail if the units specified by **Requires=** fail to start.
Wants=	Units listed will be started if possible, but the primary unit will still launch even if the units specified by **Wants=** fail to start.
Type=	Configures the startup type for the service. Values include simple, exec, forking, oneshot, dbus, notify, and idle.

Directives for .service Unit Files	Purpose
User=	Specifies the user under whose authority the service runs (usually root).
ExecStart=	Executes commands along a specified absolute path upon startup to start a service.
ExecStop=	Executes commands along a specified absolute path upon shutdown to stop a service.

Network services, for example, may be configured via .service unit files. Here is a very basic firewall configuration example.

```
[Unit]
Description=Firewall

[Service]
Type=oneshot
RemainAfterExit=yes
ExecStart=/usr/local/sbin/simple-firewall-start
ExecStop=/usr/local/sbin/simple-firewall-stop

[Install]
WantedBy=multi-user.target
```

Timer Unit Files

Systemd is also capable of managing time-based events by using .timer files. A time expression is written in the unit file and specifies what event is to be executed and defines the time interval.

Time Expression	Purpose
OnBootSec	(monotonic) Time spanning from a specific event, such as system startup.
OnCalendar	(realtime) Time referenced from the system clock.

OnCalendar events are displayed as DayOfWeek, Year-Month-Day, and as Hour:Minute:Second.

For example, a timer running daily at 3:00 a.m. displays as:

- OnCalendar=*-*-* 3:00:00

Another example is an event that runs at 9:00 p.m. on the first Friday of the month:

- OnCalendar=Fri *-*-*1..7 21:00:00

Systemd .timer files can be used to replace schedulers such as cron. Schedulers permit administrators and users to specify when an event should occur. The classic example of a timer is to schedule a system backup for the middle of the night.

The cron scheduler is discussed in a later section.

```
[student@fedora system]$ cat logrotate.timer
[Unit]
Description=Daily rotation of log files
Documentation=man:logrotate(8) man:logrotate.conf(5)

[Timer]
OnCalendar=daily
AccuracySec=1h
Persistent=true

[Install]
WantedBy=timers.target
```

Timer file for the logrotate service.

Mount Unit Files

Mount points may also be managed by systemd. A mount point is a directory within the filesystem where storage space is associated. Mount points managed by systemd rely on .mount unit files.

Mount points managed by systemd are defined in .mount unit files that contain a **[Mount]** section. This section defines the attributes of the mount action. Four of the more common options are listed in the table below.

Options for .mount Unit Files	Purpose
What=	Absolute path to storage to mount.
Where=	Absolute path to mount point directory.
Type=	Define the filesystem type (optional).
Options=	Any additional required options for the mount action.

Mount points managed via systemd reference paths use a slightly different naming convention than ones managed via normal Linux paths. Where Linux paths contain forward slashes as delimiters, systemd .mount unit files use the dash character instead. A path that might normally read `/mnt/projects/servers` becomes `mnt-projects-servers`. There are also a few replacements for special characters and punctuation.

```
[Mount]
What=tmpfs
Where=/tmp
Type=tmpfs
Options=mode=1777,strictatime,nosuid,nodev,size=50%,nr_inodes=400k
```

The [Mount] portion of a .mount file.

Target Unit Files

Manage Target Unit Files

Systemd targets represent system startup configurations. These targets define what services start when the system starts, often by chaining multiple configuration files. Four of the most commonly used targets are listed in the table below.

Common .target Files	Purpose
default	The target to which the system boots by default.
multi-user.target	Starts the enable services and the system to the CLI.
graphical.target	Starts the enable services and the system to the GUI.
network-online	Starts the specified network services, and delays the target until network service is established.

Here is a sample .target file from the man page:

```
# emergency-net.target

[Unit]
Description=Emergency Mode with Networking
Requires=emergency.target systemd-networkd.service
After=emergency.target systemd-networkd.service
AllowIsolate=yes
```

This example contains a **[Unit]** section. Other .target files may also contain an **[Install]** section. This file includes a user-friendly description, a requirements statement (for other targets or services that are required), an **After** field for when the target should load, and a field indicating whether the target can be switched manually.

Configure Targets

The `default.target` unit file points to the selected target—either CLI (`multi-user.target`) or GUI (`graphical.target`). When the default startup option is changed, this file is modified.

```
[Unit]
Description=Graphical Interface
Documentation=man:systemd.special(7)
Requires=multi-user.target
Wants=display-manager.service
Conflicts=rescue.service rescue.target
After=multi-user.target rescue.service rescue.target display-manager.service
AllowIsolate=yes
```

[Unit] section of the default target unit file.

The `systemctl` command allows manipulation of the targets. To display the default target, type:

```
# systemctl get-default
```

```
[student@fedora system]$ systemctl get-default
graphical.target
[student@fedora system]$
```

Displaying the default target.

To move the system to the graphical target, type:

```
# systemctl isolate graphical.target
```

To set the graphical target as the default, type:

```
# systemctl set-default graphical.target
```

 Remember that Linux servers often run at the CLI (`multi-user.target`*) so that all available resources can be dedicated to services. End-user Linux workstations usually run at the GUI (*`graphical.target`*).*

Identify Service Failures

Most services are configured to start when the system boots, though some are called by other services or by users.

When systemd manages service startup, use the `systemctl` command to troubleshoot and identify issues.

First, check the status of the service (using sshd as the example):

```
# systemctl status sshd
```

Next, ensure the service is enabled:

```
# systemctl enable sshd
```

```
[student@fedora ~]$ sudo systemctl status sshd
o sshd.service - OpenSSH server daemon
     Loaded: loaded (/usr/lib/systemd/system/sshd.servi>
     Active: inactive (dead)
       Docs: man:sshd(8)
             man:sshd_config(5)

Apr 14 13:08:37 fedora systemd[1]: Starting OpenSSH ser>
Apr 14 13:08:37 fedora sshd[2540]: Server listening on >
Apr 14 13:08:37 fedora sshd[2540]: Server listening on >
Apr 14 13:08:37 fedora systemd[1]: Started OpenSSH serv>
Apr 14 13:11:13 fedora systemd[1]: Stopping OpenSSH ser>
Apr 14 13:11:13 fedora sshd[2540]: Received signal 15; >
Apr 14 13:11:13 fedora systemd[1]: sshd.service: Deacti>
Apr 14 13:11:13 fedora systemd[1]: Stopped OpenSSH serv>
[student@fedora ~]$ sudo systemctl enable sshd
Created symlink /etc/systemd/system/multi-user.target.wa
nts/sshd.service → /usr/lib/systemd/system/sshd.service.
[student@fedora ~]$ █
```

Output from the systemctl status and enable commands.

Remember, if a service is disabled, it may still be launched by other services. To truly prevent a service from starting, use the `systemctl mask` subcommand.

In some cases, one service depends on another to start. In this case, ensure the primary service is not masked or disabled, but rather set to enabled.

Recognize Older SysVinit Startup

SysVinit is an older init method that has been largely replaced by systemd. However, some distributions still support SysVinit. Like systemd, SysVinit provides you with various tools to manage services and the state of the system.

Aside from systemd's improvements, one major difference between it and SysVinit is that SysVinit has runlevels. Runlevels control the state of the operating system in much the same way that systemd targets do; they determine what types of daemons should be running in order to create a specific type of environment. In fact, systemd targets were created to map to existing runlevels. As with systemd targets, you can change a system's runlevel and set a default.

 SysVinit was popularized in the UNIX System V (pronounced "System Five") family of operating systems.

Runlevel	Purpose
0	Halt or shut down the system.
1	Start single-user mode.
2	Start multi-user mode at CLI without networking.
3	Start multi-user mode at CLI with networking.
4	Unused
5	Start multi-user mode with GUI and networking.
6	Restart the system.

The `/etc/inittab` file stores details of various processes related to system initialization on a SysVinit system. It also stores details of the runlevels in use. The init daemon reads from this file to determine what runlevel to boot into, what daemons to start, and what to do if the runlevel changes. Each entry in the `/etc/inittab` file takes the format:

    id:rstate:action:process

The **id** is just a unique identifier for the entry, **rstate** defines what runlevels the entry applies to, and **action** specifies one of several tasks that determine how SysVinit handles the command defined in the process field.

Use SysVinit Commands

Two commands manage enabling and starting services under SysVinit: `service` and `chkconfig`.

The `service` command is another way to control SysVinit services through SysVinit scripts. It supports the subcommands listed below.

Subcommands for the service Command	Purpose
`status`	Print the current state of a service.
`start`	Start (activate) a service immediately.
`stop`	Stop (deactivate) a service immediately.
`restart`	Restart a service immediately.
`reload`	Reread a service's configuration files while the service remains running.

The syntax of the `service` command is `service [options] [service] [subcommand]`

The `chkconfig` command can be used to control services in each runlevel. It can also be used to start or stop services during system startup. The following are some subcommands and options that can be used with `chkconfig` to control services.

Subcommands and Options for the chkconfig Command	Purpose
`{service} on`	Enable a service to be started on boot.
`{service} off`	Disable a service so that it is no longer started on boot.
`{service} reset`	Stop (deactivate) a service immediately.
`restart`	Reset the status of a service.
`--level {runlevel}`	Specify the runlevel in which to enable or disable a service.

The syntax of the `chkconfig` command is `chkconfig [options] [service] [subcommand]`

Review Activity:

System Services

Answer the following questions:

1. When using the systemctl command, how does enabling a service differ from starting a service?

2. What command restarts the sshd service after a configuration change?

3. What are the target names for the GUI and CLI startup options?

Topic 9B

Configure Common System Services

EXAM OBJECTIVES COVERED
1.4 Given a scenario, configure and use the appropriate processes and services.
1.7 Given a scenario, manage software configurations.

One of the sysadmin's primary roles is to ensure the services users and systems rely on are available and configured. There are many possible services. Some servers are configured with multiple services, while others are dedicated to a single function. This Topic reviews several common services that sysadmins are regularly responsible for, including task scheduling, remote administration, and sharing resources from a centralized file server.

Basics of Configuration

System and service configuration files store the settings necessary to manage the system. Linux reads these configuration files as part of the startup process and loads the services accordingly. If you make a change to a configuration, the system must reread the file to implement the updates. This can be accomplished by rebooting, reloading, or restarting the service.

For example, to restart a service after editing a configuration file, type:

```
# systemctl restart {service-name}
```

Reloading a service is a similar command:

```
# systemctl reload {service-name}
```

There are several common services that Linux administrators configure. This section covers SSH, rsyslog, NTP, scheduling, web services, NFS, and CUPS.

Understand Secure Shell (SSH)

The Secure Shell (SSH) provides authenticated and encrypted remote connectivity. It is generally used for remote administration and is the standard for managing Linux systems as well as many network devices. On the destination SSH server, the primary configuration file is `/etc/ssh/sshd_config`.

Here are a few common SSH settings:

* Default port number is 22/tcp.

* Disable root authentication over SSH.

* Configure a banner message that warns users of proper use.

* Configure key-based authentication for greater security and convenience.

The actual configuration of SSH services is presented in a later section.

Configure rsyslog

Log files are a critical component of system administration. Log files display information on failed services, system restarts, configuration changes, user authentication, and more. By default, log files are stored locally on each Linux system. However, the rsyslog logging utility is capable of forwarding log files to remote systems.

rsyslog Severities and Facilities

The standard logging mechanism for Linux is rsyslog. This utility is an update to the older syslog system. In most instances, the two are the same. Rsyslog uses two values to manage entries: severities and facilities.

rsyslog Severities	Level
emerg	0
alert	1
crit	2
error	3
warn	4
notice	5
info	6
debug	7

Many services and daemons log messages. These services are referred to as "facilities." Here are a few sample facilities:

- cron

- kernel

- ftp

- ntp

```
##################
#### MODULES ####
##################

module(load="imuxsock") # provides support for local system logging
#module(load="immark")  # provides --MARK-- message capability

# provides UDP syslog reception
#module(load="imudp")
#input(type="imudp" port="514")
```

The Modules portion of the rsyslog.conf file.

There are many possible facilities, depending on what services and applications are installed on the system.

The rsyslog configuration file is found at `/etc/rsyslog.conf`. Additional configurations may be found in `/etc/rsyslog.d/50-default.conf`. Each line represents a different log configuration for the identified facility, such as:

```
cron.error  -/var/log/cron
```

This entry logs all cron messages from error upwards to `/var/log/cron`.

```
#cron.*                          /var/log/cron.log
#daemon.*                       -/var/log/daemon.log
kern.*                          -/var/log/kern.log
#lpr.*                          -/var/log/lpr.log
mail.*                          -/var/log/mail.log
#user.*                         -/var/log/user.log
```

Common facilities and severities.

Display and Forward Logs

Searching Local Logs in /var/log

The operating system and applications log entries into files stored at `/var/log`. Some applications write to their own log files, while others write to a standard system log file.

Essential Log Files	Purpose
`/var/log/syslog`	General system-related logs, found on Red Hat–derived distributions
`/var/log/messages`	General system-related logs, found on Debian-derived distributions
`/var/log/secure`	Authentication logs, found on Red Hat–derived distributions
`/var/log/auth.log`	Authentication logs, found on Debian-derived distributions
`/var/log/yum.log`	Logs YUM package management
`/var/log/httpd/`	A directory for Apache webserver to log information

Log files are simple text documents, so commands such as `tail`, `cat`, and `grep` are very useful for displaying entries. The tail command is particularly useful because rsyslog places the most recent log file entries at the bottom of the file.

```
student@ubuntu20:/var/log$ tail -n 3 dpkg.log
2021-11-11 14:40:13 status half-configured linux-image-5.8.0-43-generic:amd64
5.8.0-43.49~20.04.1
2021-11-11 14:40:13 status installed linux-image-5.8.0-43-generic:amd64 5.8.0-
43.49~20.04.1
2021-11-11 14:41:30 startup packages purge
```

The three most recent entries in the dpkg.log file.

Remote Log Forwarding

Helpdesk Ticket #01997

Submitted by:	Department:	Assigned to:	Date Opened:
Risha Patel	Information Services	*you*	2024-06-02

Subject	Configure server04 and server07
Ticket Detail	Can you set up and test log forwarding for two of our Linux servers, 04 and 07? We need server04 to be the centralized log file repo, and server07 to forward all its logs to that repo on server04. Let me know if any questions, thanks Risha
Date last updated	2024-06-02

Forwarding log files from multiple servers to a single server makes archiving and parsing the files much simpler.

The first configuration occurs on the computer where logs will be centralized. You must configure it to listen for inbound rsyslog connections.

1. Uncomment the following lines in the `/etc/rsyslog.conf` file. You will find these lines in the Modules section of the file:

    *   # Provides UDP syslog reception

    * $ModLoad imudp.so

    * $UDPServerRun 514

2. Configure a template to organize the storage of the inbound logs. The %HOSTNAME% variable means the logs will be organized based on the hostname of the sending server. The following setting is placed in the Templates section of the file:

    * $template DynamicFile,"/var/log/%HOSTNAME%/forwarded-logs.log" *.* -?DynamicFile

3. Configure the firewall to accept inbound connections over port 514/udp.

    *   On the forwarding server, edit the `/etc/rsyslog.conf` file and add the following line to the Rules section: *.* @IP

    *   Where IP is the IP address of the destination log storage server.

    *   Restart the rsyslogd on both servers.

4. Finally, test the configuration. On the source computer, type `logger TEST`. On the destination log storage computer, search `/var/log` for a directory with the source computer's name and an entry that reads "TEST".

Tools such as logrotate automate log file archiving.

Configure Network Time

Many critical services on the network rely on time synchronization, so it's imperative that all devices agree on the current time. Linux administrators select one of two daemons to manage time synchronization against public time servers. The older service is ntpd, and the more recent service is chronyd. Either may be installed, depending on the distribution. Only one time service should be active at a time.

Configure ntpd

The **Network Time Protocol** daemon (ntpd) synchronizes system time against one or more specified time servers over port 123/tcp. You can define the time servers by editing the `/etc/ntp.conf` file.

> server timeserver-IP-address

Don't forget to restart the service, since you made a configuration change:

> # systemctl restart ntp

 Often the `/etc/ntp.conf` file is configured for you by the Linux distribution vendor.

Configure chrony

In some cases, the ntpd may not be responsive enough for certain systems. Linux deployments that do not have constant or consistent network connections may not accurately or immediately synchronize time settings via the ntpd. The chrony service provides a more flexible and consistent time synchronization service in these cases. Like ntpd, chrony uses port 123/tcp.

Two components make up the chronyd service: the chronyd daemon and the chronyc command.

The chrony configuration file is `/etc/chrony.conf`. The file contains a list of the time servers chrony will synchronize with. Here is a sample of the configuration:

```
server 0.pool.ntp.org iburst
server 1.pool.ntp.org iburst
server 2.pool.ntp.org iburst
server 3.pool.ntp.org iburst
```

To see detailed configuration, status, and synchronization information, use the following commands:

```
# chronyc -n tracking
# chronyc activity
```

 Sysadmins must select one or the other time service; either ntpd or chronyd. Do not use both time services simultaneously.

Configure Scheduling

The primary Linux task scheduler is cron. This tool references a crontab file to determine whether any tasks have been assigned to a specific minute. A system-wide crontab file is located at `/etc/crontab`, and a per-user crontab is at `/var/spool/cron/crontabs`.

Helpdesk Ticket #01998

Submitted by: Kai Garcia	Department: Engineering	Assigned to: *you*	Date Opened: 2024-06-05

Subject	setting up a regular backup
Ticket Detail	Hi, can you help me figure out how to back up my files? I want to do this daily during off hours, something like 10 pm. Thanks, KG
Date last updated	2024-06-05

Cron jobs can be used to specify tasks each minute, hour, day, month, and any day of the week. This makes them extremely flexible.

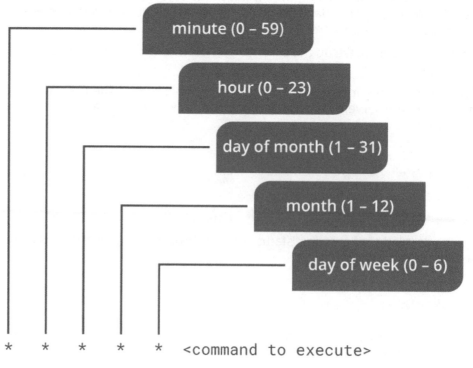

Illustration of cron component placement.

Configure cron

The cron configuration relies on a crontab file. To schedule an event, edit the crontab file using the `crontab -e` command.

The syntax of the `crontab` command is `crontab [options]`

 Do not use a regular editor for managing the cron daemon. The `crontab -e` command includes other features for managing the cron daemon. For example, after editing the file, it automatically restarts cron.

Helpdesk Ticket #01998-r

Submitted by:	Department:	Assigned to:	Date Opened:
Kai Garcia	Engineering	*you*	2024-06-05

Subject	setting up a regular backup
Ticket Detail	Hi, can you help me figure out how to back up my files? I want to do this daily during off hours, something like 10 pm.
	Thanks, KG
Response	Hey Kai, absolutely. Call the script "backup.sh" and, at the prompt, type in: `0 22 * * * /home/kgarcia/backup.sh`
Date last updated	2024-06-06

Here are a few other examples you could show the user who requested help.

To run the `curl` command to download a file daily at 10 p.m., type:

```
0 22 * * * curl -s http://sample.com/updated-file.txt
```

To execute the command at 8 p.m. Monday through Friday, type:

```
* 20 * * 1-5 /path/to/command
```

To execute the command at 2:15 a.m. daily, type:

```
15 2 * * * /path/to/command
```

To execute the command at 4:30 a.m. on the first day of each month, type:

```
30 4 1 * * /path/to/command
```

To see scheduled cron jobs for the current user, use the `cron -l` command.

Configure at

The `at` command runs a task once at a specified time. It is not designed for repetitive or regularly scheduled tasks. The `at` command is very flexible. Users can specify a particular date and time, or they can cause the scheduled command to run after a given period of time.

The command is typically used in an interactive manner, where the `at` command and time interval are specified, and then a task is defined in an interactive prompt. This enables the user to enter a path to a script or a command to be run. Pressing `Ctrl+D` exits the interactive mode.

The syntax of the `at` command is `at [options] {time}`

```
[student@fedora ~]$ at 3 PM
warning: commands will be executed using /bin/sh
at Sat Feb 19 15:00:00 2022
at> echo "Hello World"
at> <EOT>
job 4 at Sat Feb 19 15:00:00 2022
[student@fedora ~]$ atq
1        Sat Feb 19 16:00:00 2022 a student
2        Sat Feb 19 16:00:00 2022 a student
3        Sat Feb 19 16:00:00 2022 a student
4        Sat Feb 19 15:00:00 2022 a student
[student@fedora ~]$
```

Scheduling a "Hello World" message at 3 p.m.

Schedule a task in noninteractive mode using pipe:

```
echo "Hello World" | at 3 pm
```

Use `at -l` or `atq` to display scheduled jobs for the current user.

The `at` command takes several possible arguments for specifying time, including those listed here in this table.

Arguments Specifying Time for the at Command	Purpose
`noon`	Specifies 12:00 p.m.
`teatime`	Specifies 4:00 p.m.
`midnight`	Specifies 12:00 a.m.
`now + 3 minutes`	Specifies the time three minutes from now.
`now + 1 hour`	Specifies the time one hour from now.

In addition to cron, systemd `.timer` files can be used to schedule events. Recall that `.timer` files were discussed in an earlier section.

Configure a Webserver

Apache webserver requires very little configuration for a basic deployment. The basic process consists of installing the service, editing a single configuration file, configuring the firewall, and creating content.

Helpdesk Ticket #01999

Submitted by:	Department:	Assigned to:	Date Opened:
Ali Selassi	Marketing	*you*	2024-06-07

Subject	internal website
Ticket Detail	Can you help me set up the internal Marketing website? I just need it to be a static landing page, nothing fancy. Thanks!
Date last updated	2024-06-07

To edit the configuration file, use a text editor such as Vim or Nano to open `/etc/httpd/conf/httpd.conf`. This file contains a great many comments and optional directives. For a basic deployment, only two directives need to be modified. Browse or search for the **Listen** and **DocumentRoot** directives, and then make the following changes:

```
Listen 127.0.0.1:80

DocumentRoot "/var/www/html"
```

```
# Change this to Listen on a specific IP address, but note that if
# httpd.service is enabled to run at boot time, the address may not be
# available when the service starts.  See the httpd.service(8) man
# page for more information.
#
Listen localhost:80
```

The listen configuration.

```
# DocumentRoot: The directory out of which you will serve your
# documents. By default, all requests are taken from this directory, but
# symbolic links and aliases may be used to point to other locations.
#
DocumentRoot "/var/www/html"
```

The document root configuration.

In this case, the webserver listens for connections to itself (hence the 127.0.0.1 loopback address) on port 80. The files that make up the website are found at `/var/www/html`.

Next, configure the firewall to permit inbound HTTP (port 80/tcp) connections.

```
# firewall-cmd --permanent --zone-public --add-
service=http

# firewall-cmd --reload
```

```
[student@fedora ~]$ sudo firewall-cmd --permanent --zone=public
--add-service=http
success
[student@fedora ~]$ sudo firewall-cmd --reload
success
[student@fedora ~]$
```

Add the http service to the firewall.

Recall that firewall management was covered in an earlier section.

Finally, use a text editor to create a simple test web page with the following content:

Hello World

Welcome to my website!

Name the file `index.html`, and store it at /var/www/html (the location specified by the **DocumentRoot** directive in `httpd.conf`).

```
Hello World
Welcome to my website!
```

Create the index.html home page.

The Apache service must own this file, so use the `chown` command to set ownership:

```
# chown apache.apache /var/www/html/index.html
```

```
[student@fedora ~]$ ls -l /var/www/html
total 4
-rw-r--r--. 1 root root 35 Feb 19 19:23 index.html
[student@fedora ~]$ sudo chown apache:apache /var/www/html/index.html
[student@fedora ~]$ ls -l /var/www/html
total 4
-rw-r--r--. 1 apache apache 35 Feb 19 19:23 index.html
[student@fedora ~]$
```

Change ownership to Apache.

Finally, start and enable the Apache httpd web service:

```
# systemctl enable httpd
# systemctl start httpd
```

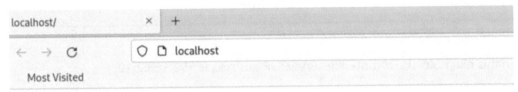

```
[student@fedora ~]$ sudo systemctl start httpd
[student@fedora ~]$ sudo systemctl enable httpd
Created symlink /etc/systemd/system/multi-user.targe
/systemd/system/httpd.service.
[student@fedora ~]$
```

Start and enable Apache.

Use a web browser on the local system to display the web page. Launch the browser, and in the address bar, type `http://localhost` to see the page.

Test the webserver deployment.

Configure NFS

One of the most common uses for a server is file storage. File servers centralize business content, making security and backups easier. The Network File System protocol permits remote client computers to connect to file servers from across the network to access shared directories.

NFS was introduced in an earlier Lesson.

NFS Server Configuration

To deploy NFS on a file server, first install, enable, and start the service. To enable and start NFS, type:

```
# systemctl enable nfs-server
# systemctl start nfs-server
```

Next, create or select directories on the file server that should be exported (shared) on the network. Note what directories these are and what access permissions might be required. Edit the `/etc/exports` file to make these resources available across the network. You will add the absolute path to the directory and various access controls.

Here are two samples:

```
/media/projects          192.168.2.0/24(rw,sync)
/media/resources         *(ro,sync)
```

In the above configuration, the projects directory will be available to any client connecting from the `192.168.2.0/24` subnet. Those clients will have read and write (rw) access. The resources directory will permit connections from any client IP and provide read-only (ro) access.

Remember to restart the service for these changes to take effect.

Configure the NFS Client

To display the available directories on the remote file server, use the `showmount -e {server}` command.

```
# showmount -e 192.168.2.10
```

On the NFS client workstation, you can mount the exported directory to a local mount point. For example, to mount the remote `/media/projects` directory to the local `/media/share` directory, type:

```
# mount -t nfs4 192.168.2.10:/media/projects
/media/share
```

In this example, the remote file server's IP address is 192.168.2.10.

 Don't forget to configure any firewalls for NFS connectivity. NFS relies on port 111/tcp (and /udp) plus port 2049/tcp (and /udp).

Configure Printing

Printing is a critical function on a network. The term *printers* refers to the software that manages the print process, while print devices are the actual hardware that applies toner (or ink) to paper. The older Linux printers were managed by a series of `lp` (line printer) commands, including the `lpr` and `lpq` commands discussed below. Modern implementations often rely on CUPS to manage the print infrastructure.

Helpdesk Ticket #02000

Submitted by:	Department:	Assigned to:	Date Opened:
Anna Tanaka	HR	*you*	2024-06-09

Subject	Print solution needed
Ticket Detail	We're trying to set up a printer managed by a website for some internal operations staff. Can you help set this up?
Date last updated	2024-06-09

Configure CUPS

CUPS is a print management system for Linux that enables a computer to function as a print server. A system running CUPS is a host that can initiate print jobs from client systems. These jobs are then processed and sent to the appropriate printer. The main advantage of CUPS is that it can process different data formats on the same print server.

CUPS is designed for scheduling print jobs, processing administrative commands, and providing printer status information to local and remote programs. CUPS provides a web-based interface for configuring the service. Changes made through this interface modify the `/etc/cups/cupsd.conf` and `/etc/cups/cups-files.conf` files.

Once CUPS is installed on the system, it must be enabled and started, just like any other service. The management interface is accessed via a web browser. Simply type `http://localhost:631` to connect to the management page.

```
# systemctl enable cups
# systemctl start cups
```

 Don't forget to open the firewall port. CUPS uses port 631/tcp.

Locally attached and network print devices are added to the CUPS configuration, enabling administrators to manage print queues, security, and availability.

The lpr Command

The `lpr` command submits files for printing. Files supplied at the command line are sent to the specified printer or to the print queue if the printer is busy. Without specifying the printer to use, the command will send the print job to the default printer, which you can configure with CUPS. The `lpr` command reads the print file from standard input if no files are supplied at the command line.

The syntax of the `lpr` command is `lpr [options] [file names]`

Options for the lpr Command	Purpose
`-E`	Force encryption when connecting to the server.
`-P {destination}`	Send the print job to the destination printer specified.
`-# {copies}`	Set the number of copies to print from 1 to 100.
`-T {name}`	Set the job name.
`-l`	Specify that the print file is already formatted and should be sent to the destination without being filtered.
`-o {option}`	Set a job option, such as printing in landscape mode, scaling the printed output, printing double-sided, etc. Job options vary depending on the printer.
`-p`	Print the specified files with a shaded header that includes the date, time, job name, and page number.
`-r`	Specify that the printed files should be deleted after printing.

While the `lpr` command submits print jobs, the `lpq` command displays existing print jobs that the printer is managing.

Review Activity:

System Service Configuration

Answer the following questions:

1. **A sysadmin has several virtual machines that are frequently on and off the development network. The administrator complains of time synchronization problems with applications on the VMs. What time service can you suggest to help?**

2. **Define some reasons to forward Linux log files to a central server.**

3. **Differentiate between the at command scheduler and the cron scheduler.**

4. **When would a script run if it were configured in cron with the following settings? 30 1 * * ***

Topic 9C

Configure Localization Settings

EXAM OBJECTIVES COVERED
1.7 Given a scenario, manage software configurations.
4.5 Given a scenario, use systemd to diagnose and resolve common problems with a Linux system.

Before users can get comfortable working in the Linux environment, they may need to have the system localized to their specific region, culture, or preferences. In this topic, you'll configure localization options for users who need them.

Manipulate System Settings

In the world of operating systems, **localization** is the process of adapting system components for use within a language or culture other than the one that the system was originally designed for. In a practical sense, this usually means translating interface components into specific languages, converting measurements into the system used in a specific region, configuring the keyboard layout to one that the user is comfortable with, and setting the date and time attributes of a specific location.

Localizing a Linux system is important for organizations that provide Linux services to personnel and customers all over the world. For example, an administrator in Japan will likely be more comfortable working on a Linux server if that server is localized to use the Japanese language rather than the English language. Working with the local time and with a compatible keyboard will also enhance the user experience for all members of an organization.

Use the date Command

The `date` command is used to print the date in a specified format. The `date` command prints the date based on the `/etc/localtime` file. By default, it prints the results in the following format:

<day of week> <month> <day> <24 hour time ##:##:##> <time zone> <year>

```
[student@fedora ~]$ date
Thu Apr 14 01:18:38 PM EDT 2022
[student@fedora ~]$ 
```

The output of the date command.

You can also format the time using a number of different formatting options. You initialize the formatting options with a plus sign (+), and each option is prefaced with a percent sign (%). For example, to retrieve the week number (out of 52 weeks a year), you'd enter:

```
date +%V
```

You can also use the `date` command to change the system's date by including the `-s` option with a provided argument.

The syntax of the `date` command is `date [options] +[format]`

Formatting Option for the date Command	Purpose
%A	Display the full weekday name.
%B	Display the full month name.
%F	Display the date in YYYY-MM-DD format.
%H	Display the hour in 24-hour format.
%I	Display the hour in 12-hour format.
%j	Display the day of the year.
%S	Display seconds.
%V	Display the week of the year.
%x	Display the date representation based on the locale.
%X	Display the time representation based on the locale.
%Y	Display the year.

Configure Localization

After you review the system settings with the date command, you can make adjustments where necessary.

Use the timedatectl Command

The `timedatectl` command is used to set the system date and time information. It can take one of several subcommands.

Subcommand for the timedatectl Command	Purpose
status	Show the current settings.
restart	Synchronize the local (system) clock based on the hardware clock when setting the hardware clock.
list-timezones	Display available time zones.
set-timezone {timezone}	Configure a specific time zone.
set-time {HH:MM:SS}	Set the system clock to the specified time.

The syntax of the `timedatectl` command is `timedatectl [options]` `[subcommand]`

The following table lists some of the options for the `timedatectl` command.

Option for the timedatectl Command	Purpose
`-H`	Execute the operation on the remote host specified by IP address or hostname.
`--no-ask-password`	Prevent the user from being asked to authenticate when performing a privileged task.
`--adjust-system-clock`	Synchronize the system clock with the real-time clock.
`-M {local container}`	Execute the operation on a local container.

For example, to configure the current time zone for Denver, Colorado, in the United States, type:

```
# timedatectl set-timezone "America/Denver"
```

 The output from the timedatectl list-timezones command is immense. Consider filtering the results with | grep or paginating the results with | less.

The localectl Command

The `localectl` command is used to view and configure the system locale and keyboard layout settings. A system's locale determines how it will represent various culture-specific elements, the most prominent of which is the language used in the interface. However, a locale can also determine factors such as how date and time are formatted, how monetary values are formatted, and more. Keyboard layouts can be configured independently of the locale and will determine how each physical key press is interpreted by the operating system. There are many keyboards with different physical layouts, so the system needs to be configured with the correct one or else the wrong character may be entered.

Like the `timedatectl` command, the `localectl` command offers various subcommands for managing the system locale and keyboard layout.

Subcommand for the localectl Command	Purpose
`status`	Show the current locale and keyboard layout. This is the same as issuing localectl by itself.
`set-locale`	Set the system locale to the locale provided.
`list-locales`	List all available locales on the system.
`set-keymap`	Set the keyboard layout to the provided layout.
`list-keymaps`	List all available keyboard layouts on the system.

The syntax of the `localectl` command is `localectl [options] [subcommand]`

The following table lists some of the options for the `localectl` command.

Option for the localectl Command	Purpose
`-H {remote host}`	Execute the operation on the remote host specified by IP address or hostname.
`--no-ask-password`	Prevent the user from being asked to authenticate when performing a privileged task.
`--no-pager`	Prevent the output from being piped into a paging utility.
`--no-convert`	Prevent a keymap change for the console from also being applied to the X display server and vice versa.

Troubleshoot Time Zone Configurations

Proper time-zone configurations enable users to better manage time. This is important when managing scheduling services such as `cron` or `at`, as well as for convenience when using the system. Linux recognizes time zones based on two primary sources.

Understand /etc/timezone and /usr/share/zoneinfo Directories

The `/usr/share/zoneinfo/` directory is a container for all of the regional time zones that you can configure the system to use. Subdirectories in this container usually organize languages by region; for example, the Africa subdirectory includes time-zone files for specific countries or cities within the continent.

The individual files are not raw text files but are special files used by the system. One way to change the system's time zone is by creating a symbolic link to one of these individual time-zone files from the `/etc/localtime` file.

```
[student@fedora zoneinfo]$ ls
Africa       Chile      Factory    Iceland
America      CST6CDT    GB         Indian
Antarctica   Cuba       GB-Eire    Iran
Arctic       EET        GMT        iso3166.tab
Asia         Egypt      GMT+0      Israel
Atlantic     Eire       GMT-0      Jamaica
Australia    EST        GMT0       Japan
Brazil       EST5EDT    Greenwich  Kwajalein
Canada       Etc        Hongkong   leapseconds
CET          Europe     HST        Libya
```

A portion of the zoneinfo directory contents on a Fedora system.

In some Debian-based distros, `/etc/timezone` can be used to view the time zone. This text file lists the time zone by the region structure you'd see in the `/usr/ share/zoneinfo` directory. For example, the file might include the text Europe/Berlin to indicate that the system is using the zone that this city is in.

```
student@ubuntu20:~$ cat /etc/timezone
America/Denver
```

The /etc/timezone file on an Ubuntu system.

Review Activity:

Localization Settings

Answer the following questions:

1. **Where are regional time-zone files stored on Red Hat–derived systems? And Debian-derived systems?**

2. **True or false? The localectl command configures the system locale and keyboard settings as one collective setting that is aligned with the locale's specific cultural elements.**

Lesson 9

Summary

The configuration services and locale settings enable users and other systems to complete business tasks and serve customers. When the system starts, it runs an initialization program to manage the necessary configurations. Most modern Linux systems rely on systemd for initialization and service management, though some older systems use SysVinit instead. These programs start web, print, file, and remote administrations services that support users.

Guidelines

These best practices and guidelines are provided for your use as revision tools or as quick references in your job role.

- Differentiate services versus daemons.

  - Services are interactive but run in the background to provide features.

  - Daemons are noninteractive and run in the background to provide features.

- Recognize the two system initialization programs: systemd and SysVinit.

- Understand service management in systemd using `systemctl` and the `start`, `stop`, `restart`, `enable`, `disable`, and `mask` subcommands.

- Understand service management in SysV using `service` and `chkconfig` commands.

- Recognize that service configurations are held in files and services must be restarted if a configuration file is changed.

- Understand the role services play in the network.

- Recognize common service configuration files for SSH, rsyslog, NTP, cron, and NFS.

- Recognize the port numbers for the services covered in this Lesson.

  - SSH default port is 22/tcp

  - ntpd default port is 123/tcp

  - chrony default port is 123/tcp

  - HTTP default port is 80/tcp

  - NFS default port is 111/tcp and 111/udp plus 2049/tcp and 2049/udp

  - CUPS default port is 631/tcp

Command Reference Table

This list of commands and their associated syntax can also be found in Appendix B.

Command	Syntax	Purpose	Covered in
systemctl	systemctl [subcommand] [argument]	Manage startup options.	Lesson 9, Topic A
service	service [options] [service] [subcommand]	Manage enabling and starting services under SysVinit.	Lesson 9, Topic A
chkconfig	chkconfig [options] [service] [subcommand]	• Control services in each runlevel. • Start or stop services during system startup.	Lesson 9, Topic A
crontab	crontab [options]	Schedule an event by editing the crontab file.	Lesson 9, Topic B
at	at [options] {time}	Run a task once at a specified time.	Lesson 9, Topic B
lpr	lpr [options] [file names]	Submit files for printing.	Lesson 9, Topic B
date	date [options] [format]	Print the date in a specified format.	Lesson 9, Topic C
timedatectl	timedatectl [options] [subcommand]	Set the system date and time information.	Lesson 9, Topic C
localectl	localectl [options] [subcommand]	View and configure the system locale and keyboard layout settings.	Lesson 9, Topic C

Lesson 10
Configuring Network Settings

LESSON INTRODUCTION

Basic networking skills are critical to Linux server administrators. The TCP/IP suite is fundamental to modern networks and is built on a series of network devices. Each node in a TCP/IP network has a unique identity, so displaying and configuring these identities is a common task for Linux admins. Many network tools exist to provide remote connectivity, whether that access is for administrative purposes or mere file transfers. And many network tools exist to help troubleshoot these network access issues.

Lesson Objectives

In this lesson, you will:

- Understand network fundamentals.

- Manage network settings.

- Configure remote administrative access.

- Troubleshoot the network.

Topic 10A

Understand Network Fundamentals

EXAM OBJECTIVES COVERED
1.5 Given a scenario, use the appropriate networking tools or configuration files.
4.2 Given a scenario, analyze and troubleshoot network resource issues.

Modern networks, including the Internet, function based on the TCP/IP protocol suite. Basic knowledge of this suite is fundamental to Linux system administration, as is general knowledge of network devices. Furthermore, sysadmins need to understand IP address assignment, classes, and relationship to network segmentation. Finally, the concept of port numbers relates particular services—such as web access or email—to numeric identifiers.

TCP/IP and Network Devices

The **Transmissions Control Protocol/Internet Protocol (TCP/IP)** suite governs network communications on internal networks, the Internet, and cloud-based networks. The protocols making up the suite manage many aspects of network communication, including addressing and identification, encryption, compression, error checking, and file transfers.

Be aware that management of features such as encryption or compression includes a lack of these features. In other words, some protocols manage encryption by not offering it as a feature. HTTP is an example.

Layers of the TCP/IP Suite

The TCP/IP protocol suite is divided into four layers, with each layer providing responsibility for one or more aspects of the communication process. Those four protocol layers are:

- **Application:** protocols that support network applications such as web browsers.

- **Transport:** protocols that support reliable communications.

- **Internet:** protocols that support addressing.

- **Network access:** protocols that support network connectivity.

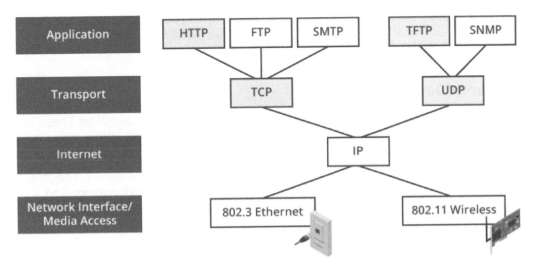

The layers of the TCP/IP suite. (Images © 123RF.com.)

Network Nodes

The term *node* refers to devices with an identity on the network. That identity may be represented by a physical address or one of two logical addresses, or any combination of the three.

Each **network interface card (NIC)** has a unique identity coded into it that identifies that NIC on the network segment. That code is referred to as a **media access control (MAC) address**. It is the most fundamental network identity and is considered a physical address.

Each NIC may be assigned a logical address called an **Internet Protocol (IP) address**. The IP address uniquely identifies the NIC in the network environment. IP addresses are shown in dotted decimal (base 10), which is a range of 0–9. The computer works with the IP address in binary (base 2), which is a range of 0–1.

Nodes may be given a human-readable name, called a **hostname**, that helps people better understand what device they are working with. This identity is often configured during the installation of the operating system and is sometimes called the "computer name." Hostnames are limited to 255 characters.

```
[student@fedora ~]$ hostname
fedora
[student@fedora ~]$ ip addr show eth0
2: eth0: <BROADCAST,MULTICAST,UP,LOWER_UP> mtu 1500 qdisc
 mq state UP group default qlen 1000
    link/ether 02:15:5d:11:b3:1e brd ff:ff:ff:ff:ff:ff
    inet 192.168.1.100/24 brd 192.168.1.255 scope global
dynamic noprefixroute eth0
       valid_lft 5632sec preferred_lft 5632sec
    inet6 fe80::1592:7c91:5619:3438/64 scope link noprefi
xroute
       valid_lft forever preferred_lft forever
[student@fedora ~]$ █
```

Output of the `ip addr show eth0` *command.*

Different devices on the network reference the different addresses. Often switches will govern traffic based on MAC addresses, while routers will manage traffic based on IP addresses.

Network Devices

There are several essential network devices and components to understand. These may be part of the troubleshooting process or network installation. Linux systems need to be configured properly to interact with these network devices and components.

A **switch** acts as a concentrator, centralizing all network connections for a segment to a single device. Switches can be used to manage traffic for performance and security concerns. As a general rule, switches work with MAC addresses at Layer 2 of the OSI model. There are switches that work at higher layers, too.

Routers act as control points for communications between network segments. Administrators can configure the router to permit or deny certain kinds of traffic, as well as pass traffic from one network segment to another. Routers work with IP addresses at Layer 3 of the OSI model.

Typically, network media is twisted-pair Ethernet cable. Twisted-pair may come **shielded (STP)** or **unshielded (UTP)**. It is inexpensive and relatively easy to work with. It is the most common type of network cable. Other cable types include coaxial (coax) and fiber optic. Wireless networks forego cables and can transmit data using radio waves.

Administrators use TCP/IP to organize networks for security and performance. Some networks are divided into multiple segments to isolate certain types of traffic. For example, traffic may be separated between production and development networks.

IP Addresses

IP addresses provide an addressing system for managing network identities. Internet Protocol version 4 was defined in 1981. The addresses are 32 bits in length, providing approximately 4.3 billion addresses. Humans usually work with IP addresses in the decimal form, such as 192.168.2.200, while network devices work with the address in binary.

IPv4 addresses are divided into at least two portions—a network identifier and a host identifier. The network identifier defines to which network segment the host belongs, and the host identifier uniquely identifies that host within the segment. Because the network ID may use different bits within the address, a second numeric value is used to show which portion of the IP address is the network ID and which part is the host ID. This value is known as the subnet mask. It is essential to understand the role of the subnet mask. It indicates where in the IP address the division is between the network ID and the host ID.

IPv6 addresses are covered in a later section.

IPv4 Address Classes

The approximately 4.3 billion IPv4 addresses are divided into five classes. These classes provide a framework for the possible segmentation of networks. Each class provides a specified number of networks, as well as a number of hosts available on each network. For the first three classes, the division between the network ID and the host ID occurs at one of the dots. Network professionals must be able to recognize all five classes by the value of the first octet and know the default subnet mask for each class.

The 4.3 billion IPv4 addresses are divided into the following five classes:

Class	Starting Address	Ending Address	Number of Networks	Hosts per Network	Default Subnet Mask
Class A	0.0.0.0	127.0.0.0	126	16,777,214	255.0.0.0 or /8
Class B	128.0.0.0	191.255.0.0	16,384	65,534	255.255.0.0 or /16
Class C	192.0.0.0	223.255.255.0	2,097,152	254	255.255.255.0 or /24
Class D	224.0.0.0	239.255.255.255	n/a	n/a	n/a
Class E	240.0.0.0	255.255.255.255	n/a	n/a	n/a

Reserved Ranges

In addition to knowing the five IP address classes, there are several other IP addresses or address ranges that are important. Due to the depletion of IPv4 addresses, there are three IP address ranges that are reserved for internal use only. You will almost always find these in use on internal business and home networks.

- **Class A Reserved:** 10.0.0.0–10.255.255.255

- **Class B Reserved:** 172.16.0.0–172.31.255.255

- **Class C Reserved:** 192.168.0.0–192.168.255.255

Subnet Masks and Network Segments

Network administrators will divide a network into segments in order to better manage network traffic. Their goal may be to manage that traffic more efficiently, resulting in better network performance, and/or to isolate that traffic for the purpose of security.

The logical divisions of the network are referred to as subnets and are identified by a network ID. This network ID is part of the IP address each node is using. All nodes in that subnet will have the same network ID in their IP address. Each node will have a unique host ID within that subnet. Recall that the subnet mask shows which part is the network ID and which part is the host ID.

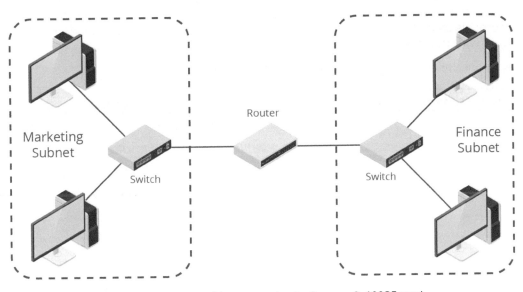

A network segmented into two subnets. (Images © 123RF.com)

Address Configuration

There are two network services that are commonly involved with TCP/IP network configuration. You will need to understand the role of both of these services in order to properly configure your Linux system.

Humans have a difficult time working with long strings of numbers such as IP addresses. The **Domain Name System (DNS)** service provides **name resolution**, a way of relating an easy-to-remember hostname with a difficult-to-remember IP address. DNS is implemented as a database hosted on one or more servers. The database may only contain the names and IPs of nodes in your own network, or it may be part of the larger Internet DNS infrastructure.

All nodes on the network must be configured with a unique IP address and other corresponding information. There are two ways of accomplishing this configuration— statically or dynamically. Static configuration is usually appropriate for servers and network devices, while dynamic configuration is typically used with end-user workstations. The **Dynamic Host Configuration Protocol (DHCP)** service provides dynamic configuration.

IPv6

The IPv4 addressing scheme has many limitations. A newer standard is being implemented in the form of Internet Protocol version 6. IPv6 addresses many of the weaknesses of IPv4 with a much larger address space, built-in encryption, and more efficient routing.

IPv6 uses 128-bit addressing, while IPv4 relies on 32-bit addressing. The result is a much larger address space. IPv6 includes more modern features and is common on large networks, such as telecom, Internet service providers (ISPs), and cloud environments.

Linux is fully compatible with IPv6, so Linux servers and workstations should not be a limiting factor in the deployment of IPv6 in a network environment.

Network Ports

Network port numbers are numeric values assigned to the various application-layer protocols. Network devices use these port numbers to understand what application will handle the communication. Humans work with the application-layer protocols by name, such as Hypertext Transfer Protocol (HTTP). Computers need to work with these by port number.

A few of the more commonly used ports are provided in this table.

Network Port Number	Application-layer Protocol
22	Secure Shell (SSH)
25	Simple Mail Transfer Protocol (SMTP)
80	Hypertext Transfer Protocol (HTTP)
123	Network Time Protocol (NTP)
443	Hypertext Transfer Protocol Secure (HTTPS)

 IT personnel, from service desk employees to infrastructure administrators, are expected to understand basic IP addressing, subnet masks, network segmentation, and IP address configuration.

Review Activity:

Network Fundamentals

Answer the following questions:

1. **Differentiate between MAC addresses, IP addresses, and hostnames.**

2. **Explain the difference between the Network ID and the Host ID portions of an IP address.**

3. **List three advantages of IPv6 over IPv4.**

Topic 10B

Manage Network Settings

EXAM OBJECTIVES COVERED
1.5 Given a scenario, use the appropriate networking tools or configuration files.

Network settings are often configured manually (or statically) on servers and dynamically on client devices. Various tools display and manage these settings, aiding administrators in system configuration and troubleshooting. As has already been covered, Linux configurations are stored in text files, and network settings are no different.

This Topic focuses on network management tools and the process of configuration IP address settings and name resolution.

Configure Network Interfaces

IP addresses are a critical identifier on the network, so configuration and troubleshooting both revolve around the proper settings. The older `ifconfig` command displays settings and allows for configuration; however, the `ip` command is the recommended solution for modern Linux distributions.

Use ip Commands

The `ip` command replaces `ifconfig` in many distributions. It provides similar information to `ifconfig`, including IP address, subnet mask, and MAC address. The `ip` command is one of the first tools used in network troubleshooting on a Linux system. Some common ways to utilize the `ip` command include:

- `ip addr show` —Displays the IP address information on all interfaces.

- `ip link` —Displays the status of each interface.

- `ip link set eth1 up` —Enables the interface identified as eth1.

- `ip link set eth1 down` —Disables the interface identified as eth1.

The syntax of the `ip` command is `ip [options] {object} [subcommand]`

```
[student@fedora ~]$ ip
address        mptcp          route
addrlabel      mroute         rule
fou            mrule          sr
help           neighbor       tap
ila            neighbour      tcpmetrics
l2tp           netconf        token
link           netns          tunnel
macsec         nexthop        tuntap
maddress       ntable         vrf
monitor        ntbl           xfrm
```

Available ip subcommands.

Viewing the IP address configuration is a critical part of network troubleshooting. The `ip` command is one of the most important tools in the administrator's arsenal.

> *The `ip` command is installed as part of the `iproute2` software package.*

Use the ifconfig Command

The `ifconfig` command enables a user to view the current IP addressing information for each NIC recognized by the system. Viewing the IP address configuration is one of the earliest steps in network troubleshooting. The `ifconfig` command shows the IP address, subnet mask, broadcast ID, MAC address, basic performance information, and NIC name. The tool also enables NICs to be placed in an up or a down configuration (enabled or disabled).

The `ifconfig` command is officially deprecated in Linux, as noted in the man page; however, it is still available in many current distributions.

The syntax of the `ifconfig` command is `ifconfig [options] [interface]`

Some of the more common uses for the `ifconfig` command are:

- `ifconfig` —Displays the configuration for all interfaces.

- `ifconfig eth0` —Displays configuration for a specific interface named eth0.

- `ifconfig eth0 up` —Enables an interface.

- `ifconfig eth0 down` —Disables an interface.

- `ifconfig eth0 192.168.2.200 netmask 255.255.255.0` —Sets a static IP address and subnet mask on eth0.

The `ifcfg` command is an alternative to `ifconfig` or the `ip` command for managing IP addressing. The command is less robust than the other two and not as commonly used.

Use the iwconfig Command

The `iwconfig` command is used to provide wireless NIC configurations, including settings like SSID and encryption information.

The syntax of the `iwconfig` command is `iwconfig [options] [interface]`

This table describes some commonly used `iwconfig` command options.

Option for the iwconfig Command	Purpose
`nick {name}`	Set a nickname for the NIC.
`mode {mode}`	Set the operating mode for the NIC that corresponds to the network topology.
`freq {number}`	Set the Wi-Fi frequency used by the NIC.
`channel {number}`	Set the Wi-Fi channel used by the NIC.
`retry {number}`	Set the maximum number of MAC retransmissions for the NIC.

Use NetworkManager

Linux distributions often include a utility called NetworkManager to aid in the proper configuration of the IP information. NetworkManager includes three different interfaces that may be used, depending on whether or not a GUI is available on the Linux system.

The nmcli Command

The `nmcli` tool is the most fundamental of the NetworkManager interfaces. It contains many subcommands that enable you to view and configure network information. Because many network servers will not include a GUI, it is important to be comfortable with `nmcli` to manage network settings.

```
[student@fedora ~]$ nmcli device status
DEVICE   TYPE      STATE       CONNECTION
eth0     ethernet  connected   Wired connection 1
lo       loopback  unmanaged   --
[student@fedora ~]$ ▮
```

The nmcli tool displaying the status of all connected network interfaces.

The syntax of the `nmcli` command is `nmcli [options] [subcommand] [arguments]`

This table outlines some often-used subcommands for `nmcli`.

Subcommand for the nmcli Command	Purpose
`general status`	View a summary of network connectivity data.
`connection show`	View identification information for each NIC.
`con up {device ID}`	Enable the specified NIC.
`con down {device ID}`	Disable the specified NIC.
`con edit {device ID}`	Enter interactive mode to configure the specified NIC.
`device status`	Display the current status of each NIC.

The nmtui Command

While Linux administrators often work at the command line, it is certainly useful to have a visual representation of network configuration options. By running the `nmtui` command, you can call up a text-based user interface, or TUI. Navigating a TUI is accomplished by using the Tab key, the Spacebar, the Enter key, and the arrow keys. The Tab key moves the cursor from field to field. The arrow keys are used to make selections within the field. The Enter key is used to activate a setting, such as OK or Quit. The Spacebar is used to check or uncheck a check box.

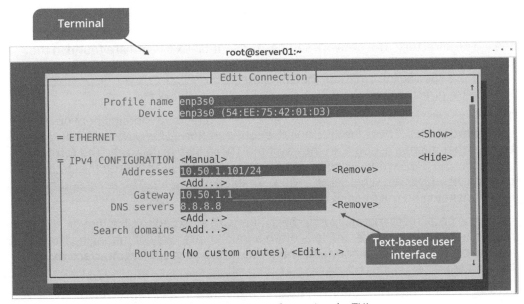

Editing a network interface using the TUI.

The nmgui Command

NetworkManager also includes a GUI tool, which is particularly helpful for managing the network connections of workstations. The `nmgui` tool enables IPv4 and IPv6 configuration, and it provides access to a wide variety of other network settings. This tool will certainly be familiar to most end-users.

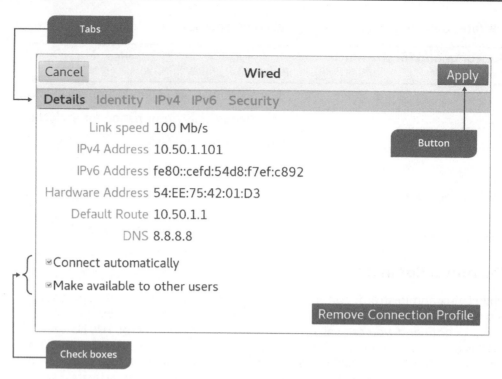

Viewing network interface details in a GUI.

Network Configuration Files

Recall that Linux system configurations are stored in text files and are found in the `/etc` directory. The network settings for your Linux system are found in the `/etc/sysconfig` directory. There are multiple subdirectories and files that store more specific information, including the `/etc/sysconfig/network-scripts` directory and the `/etc/sysconfig/`network file.

The `/etc/sysconfig/network-scripts` directory contains network device configuration files. These files include the configurations of any NICs, bonds, and bridges that might exist on the Linux system. These files usually take the form of `ifcfg-<NIC>`. Settings can include whether the NIC is configured for static or dynamic IP addresses, whether the NIC is enabled or not, etc. The exact settings vary depending on the needed configuration and device type.

While it is possible to manually edit these files with a text editor like Vim or nano, the NetworkManager utility is often a much better way of managing the interfaces. There is a command-line, text interface, and graphical interface for NetworkManager.

For Debian-derived distributions, network configuration files representing the interfaces can be found in the `/etc/network` directory. Many Debian-based distributions also use NetworkManager, so editing the files in `/etc/network` is usually not necessary.

The `/etc/sysconfig/network` file is used to configure whether networking should be enabled at boot and to configure hostname information, gateway information, etc. These settings may instead be configured on a per-interface basis in the `/etc/sysconfig/network-scripts/ifcfg-<NIC>` files.

Use ethtool

The `ethtool` is used to manage NIC driver and network configurations. Whether or not it is installed by default will depend on the distribution in use. The `ethtool` utility has a great many options for gathering information. The basic output displays interface options such as modes, speed, duplex configuration, Wake-on-LAN settings, etc. Not only does the `ethtool` command allow admins to see these settings, but it also allows them to change these options.

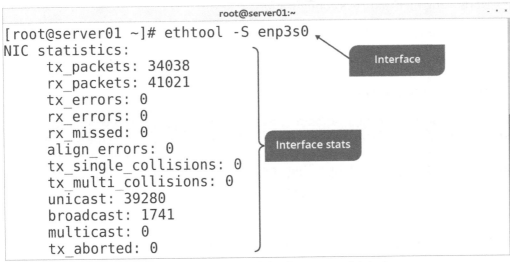

`ethtool` *displaying statistics for a network interface.*

The syntax of the `ethtool` command is `ethtool [options] {device name}`

The following table describes some common `ethtool` command options.

Option for the ethtool Command	Purpose
`-S {interface}`	Show statistics for a NIC.
`-i {interface}`	Show driver information for a NIC.
`-t {interface}`	Execute a self-test on the NIC.
`-s {interface} {setting} {value}`	Change some of a NIC's settings, such as its speed and duplex mode.
`-f {interface}`	Write ("flash") a firmware image to the NIC.

Assign IP Addresses

IP address configurations can be set in two ways: statically or dynamically. Each method has advantages and disadvantages. It is important to know when to use each method. Administrators will statically (or manually) configure IP addresses on some types of network nodes. Client devices, however, are usually configured with dynamic IP address settings. IP address configurations are then leased from a DHCP server. The result is that both methods are used in most networks, not just one method or the other.

Static IP Addresses

Static IP address configuration means that the settings are implemented manually by an administrator. This method increases the risk of mistakes but also ensures the system always has the same identity. Static IP address configurations are usually appropriate for network devices (such as routers and network switches) and servers. They may also be used for network print devices.

Static configurations are characterized by:

• Non-changing IP address configuration.

• Heightened possibility of mistakes when entered manually.

• Increased administrative workload when configured and reconfigured.

Dynamic IP Addresses

Dynamic IP address configuration means that the settings are retrieved from a server. This method decreases the risk of mistakes but also means the system may not always have the same IP address. Dynamic IP address configurations are usually appropriate for client machines. They may also be used for network print devices.

Consider these traits of dynamic configurations:

• IP address configuration may fluctuate over time.

• Reduced risk of typographical errors during configuration.

• Decreased administrative workload when configured and reconfigured.

Dynamic IP Addressing Components

There are two components to a dynamic IP lease generation process. The first is the DHCP server, and the second is the client that will lease the IP address configuration.

Understand the DHCP Server

A **Dynamic Host Configuration Protocol (DHCP)** server contains one or more pools of IP addresses and related configuration options that client machines can lease. This saves a significant amount of administrative effort since IP address information does not have to be configured statically for each system.

DHCP servers are configured with a scope, or a range of available IP addresses, along with additional options. The DHCP service must be installed on the server that will host the service and allow client machines to lease configurations.

Understand the DHCP Client

Workstations lease their IP address configurations from a DHCP server. The process consists of four steps, initiated by the clients. The leases are temporary, so periodically the clients will be required to renew their leases. The renewal process provides an opportunity to update the clients if there have been network configuration changes.

The lease typically includes the IP address for the client, the associated subnet mask, the IP address of the default gateway (router), the IP address of one or more DNS servers, and the length of time the lease is valid. There are additional options that may be configured as well.

Periodically, DHCP clients must renew their leased IP address configuration. If the DHCP server detects that the client has out-of-date information, it will force the client to lease a new configuration. If there have been no changes, the renewal will succeed. The lease renewal process is steps three and four of the initial lease generation process.

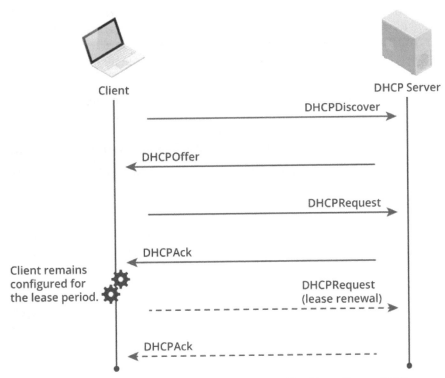

The process of a DHCP client leasing and renewing an IP address from a DHCP server.
(Images © 123RF.com.)

Use the dhclient.conf Config File

The primary DHCP client reference file is the `/etc/dhcp/dhclient.conf` file. This file enables the configuration of DHCP client settings, including timeout values, dynamic DNS configurations, etc. The file is called and managed by NetworkManager, which serves as a network configuration service for multiple network settings, including the DHCP client configuration. It is typically appropriate to manage DHCP client configurations by using NetworkManager rather than editing the `/etc/dhcp/dhclient.conf` file directly.

Use the dhclient Command

The `dhclient` command allows administrators to manage the current configuration. When run without options, `dhclient` broadcasts a DHCPDiscover on the network. Add the `-r` option to release the current IP address configuration. This is an important strategy in network troubleshooting.

Configure Name Resolution

TCP/IP data packets must include a source IP address and a destination IP address. Humans have a very difficult time remembering long strings of numbers. For example, imagine if every website you have bookmarked or every email address you have in your contacts information was noted for you as an IP address instead of a name!

Humans work with easy-to-remember names, such as www.redhat.com or www.ubuntu.com. Such information is virtually useless to computers, which need the IP address information in order to properly find the resource. Names are a description, whereas addresses are a location. Some names, such as webserver01.devnetwork.internal, are **fully qualified domain names (FQDNs)**, while others, such as server01, are simple hostnames.

On the network, it's relatively easy for users and administrators to rely on descriptive names, such as webserver01 or sales-color-printer. Network protocols, however, must rely on numeric addresses. Name resolution is the process of relating these two values. It allows an administrator to specify a connection to sales-color-printer and the network to understand that as 192.168.2.42.

Name resolution is the process of relating these easy-to-remember names with difficult-to-remember IP addresses. There are two general ways in which name resolution works. The first is via static text files such as the /etc/hosts file. The second method is via a dynamic database called **Domain Name System (DNS)**.

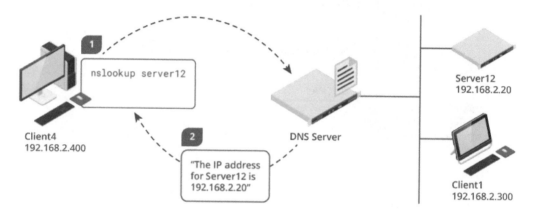

The name resolution process using a DNS server. (Images © 123RF.com.)

The hostnamectl Command

The systemd hostnamectl command enables you to view the system's network hostname and other information about the system's hardware and the Linux kernel it is running. You can also use this command to change the system's hostname.

The syntax of the hostnamectl command is hostnamectl [options] [subcommand] [arguments]

For example, to set the hostname to server01, enter: hostnamectl set-hostname server01

The hostname command displays the system's current network name configuration and is a useful troubleshooting reference. To display the network name, simply type hostname.

Like other Linux settings, name resolution configurations are stored in various text files, including /etc/hosts, /etc/resolv.conf, and /etc/nsswitch.conf.

Understand Name Resolution Files

Early network environments were relatively small, and the identities of network nodes did not change frequently. Name resolution could be managed by using a text file, stored locally on each system, that contained all the systems and their related IP addresses. This file would have to be manually updated if there were any name or IP address changes, additions, or deletions. In today's modern, transient networks, this method is not realistic. The number of entries in the file and the frequent changes to the identity entries would be overwhelming.

Helpdesk Ticket #02001

Submitted by:	Department:	Assigned to:	Date Opened:
Kai Garcia	Engineering	*you*	2024-06-14

Subject	test server connection request
Ticket Detail	Hey, I need some help getting connected to a test server by name, not IP address. I only need this access for the next two weeks for the project I'm working on, and I need the name access limited to just me. Can you let me know how to manage this?
	Thanks,
	KG
Date last updated	2024-06-14

The `/etc/hosts` file is still important, however, because it can be used in special case situations where a particular system—perhaps a developer's workstation—needs to connect to an experimental server that is not registered on the network. While the `/etc/hosts` file is not commonly used, it is essential in certain scenarios.

Locally configuring name resolution.

The /etc/resolv.conf File

Modern networks use a name resolution service like DNS to relate computer names and IP addresses. Network devices will query a DNS server in order to resolve a name and IP address relationship. The DNS server contains resource records that will provide answers to the query. DNS servers are centralized and much easier to maintain and keep current than `/etc/hosts` files are.

The `/etc/resolv.conf` file is stored locally on each system, informing that system of the IP address of one or more DNS servers. DNS is an essential service, so it is a good practice to have at least two DNS servers listed in the `/etc/resolv.conf` file.

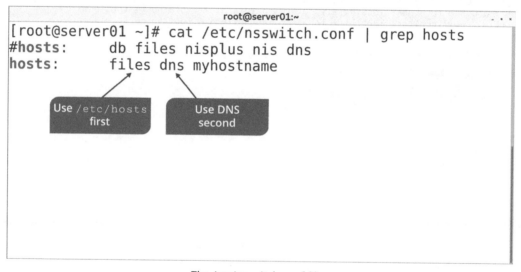

```
                              root@server01:~                          _  ·  ×
[root@server01 ~]# cat /etc/resolv.conf
# Generated by NetworkManager
nameserver 8.8.8.8 ⎤
                   ⎬   DNS servers
nameserver 8.8.4.4 ⎦
[root@server01 ~]#
```

Configuring name resolution using public DNS servers.

The /etc/nsswitch.conf File

The `/etc/nsswitch.conf` file includes several configuration options. The option related to name resolution defines the order in which name resolution methods will be used by the system. The order may be the `/etc/hosts` file first, then DNS; or DNS first, then the `/etc/hosts` file. The preferred configuration is `/etc/hosts` then DNS.

```
                              root@server01:~                          _  ·  ×
[root@server01 ~]# cat /etc/nsswitch.conf | grep hosts
#hosts:       db files nisplus nis dns
hosts:        files dns myhostname
                       ↗       ↖
            Use /etc/hosts   Use DNS
                first        second
```

The /etc/nsswitch.conf file.

Responding to Ticket #02001

You decide to edit the `/etc/hosts` file on Kai Garcia's workstation. You then verify the `/etc/nsswitch.conf` file directs the system to the `/etc/hosts` file before a name resolution server. You also confirm that the contents in `/etc/resolv.conf` are accurate for any other name resolution queries. If the test server is named test-server01 and it has an IP address of 192.168.2.42, you would add the following to the `/etc/hosts` file:

```
192.168.2.42  test-server01
```

Use the route Command

The `route` command manages the route table on the local system after any IP address configurations, such as IP address, subnet mask, and default gateway, have been set. Static routes can be added or removed from the system, and the existing routing table can be displayed.

To display the current route table, type:

```
# route
```

To add a route to the 192.168.2.0/24 network for interface eth0, type:

```
# route add -net 192.168.2.0 netmask 255.255.255.0
dev eth0
```

The route table permits the system to direct network traffic out through the appropriate interface to move the traffic nearer to the destination network.

Review Activity:

Network Settings

Answer the following questions:

1. **Why would an administrator need to use the ip link set eth0 up command?**

2. **Describe the dynamic and static IP address assignment processes, and list the types of devices that likely rely on each process.**

3. **What commands are needed to refresh dynamically assigned IP settings?**

4. **What is the purpose of the /etc/resolv.conf and /etc/nsswitch.conf files?**

Topic 10C

Configure Remote Administrative Access

EXAM OBJECTIVES COVERED
1.5 Given a scenario, use the appropriate networking tools or configuration files.
2.4 Given a scenario, configure and execute remote connectivity for system management.

Administrators often take advantage of the convenience and security of remote administration. Command line tools, such as SSH, and GUI utilities like VNC allow administrators to remotely manipulate the system as if they were physically present. If the goal is merely to move files from one system to another, data transfer tools exist—several of which can provide encrypted connections.

The following Topic defines SSH settings, explains downloading files using a multitude of protocols, and explores GUI-based remote connectivity.

Configure SSH

The primary remote administration tool in Linux is Secure Shell (SSH). SSH provides encrypted and authenticated remote access to Linux systems. However, it is also very common to use SSH to connect to network devices such as routers and switches. Linux, Unix, and macOS systems include SSH by default, and the protocol can be added to Microsoft Windows.

SSH has become an even more critical tool with the rapid growth of cloud computing. SSH enables cloud administrators to securely connect to remote cloud resources and is an essential tool.

SSH Server Configuration Files

Two configuration files manage SSH on Linux. The first, `/etc/ssh/ssh_config`, defines SSH client settings and usually is not customized. The second, `/etc/ssh/sshd_config`, has many configuration options (most of which are security-oriented).

Be careful not to get confused by the similar names of the SSH configuration files (`ssh_config` versus `sshd_config`).

Common SSH server configurations with the `/etc/ssh/sshd_config` include changing ports, preventing the root user from connecting over the network via SSH, and requiring key-based authentication.

To change the port number, search for the port value and assign a port number:

    Port 2222

To block the root user from authenticating over SSH, set the following value to no:

PermitRootLogin no

To both prevent password-based authentication and permit key-based authentication, set the following two values (be sure you have configured key-based authentication first!):

PasswordAuthentication no

PublicKeyAuthentication yes

 Don't forget to restart `sshd` *if you make changes to the configuration file.*

Additional SSH Configurations

The first time a user runs an `ssh` command, a hidden directory is created in the user's home folder. The directory is `~/.ssh`, and it may store multiple files related to the user's SSH connections.

The `~/.ssh/config` file allows the user to configure specific settings for specific connections. Administrators may connect to many systems, and some of those systems may have custom or specific requirements. For example, perhaps dev-server01 uses the default port 22 for SSH, but dev-server02 uses port 2222. Without the config file, the user would have to remember these different settings. The `config` file permits the user to store connection-specific information.

```
HOST server01
        HostName server01.example.com
        User admin
        Port 2222


HOST server02
        HostName server02.example.com
        User dev
        Port 22
```

A sample SSH config file.

The `~/.ssh/authorized_keys` file stores the keys on the remote SSH servers the client machine connects to, allowing key-based authentication to occur. Note that this file resides on the remote SSH server.

The `~/.ssh/known_hosts` file stored the public keys of remote systems the client has connected to. The goal is to protect the client from man-in-the-middle or impersonation attacks. Note that this file resides on the local SSH client.

Configure Key-Based Authentication

The standard SSH authentication process is a password challenge. The connecting user submits a username and password that is recognized on the local system. Password-based authentication, however, has some significant limitations: passwords may be intercepted, guessed, or found after being written down. Automated processes, such as remote backup scripts that connect over SSH, can be interrupted by password challenges and passwords for multiple remote systems may be difficult for administrators to recall.

Key-based authentication generates a public-private key pair that uniquely identifies the user. The private key remains on the user's workstation, and the public key is stored on the remote system. When the user attempts to connect, the keys are checked to ensure they match, thus guaranteeing the user's identity. This is more secure and much easier to automate for automated connections, such as remote backup scripts. A single key pair can be used for multiple systems.

Helpdesk Ticket #02002

Submitted by:	Department:	Assigned to:	Date Opened:
Risha Patel	Information Services	*you*	2024-06-22

Subject	Authentication on remote server
Ticket Detail	Can you please configure key-based authentication on server29, repurposing as a remote server.
Date last updated	2024-06-22

Cloud service providers strongly urge administrators to administer systems via SSH key-based authentication. Many organizations rely on SSH authentication keys for on-premises and cloud resources.

The use of public and private keys is covered in more detail in a later section.

Configuring Key-Based Authentication

To close the assigned Help Desk ticket requesting a key-based authentication configuration on a remote SSH server, follow these steps.

1. Generate the public-private key pair:
   ```
   # ssh-keygen
   ```

2. Next, transfer the public key to the remote system. For example, to transfer your user01 key to remote system 192.168.2.200, type:
   ```
   # ssh-copy-id user01@192.168.2.200
   ```

Note that you'll be challenged for a password for this connection as the configuration for key-based authentication is not yet complete.

3. Finally, test the connection. To connect to 192.168.2.200 with the user01 key, type:

```
# ssh user01@192.168.2.200
```

Observe that you are not challenged for a password. The key exchange quickly authenticates you.

Key-based authentication is managed by the ssh-agent tool, and it needs to be aware of existing keys. These keys are automatically added to the agent when generated, but the ssh-add command allows a user to manually add an existing key to the agent if it's not already aware of the key.

Understand SSH Tunneling

SSH can be used to secure other TCP-based network connections for applications or protocols that don't provide their own authentication and encryption methods.

The process of tunneling an application through SSH to secure it during transmission is called **SSH port forwarding**. There are two main types: local forwarding and remote forwarding.

In local forwarding, the local client listens for connections on a port and then tunnels any active connection to a remote server using SSH. One use case for local forwarding is to remotely access a system over the Internet using a protocol like VNC. When you connect to the VNC server with your local VNC client, that traffic (usually over a port like 5900) will be forwarded through SSH, securing it.

In remote forwarding, the SSH server forwards inbound client traffic to another system on a different port. One use case for remote forwarding is setting up a VNC server on a local system and forwarding all VNC traffic to a port on a remote client. Whenever the remote client connects to this port using localhost (their own network address), they can establish a **remote desktop** connection with the local server.

Dynamic port forwarding creates a proxy that is then used by other applications for SSH connectivity. A range of ports is used rather than a single port, as with standard forwarding. The advantage over the other two methods is the ability to connect to multiple destinations simultaneously via different port numbers without having to tear down and rebuild the connections each time. Applications such as web browsers can be configured to use the connections established by SSH dynamic port forwarding for web administration of multiple systems.

Other CLI Remote-access Tools

Often, users do not need a full command-line connection to a remote system. Instead, the user may simply be uploading or downloading files between the local and remote systems. In some cases, administrators may be making configuration changes to the remote system but prefer a GUI interface, such as Cockpit.

Use the curl and wget Commands

Helpdesk Ticket #02003

Submitted by:	Department:	Assigned to:	Date Opened:
Kai Garcia	Engineering	*you*	2024-06-24

Subject	constant download
Ticket Detail	Hi, I'm always downloading a configuration file from the internal server -- is there a better way to do this? I was trying to schedule this operation with c r o n, but that's proving to be challenging. What else can I try? Thanks, KG
Date last updated	2024-06-24

Wget and cURL are HTTP clients capable of downloading files from remote webservers. Most HTTP connections occur using web browsers and download a series of files that are assembled into a web page. Simple downloads, however, don't justify the use of a browser. Furthermore, it's difficult to script or automate browser-based downloads.

The following is an example of using the cURL tool to download a file from the Nmap website:

```
# curl -o nmap-7.70.tar.bz2 https://nmap.org/dist/
nmap-7.70.tar.bz2
```

The following is an example of using wget to download a file from the Samba website:

```
# wget http://download.samba.org/pub/samba/samba-
latest.tar.gz
```

While curl and wget perform the same basic function, there are some key differences. wget is a command-line utility only, whereas curl is implemented using the cross-platform libcurl library and is, therefore, more easily ported to other systems. wget can download files recursively, whereas curl cannot. curl supports many more network protocols than wget does (wget only supports HTTP/S and FTP). wget is better suited for straightforward downloading of files from a web server, while curl is better suited to building and managing more complex requests and responses from web servers.

Use the netcat Command

The netcat or nc command can be used to test connectivity and send data across network connections. The command may be spelled out as "netcat" or abbreviated as "nc" depending on the distribution. Systems may be identified by IP address or by hostname.

When troubleshooting, use netcat to listen on the destination computer and attempt a connection from the source computer in order to verify network functionality.

The syntax of the netcat command is netcat [options]

The following table provides some example use cases for the netcat command.

Use Case	Example Command
Port scan a computer.	`netcat -z -v domain.tld 1-1000` (scans ports 1 to 1000)
Transfer file content between two computers.	**1.** On comp1 (listen on port): `netcat -l 4242 > received.file`
	2. On comp2 (connect to listener): `netcat comp1 < original.file`
Connect two computers for the purpose of transferring information.	**1.** On comp1 (listen on port): `netcat -l 4242`
	2. On comp2 (connect to listener): `netcat comp1 4242`

Use Data Transfer Tools

Other data transfer tools, such as SCP and SFTP, use SSH connectivity to more securely copy files. The rsync utility is distinguished by its ability to only transfer changed files, which can drastically reduce network traffic by avoiding copies of duplicate information that already exist at the remote destination.

The scp Command

The SCP tool is used to copy data to or from a remote host over SSH. Because it uses SSH, data you send to an off-site backup will be encrypted in transit, protecting its confidentiality. Like SSH, SCP uses TCP port 22 by default.

The following is an example of copying a file to a remote host using the `scp` command:

```
# scp file.txt user@host:/home/dir
```

 Other commands, such as nc, may also be used to transfer files across the network. However, nc may be more difficult to set up than establishing a basic scp connection.

The sftp Command

The `sftp` command is the implementation of the Secure File Transport Protocol (SFTP). SFTP uses an SSH tunnel as a transportation mechanism to encrypt data. Whereas `scp` is used purely for transferring files, sftp can transfer files and manage files and directories. So, you can list, create, and remove directories on the remote system. The `sftp` command also supports resuming file transfers, whereas `scp` does not.

Just like with the standard `ftp` command, you can use `sftp` interactively or noninteractively. For example, to retrieve a file noninteractively, type:

```
# sftp user@host:file.txt
```

The rsync Command

Sysadmins use the rsync tool to copy files both locally and on remote systems. Its real power lies in its efficient use of network bandwidth; instead of copying all files, it only copies differences between files. So, if you use rsync on all files in a directory, it will check the destination directory to see if those exact files already exist. Only files that aren't already in the destination will be copied.

The `rsync` command can copy files over SSH, or it can use the rsyncd daemon if you set it up on the remote system. In the latter case, rsync must be installed and running on the source and destination systems.

The following is an example of synchronizing the files in a local directory to a remote directory over SSH:

```
# rsync -a /home/mydir/ user@host:/home/mydir/
```

The `rsync` command is used for network file transfers, where bandwidth may be at a premium. This is different from a local move action, such as using the `mv` command to move a file from one directory to another on a local filesystem.

Understand Remote GUI Tools

Tools such as SSH, rsync, cURL, and others rely on CLI environments. This makes them uniquely suited for automation via scripting or remote administration by those comfortable with Bash command line commands. The convenience and flexibility of a GUI are undeniable, and in many cases, a sysadmin might prefer a GUI-based remote-access method. Some GUI-based options are Cockpit, VNC, XRDP, and X FORWARDING.

Cockpit provides remote administration options over a web-based connection. It includes an intuitive interface and many configuration options. It is not installed by default on all distributions. To connect to a Cockpit-enabled system, type:
`http://{IPaddress}:9090`

Virtual Network Computing (VNC) offers complete access to a remote desktop and is very common for administration. VNC relies on a client-server model that gives the remote administrator complete access to the system.

XRDP is open-source implementation of Microsoft's Remote Desktop Protocol (RDP) to provide remote desktop access across a network.

X FORWARDING is the X Windows System (X11) that provides the graphical interface for Linux systems. Desktop environments rely on X to enable GUI services. X is network-aware and can enable clients to access GUI elements over a network. You can forward X traffic through an SSH tunnel in order to encrypt these communications.

Review Activity:

Remote Administrative Access

Answer the following questions:

1. A developer wants to integrate an SSH connection to a remote server into a script. The developer needs to avoid a password challenge for the SSH connection. What solution can you recommend?

2. Why might a sysadmin use the curl or wget commands?

3. What advantage does the rsync utility have over SCP and SFTP? What disadvantage does it have?

Topic 10D

Troubleshoot the Network

EXAM OBJECTIVES COVERED
1.5 Given a scenario, use the appropriate networking tools or configuration files.
4.2 Given a scenario, analyze and troubleshoot network resource issues.
4.5 Given a scenario, use systemd to diagnose and resolve common problems with a Linux system.

Network troubleshooting involves many layers and components. It may also span areas of IT influence, such as between the server team (managing Linux servers) and the network team (managing routers and switches). Often, troubleshooting scenarios involve a fairly discrete part of the network. There may be issues with the server's network configuration or with the remote system's network settings. There may be network bandwidth, latency, or performance issues. Many issues revolve around name resolution challenges. This section breaks down the tools and approaches necessary for Linux admins to troubleshoot network problems.

Identify Network Configuration Issues

Troubleshooting network clients begins by understanding the system's current network configuration and whether that configuration was set statically or dynamically.

Helpdesk Ticket #02004

Submitted by:	Department:	Assigned to:	Date Opened:
Rey Harper	Information Services	*you*	2024-07-12

Subject	Server connectivity issues
Ticket Detail	Hi, I'm working on a connection issue between a client and server, and could use your help getting started.
	Thank you, Rey Harper Jr Sysadmin
Date last updated	2024-07-12

Use the following steps as a guide when troubleshooting failed network connectivity between a client and an NFS, web, or SSH server located on a separate segment.

1. Display the current IP address configuration by using commands such as `ip addr` or `ifconfig`. Verify the address and subnet mask values are accurate with no typographical errors. Confirm the gateway value is the IP address of the NIC in the router connected to this client's subnet.

Recall that 127.0.0.1 is the loopback address, and it is not valid on the network. An address of 169.254.x.x indicates the client attempted to lease an IP configuration from a DHCP server but failed.

2. Use the `route` command to display the system's routing table. This table lets the system know which interface is connected to which subnet.

3. Initiate a `ping` test against the remote server and the gateway address. Ping the remote server by name and by IP address. Use the `traceroute` or `tracepath` command to display the network path between the client and server.

Statically-assigned IP addresses were manually entered by an administrator and may contain typographical errors or duplicate IPs. Carefully confirm these settings.

Dynamically-assigned IP addresses from a DHCP server rarely contain typographical errors (unless the DHCP server is misconfigured). Ensure the IP address assignment is current. Use the `dhclient -r` and `dhclient` commands to release and acquire the IP address configuration.

4. Confirm the remote server is online and has a valid IP address configuration.

 These steps will generally be followed in this order.

Test Remote Systems

Various other tools exist that allow administrators to discover and view information about remote nodes. The Nmap network mapper is one of the most powerful tools sysadmins have for understanding the network and the nodes connected to it. It's also useful to view certificate information from web servers or other nodes that guarantee identities via SSL.

In addition to commands such as `ping` and `traceroute` to test connectivity to remote clients, tools such as Nmap and OpenSSL s_client can provide more detailed and specialized results.

Display Network Nodes with Nmap

Nmap is highly configurable, but at its most basic it displays the network configuration of the remote system. Nmap reports connectivity, listening ports, firewall status, operating system identification, and a host of other values.

To display basic configuration, type the following Nmap command:

```
nmap -sn {destination IP address}
```

```
[student@fedora ~]$ nmap -sn localhost
Starting Nmap 7.92 ( https://nmap.org ) at 2022-02-27 11:16 EST
Nmap scan report for localhost (127.0.0.1)
Host is up (0.00019s latency).
Other addresses for localhost (not scanned): ::1
Nmap done: 1 IP address (1 host up) scanned in 0.05 seconds
```

Output of a simple Nmap scan of the localhost.

Nmap is covered in more detail in a future Lesson.

Test Certificates with the openssl s_client Command

OpenSSL provides SSL connectivity between clients and servers. SSL relies on certificates generated as part of the public-private key PKI design. When there are issues connecting to webservers using SSL or TLS, the `openssl s_client` command helps identify the problem.

To display connectivity information, including the server's certificate, type:

```
# openssl s_client -client foo.com:443
```

The term "foo" is a common example file or URL name that means nothing or a changeable value. The focus is not on the actual object, but rather on the command(s) associated with it.

Compare the returned certificate and trust information to determine whether there is a problem with the remote server's certificate.

Identify Network Interface Errors

Frequently the network itself is to blame for connectivity issues rather than the Linux systems connected to it. Such network errors may include dropped packets or collisions.

Data moves across the network in small packets. The data is disassembled and addressed on the sending end and reassembled at the receiving endpoint. Unfortunately, these small data packets are sometimes lost. Linux administrators can help narrow the scope of network problems by determining whether data is lost at the server or along the network path. Because packet loss can be caused by software bugs or failing server components (such as NICs), the Linux system may be to blame. However, overtaxed or failing network devices (such as routers and switches) may also be at fault, so correctly identifying where the loss occurs is helpful in solving dropped packet issues.

Network collisions occur when systems send information on the network simultaneously and result in none of the communications being valid. Often, collisions are related to older network hardware, such as using hubs as concentrators instead of enterprise-class switches.

Hubs, switches, and **network interface cards (NICs)** feature LED indicators to report basic connectivity information. A status light shows whether connectivity exists at all, and green or amber LEDs display connectivity speeds. Many networks will operate at 1Gbps speeds, as 100Mbps speeds are often no longer sufficient. Review the network device's configuration for details. Also, review the type of ethernet cable in use.

Various network tools help identify bandwidth and latency issues. Bandwidth measures how much data can be moved on the network in a specified time. Latency measures how much time is required for a network signal to travel from the source to the destination and back.

iftop

The `iftop` command displays bandwidth usage information for the system, helping to identify whether a particular NIC or protocol is consuming the most bandwidth. The `iftop` command may not be installed on all Linux distributions.

This command can help you identify why a particular link may be slow by showing the traffic on that connection. You can use it to check to see what is consuming the most bandwidth on an interface. For example, `iftop -i eth0`

Network slowness is often a symptom of bandwidth saturation, in which a network link's capacity is exceeded, i.e., all bandwidth is being used up. This can lead to degraded network performance or even service outages. With the `iftop` command, you can investigate any NICs on a network link that you suspect may be sending or receiving excessive sums of traffic across that link. For example, one host might be making repeated requests to an internal web server, and both hosts might be flooding the network with their requests and responses. Once you've identified the source of the issue, you can then take steps to stop the offending host from making these requests, such as terminating the service responsible for the requests.

The syntax of the `iftop` command is `iftop [options] [-i {interface}]`

Output showing the connection bandwidth statistics.

iperf

The `iperf` command is used to test the maximum throughput an interface will support. The utility must be installed on both endpoint systems. One system is designated as a "server" and the other as a "client." It is the `iperf` client that is getting tested. You can use this command to ensure that throughput is meeting your expectations.

A basic test uses these steps:

1. On the server, run `iperf -s`

2. On the client, run `iperf -c {server address}`

3. Examine the results that appear.

```
                         root@server01:~                         _ . x
                                              ┌─────────────────┐
[root@server01 ~]# iperf -c server02 ◄────────┤  Remote host    │
------------------------------------------------└─────────────────┘
Client connecting to server02, TCP port 5001
TCP window size: 85.0 KByte (default)
------------------------------------------------------------
[  3] local 10.50.1.101 port 54382 connected with 10.50.1.102 port 5001
[ ID] Interval       Transfer     Bandwidth
[  3]  0.0-10.0 sec   112 MBytes   94.3 Mbits/sec
[root@server01 ~]#                    ▲
                          ┌───────────┴──────┐
                          │   Test results   │
                          └──────────────────┘
```

Testing network bandwidth between two hosts.

The tracepath and traceroute Commands

The `traceroute` command is used to report the network path between the source and destination computers, including any routers the connection uses. The process of a packet traveling from one router to the next is called a hop. The `traceroute` command, therefore, outputs each hop along the path. This is particularly effective when troubleshooting Internet connectivity or connections within very large routed environments. If the `traceroute` fails, being able to identify where along the path it failed is useful for troubleshooting.

The `tracepath` command is a simplified version of `traceroute` that does not require administrative privileges to run. It also contains fewer options.

The syntax of the `traceroute` and `tracepath` commands is `traceroute/ tracepath [options] {destination}`

```
┌──────────┐                              ┌─────────────────┐
│   Hops   │                              │  Remote host    │
└──────────┘                              └─────────────────┘
                         root@server01:~                         _ . x
  [root@server01 ~]# traceroute -I -m 10 comptia.org
  traceroute to comptia.org (198.134.5.6), 10 hops max, 60 byte packets
   1  gateway (10.50.1.1)  0.511 ms  0.804 ms  1.697 ms
   2  192.168.38.1 (192.168.38.1)  3.895 ms  4.009 ms  4.114 ms
   3  rrcs-24-213-135-1.nys.biz.rr.com (24.213.135.1)  5.465 ms * *
   4  * * *
   5  * * *
   6  * be28.albynyyf01r.northeast.rr.com (24.58.32.70)  12.137 ms  12.311 ms
   7  bu-ether16.nycmny837aw-bcr00.tbone.rr.com (66.109.6.74)  18.020 ms  21.875 ms  22.
  045 ms
   8  66.109.5.119 (66.109.5.119)  17.791 ms  58.801 ms  58.934 ms
   9  38.142.136.185 (38.142.136.185)  18.192 ms  18.292 ms  18.378 ms
  10  qwest.iad01.atlas.cogentco.com (154.54.10.26)  17.758 ms  17.969 ms  17.845 ms
```
```
        ┌──────────────────┐              ┌──────────────────┐
        │  Router address  │              │   Round-trip     │
        └──────────────────┘              │   times (RTTs)   │
                                          └──────────────────┘
```

Following the route between two network hosts.

While tools such as `itop` and `iperf` give information about the quality of the connection, `tracepath` and `traceroute` display the network path followed by the connection.

Troubleshoot High Network Latency

Users may complain of slow web pages, slow web apps, and messages or file transfers that take a long time. All of these are signs of high latency. Latency issues can be caused by many network components, and troubleshooting begins with determining whether the problem is with the local Linux system or with network components such as routers or switches elsewhere on the network.

Begin with `ping`. While `ping` is normally used to determine whether connectivity exists, it also reports back travel time for the echo messages. This report helps determine the scope of the problem and may provide insights on where the issue resides. The `traceroute` utility also helps narrow down whether you have a local host issue or a remote network device issue. Finally, tools such as `iperf` provide detailed network analysis.

The information gained with these tools will guide you to the cause of high latency. Some of the most common causes are:

- **Router issues:** hardware problems with the router or its NICs.

- **Switch issues:** problems with the switch hardware or its ports.

- **Routing issues:** errors in the router configuration.

- **Switching issues:** errors in the switch configuration.

- **Network or router saturation:** too much network traffic.

It's also possible the NIC in the local machine is misconfigured or failing. Ensure it's using a current device driver and that no system errors are associated with the NIC. Consider replacing the NIC with a known-good spare.

Identify Name Resolution Failures

One of the most important network services is name resolution. If systems are not able to reach or use DNS name resolution servers, they are not likely to be able to access the needed network services.

Helpdesk Ticket #02005

Submitted by:	Department:	Assigned to:	Date Opened:
Rey Harper	Information Services	*you*	2024-07-19

Subject	Testing name resolution issues
Ticket Detail	Hi, can you share some suggestions for name resolution testing utilities that might be installed on the variety of distros we have on the network?
	Thank you, Rey Harper Jr Sysadmin
Date last updated	2024-07-19

Many different tools test and troubleshoot name resolution. These tools should be used after you have confirmed that the system is configured with the proper IP address of one or more DNS servers (use `cat /etc/resolv.conf` to verify) and after using `ping` to test connectivity to the DNS server.

To quickly display the hostname for the system, type the `hostname` *command.*

Use the resolvectl Command

The `resolvectl` command allows troubleshooters to manually query name resolution services to confirm names and IP addresses are accurately returned. `Resolvectl` is part of the systemd suite, and it uses command subcommand syntax.

To make a basic name resolution query, type:

```
resolvectl query {domain-name}
```

For example, to resolve the comptia.org domain name, type:

```
# resolvectl query comptia.org
```

```
[student@fedora ~]$ resolvectl query comptia.org
comptia.org: 104.18.16.29                    -- link: eth0
             104.18.17.29                    -- link: eth0
             2606:4700::6812:101d            -- link: eth0
             2606:4700::6812:111d            -- link: eth0
```

Resolving the comptia.org domain name using the `resolvectl` *query.*

Use the dig Command

The `dig` command is a powerful tool for gathering information and testing name resolution. It is installed on most Linux distributions. Output is displayed in an answer section. The output includes the IP address mapped to the domain name, the DNS server that answered the query, and how long it took to receive that answer.

The basic syntax is `dig {domain name}`

The command `dig @{IP address} {domain name}` will resolve the domain name against the DNS server specified by the IP address field.

```
[student@fedora ~]$ dig comptia.org

; <<>> DiG 9.16.21-RH <<>> comptia.org
;; global options: +cmd
;; Got answer:
;; ->>HEADER<<- opcode: QUERY, status: NOERROR, id: 2170
;; flags: qr rd ra; QUERY: 1, ANSWER: 2, AUTHORITY: 0, ADDITIONAL: 1

;; OPT PSEUDOSECTION:
; EDNS: version: 0, flags:; udp: 65494
;; QUESTION SECTION:
;comptia.org.                    IN      A

;; ANSWER SECTION:
comptia.org.            118     IN      A       104.18.17.29
comptia.org.            118     IN      A       104.18.16.29

;; Query time: 1 msec
;; SERVER: 127.0.0.53#53(127.0.0.53)
;; WHEN: Sun Feb 27 11:24:38 EST 2022
;; MSG SIZE  rcvd: 72
```

Output of a `dig` *query.*

Use the nslookup Command

The `nslookup` command gathers name resolution information and tests name resolution. It is available on most Linux distributions as well as Microsoft Windows. This command has a noninteractive mode, in which you can provide a domain name in a single command, and an interactive mode, in which you can issue the command by itself and then provide domain names on separate consecutive prompts.

The syntax for noninteractive mode is `nslookup {domain name}`

```
[student@fedora ~]$ nslookup comptia.org
Server:         127.0.0.53
Address:        127.0.0.53#53

Non-authoritative answer:
Name:   comptia.org
Address: 104.18.16.29
Name:   comptia.org
Address: 104.18.17.29
Name:   comptia.org
Address: 2606:4700::6812:101d
Name:   comptia.org
Address: 2606:4700::6812:111d
```

Output of an `nslookup` *query.*

Use the host Command

Another simple tool capable of gathering information and testing name resolution is the `host` command. It is installed on most Linux distributions.

The basic syntax is `host {domain name}`

The command `host {domain name} {IP address}` will resolve the domain name against the DNS server specified by the IP address.

```
[student@fedora ~]$ host comptia.org
comptia.org has address 104.18.17.29
comptia.org has address 104.18.16.29
comptia.org has IPv6 address 2606:4700::6812:101d
comptia.org has IPv6 address 2606:4700::6812:111d
```

Output of a `host` *query.*

 The dig, nslookup, and host utilities are installed as part of the `bind-utils` package.

Use WHOIS

WHOIS is a name resolution protocol that queries DNS servers to display the hostname, fully qualified domain name (FQDN), IP address, and other information about a given host.

The syntax of the `whois` command is `whois [options] {domain name}`

For example, type `whois comptia.org` to display the related information.

```
Registrant Organization: CompTIA
Registrant State/Province: Illinois
Registrant Country: US
Name Server: JADE.NS.CLOUDFLARE.COM
Name Server: ARMANDO.NS.CLOUDFLARE.COM
```

Partial output of the `whois comptia.org` *query.*

Clear the ARP Cache

As you know, nodes on the network typically have three identities: hostname, IP addresses, and MAC addresses. DNS translates hostnames to IP addresses. The **Address Resolution Protocol (ARP)** is used to relate IP addresses and MAC addresses. There is also an arp command that administrators can run to discover information about known MAC addresses.

Computers will cache recently resolved MAC and IP address combinations. If a computer has cached incorrect or out-of-date information, connectivity may be lost to a particular node. The ARP cache can be cleared as part of the troubleshooting process. For example, you can run `arp -d {IP address}` to a clear entry for a particular IP address, and then try to `ping` the host again. Use `arp -a` to view the cache.

The syntax of the `arp` command is `arp [options]`

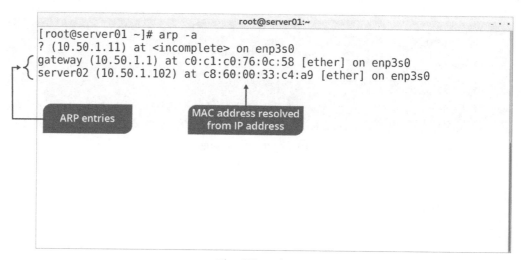

The ARP cache.

Review Activity:

Network Troubleshooting

Answer the following questions:

1. **A helpdesk technician approaches you for help with a network troubleshooting challenge. The tech states that the workstation shows two IP addresses, neither of which matches the expected configuration. The first IP address is 127.0.0.1 and the second is 169.2540.99.42. What can you explain about each address?**

2. **A helpdesk technician approaches you for help with a network troubleshooting challenge. The tech states that a workstation can ping a remote server by IP address but cannot ping it by name. What type of problem is this?**

Lesson 10

Summary

Knowledge of TCP/IP, including IP addressing, is essential for Linux administrators. Administrators are often asked to troubleshoot IP address assignments, name resolution, and network performance issues. As a server platform, Linux has a great many tools available to help with these configurations and supporting tasks. Of these, SSH is one of the most important.

Guidelines

These best practices and guidelines are provided for your use as revision tools or as quick references in your job role.

- Understand that different distributions use different network configuration tools.

- Recognize the three identities of a network node:

  - hostname

  - IP address

  - MAC address

- Understand how to check and set IP address configurations:

  - ip addr and ifconfig display and configure settings

  - hostname and hostnamectl display and configure hostname settings

  - dhclient initiates the DHCP lease-generation process

- Recognize network configuration files:

  - /etc/sysconfig/network-scripts - contains files that configure individual NICs with IP settings, enable/disable status, etc.

  - /etc/sysconfig/network - contains global network settings

  - /etc/dhcp/dhclient.conf - configures how the DHCP client is configured

  - /etc/nsswitch.conf - defines whether name resolution requests use /etc/hosts or /etc/resolv.conf first

  - /etc/resolv.conf - lists DNS name resolution servers and their IP addresses

  - /etc/hosts - manually configured list of hostnames and IP addresses for name resolution

Command Reference Table

This list of commands and their associated syntax can also be found in Appendix B.

Command	Syntax	Purpose	Covered in
ip	ip [options] {object} [subcommand]	Display IP address, subnet mask, and MAC address settings.	Lesson 10, Topic B
ifconfig	ifconfig [options] [interface]	Display current IP address information for each NIC recognized by the system.	Lesson 10, Topic B
iwconfig	iwconfig [options] [interface]	Provide wireless NIC configurations and settings.	Lesson 10, Topic B
nmcli	nmcli [options] [subcommand] [arguments]	View and manage network settings.	Lesson 10, Topic B
ethtool	ethtool [options] {device name}	Manage NIC driver and network configurations.	Lesson 10, Topic B
hostnamectl	hostnamectl [options] [subcommand] [arguments]	View system's network hostname.	Lesson 10, Topic B
netcat	netcat [options]	Test connectivity and send data across network connections.	Lesson 10, Topic C
iftop	iftop [options] [-i {interface}]	Display bandwidth usage information.	Lesson 10, Topic C
traceroute	traceroute [options] {destination}	Report the network path between the source and destination computers.	Lesson 10, Topic C
tracepath	tracepath [options] {destination}	Report the network path between the source and destination computers.	Lesson 10, Topic C
resolvectl	resolvectl query {domain-name}	Manually query name resolution services.	Lesson 10, Topic D
dig	dig {domain name}	Test name resolution.	Lesson 10, Topic D
nslookup	nslookup {domain name}	Gather information about and test name resolution.	Lesson 10, Topic D

Command	Syntax	Purpose	Covered in
host	host {domain name}	Gather information about and test name resolution.	Lesson 10, Topic D
whois	whois [options] {domain name}	Display hostname, FQDN, IP address, and other information about a given host.	Lesson 10, Topic D
arp	arp [options]	Discover information about known MAC addresses.	Lesson 10, Topic D

Lesson 11

Configuring Network Security

LESSON INTRODUCTION

It's critical for administrators to understand what's happening on the network and how that impacts servers and clients. Administrators can use firewalls to control the flow of traffic into and out of individual nodes, network segments, or even entire networks. Firewalls contain rules that define what traffic is permitted and what traffic is not.

Ensuring network traffic flows as it should also includes monitoring and troubleshooting connectivity issues, as well as understanding exactly what data is moving on the network. The network map helps make the task of securing and monitoring the network easier.

Lesson Objectives

In this lesson, you will:

- Configure the firewall.

- Monitor network traffic.

Topic 11A

Configure the Firewall

 EXAM OBJECTIVES COVERED
2.3 Given a scenario, implement and configure firewalls.

Firewalls are one of several tools administrators use to mitigate threats. Most operating systems provide firewalls for the location computer, and most networks have perimeter firewalls to control the flow of traffic. This Topic covers firewall use cases, types, and configurations.

Firewall Use Cases

A **firewall** is a hardware device or software service that monitors inbound and outbound network traffic and either permits or denies that traffic based on a series of rules. Administrators customize the rules to meet requirements and log files to maintain a record of rule application.

Firewalls are found in three major areas of the enterprise network: host-based, segment network-based, and perimeter network-based.

Host-based software firewalls protect a workstation or server by filtering inbound and outbound network traffic for that host specifically. Host-based firewalls mitigate threats to the host from other systems and protect other systems from it.

Segment network-based hardware or software firewalls protect one network segment from another within the boundaries of a larger private, internal network. Administrators divide the network and enforce rules governing the flow of traffic between network divisions. This firewall mitigates threats to the devices in one segment from the devices in another segment.

Perimeter network-based hardware or software firewalls define the boundary between the internal private network and external untrusted networks, such as the Internet. This firewall mitigates threats to internal systems from external threats.

Sysadmins use firewalls to separate one type of traffic from another.

Understand Firewall Actions

The most fundamental function of a firewall is to permit or deny traffic. This decision is made based on a series of rules controlled by the administrator. Initially, the rules are based on a series of simple elements:

- Traffic type (defined by service name or application layer port number)

- Traffic destination (inbound or outbound)

- Traffic interface (the interface where the rule is applied)

To summarize, a firewall rule might specify these elements: **permit inbound HTTP traffic on eth0.**

How sysadmins write these rules varies depending on the type of firewall. For example, *permitting* or *denying* traffic by port or protocol is referred to as *opening* or *closing* the port in some configurations or instructions.

Firewall rules are processed in order, with the most specific rules applied first and the most general rules applied last. Nearly every firewall uses a generic "deny all" rule as the final rule. A simplified explanation might look like this:

- Rule 1: Permit inbound port 80 to webserver01.

- Rule 2: Permit inbound port 21 to the 192.168.2.0/24 segment.

- Rule 3: Block all inbound connections.

Any inbound connection that matches a rule is processed against that rule. Observe that all inbound connections would eventually match the final rule. In this scenario, any connection that is not inbound HTTP to webserver01 or not inbound FTP to the 192.168.2.0/24 segment is blocked.

Understand Port Forwarding

Some firewalls also forward specific types of traffic to specific destinations. Using a process called **port forwarding**, administrators can define an external port number that the firewall then maps or associates with a particular system within the protected network or network segment. This allows a more controlled level of access to a particular system through the firewall or router.

Key Firewall Features

Firewalls use services and ports to identify traffic and control access through one or more interfaces. Some firewall devices have several interfaces that connect to different segments. Stateless and stateful firewalls differ by exactly what criteria are checked to match traffic against rules.

Firewall Zones

Firewalls recognize different zones or groups of interfaces. A firewall device may have multiple interfaces connecting to various network segments, such as the Internet (untrusted), a perimeter network (semi-trusted), and an internal network (trusted). Zones define a set of rules for each connection, simplifying the administrative process. In addition, many firewalls come with pre-defined zones, offering administrators common configurations so they don't have to create all rules themselves. Which zones exist by default varies by firewall service.

Stateful and Stateless Firewalls

The simplest firewalls are stateless. These firewalls merely check individual packet address information, such as source, destination, and protocol. These values are checked against the firewall rules.

Like a stateless firewall, stateful firewalls check source, destination, and protocol values against rules. Stateful firewalls, however, delve into more detail. They inspect the packet contents and identify the behavior of the connection and how the data changes throughout the network communication process. These firewalls are significantly more robust than stateless firewalls.

Firewall Types

While Linux devices may perform as a network segment or perimeter firewalls, those devices are usually dedicated hardware components. In the context of Linux systems, host-based firewalls are the main focus.

Most Linux distributions ship with a firewall, and it is usually enabled by default. After the operating system is installed, it often has limited network connectivity or it may even be completely isolated. This is a good default because it allows administrators to define exactly what connections should be permitted or blocked.

Linux firewall capabilities are managed by iptables or nftables. These services have their own command sets or tools, such as firewalld, or UFW can be used to establish rules.

 UFW and firewalld are covered later in this Topic.

Manage the Firewall with iptables and nftables

Nearly every Linux distribution ships with a firewall, however, different distros select various firewall technologies and user interfaces. Fedora Linux and RHEL rely on firewalld for basic firewall configuration, while Ubuntu Linux uses the **Uncomplicated Firewall (UFW)** interface to configure iptables. However, iptables is being replaced with nftables on many distributions.

Configure iptables

The iptables tool enables you to manage packet filtering as well as stateful firewall functionality within Linux through various tables. Each table applies to a certain context and consists of rule sets, called chains, that the table uses to implement the firewall. A packet is compared to the first rule in the appropriate chain, and if it does not match that rule, it is compared to the next rule in the chain, and so on. If the packet matches a rule, it can either be evaluated by a new chain or have one of three actions applied to it: ACCEPT, DROP, or RETURN (skip to next rule in previous chain).

Each table has one or more built-in chains, but you can also define your own chains as desired.

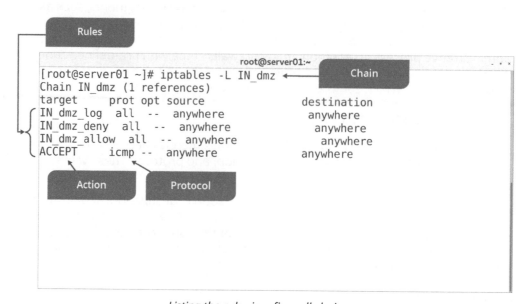

Listing the rules in a firewall chain.

The syntax of the `iptables` command is `iptables [options]
[-t table] [commands] {chain/rule specification}`

Five default tables may be active depending on how the kernel is configured:

Table	Purpose
filter	The default table used for typical packet filtering functionality.
nat	Used to implement Network Address Translation (NAT) rules.
mangle	Used to alter packets' TCP/IP headers.
raw	Used to configure exceptions for packets involved in connection tracking.
security	Used to mark packets with SELinux security contexts.

By default, rules set with the `iptables` command are lost on reboot. In CentOS/RHEL, you can install the iptables-services package and issue the `service iptables save` command to ensure your changes persist. For Debian-based distros, you can install the iptables-persistent package. After installation, you'll be asked to confirm that you want your current rules to persist. The iptables-persistent service will then automatically run at boot and load your rules.

Configure nftables

The nftables firewall is a modern, scalable, high-performance replacement for iptables. It uses similar logic but includes enhancements that make the lives of sysadmins easier. For example, management of IPv4 and IPv6 rules is integrated rather than separate as in the older iptables. Other improvements include simplified syntax, modernized security, and increased performance.

For example, to add a rule to the input chain of the traffic-filter table that permits inbound IPv4 or IPv6 HTTP traffic, type:

```
# nft add rule inet traffic-filter input tcp dport
80 accept
```

Netfilter, the developer of nftables, has included translation options for converting complex iptables rules into the nftables syntax.

Manage the Firewall with firewalld

The firewall daemon (firewalld) dynamically manages a firewall without requiring the firewall to restart upon modification. It uses the concepts of zones and services rather than chains and rules. However, firewalld uses the underlying nftables firewall backend. It receives its own table within which configurations are set via the firewall-cmd command.

Firewall zones are the rule sets that can apply to specific network resources, like a network interface. You'd typically place resources in a zone to group them with resources having similar security requirements or similar levels of trust. There are various default zones, each with different levels of trust. For example, the zone with the lowest level of trust is called *drop*, and it immediately drops all incoming connections. Firewall services are the rules that apply to specific services that operate within a zone. For example, you can add a service like HTTP to the perimeter network zone to allow incoming connections from untrusted networks like the Internet, while denying outgoing access to the rest of the network.

The `firewall-cmd` command enables you to configure firewalld by querying, adding, modifying, and deleting zones and services as desired. Because firewalld is the default firewall service for many Linux distributions, including Red Hat® Enterprise Linux® and CentOS®, you will be using the `firewall-cmd` command regularly. The command includes options to identify which zone and which interface you want to configure, as well as the ability to permit services by name or by port number.

The syntax of the `firewall-cmd` command is `firewall-cmd [options]`

The following are some common examples of using the `firewall-cmd` command and its options:

Command String for firewall-cmd	Purpose
`firewall-cmd --get-zones`	List all available firewalld zones.
`firewall-cmd --zone=dmz --list-all`	List all details of the perimeter network zone, including the interfaces, ports, services, protocols, and more that the zone applies to.
`firewall-cmd --zone=dmz --change-interface= <device ID>`	Add the specified interface to the perimeter network.
`firewall-cmd --zone=dmz --add-service=http`	Add the HTTP service to the perimeter network.
`firewall-cmd --zone=dmz --add-port=21/tcp`	Add TCP port 21 (FTP) to the perimeter network.
`firewall-cmd --zone=dmz --remove-service=http`	Remove the HTTP service from the perimeter network.
`firewall-cmd --zone=dmz --remove-port=21/tcp`	Remove TCP port 21 (FTP) from the perimeter network.
`firewall-cmd --reload`	Reload the zone's configuration.

The command option uses the now-deprecated term "dmz" to describe the perimeter network. Terminology within the field has evolved, but the command syntax is likely to remain the same for some time.

Settings configured with the above sample commands affect the current runtime after the `--reload` *flag is used. If the system restarts, these settings will be lost. To make the settings persistent (survive restarts), add the* `--permanent` *flag to the commands.*

Example of persistently opening a port for web services:

```
# firewall-cmd --permanent --zone=dmz --add-
service=http
# firewall-cmd --reload
```

```
[student@fedora ~]$ sudo firewall-cmd --list-all --zone=public
public
  target: default
  icmp-block-inversion: no
  interfaces:
  sources:
  services: dhcpv6-client mdns ssh
  ports:
  protocols:
  forward: yes
  masquerade: no
  forward-ports:
  source-ports:
  icmp-blocks:
  rich rules:
```

Listing the permitted connections.

```
[student@fedora ~]$ sudo firewall-cmd --permanent --zone=public
 --add-service=http
success
[student@fedora ~]$ sudo firewall-cmd --reload
success
[student@fedora ~]$ 
```

Permit the HTTP service.

Manage the Firewall with the UFW

The **Uncomplicated Firewall (UFW)** is a firewall management tool that makes it easier to configure the nftables or iptables service. UFW originated with Ubuntu® but can be downloaded and installed on other distributions. It is primarily useful for home users who don't have experience with the intricacies of firewall configuration.

The syntax of the `ufw` command is `ufw [options] {action}`

A portion of the UFW graphical user interface.

The `ufw` command enables you to work with the command line interface. For example, the following commands set up an allow rule for HTTP, turn on logging, and enable the firewall:

```
# ufw allow http/tcp
# ufw logging on
# ufw enable
```

This automatically creates a default deny configuration for incoming traffic. In other words, everything without an explicit allow rule is dropped.

Advanced UFW Settings

If you want to use UFW to employ a more complex firewall configuration, you'll need to edit text files rather than use the `ufw` command. The `/etc/default/ufw` file configures high-level settings like policy defaults and kernel module usage. More granular configuration files are found in the `/etc/ufw/` directory. You can edit these files to control when rules are applied, when customizations are run for the `ufw` command, and more.

For example, UFW defaults to accepting outgoing traffic through the firewall. You change this behavior by specifying a different policy directive in `/etc/default/ufw` in this way:

```
DEFAULT_OUTPUT_POLICY="DROP"
```

As a more granular example, you can configure `/etc/ufw/applications.d/myapp` to instruct UFW to recognize your app and its port and protocol information:

```
[My App]
title=My App
```

```
description=My custom application
ports=23534/tcp
```

Selecting a Firewall

For Linux servers, workstations, and laptops, the simple interface of firewalld or UFW is sufficient. These systems are simple with basic filtering requirements and are not likely to service vast amounts of network traffic. When high performance or complexity is needed, working directly with nftables may be beneficial. One example of such a configuration is establishing a complex set of filtering rules between two internal network segments.

In summary, you will:

- Use firewalld for simple, host-based situations.

- Use nftables for complex, high-performance, segmentation situations.

Troubleshoot Common Firewall Issues

As you configure and implement a firewall, you may run into a common issue: The firewall blocks traffic that it shouldn't. Firewall rules can easily become confusing and complex. While the symptom is easy (traffic is or is not getting through), finding and correcting the related setting may be very difficult.

Review the following areas of the firewall configuration:

- Check the firewall rules to ensure that they are not blocking a port that your system needs.

- Check whether the default deny-all rule for incoming connections is processed before permit rules.

- Consider whether you have confused inbound versus outbound traffic.

- Ensure rules exist that match the traffic type.

- Check whether you've blocked or allowed the incorrect transport layer protocols (TCP, UDP, or both).

- Ensure application-layer firewalls are properly configured to manage packets whose contents match a specific application-layer protocol (e.g., HTTP, FTP, SSH).

- Be sure you have reloaded the firewall after configuration changes.

 Remember that the misconfiguration may be that traffic is getting through that should not.

While examining the firewall's configuration is certainly helpful for troubleshooting, it may also be useful to use an outside tool to display firewall configurations. A network scanner such as Nmap may be helpful for identifying misconfigurations.

Review Activity:

Firewall Configuration

Answer the following questions:

1. How does a firewall help mitigate threats between two network segments?

2. What commands are necessary to persistently permit custom TCP port 9876 through the local firewalld configuration on the public zone?

3. Explain the purpose of a firewall's default deny rule.

Topic 11B

Monitor Network Traffic

EXAM OBJECTIVES COVERED

1.5 Given a scenario, use the appropriate networking tools or configuration files.
4.2 Given a scenario, analyze and troubleshoot network resource issues.

Systems administration and network administration are closely linked. Sysadmins are often required to understand how network performance impacts servers and workstations. In addition, proper use of monitoring tools helps narrow the scope of problems to either the network infrastructure or the server's configuration. This Topic covers several common network troubleshooting tools.

Many of the tools network and system administrators rely on daily are the same tools used by threat actors. It's just as useful to detect nodes, services, and network devices for admins as for malicious persons, and penetration testers will use the same utilities as the threat actors they are imitating. It is critical that you have authorization to use security tools in a production network. Intrusion detection software, written security policies, and the organization's cybersecurity staff can and will detect the use of such tools.

Use Basic Network-Monitoring Tools

Administrators rely on network monitoring for many purposes, including troubleshooting, monitoring performance, security, penetration testing, and service availability.

Many monitoring and troubleshooting tools are quite basic, such as ping and tracepath, while others are somewhat more complex, such as tcpdump and **Wireshark**. Still others, such as Nmap, may have very advanced capabilities. It's important to know what tools to use and when. To that end, you can categorize monitoring tools in the following ways.

1. **Basic connectivity.** These tools test the ability to communicate between two nodes and report information about the network path, including performance information. The ping and tracepath tools are examples of basic tools.

2. **Packet capturing.** These tools intercept and display the contents of network traffic. If the traffic is not encrypted, the contents are readable by whoever conducted the capture. Wireshark and tcpdump are examples of packet-capturing tools. Another name for this category of tools is protocol analyzers.

3. **Scanning.** These tools attempt to connect to the addresses of specified nodes or segments and report whether the connection was successful and what type of connection was permitted. Nmap is an example of a scanning tool.

Begin network troubleshooting and monitoring with basic tools, and move toward the more complex utilities as circumstances dictate. This section begins with checking connectivity before moving into intercepting network traffic.

Test Connectivity with Path Tools

Network troubleshooting almost always involves confirming connectivity. There are many levels of detail for the confirmation, from a basic connection to understanding how the network path is traversed to seeing what connections currently exist. Many of the following tools are fundamental to any networking situation, but they are still critical. This section covers commands such as `ping`, `traceroute`, `ss`, and others.

Use ping

One of the earliest parts of network troubleshooting is sending test packets between two systems. This is done using a TCP/IP utility called ping. The `ping` command generates a response request from the sending, or source, computer and should receive a reply from the destination computer.

Possible outcomes of the `ping` command include:

- **Reply from <host>**: The connection was successful.

- **Destination unreachable**: The source computer cannot find a path to the destination. This often indicates the problem is with the source computer.

- **Timeout**: The request reached the destination computer, but a response did not return to the source computer before the source computer timed out. This often indicates the problem is with the destination computer.

Although using `ping` is one of the earliest steps in the network-troubleshooting process, it only tells you that something is wrong—not what is wrong.

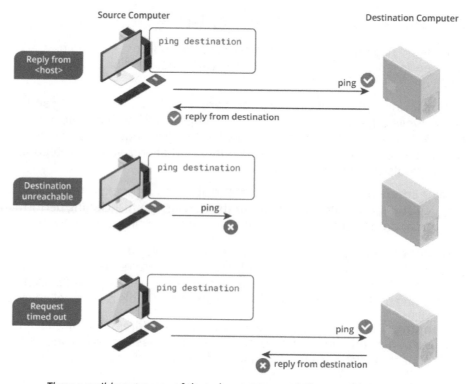

Three possible outcomes of the `ping` command. (Images © 123RF.com.)

The syntax of the `ping` command is `ping [options] {destination}`

The {destination} can be an IP address, such as 192.168.1.1, or it can be a hostname, such as server01.

Options for the ping Command	Purpose
`-c {number}`	Send only a specified number of pinging attempts.
`-v`	Specify verbose output.

By default, Linux systems send continuous pings, until interrupted with `Ctrl + C`, unless you deliberately define a ping count. The `-c {number}` option defines the count. For example, to send five pings, type: `ping -c 5 192.168.2.200`

```
[student@fedora ~]$ ping -c 1 192.168.1.101
PING 192.168.1.101 (192.168.1.101) 56(84) bytes of data.
64 bytes from 192.168.1.101: icmp_seq=1 ttl=64 time=0.230 ms

--- 192.168.1.101 ping statistics ---
1 packets transmitted, 1 received, 0% packet loss, time 0ms
rtt min/avg/max/mdev = 0.230/0.230/0.230/0.000 ms
[student@fedora ~]$ ping -c 1 192.168.1.99
PING 192.168.1.99 (192.168.1.99) 56(84) bytes of data.
From 192.168.1.100 icmp_seq=1 Destination Host Unreachable

--- 192.168.1.99 ping statistics ---
1 packets transmitted, 0 received, +1 errors, 100% packet lo
ss, time 0ms

[student@fedora ~]$
```

Examples of successful and failed `ping` *results.*

Continuous `ping` *is a surprisingly useful tool. For example, if you are rebooting a remote computer via SSH, you could set up a continuous* `ping`*. While the remote system is restarting, the* `pings` *will fail. However, once the startup process is complete, the remote system is again available for you to reconnect to it.*

Use traceroute and tracepath

The `traceroute` command reports the network path between the source and destination computers, including any routers the connection uses. The process of a packet traveling from one router to the next is called a **hop**. The `traceroute` command, therefore, outputs each hop along the path. This is particularly effective when troubleshooting Internet connectivity or connections within very large routed environments. If the `traceroute` fails, identifying where along the path it failed is useful for troubleshooting.

The `tracepath` command is a simplified version of `traceroute` that does not require administrative privileges to run. It also contains fewer options.

The traceroute command output following the route between two network hosts.

The syntax of the `traceroute` and `tracepath` commands is `traceroute/ tracepath [options] {destination}`

Use mtr

The mtr utility is a combination of the ping and traceroute tools, with additional improvements to enable testing of the quality of a network connection. Ping packets are sent to the destination in large groups, with mtr noting how long responses take to arrive at the packets.

The `mtr` command also takes note of lost packets, a symptom of a problem called packet drop or packet loss. This occurs when one or more packets sent from a source cannot reach their intended destination. Packet loss can cause latency if the packets are queued for retransmission, or the data may not be successfully transmitted at all. A large number of lost packets is a strong indicator of a network issue along the path. By identifying that the issue exists, as well as where in the path it exists, the mtr utility enables an administrator to find potentially failed networking components.

The output of the `mtr` command identifies the percentage of packets along the path that are dropped, and one or more nodes in that path experiencing a high percentage of packet loss may be at fault.

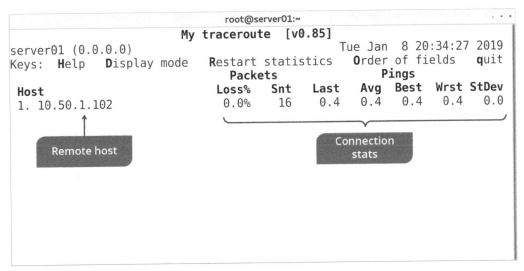

Analyzing connection information to a remote host with the mtr utility.

The syntax of the `mtr` command is `mtr [options] [hostname]`

Test Connectivity with Socket Tools

Helpdesk Ticket #02006

Submitted by:	Department:	Assigned to:	Date Opened:
Kai Garcia	Engineering	*you*	2024-08-09

Subject	network monitoring tools
Ticket Detail	Hello, I'm trying to monitor a network connection for the new application my team is working on. I need to see what ports the application is available on, and which systems are connected to the network application. Which tools do I need to make this happen?
	Thanks, KG
Date last updated	2024-08-09

Use netstat

The `netstat` (network statistics) command gathers information about TCP connections to the system. Depending on the options used, the netstat tool informs the user of existing connections, listening ports on the server, NIC information, and more.

The syntax of the `netstat` command is `netstat [options]`

Common options for the `netstat` command are listed in the table below.

Option for the netstat Command	Purpose
-v	Activate verbose mode.
-i [interface]	Display information about all network interfaces or the specified interface.
-c	Continuously print information every second.
-l	Show only what ports are being listened on.

The default output of `netstat` is in columnar format, as follows:

- The protocol used by the socket.

- The number of processes attached to the socket.

- Flags that give further information about the socket's status.

- The type of socket access.

- The state of the socket.

- The ID of the process attached to the socket.

- The path of the process attached to the socket.

Use ss

The `ss` (socket state) command is an information-gathering utility similar to netstat but provides simpler output and syntax. The ss tool provides information about established TCP connections or which ports the system may be listening on for inbound connections. This can help you diagnose problems related to clients and servers being unable to communicate with one another over the desired protocol; a missing socket could mean that the service isn't running, and a closed socket could mean that either the client or the server is prematurely terminating the connection. Another way to use the `ss` command is to gather information about a particular client that may be connected.

The syntax of the `ss` command is `ss [options]`

Subcommand for the ss Command	Purpose
src {ip-address}	Display connections from a specific IP.
dst {ip-address}	Display connections to a specific IP.

Option for the ss Command	Purpose
-l	Display only listening sockets.
-a	Display all listening/non-listening ports.
-t	Display TCP connections only.
-u	Display UDP connections only.

```
                                              root@server01:~                          - · ·
[root@server01 ~]# ss -l | grep ssh
u_str  LISTEN    0      128     /tmp/ssh-anqcWhPB1Axb/agent.2329 35364
              * 0
u_str  LISTEN    0      128     /run/user/1000/keyring/ssh 37090
        * 0
tcp    LISTEN    0      128     *:ssh                    *:*

tcp    LISTEN    0      128     :::ssh                   :::*

[root@server01 ~]#
```

Listening sockets

The ss command displaying the listening sockets related to SSH.

The `ss` command is useful when troubleshooting errors such as ports that are already in use by one application when another application starts or when tracing existing connections to or from the server for security purposes.

Use lsof

The `lsof` command displays files in use by active processes. However, by adding the `-i` switch, it displays network sockets in use. The `lsof` command can be used instead of (or in addition to) the `netstat` and `ss` commands.

```
[student@fedora ~]$ lsof -i
COMMAND      PID    USER    FD   TYPE DEVICE SIZE/OFF NODE NAME
dleyna-re 33701 student     9u  IPv4  72174      0t0  UDP localhost:ssdp
dleyna-re 33701 student    10u  IPv4  72175      0t0  UDP 239.255.255.250:ssdp
dleyna-re 33701 student    11u  IPv4  72177      0t0  UDP localhost:41254
```

Output of the `lsof  -i` *command.*

Another useful troubleshooting utility is netcat. Recall that the `netcat` *(or* `nc`*) command can test connectivity and transfer files. This tool was covered in Topic 10C.*

Analyze Network Traffic

Protocol analyzers intercept and read network traffic. Recall that data is broken down into small packets and addressed before being sent across the network. The data is reassembled at the destination node. The addressing and protocol information can easily be read, as can the actual data content if it's not encrypted.

The two common protocol analyzers for Linux are tcpdump and Wireshark.

Use tcpdump

Linux admins often rely on the tcpdump utility for packet captures. Created in 1987, tcpdump remains one of the most popular packet sniffers available. It is installed by default on many Linux distributions. Users can determine traffic type and content using this command. It provides similar information to Wireshark, and you can use it in a similar troubleshooting process.

The syntax of the `tcpdump` command is `tcpdump [options] [-i {interface}] [host {IP address}]`

The following table provides some common `tcpdump` options.

Subcommand for the service Command	Purpose
`-i`	Specify the interface to use.
`-n`	Not resolve hostnames, speeding up the capture.
`-v`	Specify verbose mode.
`-w {filename}`	Write the results to the specified file.
`-r {filename}`	Use tcpdump to read the results.

When writing the results to a file, tcpdump does not provide a human-friendly format. The file can be read by using `tcpdump -r` or Wireshark. The file extension is usually .pcap.

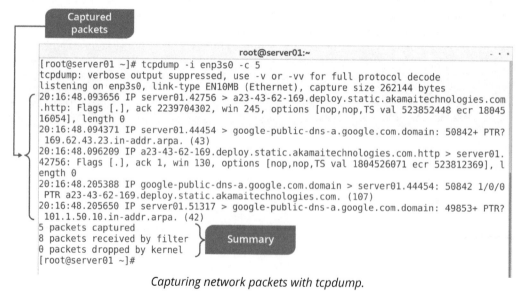

Capturing network packets with tcpdump.

To capture DNS traffic, use port 53 as part of the capture:

```
# tcpdump -i enp0s8 port 53
```

To write the verbose results of the capture on interface enp0s8 to a file named capture-results.pcap, type:

```
# tcpdump -i enp0s8 -w capture-results.pcap -v
```

```
[student@fedora ~]$ sudo tcpdump -i eth0 -w capture-results.pcap -v
dropped privs to tcpdump
tcpdump: listening on eth0, link-type EN10MB (Ethernet), snapshot length 262144 byte
s
^C15 packets captured
15 packets received by filter
0 packets dropped by kernel
```

Writing a tcpdump capture to a file.

 Ensure you have authorization before using this security tool.

Use Wireshark

Wireshark is a very common packet sniffer and network analyzer. Network analyzers intercept and potentially read network traffic. These tools may be used for eavesdropping attacks but are also commonly used for network troubleshooting. When network traffic is intercepted, information such as source/destination MAC address, source/destination IP address, port numbers, and packet payload (data) is exposed. One advantage of a tool like Wireshark is seeing exactly which packets are moving through a network segment or NIC and which packets are not. This is very useful for troubleshooting.

 Ensure you have authorization before using this security tool.

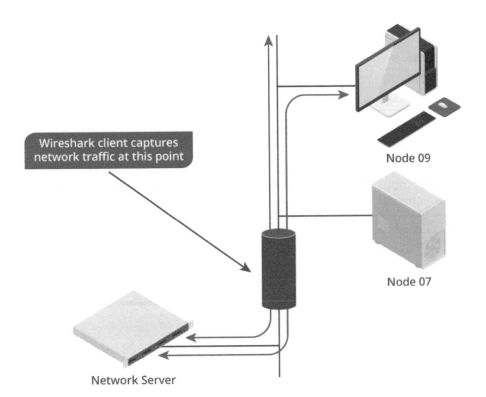

Node 09

Wireshark client captures network traffic at this point

Node 07

Network Server

Wireshark capturing network traffic as it flows between two hosts. (Images © 123RF.com.)

Wireshark is primarily used with a GUI, but it does include the `tshark` command for CLI use or scripting.

The `tshark` utility functions much like `tcpdump`. It even outputs capture results in the same PCAP format. The results are a little more user friendly when generated by `tshark` as compared to `tcpdump`.

The basic process for using `tshark` is the same as any other capture: Define the interface you want to capture on, begin the capture, and then end the capture.

To identify the available interfaces, type:

```
# tshark -D
```

To begin a capture on the eth0 interface, type:

```
# tshark -i eth0
```

Use `Ctrl+C` to end the capture.

You could also use the `-c {number}` option to limit the capture to a specified number of packets.

Map the Network

In order to illustrate how various tools can be used, you'll walk through a common workplace scenario. In this scenario, you are a junior sysadmin involved in an upcoming network security audit. In preparation for the audit, you have been tasked with conducting a network inventory. Your project parameters include operating system identification, port status (open, closed, or filtered), and the use of nontraditional ports for network services.

Use Nmap

The Nmap utility is an incredibly powerful network-mapping tool. It scans individual network nodes, subnets, or entire networks and can report extremely detailed results. The most basic scan shows the status and listening ports on a target, while more advanced scans display target vulnerabilities, the presence of web application firewalls, rogue DHCP servers, and more.

Ensure you have authorization before using this security tool.

Nmap is a CLI tool, but there is an available GUI named Zenmap, which is powerful and convenient. Both utilities are examples of open-source software.

Recall that the advantage of CLI tools is the ability to automate or script their functionality. For example, the Nmap-based network inventory objective in this example could be scripted and scheduled to run every 90 days, providing a quarterly report to administrators that shows changes to the network environment over time.

The syntax for the `nmap` command is `nmap [options] [target]`

For example, to conduct a basic port scan of the 192.168.2.200 node, type:

```
# nmap -Pn 192.168.1.1
```

```
[student@fedora ~]$ nmap -Pn 192.168.1.1
Starting Nmap 7.92 ( https://nmap.org ) at 2022-03-06 09:30 EST
Nmap scan report for lodSense.localdomain (192.168.1.1)
Host is up (0.00092s latency).
Not shown: 997 filtered tcp ports (no-response)
PORT    STATE SERVICE
22/tcp open  ssh
53/tcp open  domain
88/tcp open  kerberos-sec

Nmap done: 1 IP address (1 host up) scanned in 6.40 seconds
```

An `nmap -Pn` *scan of a router.*

To conduct a basic port scan of the Class C 192.168.2.0/24 subnet, type:

```
# nmap 192.168.2.0/24
```

Option for the nmap Command	Purpose
`-sP`	Ping-only scan.
`-sT`	TCP-connect scan.
`-F`	Fast scan.
`-p [ports]`	Scan for specific ports.
`-top-ports [number]`	Scan for common ports (however many specified by [number]).
`-O`	Detect operating system.

Result of the Nmap Port Scan	Explanation
open	Ports accepting connections.
closed	Ports are reachable by Nmap but have no associated service.
filtered	Ports are protected by packet filtering and provide little information.

Depending on one's goals, open ports represent network services available for use, or they represent attack paths.

There are other port results, but these are the three most commonly seen in Nmap results.

Conduct Basic Nmap Scans

There are many ways of using the `nmap` command. It is a very robust and complex tool. Basic scans of a single workstation or a single network segment are fairly straightforward, however.

Checking the status of IP addresses is one example of a basic scan. Recall the scenario described at the beginning of this page. To begin the network inventory assignment, you can scan for available systems on the network segment. This scan uses the `-sn` options, which does not report listening ports but merely checks the status of IP addresses to see whether a host responds to a query. The result is a basic list of IP addresses in use.

```
# nmap -sn 192.168.1.0/24
```

```
[student@fedora ~]$ nmap -sn 192.168.1.0/24
Starting Nmap 7.92 ( https://nmap.org ) at 2022-03-06 09:39 EST
Nmap scan report for fedora (192.168.1.101)
Host is up (0.00012s latency).
Nmap done: 256 IP addresses (1 host up) scanned in 7.08 seconds
```

Nmap scan of a network segment.

Nmap can also detect the operating systems of scan targets. This type of basic scan does more than simply identify Linux, Windows, or macOS; instead, it is usually capable of accurately identifying specific versions, kernels, and roles (servers). While many of the default scans include OS detection, to specifically identify operating systems, add the `-O` option.

OS detection works against entire subnets, but here is an OS detection scan against just the 192.168.2.200 host:

```
# nmap -O 192.168.1.1
```

```
[student@fedora ~]$ sudo nmap -O 192.168.1.1
Starting Nmap 7.92 ( https://nmap.org ) at 2022-03-06 09:41 EST
Nmap scan report for lodSense.localdomain (192.168.1.1)
Host is up (0.0013s latency).
Not shown: 997 filtered tcp ports (no-response)
PORT   STATE SERVICE
22/tcp open  ssh
53/tcp open  domain
88/tcp open  kerberos-sec
MAC Address: 02:15:5D:16:AC:19 (Unknown)
Warning: OSScan results may be unreliable because we could not f
and 1 closed port
Device type: general purpose
Running (JUST GUESSING): FreeBSD 11.X (93%)
OS CPE: cpe:/o:freebsd:freebsd:11.2
Aggressive OS guesses: FreeBSD 11.2-RELEASE (93%)
```

Nmap guessed the BSD operating system.

Nmap Output Redirection

Rather than using the traditional > redirector, Nmap has its own options for saving the output to a file. Two common output methods (there are others) are listed in the table below.

Redirector for the nmap Command	Purpose
`-oN`	Generate a basic text file in human-readable format.
`-oG`	Generate a text file useful for `grep`, `awk`, `diff`, and other commands.

Generate a basic text file named `net-scan.txt` from an Nmap scan in the `~/scans` directory:

```
# nmap -oN ~/scans/net-scan.txt 192.168.2.200
```

Conduct Detailed Nmap Scans

Be aware that Nmap scans of large groups of nodes can take a long time. Nmap has a variety of features designed to avoid detection or gather immense amounts of information. In addition, scanning a large segment, such as a heavily populated Class C or a Class B subnet, targets a lot of machines.

Some advanced scans speed this process up. Other advanced scans focus on more stealthy scans to avoid detection.

Here is an example of a fast scan designed to check for common port numbers, including 22 (SSH), 80 (HTTP), 443 (HTTPS), and others:

```
# nmap -F 192.168.1.1
```

```
[student@fedora ~]$ sudo nmap -F 192.168.1.1
Starting Nmap 7.92 ( https://nmap.org ) at 2022-03-06 09:44 EST
Nmap scan report for lodSense.localdomain (192.168.1.1)
Host is up (0.0013s latency).
Not shown: 97 filtered tcp ports (no-response)
PORT    STATE SERVICE
22/tcp  open  ssh
53/tcp  open  domain
88/tcp  open  kerberos-sec
MAC Address: 02:15:5D:16:AC:19 (Unknown)

Nmap done: 1 IP address (1 host up) scanned in 1.71 seconds
```

Fast Nmap scan of a router.

Another example is a TCP connect scan. This scan attempts TCP connects via the three-way handshake, which may leave entries in the target's log file. This scan is slower than some other scans.

```
# nmap -sT 192.168.1.1
```

Some administrators use nontraditional port numbers to help camouflage network services. For example, port 22 is a well-known port associated with the SSH service. An administrator might set that service to port 2222 as a way of hiding the service from basic scans. However, nontraditional ports could mean unexpected configurations are in place that require further investigation.

The following example scans for nontraditional ports:

```
# nmap -sV 192.168.1.1
```

Nontraditional ports, however, may represent an entirely different security concern. Nontraditional ports may represent rogue network services (services the administrator is not aware of). Such services might be the result of malware or other unauthorized and unwanted software running on the network. Such software could offer backdoor access to the network or direct network traffic outside the network to a threat actor.

The nmap.org website also contains a large library of Nmap scripts that automate very specific and detailed scans. These can be very useful for network administrators.

Nmap is a powerful but simple tool to use for network inventories, security audits, and troubleshooting. Once you've completed your Nmap scans, reporting such details as operating systems, port status, and any nontraditional reports should be straightforward. Reports may be generated directly from Nmap output, integrated into spreadsheets, or added to text files.

Ensure you have authorization before using this security tool.

Troubleshoot Connectivity Issues

The following is an example network-troubleshooting process. The process varies based on the symptoms of the problem. For example, a failed connection probably would not require packet sniffing to resolve.

1. `ip addr` —Does the local host have the correct IP configuration?

2. `ping {destination}` —Is traffic able to flow from the source to the destination and back?

3. `traceroute, tracepath` —Is traffic moving along the expected network path? Is it blocked at a specific router or firewall device?

4. `ss, netstat, lsof -i` —Display current connections and listening ports.

5. `firewall-cmd --list-services` —View what traffic may be filtered by the local firewall.

6. Wireshark or tcpdump —Identify what network traffic is moving in a given network subnet.

7. Nmap —Scan hosts or networks for configurations.

Review Activity:

Network Traffic

Answer the following questions:

1. An administrator wants to better understand the structure of TCP/IP packets, including addressing, transport layer protocols, and the data payload. How would the Wireshark utility help with this understanding?

2. A developer is working on a custom application that sends data to three different remote servers. The developer wants to see, at the network level, what data is sent to each server. What tools can you suggest to help with this, and what selection criteria might you suggest for those tools?

3. A junior administrator needs to generate a report displaying the operating systems running on all nodes on the 192.168.1.0/24 network segment. What command might you suggest?

Lesson 11

Summary

The tools that threat actors use to understand the network are the same tools that help administrators mitigate threats. Protocol analyzers intercept and read network traffic, so firewalls help to isolate and manage that traffic. Network mappers such as Nmap display potential vulnerabilities, misconfigurations, or unexpected services exposed to remote devices.

Because both administrators and threat actors use these tools, it is critical to have authorization to use them on the network.

Command Reference Table

This list of commands and their associated syntax can also be found in Appendix B.

Command	Syntax	Purpose	Covered in
`iptables`	`iptables [options] [-t table] [commands] {chain/rule specification}`	Manage packet filtering and stateful firewall functions.	Lesson 11, Topic A
`firewall-cmd`	`firewall-cmd [options]`	Configure firewalld by querying and modifying zones or services as desired.	Lesson 11, Topic A
`ufw`	`ufw [options] {action}`	Configure nftables or iptables.	Lesson 11, Topic A
`ping`	`ping [options] {destination}`	Generate a response request from the sending computer, which should receive a reply from the destination computer.	Lesson 11, Topic B
`traceroute`	`traceroute [options] {destination}`	Display each hop along the network path.	Lesson 11, Topic B
`tracepath`	`tracepath [options] {destination}`	Display each hop along the network path.	Lesson 11, Topic B
`mtr`	`mtr [options] [hostname]`	Test network connection quality and packet loss.	Lesson 11, Topic B

Command	Syntax	Purpose	Covered in
netstat	netstat [options]	Gather information about TCP connections to the system.	Lesson 11, Topic B
ss	ss [options]	Gather information about TCP connections and display in a simple output.	Lesson 11, Topic B
tcpdump	tcpdump [options] [-i {interface}] [host {IP address}]	Determine traffic type and content.	Lesson 11, Topic B
nmap	nmap [options] [target]	Report extremely detailed information about a network.	Lesson 11, Topic B

Lesson 12
Managing Linux Security

LESSON INTRODUCTION

System security mitigates threats and vulnerabilities by ensuring Linux devices match required configurations. These configurations, implemented via a process called hardening, are supplemented by encryption, strong authentication methods, and mandatory access controls. This Lesson provides configuration steps and commands to manage security tools.

Lesson Objectives

In this lesson, you will:

- Harden a Linux system.

- Manage certificates.

- Understand authentication.

- Configure context-based permissions with SELinux and AppArmour.

Topic 12A

Harden a Linux System

EXAM OBJECTIVES COVERED

2.1 Summarize the purpose and use of security best practices in a Linux environment.

Security is a critical part of every administrator's role. With the advent of DevSecOps, security becomes part of the development, integration, and maintenance life cycles. Basic server security begins with hardening—ensuring the system is configured in a manner that mitigates threats and assures availability. Hardening also includes the use of encryption to confirm data confidentiality, data origin, and data integrity.

This Topic provides hardening techniques, an explanation of security goals, and an introduction to encryption concepts.

Hardening Servers

There are many steps administrators can take to mitigate threats to Linux systems. The process of managing such mitigations is known as **hardening**. Two of the most crucial aspects of hardening are removing anything from the system that it does not need and then using the most current version of whatever software and services remain. There are many more tasks involved in hardening, however.

The **principle of least privilege** guides many hardening techniques. The principle states that users and services should be granted as little access as possible while still allowing them to function. In other words, if a user only needs read access to a file, do not grant them both read and write.

Understand Hardening Steps

Server security requires many steps, and some basic practices are listed here. In general, the guiding principle is to remove everything the system doesn't need and use the most current version of whatever remains.

Hardening Practice	Implementation
Integrate strong physical security	Enforce restricted areas, require guest badges, ensure doors lock properly, and monitor physical access.
Implement security scans	Utilize vulnerability scanners and network tools such as Nmap to automate security auditing and ensure compliance.
Configure secure boot with UEFI	The use of UEFI firmware ensures only digitally signed software is loaded at boot time.

Hardening Practice	Implementation
Configure system logging	Configure rsyslog service to log significant system and application events. System access by the root account should particularly be logged.
Set a strong default umask	Configure an appropriate set of default permissions via umask to enforce the principle of least privilege.
Manage file access	Carefully configure permissions and ACLs according to the principle of least privilege, and utilize SELinux.
Configure the host firewall (elsewhere)	Configure the firewall to enforce the principle of least privilege on network connectivity.
Configure secure SSH connectivity	Configure the SSH service to deny root logins via network connections, display warning banners to remote users, disallow blank passwords, and require key-based authentication.
Disable and remove insecure services	Carefully audit for running services that become unneeded as the server's role changes throughout its life cycle. Remove unnecessary services via tools such as the DNF and APT package managers. Mask services with the `systemctl` command.
Secure service accounts	Audit service accounts stored in `/etc/passwd` to ensure they do not have shell privileges that would permit privilege escalation. Block shell access by placing `/sbin/nologin` in the account's shell field of the `/etc/passwd` file.
Enforce strong password requirements	Enforce strong password requirements by using the `chage` command. Pluggable Authentication Modules (PAM) also help enforce password settings.
Remove unused software packages	Remove unneeded software via tools such as the DNF and APT package managers.
Tune kernel parameters	Tune kernel parameters to match the server's role, installed services, network capabilities, performance requirements, and service levels.
Automate updates	Automate the application of patches and audit the results to ensure all systems receive the appropriate updates.

 UEFI will be covered in Topic 16A. Logging was covered in Topic 9B.

Where possible, use automation to provide consistency and reduce errors. Automated scanning, deployments, updates, and configuration all contribute to more secure environments.

Security Goals

One useful way of considering security is to define goals. System security attempts to satisfy three primary goals: confidentiality, integrity, and availability. These goals are known as the **CIA Triad**.

Confidentiality ensures that only the authorized user has access to data. Establishing confidentiality may include encryption of network traffic against interception, permissions to manage access to files or databases, and authentication to manage access to system resources and other sensitive assets.

Integrity ensures that data has not changed unexpectedly. Such changes may occur because of data corruption during network transfer, malicious users altering data, non-malicious users accidentally changing or deleting data, and other similar activities.

Availability ensures that users and services have access to the resources they need when they need them. Availability includes system uptime, appropriate network performance, and access to resources. Solutions such as backups, load balancing, and low latency network connections are all part of the availability goal.

Observe how many Linux topics deal with availability. A few examples include RAID for storage disks, the df *and* du *commands to measure storage disk capacity,* iftop *for overcoming network bandwidth limitations, and tools such as* top *to maintain processor/memory utilization.*

Notice in security discussions that there is no real guarantee or absolute statement of security. In general, security professionals use the term "mitigate" rather than "eliminate" when discussing threat management.

DevSecOps Concepts

Development processes have changed in recent years, moving toward a more frequent and short release cycle. This practice is referred to as DevOps, and it is a common part of application development in modern IT teams.

The shorter development cycle and more frequent release schedule for applications have changed the approach for security. Security teams must now be integrated into the development process rather than viewed as a single step toward the end of the life cycle. This integration is **DevSecOps**, and it associates a development culture, automation practices, and design based on blending security and development practices throughout the process. DevSecOps does not really refer to the surrounding security environment (firewalls, network encryption, server hardening), but Linux sysadmins are still part of the process and must understand the concept.

Understand Encryption

Encryption is a cryptographic technique that converts data from plaintext form into coded, or ciphertext, form. Decryption is the companion technique that converts ciphertext back to plaintext. An algorithm called a cipher is responsible for the conversion process.

When a message is encrypted, only authorized parties with the necessary decryption information can decode and read the data. This information is called a key, and it is used with the cipher to ensure the message is unreadable to those not in possession of the key. Encryption is therefore one of the most fundamental cybersecurity techniques for upholding the confidentiality of data.

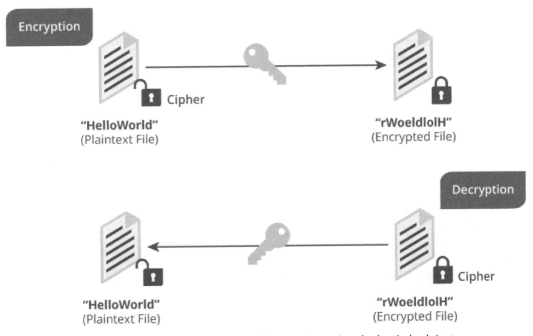

The basic process of both encryption and decryption, using the key in both instances.
(Images © 123RF.com.)

Encryption can be applied to data in three different states: when the data is passing through a network (in transit), when the data is accessed in memory (in use), and when the data is stored on a device such as a storage disk (data at rest).

There are several subtypes of encryption for data at rest, with two of the most prominent being **full disk encryption (FDE)**, which encrypts an entire storage drive, partition, or volume using either hardware or software utilities, and file encryption, which encrypts individual files and folders on a file system using software utilities.

Encryption Goals

Encryption attempts to satisfy the three primary goals of confidentiality, integrity, and non-repudiation.

 While the encryption goals look similar to the security goals, there are differences. One primary difference is the encryption goal of non-repudiation as compared to the security goal of availability.

Users often assume that encryption is synonymous with confidentiality. Encryption may provide confidentiality, but there are other possibilities. Some encrypted information is easily read or easily decrypted because the goal may not have been secrecy.

Data encrypted for confidentiality should only be decrypted by those authorized to do so. The authorization is proven by the fact that they have the ability to decrypt the content. In this case, the goal is to keep the data private.

Data encrypted for integrity is usually easily readable by anyone who might intercept the transmission or otherwise gain access to the content. By using the same encryption method twice, the encrypted result should be the same, proving the data is unchanged. If the data is encrypted the same way twice and the results are different, the data changed between the two encryption events.

Non-repudiation ensures that a sending party cannot deny the origin of a transaction. The sender encrypted the data in a manner that only the sender is capable of, proving the source. The data is usually easily decrypted because the goal is not confidentiality but origin.

These goals describe ways encryption might be used. The next section covers specific encryption methods for each way.

Encryption Types

Two of the most common ways of encrypting and decrypting information are symmetric key encryption, which is the use of a single key to both encrypt and decrypt data, and asymmetric key encryption. Asymmetric encryption uses a pair of mathematically related keys, where one key encrypts and the other key decrypts data. One key is referred to as the public key, and the other is referred to as the private key.

 A third encryption method, hashing, is covered below.

The use of a single key (symmetric) for both encryption and decryption performs well but introduces a problem: how to securely deliver the key to the endpoint.

The asymmetric key-pair approach solves the security problem, though at the expense of speed. Asymmetric encryption is more secure because the public key is available for transport across a network or other media and is viewable by anyone, while the private key must remain on the local system and is available only to the authorized user or service. Finally, the asymmetric key pair is governed by the rule that if data is encrypted with one key, the data must be decrypted by the other key. This lends increased security over symmetric encryption because one key remains private at all times. However, the process of encrypting and decrypting content is slower due to the use of two keys.

The use case for each type varies depending on the goal (confidentiality, integrity, non-repudiation). The following sections summarize these use cases and the role the keys play in managing data.

Public Key Encryption

One use of asymmetric encryption is in e-commerce. In this scenario, you may encrypt content, such as a bank account number, with the public key. When this occurs, the only option for decryption is the related private key, which is available only to the authorized user or service. Anyone can encrypt the data, but only the possessor of the private key may decrypt the information.

The primary goal with public-key encryption is keeping one's personal information confidential.

Private Key Encryption

Another use of the asymmetric key pairs involves encrypting information with the private key. This means, of course, that only the related public key can decrypt the content. Only the holder of the private key could have encrypted the information, and therefore the transmission must have originated from that user or service. No other user or service could have encrypted the data in that way. Anyone possessing the public key can decrypt the information, which is acceptable since the goal is not confidentiality.

This method proves authenticity and meets the goal of non-repudiation. In other words, it proves that the content came from the specified source. This is known as a **digital signature**.

Hashing

The **hashing** encryption method uses a single-key symmetric encryption, but the goal is to provide integrity, not confidentiality. The information is encrypted using a key, and the encryption process generates a resulting encrypted value. If another party encrypts a copy of the same original data, they would expect to get the same result. If a different result is generated, the data copy is different from the original.

For example, an administrator stores a file on a Linux server and uses a hash algorithm to encrypt the file. The hash generates a unique string. The administrator makes both the file and hash available to users to copy. A user who copies the file to their workstation and runs the same hash algorithm should see the same hash result as the administrator sees. If the result is the same, the data is identical on the server and the user's workstation. If the result is different, the copy on the workstation is not the same as the copy on the server. Observe that hashing does not indicate what changed, only that something changed. Files might change based on events such as user updates, file corruption, or malicious alteration.

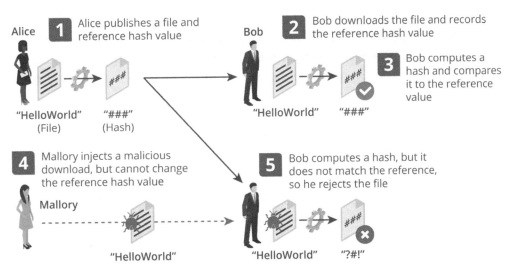

Outcome of hashing. Alice, the administrator, has made the file available (1) to Bob, who runs the hash algorithm and is able to see the correct file (2 and 3). If Mallory is able to inject a malicious download (4), Bob would run the hash algorithm, see that it's different from the reference file (5), and reject it. (Images © 123RF.com.)

Hashing proves file integrity, ensuring that two copies of the same data are indeed identical.

 You will work with hashing utilities later in this lesson.

Review Activity:

System Hardening

Answer the following questions:

1. Explain the principle of least privilege, and provide at least two examples of its use.

2. Explain the three components of the CIA Triad.

3. Explain the three goals of encryption.

4. Differentiate between symmetric and asymmetric encryption, and explain the rule associated with asymmetric encryption.

Topic 12B

Manage Certificates

EXAM OBJECTIVES COVERED
2.1 Summarize the purpose and use of security best practices in a Linux environment.

Digital certificates provide a medium to transport public keys and information about key holders. The certificates may be integrated into websites for e-commerce, stored on smart cards for authentication, or utilized with email to provide confidentiality and non-repudiation.

Public key encryption relies on the Public Key Infrastructure (PKI) to manage the certificate lifecycle, from request to issue to expiration or revocation. Many different certificate types exist.

Certificate Use Cases

When a public/private key pair is generated, the public key is often embedded in a **digital certificate**. The certificate includes a great deal of information, including the owner's public key, the issuer of the key pair, the holder of the key pair, the certificate expiration date, and the issuer's digital signature.

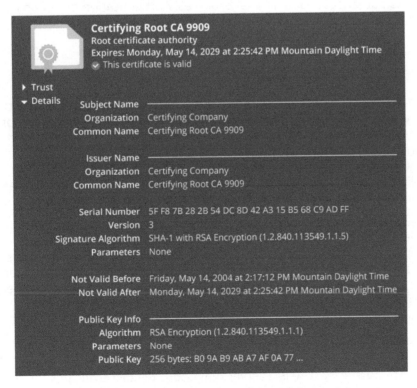

The public key portion of a digital certificate.

A digital certificate is an electronic document that associates credentials with a public key. Both users and devices can hold certificates. The certificate validates the certificate holder's identity through a digital signature and is also a way to distribute the holder's public key. In addition, a certificate contains information about the holder's identity.

There are many use cases for asymmetric public/private key encryption and the related digital certificates. **E-commerce:** Guarantees the identity of remote servers from which customers may purchase goods and provides a means for protecting the purchaser's personal information. **Secure email:** Guarantees the identity of an email sender to the receiving party. **Smart cards:** Guarantees the identity of a user to a system.

Recognize SSL/TLS

Security professionals must protect web traffic, and public key encryption helps with that process. Transport Layer Security (TLS) relies on digital certificates to provide confidentiality, integrity, and authenticity for web connections.

Secure Sockets Layer (SSL) is an earlier implementation of TLS, and often the two acronyms are used interchangeably. The actual SSL protocol is deprecated but often referenced due to its name recognition.

Websites that rely on TLS security contain HTTPS in the URL. This indicates that in the background, the certificate information is exchanged between the web client and the webserver to negotiate a secure connection. Web connections that use HTTP do not negotiate this same information, leaving the connections vulnerable to eavesdropping, impersonation, on-path, and other forms of attacks.

Certificate Authentication

Certificates are also used to allow users, applications, services, devices, and other identities to authenticate and access resources. Authentication based on certificates is more secure than password authentication and is usually more flexible. Certificates may be stored on smart cards or hardware devices.

Manage PKI Certificates

Certificates have a life cycle consisting of enrollment (requesting a certificate), issue, use, and expiration. Certificates can be revoked before their expiration if the identity they guarantee is no longer valid. The servers and organizations that manage this life cycle are called the Public Key Infrastructure, or PKI. PKIs may manage third-party certificates, self-signed certificates, and even wildcard certificates. These certificates are used for everything from secure web communications to encrypted email.

A **public key infrastructure (PKI)** is a system that is composed of certificate authorities, certificates, software, services, and other cryptographic components to enable authenticity and validation of data and entities. The PKI can be implemented in various hierarchical structures and can be publicly available or maintained privately by an organization. As its name implies, a PKI implements asymmetric cryptography for the encryption and decryption of network data, including transactions over the Internet.

Certificate Authorities

A **certificate authority (CA)** is a server that issues digital certificates for entities and maintains the associated private/public key pair. CAs sign digital certificates so that clients can validate the authenticity of certificates owned by entities. CAs may be third-party or internal.

Third-party CAs issue certificates that guarantee identities in public settings, such as the Internet. The CA acts as a trusted third party—trusted by the entity claiming an identity and trusted by the entity confirming the identity. For example, an e-commerce site will request a certificate from a third-party CA that confirms its claimed identity. E-commerce customers trust that the certificate confirms the website's identity.

Third-party certificates issued by CAs are used when the two parties don't trust each other's identities, such as when an anonymous customer makes a purchase on a vendor's website.

Self-Signed Certificates

Internal CAs issue self-signed certificates—certificates that are owned by the same entity that signs them. In other words, the certificate does not recognize any authority and is essentially certifying itself. Self-signed certificates require the client to trust the entity directly.

Self-signed certificates issued by an internal CA are used when the two parties each trust the organization, such as when an internal workstation connects to an internal server.

Wildcard Certificates

Most certificates are associated with a single identity, such as a website at www. [example].com. These types of certificates will not guarantee other identities related to that domain, such as mail.[example].com. Hence, an organization would need to purchase two certificates; one for the website and one for the mail subdomain.

Wildcard certificates support multiple subdomains of a single parent domain, such as www.[example].com, mail.[example].com, and ftp.[example].com.

Common certificate use cases include HTTPS web connections, smart-card authentication, and digitally signed files.

Integrity Checking

Integrity checking is the process of verifying that data has not been intentionally or unintentionally modified in any way. In other words, an integrity check can validate the security goal of integrity. It is good practice to perform integrity checking after you finish compressing and archiving a backup file to confirm that the data has not changed. This will help you avoid storing corrupted and inaccurate archives for future recovery, only to find out too late that the data was not properly backed up.

Several methods enable you to check data integrity, each of which may vary based on its security requirements or goals. One of the most common and secure methods of checking data integrity is through the use of hashing. By calculating the hash of a file like a backup archive, you can compare that hash to past values, and if both are the same, you can be reasonably sure the data has not changed in the meantime.

Hash Functions

A hash function is an algorithm that performs a hashing operation. There are many different hash functions, each of which may have its own security strengths and weaknesses. The two most common hash functions for checking data integrity on Linux systems are MD5 and SHA.

The **Message Digest 5 (MD5)** algorithm produces a 128-bit message digest. It was created by Ronald Rivest and is now in the public domain. MD5 is no longer considered a strong hash function and should be avoided for sensitive operations like storing passwords; however, it is still used in integrity checking.

The **Secure Hash Algorithm (SHA)** is modeled after MD5 and is considered the stronger of the two. Common versions of SHA include SHA-1, which produces a 160-bit hash value, while SHA-256, SHA-384, and SHA-512 produce 256-bit, 384-bit, and 512-bit digests, respectively. SHA-1 is being deprecated due to some security weaknesses.

The md5sum Command

Helpdesk Ticket #02007

Submitted by:	Department:	Assigned to:	Date Opened:
Ali Selassi	Marketing	*you*	2024-08-17

Subject	is this file safe??
Ticket Detail	I'm trying to download this file from a website, and the instructions say "check the checksum value produced with an MD5 hash." What does this mean? Is this a reliable website?
Date last updated	2024-08-18

The `md5sum` command is used to calculate the hash value of a file or standard input using the MD5 hash function. You can also use the `-c` option to specify a file containing MD5 hashes and the file names they apply to; `md5sum` will calculate the hashes of the files listed and then compare them to the hash values listed. The results will let you know whether each file passed, failed, or could not be found.

MD5 hashes are 128-bits in length. Like many other hash values, they are typically represented in hexadecimal format (32 characters for MD5). The following is the hash value of the string "Linux":

edc9f0a5a5d57797bf68e37364743831

The syntax of the `md5sum` command is `md5sum [options] [file name]`

To use the `md5sum` command, create a test file by using Vim (or another text editor). Type a basic sentence or phrase in the file, and then save and close the file. Next, run the `md5sum` command using the file name as the argument. You'll see hash value output on the screen. Now, make a change to the file contents, then save and close the file. Run the same `md5sum` command using the file name as the argument. Compare the new hash. Because the contents are different, the hashes are different.

Here's an example:

```
md5sum {filename} >> hashresults.txt
```

```
[student@fedora ~]$ cat myfile.txt
Hello World!
[student@fedora ~]$ md5sum myfile.txt
8ddd8be4b179a529afa5f2ffae4b9858  myfile.txt
[student@fedora ~]$ echo Hello again >> myfile.txt
[student@fedora ~]$ md5sum myfile.txt
926c68c27aaa03fa77497929164ddb07  myfile.txt
[student@fedora ~]$
```

Checksums from `md5sum` *after a file changes.*

Note that using `md5sum` to confirm the file is unchanged does not prove its authenticity or guarantee confidentiality. It also does not prove the file contents are safe. Hashing shows that the file contents—whatever they may be—are unchanged.

SHA Commands

There are several different commands that you can use to calculate SHA hash values. These commands are functionally identical to md5sum but use the SHA function with the applicable bit size.

- `sha1sum`

- `sha256sum`

- `sha384sum`

- `sha512sum`

The syntax of the `sha#sum` commands is `sha#sum [options] [file name]`

```
[student@fedora ~]$ sha1sum myfile.txt
261d887fb532dde847ce3a61db5908b13840c22a  myfile.txt
[student@fedora ~]$ echo Hello again >> myfile.txt
[student@fedora ~]$ sha1sum myfile.txt
8bfe72dc5bddcfbb80ab39dcb8a94fb3d177a419  myfile.txt
```

Checksums from `sha1sum` *after a file changes.*

Review Activity:

Certificates

Answer the following questions:

---

1. **What are some of the contents of a digital certificate?**

2. **Differentiate between self-signed certificates and third-party certificates.**

3. **When might checking file integrity with hashing tools be useful?**

Topic 12C

Understand Authentication

EXAM OBJECTIVES COVERED
2.1 Summarize the purpose and use of security best practices in a Linux environment.
2.2 Given a scenario, implement identity management.

Identity and Access Management refers to identifying and authenticating users, whether on a standalone system or in a network environment. Various approaches, from tokens to multifactor authentication to LDAP, exist to guarantee the identity of a user. Authentication controls, such as Pluggable Authentication Modules (PAM), allow Linux administrators to tailor server configurations to the organization's written security policies.

This Topic explores authentication methods and basic PAM configurations.

What is Identity and Access Management?

Identity and access management (IAM) is a security process that provides identity, authentication, and authorization mechanisms for users, computers, and other entities to work with organizational assets such as networks, operating systems, and applications. IAM enables you to define the attributes that comprise an entity's identity, such as its purpose, function, security clearance, and more. These attributes subsequently enable access management systems to make informed decisions about whether to grant or deny an entity access and if granted, decide what the entity is authorized to do. For example, an individual employee may have their own identity in the IAM system. The employee's role in the company (e.g., the department in which the employee works and whether or not the employee is a manager) factors into their identity.

In most business environments, IAM is a crucial service for provisioning and managing access, as well as bolstering the overall security of the IT infrastructure.

One goal of IAM is **single sign-on (SSO)**. An SSO implementation requires a user to authenticate only once to get access to multiple systems. For example, a user could authenticate with a name and password and then access a customer database, a secure webserver, and a remote file server, all without being challenged for credentials.

Review Standard Authentication

Recall that the primary way of authenticating to a Linux system is a name and password that are checked against the `/etc/passwd` and `/etc/shadow` file. A hashed version of the password is stored in the `/etc/shadow` file. When you type in your password, it is hashed using the same algorithm as the file and then compared against what the file expects.

This type of local authentication is fine for standalone systems or workstations used only by a few people. However, in larger environments, centralized authentication is far more efficient. Centralized authentication services store name and password combinations on one or more servers. Users can log in to any system, with their identity checked against the authentication server. This approach is easier than maintaining user accounts on each independent standalone system.

Centralized authentication is covered in more detail later in this section.

Authentication Methods

There are multiple ways of proving identities beyond the use of passwords. Tokens and biometrics enhance password-based authentication methods. Linux servers are configured via the System Security Services Daemon (sssd) to use these methods for centralized authentication with services such as Lightweight Directory Access Protocol (LDAP) servers.

Tokens

A **token** is any unique physical or digital object that you can use to verify your identity. Tokens are typically used to generate **one-time passwords (OTP)**, which are passwords that either expire after first use or within a small time period, or both. In either case, OTPs are not meant to be memorized like normal passwords. Tokens can also leverage digital certificates as authentication information.

A hardware token is a physical device that generates and stores the authentication information, and that information is tied to that particular device. One common example is a key fob that generates and displays a numeric token on the key fob's small screen. RSA SecurID® is the most popular security key fob.

Software tokens, on the other hand, are generated by a system that can distribute the authentication information to authorized general-purpose devices, including smartphones and desktop computers. RSA SecurID also has a mobile app for this purpose, and apps like Google Authenticator can generate one-time tokens.

Multifactor Authentication

Authentication methods can make use of several factors. These factors are typically expressed as something you know, something you have, and something you are.

Multifactor authentication (MFA) is the practice of requiring the user to present at least two different factors before the system authenticates them. This helps prevent unauthorized access when one factor is compromised (for example, when an attacker guesses a user's password). Tokens and OTPs (something you have) are commonly used as the second factor after the user's standard password. On more advanced systems, biometrics (something you are) is also used as a factor.

For a system to enforce MFA, it must incorporate more than one factor, not more than one method. For example, using a hardware token and a software token would not qualify because they are the same factor (something you have).

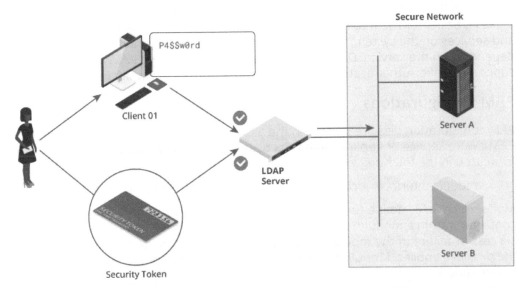

A user employs both a password and a security token as part of the multifactor authentication (MFA) process. When the LDAP server confirms both elements as correct, the user may access the secure network. (Images © 123RF.com.)

System Security Services Daemon

The System Security Services Daemon (sssd) connects the local system to remote authentication services. The local system, known as the sssd client, caches authentication information from the remote authentication provider. The user can then use these cached credentials to access resources, including those protected by PAM configurations. The remote provider might use authentication services such as LDAP, Kerberos, or Microsoft Active Directory.

By caching credentials, the service helps reduce the workload on the authentication providers and allows offline authentication. SSSD also provides single sign-on capabilities.

Lightweight Directory Access Protocol (LDAP)

Lightweight Directory Access Protocol (LDAP) is a directory service protocol that runs over **Transmission Control Protocol/Internet Protocol (TCP/IP)** networks. LDAP clients authenticate to the LDAP service, and the service's schema defines the tasks that clients can and cannot perform while accessing a directory database, defines the form the directory query must take, and defines how the directory server will respond.

Secure LDAP (LDAPS) is a method of implementing LDAP using **Secure Sockets Layer (SSL)** or **Transport Layer Security (TLS)** encryption protocols to protect the confidentiality and integrity of directory service transmissions.

Pluggable Authentication Modules

A **Pluggable Authentication Module (PAM)** defines the underlying framework and centralized authentication method leveraged by authentication services, such as **Kerberos** and LDAP. This provides a common mechanism for many different authentication services and applications. Authentication can therefore be streamlined within that single framework rather than be different for each application and service.

The streamlining of authentication also benefits administrators because PAM makes it easier for them to configure authentication policies across all applications and services on the system, as opposed to configuring policies in different formats depending on the service. Developers can also write their own PAM modules to support specific authentication and authorization functions within an app.

PAM Configurations

PAM configuration files are located in the `/etc/pam.d/` directory, where each PAM-aware service or application has its own file. Each file includes directives, formatted in the following way:

<module interface> <control flag> <module name> <module arguments>

Module interfaces define functions of the authentication/authorization process contained within a module. Control flags indicate what should be done upon the success or failure of the module. The module name defines the module to which the directive applies. Module arguments are additional options you can pass into the module.

The four module interfaces are account, auth, password, and session. **Account** checks to see whether a user is allowed access to something, **auth** is used to verify passwords and to set credentials (such as Kerberos tickets), **password** is used to change passwords, and **session** is used when performing tasks in a user session that are required for access (such as mounting home directories).

There are also four control flags. When the **optional** flag is set, the module result is ignored. The **required** flag mandates that the module result must be successful to continue the authentication, and the user is notified when all tests in the module interfaces are finished. The **requisite** flag is the same as the required flag except for the requisite flag's directive to notify the user immediately upon failure. The **sufficient** flag states that the module result is ignored upon failure.

```
[student@fedora etc]$ cat /etc/pam.d/sudo
#%PAM-1.0
auth        include      system-auth
account     include      system-auth
password    include      system-auth
session     optional     pam_keyinit.so revoke
session     required     pam_limits.so
session     include      system-auth
```

Viewing the /etc/pam.d/ directory and pluggable authentication modules.

 In some distributions, you may be able to configure PAM directly through the `/etc/pam.conf` file. The syntax of this file is similar to individual files in the `/etc/pam.d/` directory.

Manage Passwords with PAM

Pluggable authentication modules have a variety of applications in password management. In this section you'll take a look at three situations in which you'd test passwords: against a dictionary attack, against policy requirements, and against the password history.

Test Passwords Against a Dictionary Attack

The following is an example of a password policy directive:

```
password required pam_cracklib.so retry=5
```

The module interface password indicates that this directive pertains to changing passwords. The required control flag means that the result of the module must be successful, or else the authentication process will not continue. The pam_cracklib.so module contains functionality that prompts a user for a password and will test that password to see whether it can be easily cracked in a dictionary attack. The retry=5 argument gives the user five chances to fail the dictionary test.

Test Passwords Against Policy Requirements

In the following example, the module will require that the user enter a "quality" (strong) password. Non-local users—those not found in /etc/passwd—are ignored:

```
password requisite pam_pwquality.so local_users_
only
```

Test Passwords Against Password History

This example enforces a password history so that users don't reuse old passwords when making password changes. Passwords are remembered for 90 days:

```
password requisite pam_pwhistory.so remember=90
```

Configure User Lockouts

There are two PAM modules you can use to trigger a temporary user lockout if multiple authentication attempts fail: pam_tally2 and pam_faillock. The pam_faillock module is recommended because it is a newer module that improves upon pam_tally2 by supporting user lockout when authentication is performed over a screen saver.

You can place these user lockout directives in /etc/pam.d/password-auth and /etc/pam.d/system-auth

To unlock a user and reset their failure count, you can issue:

```
# pam_tally2 -r -u user
```

Review Activity:

Authentication

Answer the following questions:

1. **What is the purpose of sssd?**

2. **What is the relationship between PAM modules and PAM control flags?**

Topic 12D

Configure SELinux or AppArmor

EXAM OBJECTIVES COVERED
2.5 Given a scenario, apply the appropriate access controls.

Standard file access relies on discretionary access controls (DAC) provided by permissions. In some situations, DAC does not provide enough security to resources. Mandatory access controls (MAC) enforce context-based permissions on processes accessing resources to provide greater security. For many Linux distributions, MAC is provided by Security-Enhanced Linux (SELinux). For other distributions, AppArmor provides similar functionality.

What is SELinux?

Security-Enhanced Linux (SELinux) is the default **context-based permissions** scheme provided with CentOS and Red Hat Enterprise Linux and is available on other distributions. It was developed by the U.S. National Security Agency (NSA). It provides additional file system and network security so that unauthorized processes cannot access or tamper with data, bypass security mechanisms, violate security policies, or execute untrustworthy programs.

SELinux enforces **mandatory access control (MAC)** on processes and resources and enables information to be classified and protected based on its confidentiality and integrity requirements. This helps mitigate the damage caused to information by malicious applications and users.

SELinux Contexts

SELinux contexts (labels) define resource access. Access issues may be related to incorrect labels, and relabeling the resources can help resolve such problems. The autorelabel feature of SELinux allows sysadmins to cause contexts to be reset throughout the filesystem.

SELinux defines three main contexts for each file and process. When you list an object's contexts, each one is delineated by a colon.

- **User:** This context defines how users can access the object. Note that this does not refer to Linux system users but rather distinct SELinux users. Each Linux system user is mapped to one of these SELinux user values. Different distributions provide different users, but common ones include:

  - **unconfined_u** —All users

  - **user_u** —Unprivileged users

  - **sysadm_u** —System administrators

  - **root** —Root user

- **Role:** This context defines what roles can access the object. SELinux users are authorized to be in roles. Roles are typically used to permit or deny users access to domains, which apply to processes. The object_r role applies to files and directories.

- **Type:** This context is the "label" portion of MAC and is perhaps the most important context for fine-grained access control. It is a way of grouping objects together that have similar security requirements or characteristics. The word *type* usually applies to files and directories, whereas a *domain* is just a type that applies to processes. For example, ssh_t is the domain for the SSH process.

Display Security Contexts

Many standard Linux commands include options to display SELinux information. For example, both the `ls` and `ps` commands display additional SELinux details.

List directory contents along with each object's security context. You can check the context of specific objects by issuing:

```
# ls -Z {file or directory name}
```

```
[student@fedora etc]$ ls -Z ~
 unconfined_u:object_r:user_home_t:s0 Desktop
 unconfined_u:object_r:user_home_t:s0 Documents
 unconfined_u:object_r:user_home_t:s0 Downloads
unconfined_u:object_r:audio_home_t:s0 Music
 unconfined_u:object_r:user_home_t:s0 myfile.txt
 unconfined_u:object_r:user_home_t:s0 Pictures
 unconfined_u:object_r:user_home_t:s0 Public
 unconfined_u:object_r:user_home_t:s0 Templates
 unconfined_u:object_r:user_home_t:s0 Videos
```

Output of the `ls -Z ~` *command displaying SELinux contexts.*

List running processes along with each process's security context. You can check the context of specific processes by issuing:

```
#ps -Z {PID}
```

Change Security Contexts

Once you understand the resource's current SELinux context, you can decide whether it's appropriate to change that context. The `chcon` command temporarily changes the security context of a file.

The basic syntax of the `chcon` command is:

```
chcon {-u|-r|-t} {context value} {file or directory
name}
```

where `{-u|-r|-t}` refers to user, role, or type, respectively.

If the filesystem is relabeled or the `restorecon` command is used, the file's context is reset, restoring the default security context.

The syntax of the `restorecon` command is:

```
restorecon {file-name or directory-name}
```

Apply SELinux Settings

SELinux relies on modes to control access to system resources. Depending on the mode, SELinux policies are applied or not. Furthermore, administrators have very granular control over the policies themselves. This control is managed via SELinux booleans, which enable or disable specific policy settings.

Configure SELinux Modes

Helpdesk Ticket #02008

Submitted by:	Department:	Assigned to:	Date Opened:
Rey Harper	Information Services	*you*	2024-08-21

Subject	Failed service - troubleshooting
Ticket Detail	Hi, can you help with a troubleshooting issue. Service00 is failing and I think it's because SELinux is misconfigured, but I still need to test that. I do know SELinux should not be permanently disabled, but I don't know what the next steps are, can you help? Thank you, Rey Harper Jr Sysadmin
Date last updated	2024-08-21

Three modes define how SELinux applies to the system. Think of these modes as either turning on or turning off SELinux security. You can switch between the modes on the fly, making configuration and troubleshooting easier.

SELinux Mode	Outcome
Enforcing	SELinux is enabled and policies are enforced. This is the normal SELinux mode that protects the system.
Permissive	SELinux is enabled, but policies are not enforced. Actions that would have been blocked by SELinux are instead logged for further examination by the administrator.
Disabled	SELinux is turned off system-wide.

The default mode is typically Enforcing. Use the `getenforce` command to display the current mode:

```
# getenforce
```

Use the `setenforce` command to temporarily change modes. Note that a value of `0` is Permissive mode and a value of `1` is Enforcing mode. For example, to temporarily change to Permissive mode while troubleshooting a resource access issue, type:

```
# setenforce 0
```

Once the problem is resolved, be sure to switch back to Enforcing mode with this command:

```
# setenforce 1
```

```
[student@fedora etc]$ getenforce
Enforcing
[student@fedora etc]$ sudo setenforce 0
[student@fedora etc]$ getenforce
Permissive
[student@fedora etc]$ sudo setenforce 1
[student@fedora etc]$ getenforce
Enforcing
```

Changing modes as part of troubleshooting.

The purpose of Permissive mode is for testing and troubleshooting. If you are attempting to resolve resource access issues that you believe may be related to SELinux, you can temporarily set the mode to Permissive and attempt the access again. Your results show you specific information:If you could not access a resource when SELinux was set to Enforcing, but you could when it was set to Permissive, then SELinux is blocking the access.If you could access the resource in Permissive mode but not in Enforcing mode, SELinux logs the policy that blocked your access. Examining the log file allows you to identify which policy needs to be updated to resolve the access control issue.If you could not access the resource in Permissive mode, then it is likely that some other security layer, such as standard permissions or access control lists, is denying access.

Setting the mode to Permissive is an important troubleshooting suggestion. Disabling SELinux is not recommended.

Configure SELinux Policy Types

A SELinux security policy defines access parameters for every process and resource on the system. It enforces rules for allowing or denying different domains and types to access each other. Configuration files and policy source files located in the /etc/selinux/ directory can be configured by the root user.

Each policy is categorized as either targeted, strict, or minimum. **Targeted policy** subjects and objects run in an unconfined environment. The untargeted subjects and objects will operate on the DAC method, and the targeted daemons will operate on the MAC method. A targeted policy is enabled by default. A **strict policy** is the opposite of a targeted policy, where every subject and object of the system is enforced to operate on the MAC method. Finally, a **minimum policy** is similar to the targeted policy in that subjects and objects run in an unconfined environment but load less configuration into memory. This policy category is appropriate for small devices, such as phones, and for experimentation with SELinux.

```
[student@fedora etc]$ sestatus
SELinux status:                 enabled
SELinuxfs mount:                /sys/fs/selinux
SELinux root directory:         /etc/selinux
Loaded policy name:             targeted
Current mode:                   enforcing
Mode from config file:          enforcing
Policy MLS status:              enabled
Policy deny_unknown status:     allowed
Memory protection checking:     actual (secure)
Max kernel policy version:      33
```

Reviewing the status of SELinux with the `sestatus` command.

An example targeted policy might leave SSH running in an unconfined environment but target httpd (Apache webserver) and MariaDB for more strict MAC-based SELinux control.

Understand System Booleans

Administrators can configure different security contexts and settings for various systems. Internal webservers, for example, likely require different security configurations than do Internet-facing webservers. Here are common commands for configuring SELinux:

Command	Purpose
`semanage`	Configure SELinux policies.
`sestatus`	Get the status of SELinux, including its current mode, policy type, and mount point.
`getsebool`	Display the on/off status of SELinux boolean values. Boolean values enable you to change policy configurations at runtime without actually writing the policy directly.
`setsebool`	Change the on/off status of an SELinux boolean value.

Additional SELinux Troubleshooting Tools

SELinux troubleshooting begins by determining whether SELinux is actually the issue. Set SELinux to permissive mode and test access. Tools such as `audit2allow` and `restorecon` can help update SELinux settings.

Use audit2allow

The `audit2allow` command converts access attempts that were denied by SELinux into allow rules. For example, after troubleshooting an access issue by checking log files, you discover that SELinux is incorrectly blocking access to a resource. Rather than generate access rules yourself, you can use `audit2allow` to generate the rules for you.

Copy versus Move and SELinux

You are assigned a helpdesk ticket stating that a user created some HTML files in their home directory and then utilized the `mv` command to move the files to Apache's default DocumentRoot location of /var/www/html (which is where the Apache webserver expects to find the files). Apache cannot use the files, and the user suspects a SELinux issue based on the error message.

One common issue deals with the inheritance of SELinux contexts when moving or copying files. When a file is moved, it does not actually change locations on the storage disk. Instead, the file's pointer changes, but the file retains its characteristics, including the SELinux context. When a file is copied, the duplicate is freshly created in the destination locations. Files created in a directory (for example, via the `cp` command) inherit the characteristics of the directory they are created in, including the SELinux context.

The reason Apache cannot access the files is because they still have the SELinux context of the user's home directory (because the files never really moved). There are two solutions: either copy the files from the user's home directory, causing the new versions to inherit that directory's SELinux context, or update the SELinux context of the files by using the `restorecon` command.

What is AppArmor?

AppArmor is an alternative context-based permissions scheme and MAC implementation for Linux. Whereas SELinux is more commonly associated with RHEL, AppArmor is packaged with Debian-based and SUSE Linux distros.

AppArmor provides the same fundamental service as SELinux provides, but its approach is different in many significant ways. Perhaps the most overarching difference is that SELinux is very complex and often difficult to configure, whereas AppArmor was designed to be much simpler.

Functionally, the main difference is that AppArmor works with filesystem objects based on paths, whereas SELinux references inodes directly. These paths are referenced in flat configuration files, or profiles, that AppArmor uses to determine how to control access. This also means that there are no types or domains in AppArmor, only these profiles.

AppArmor Profiles

Each executable can have an associated AppArmor profile. Profiles are located in the `/etc/apparmor.d/` directory. Within this directory are several text files that are named in a path.binary format. For example, the `/bin/dig` command binary's AppArmor configuration file would be located at `/etc/apparmor.d/bin.dig`.

Within a profile, you can configure two main types of rules: capabilities and path entries. Capabilities provide the executable in question access to some sort of system functionality. For example, the net_bind_service capability enables the executable to bind to a well-known TCP/IP port (port numbers below 1024).

Path entries enable the executable to access a specific file on the file system. As the name suggests, you reference the files by their paths. After the path, you specify what permissions you want to grant to this executable for the files. There are several possible permissions, including r for read, w for write, ux for unconfined execute (file being accessed doesn't have a profile), l for link, and so on.

Each profile operates in one of two modes: complain and enforce. In complain mode, profile violations are logged but not prevented. In enforce mode, profile violations are both logged and prevented.

AppArmor Tunables

Tunables enable you to configure AppArmor functionality without directly modifying profiles. For example, profiles may reference a common object or path using a variable name, such as @{HOME} to refer to the user's home directory. If the user's home directory is not in the default location, you can adjust the appropriate tunable file to account for this. Tunable files are located in the `/etc/apparmor.d/tunables/` directory.

AppArmor Commands

The following table describes some of the major commands that you can use to configure an AppArmor environment.

AppArmor Command	Purpose
`apparmor_status`	Display the current status of AppArmor profiles.
`aa-complain`	Place a profile in complain mode. The basic syntax is `aa-complain {path to profile}`
`aa-enforce`	Place a profile in enforce mode. The basic syntax is `aa-enforce {path to profile}`
`aa-disable`	Disable a profile, unloading it from the kernel. The basic syntax is `aa-disable {path to profile}`
`aa-unconfined`	List processes with open-network sockets that don't have an AppArmor profile loaded.

```
student@ubuntu20:~$ sudo apparmor_status
[sudo] password for student:
apparmor module is loaded.
37 profiles are loaded.
35 profiles are in enforce mode.
   /snap/snapd/11036/usr/lib/snapd/snap-confine
   /snap/snapd/11036/usr/lib/snapd/snap-confine/
   /snap/snapd/15177/usr/lib/snapd/snap-confine
```

Partial output from the `apparmor_status` *command.*

Review Activity:

SELinux and AppArmor

Answer the following questions:

1. What command displays the SELinux context for files?

2. You're troubleshooting a file-access issue and wish to see whether SELinux is to blame. What is one way you could test this by using the Permissive and Enforcing modes?

3. Differentiate between targeted and strict policy types in SELinux.

Lesson 12

Summary

Solid hardening practices are critical to Linux system security. Begin with a security-oriented mindset by integrating DevSecOps practices into all aspects of system and application development security. Use encryption as appropriate to secure data in transit, in use, and in storage. Carefully control authentication processes to ensure only authorized users access your systems. Finally, rely on technologies such as SELinux and AppArmor to provide more granular control to access your resources.

Command Reference Table

This list of commands and their associated syntax can also be found in Appendix B.

Command	Syntax	Purpose	Covered in
md5sum	md5sum options] [file name]	Calculate the hash value of a file with the MD5 hash function.	Lesson 12, Topic B
sha#sum	sha#sum options] [file name]	Calculate the hash value of a file with the SHA hash function.	Lesson 12, Topic B
chcon	chcon {-u|-r|-t} {context value} {file or directory name}	Temporarily change the SELinux context of a resource.	Lesson 12, Topic D
apparmor_status	*No additional options or subcommands.*	Display the current status of AppArmor profiles.	Lesson 12, Topic D
aa-complain	aa- complain {path to profile}	Place an AppArmor profile in complain mode.	Lesson 12, Topic D
aa-enforce	aa- enforce {path to profile}	Place an AppArmor profile in enforce mode.	Lesson 12, Topic D
aa-disable	aa-disable {path to profile}	Disable an AppArmor profile, unloading it from the kernel.	Lesson 12, Topic D
aa-unconfined	*No additional options or subcommands.*	List processes with open network sockets that don't have an AppArmor profile loaded.	Lesson 12, Topic D

Lesson 13

Implementing Simple Scripts

LESSON INTRODUCTION

The ability to automate and schedule complex tasks on a Linux system relies on Bash scripting. Scripts can be as simple or complex as necessary to accomplish the goal. One of the benefits of a script is that it executes the same way every time, rather than relying on an administrator to recall the proper order of operations or avoid typographical errors.

Scripts are also capable of running a set number of times, for example, while a value is true. They can also compare values and use if/then logic to process information differently depending on the contents.

This Lesson begins with simple scripting basics and then addresses various scripting techniques that increase flexibility.

Lesson Objectives

In this lesson, you will:

- Understand Bash scripting basics.

- Use shell script elements.

- Implement scripts with logical controls.

Topic 13A

Understand Bash Scripting Basics

EXAM OBJECTIVES COVERED
3.1 Given a scenario, create simple shell scripts to automate common tasks.

Scripts provide scheduled, repeatable sets of commands that run the same way each time they execute. Such consistency and flexibility make them a powerful tool for administrators. You must understand how to write scripts that call the appropriate shell and are well-documented. In addition, scripts need the execute permission to run and must either be placed in specific locations or you must issue special instructions to Bash to run them.

The Purpose of Scripts

Linux sysadmins find themselves repeating tasks on a regular basis. These tasks might include backing up and archiving files, managing system updates, downloading files, or doing a host of other basic jobs. Accomplishing these tasks manually may be tedious, time-consuming, and error-prone.

Scripting allows an administrator to place commands in a file. The system then reads the file and executes the commands exactly as written. Assuming the file is accurate, the commands are run the same way every time. Furthermore, the file can be run on a schedule, allowing automatic backups during nonbusiness hours, for example.

The many advantages of scripting include:

- **Consistency:** Scripts run the same way every time they operate.

- **Speed:** Scripts execute commands more quickly than humans can type them.

- **Accuracy:** Scripts are less likely to produce errors than humans would likely produce them when typing commands.

- **Customization:** Combining commands allows you to create your own custom tools that meet your needs.

- **Scheduling:** Using tools such as cron and systemd timers, you can schedule scripts to begin at certain times.

Script Comments

In the world of programming, comments are a method of annotating source code so that it is easier for the author and other programmers to understand. In most languages, comments are ignored by the system that compiles, interprets, or otherwise executes the program. Therefore they exist as a way to document various elements of the code within the code itself.

In Bash, the number or pound sign (#) indicates that every character after it on that line is part of a comment and is not to be executed. Although you are free to comment your code how you want, it's usually good practice to include one or more comment lines at the top of the script that explain what that script does and to comment each line or code block that may require explanation. You should refrain from commenting on a line of code with an obvious purpose. Too many comments can clutter the source code and make it harder to understand.

This is an example of a short script with comments:

```
# This script determines how many files are remaining
to process in a directory.
num_files=432        # current number of files
                     processed
total_files=512      # total number of files to process
echo "There are $((total_files - num_files)) files
remaining."
```

How to Run Scripts

Scripts require the executable permission to run and are usually identified by the .sh file extension. This extension isn't required but often makes identifying scripts easier when displaying the contents of a directory. In addition, scripts must either be stored along the system $PATH or must be called directly from the local directory.

Call Scripts from Local Directory

Helpdesk Ticket #02009

Submitted by:	Department:	Assigned to:	Date Opened:
Rey Harper	Information Services	*you*	2024-08-28

Subject	Archive script
Ticket Detail	I'm trying to run a script to archive files older than 120 days, but every time I go to execute it the system says it can't be found. Oddly, executing ls on my home directory shows me the script with no problem. I set up (and double-checked) the permissions, and I'm out of ideas. Can you help me figure this out?
	Thank you, Rey Harper Jr Sysadmin
Date last updated	2024-08-28

One of the system variables is $PATH. This value specifies where Bash looks for executable files. When you run a command, Bash doesn't search every directory on the storage disk looking for the command's executable. That would be very inefficient and time-consuming. Instead, Bash standardizes a few specific locations for executables and only checks there. For example, Bash knows to check the /bin and /sbin directories.

Bash doesn't check custom directories or user home directories (even the /root directory). However, it's common for administrators to write and save scripts in their home directory. To cause a script to execute from a directory that is not part of $PATH, you must type ./ before the script name. This causes Bash to check the current directory for the executable, which it normally would not do.

In the scenario above, the jr admin needs to type the following:

```
$ ./myscript.sh
```

```
[student@fedora ~]$ ./myscript
```

Use ./ to tell Bash to "look here" for the script.

Script Permissions

Remember, your ability to use any file, including a script, is constrained by the permissions assigned to that script. Even though you created the script, you won't automatically have permission to run it. You need to make sure two permissions are set for each user who needs to run the script: the execute (x) bit on the script itself and the (w) and execute (x) bits on the directory containing the script.

You can set these permissions using `chmod` just as you would with any other file.

File Extensions

For the most part, file extensions in Linux are optional. Linux checks a file's metadata to determine what type of file it is. This goes for Bash scripts as well—you don't need to name your scripts with an extension. However, many developers have adopted the convention of adding .sh as an extension to their shell scripts, such as myscript.sh. While this does not imbue the script with any special meaning, it can make it easier for a person to identify that a file is indeed a script. Including a file extension can also help search operations in which you only want to look for or within shell scripts.

Script Syntax

Not only is Bash the default shell in Linux, but it is also a powerful scripting language. Creating Bash scripts is incredibly useful in increasing the efficiency and productivity of your Linux administration tasks. Bash scripts can make Linux system calls and leverage existing tools in the user space. Essentially any program, tool, utility, or system function that you can call at the command-line, you can also invoke in a Bash script. Likewise, Bash scripts support modern programming elements like loops and **conditional statements** to enhance the logic of the task(s) being automated.

Just as commands at the CLI have a syntax, so too do scripting languages. A language's syntax defines the rules for how you write the code. Each language has its own syntax, but many share a few commonalities. Because of its association with the underlying Linux operating system, the syntax of a Bash script is very similar to what you'd input line-by-line at a CLI.

sh-bang

Bash scripts contain shell-specific instructions that may not be compatible with other Linux shells. This will result in a Bash script running on Bash shells correctly, while failing on other non-Bash shells in Linux. To specify that your script is written for the Bash shell, you need to add the line `#!/bin/bash` at the beginning of each script. This line will instruct the operating system to use the Bash shell interpreter when executing a script on an incompatible Linux shell.

The `#!/bin/bash` string at the front of a script is known as "sh-bang."

Review Activity:

Script Basics

Answer the following questions:

1. **What is the purpose of sh-bang, and how would you configure the value for Bash?**

2. **How does Bash handle lines that begin with the # character?**

Topic 13B

Use Shell Script Elements

EXAM OBJECTIVES COVERED
3.1 Given a scenario, create simple shell scripts to automate common tasks.

This topic introduces the elements of a script. The features discussed can be combined and used in an almost unlimited manner to gather the information Linux users need. Bash scripts use many of the same commands as users do at the command prompt, but the ability to combine these commands and the output they generate makes scripting incredibly powerful.

Use Built-in Shell Commands

Scripts use many of the same commands as Linux users do; however, there are some commands that are more commonly found in scripting. For example, `echo` and `read` work together to allow scripts to query users. Other commands, such as `exec` and `source`, run additional executables.

The echo and read Commands

These two commands often work in tandem, allowing the script to ask users for input and then read the input offered. Combining the commands adds a powerful interactive capability to even the simplest Bash scripts.

The `echo` command has many uses. When integrated into scripts, `echo` displays text to users during the script's execution. This text might include questions the user must answer, additional instructions, or even a progress report on the script's execution.

Assuming you use the `echo` command to ask the user a question, how does the script receive the reply? The `read` command causes Bash to expect input and process that input as part of the script.

Here is a simple example you might find in a script:

```
$ echo "What is your name?"
$ read username
```

The exec and source Commands

The `exec` command is used to execute another command, replacing the current shell process with this new program's process (no new process is created). This can be useful when you want to prevent the user from returning to the parent process if an error is encountered. For example, you may want to terminate a privileged shell if a command fails.

You can also use the `exec` command without another command as an argument to redirect all output in the shell to a file. This is commonly used in scripts to suppress stdout at the CLI and instead send it only to one or more files. For example:

```
#!/bin/bash
exec > out.txt
pwd
ls -al
```

The current working directory and directory listing will output to out.txt and not the CLI.

The `source` command is used to execute another command within the current shell process. In this sense, it performs the opposite functionality of the `exec` command. This is useful when you'd like to stay within your current shell while executing a script. One example is sourcing a script that performs a change of directory (`cd`). After the script executes, your location will be whatever the directory was changed to, whereas executing the script normally would keep you where you are.

Another situation where you might want to source a script is when your script changes or defines environment variables. For example, the following script (export.sh) exports a custom environment variable named MYVAR:

```
#!/bin/bash
export MYVAR=1
```

If you execute this script normally and issue the `env` command, you'll see that MYVAR is not listed. This is because the script spawned a new shell process, and once it terminated, its changes to the shell environment were destroyed. However, if you enter the command `source export.sh`, then the environment variable will be maintained because the script executes in your current shell.

Identify Script Components

Scripts contain a great deal of functionality and take advantage of many programming techniques. For example, scripts encourage reusing existing code rather than writing the same code repeatedly. There are many ways of calling values and using code blocks, including arrays and functions.

In addition, you may need to explicitly state values that normally have a meaning in Bash. For example, sometimes you may actually mean the asterisk character (*) rather than the wildcard expression *. String literals and escape characters make this possible.

String Literals

A string literal is any fixed value that represents a string of text within the source code.

String literals are enclosed in single (') or double (") quotation marks. As long as you are using them consistently, either type of mark is acceptable for basic string output. However, there are circumstances where double quotes won't preserve the literal value of all characters within the quotes.

For example, say you've defined the my_str variable mentioned previously. You then want to substitute this variable into a larger string literal:

```
echo "My variable is $my_str"
echo 'My variable is $my_str'
```

The first line, because it is using double quotes, will print "My variable is Hello, World!" The second line, because it uses single quotes, will literally print "My variable is $my_str". Therefore, you must be careful to use the correct type of quotation mark depending on your intent.

It's not always necessary to use a string literal. If you don't wrap the previous `echo` example in any quotation marks, then it will by default produce the same output as if you had wrapped it in double quotes. However, it's still good practice to wrap strings of text in quotes just to be sure. When you assign values with spaces in them to variables, you are required to use quotes.

Escape Characters

In any language, Bash included, certain characters have special meaning. An **escape character** is used to remove that special meaning so the character can be used literally rather than interpreted as something else by the system. This is similar to using a string literal, but in the case of an escape character, you're only removing the special meaning from one character at a time.

In Bash, the escape character is a single backslash (\). For example, let's say you want to print a string to the command-line that contains a dollar sign. The dollar sign has a special meaning—it is used in variable substitution. You can handle this by using single quotation marks:

```
echo 'This $var is escaped'
```

Alternatively, if you wanted to use double quotes or no quotes at all, you could enter either of the following:

```
echo "This \$var is escaped"
echo This \$var is escaped
```

Notice how the backslash escape character precedes the dollar sign, which is the character you want to be interpreted literally.

Arrays

An array is a collection of values. In other words, an array enables you to store multiple values in a single variable. This can make your code much easier to read and maintain. For example, you might want to perform a single mathematical operation on dozens of different values. Instead of creating a variable for each value, you can create an array to simplify your code. Another benefit of arrays is that you can easily update their values throughout the code.

Arrays are ordered based on their indices. Most languages start an array with an index of 0. When you assign values to an array, you can usually perform a compound assignment to assign all values at once. The order you place each value in the compound assignment will determine its index—i.e., the first value will be at index 0, the second at index 1, and so on. Languages like Bash can also use individual assignments to assign specific values to each index.

Compound assignment in Bash arrays uses parentheses with each value separated by a space:

```
my_arr=(1 "Hello" 3.1)
```

Individual assignment adds a value to a specific index in brackets:

```
my_arr[0]=1

my_arr[1]="Hello"

my_arr[2]=3.1
```

You can reference an array by wrapping it in curly braces. You can reference a specific index of the array as follows:

```
echo ${my_arr[0]}
```

This will print "1". You can also reference all of the values in an array by using the asterisk (*) or at symbol (@) in place of the index:

```
echo ${my_arr[*]}
```

Functions

A function is a block of code that you can reuse to perform a specific task. Calling a function is efficient because it means you do not need to repeatedly write the same or similar code. You can define your own functions that you can call in other parts of the script, or even call from other scripts.

Like variables, you define a function with a unique identifier. You use this identifier to reference the reusable code within the function.

In Bash, there are two ways of writing functions. Both involve placing the desired code in between curly braces. The first method is:

```
function my_func {

code...

}
```

If you're familiar with object-oriented programming languages like C, you might be more comfortable with the second method:

```
my_func() {

code...

}
```

However, note that the open and closed parentheses are just there for visual clarity. In Bash, you don't pass in arguments to a function like you would with other programming languages. Instead, you pass in arguments similar to how you would at the command-line.

Understand Exit Codes

An **exit code**, or exit status, is a value that a child process passes back to its parent process when the child process terminates. In the Linux world, a status code of 0 indicates that the process was executed successfully. The exit code 1 or any number higher indicates that the process encountered errors while executing. The precise codes and their meanings vary by command. Use the command's man page to see its exit values.

Display the exit code for the most recent command by using the following command:

```
# echo $?
```

```
[student@fedora ~]$ useradd newuser
useradd: Permission denied.
useradd: cannot lock /etc/passwd; try again later.
[student@fedora ~]$ echo $?
1
[student@fedora ~]$
```

Attempting to add a new user resulting in the error message "Permission denied." The CLI output, when queried with `echo $?`, *shows the error code 1. All failures will result in an exit code that is a nonzero number.*

Many Bash scripts call upon other scripts or enable the user to leverage system commands with the script. Exit codes are useful because they can help these external entities detect whether initial script execution was successful and then potentially change their behavior based on this exit code.

By default, a Bash script will generate an exit code of the last command that was run. You can also specify exit code behavior yourself. The exit code of the last run command is represented by the $? special variable. You can, for example, redirect the exit code to standard output (stdout) and/or standard error (stderr). For example:

```
#!/bin/bash
chmod 888 file
echo $? >&2
```

The script contains an error (there is no permission 888 value). These instructions will redirect the exit code 1 to stderr. Likewise, you can use input redirection to take an exit code from standard input (stdin) into a Bash script.

 Exit codes are discussed again in greater detail in Topic 13C.

The exit Command

You can use the `exit` command in a script to force the shell to terminate with whatever exit code you provide. For example, `exit 1` will cause the script to terminate with a failure status. If you don't provide a number, `exit` will terminate with the exit code of the last command that was run.

Add the `exit` command to if/then in scripts to cause the script to react to success or failure.

Common Script Utilities

Scripts use many of the same basic Linux commands as do users. Scripts can search for files, display file content, sort information, extract data, and perform basically any other file manipulation function you might do at the command prompt.

Regular Expressions

Regular expressions (or "regex" for short) are designated characters that make pattern-matching and searching easier by representing different types of data. Tools such as `grep`, `sed`, `tr`, and others use regular expressions as part of their pattern-matching function.

Regular Expression	Function
.	Replace any character.
^	Match the start of a string of characters.
$	Match the end of a string of characters.
?	Match any one character.

Here are a few simple examples of using regex. Regex is capable of providing very complex pattern-matching to find exactly the information requested.

To search for strings that begin with the character d, type:

```
$ cat textfile | grep ^d
```

To search for strings that end with the character z, type:

```
$ cat textfile | grep z$
```

The xargs Command

The `xargs` command reads from standard input and executes a command for each argument provided. Each argument must be separated by blanks. The pipe operator is used to make the output of the first command the input for the second command. The `xargs` command is commonly used with the `find` command to operate on each result that is found within the file or directory search.

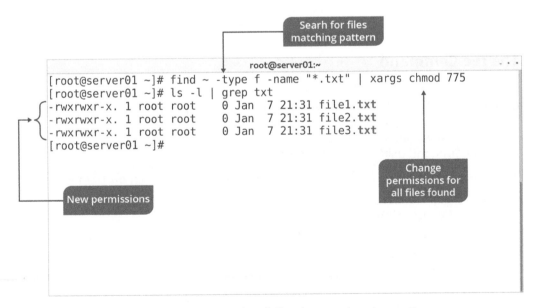

Changing the permissions for all files that match a given pattern.

The general syntax of the `xargs` command is `command [options] [arguments] | xargs [options] {command}`

Let's say you want to delete all of the files in the /foo directory that have a .pdf extension. You can use `xargs` to automate the process:

```
# find /foo -type f -name ".pdf" | xargs rm
```

The `find` command searches for all files in /foo that have a .pdf extension, then pipes the result to the `xargs` command. Because the results are delimited by a space, the `xargs` command will execute the `rm` command for each file in the results— removing all PDF files in the directory.

The `xargs` command includes the options listed in this table.

Option for the xargs Command	Purpose
`-I {replacement string}`	Consider each line in the standard input as a single argument.
`-L {number of lines}`	Read a specified number of lines from the standard input, and concatenate them into one long string.
`-p`	Prompt the user before each command.
`-n {number of arguments}`	Read the maximum number of arguments from the standard input, and insert them at the end of the command template.
`-E {end of string}`	Represent the end of the standard input.
`-t`	Write each command to the standard error output before executing the command.
`-s {max size}`	Set the maximum allowable size of an argument list to a specified number of characters.

The tee Command

The `tee` command reads the standard input, sends the output to the default output device (the CLI), and copies the output to each specified file. This command enables you to verify the output of a command immediately as well as store that output in a file for later reference. Like `xargs`, `tee` typically accepts input from another command using the pipe operator.

When used with the `-a` option, `tee` appends the output to each output file instead of overwriting it.

The general syntax of the `tee` command is command `[options] [arguments] | tee [options] {file-names}`

Let's say you want to check the contents of a directory and output those contents to a file to process later. You could issue separate commands to do this, or you can use the `tee` command:

```
$ ls -l | tee listing.txt
```

The output appears on the screen but is also written to the file.

File Manipulation Commands in Scripting

Commands such as `sed`, `awk`, `find`, `grep`, `wc`, and `cut` have already been introduced as tools to manage files. Here, the spotlight is on their use in automated scripts.

The `sed` command modifies text files in several ways, one of which is with its search-replace capability.

For example, to search for and replace a value in the usernames.txt file, use the `s` (substitute) command and the `g` (global replace) action. To replace the string 'identity' with the string 'username' in a file named users.txt, type:

```
$ sed 'a/identity/username/g' users.txt
```

The syntax of the `sed` command is `sed {'options/address/action'} {file-names}`

The `awk` command is a powerful pattern-matching utility. The command searches for the specified information and can take action when the string is found.

The syntax of the `awk` command is `awk [options] ['patterns {actions}'] | {file-names}`

It may be difficult for users to find files they've created, or you may need to search for files based on criteria other than filename. For example, in a security audit, you might want to search for files that don't match a particular permissions assignment.

The syntax for the `find` command is `find {where to search} {search criteria}`

As an example, to search the /etc directory for any files with the 777 (rwx for all users) permission, type:

```
# find /etc -perm 777
```

Some of the search criteria for the `find` command include -name, -type f, -type d, and -perm.

The `grep` utility is a pattern matcher. It can be used on its own, but it's very common to find it used in conjunction with other commands. Sysadmins will run a command and then use the | character to direct the output into `grep` to search for specific information. Administrators might use the `cat` command to display the contents of the `/etc/groups` file and then use `grep` to search the results for a group named sales:

```
# cat /etc/groups | grep -i sales
```

The `-i` option causes grep to ignore case.

The `egrep` utility is deprecated. It offers the same functionality as `grep -E`, which is to allow extended regex values to be used. Rely on the `grep -E` command instead.

What if you need to count words (or other values) in a file? The `wc` command provides this functionality. It can also count lines, characters, or bytes.

`# wc /etc/passwd` displays the total number of words in the `/etc/passwd` file.

wc -l /etc/passwd displays the number of lines in the file.

```
[student@fedora ~]$ wc -l /etc/passwd
48 /etc/passwd
[student@fedora ~]$
```

Counting the number of lines in the /etc/passwd file.

The cut command extracts the specified lines of text from a file. Cut is another example of a command you might find in a file manipulation script.

Standard Stream Redirection

Redirection permits data to flow into or out of the computer by a means other than the default. The system expects information to enter via the keyboard, and it typically returns information via the monitor. However, these abilities can be changed, allowing data to be pulled in from sources such as text files or for data to be written out to text files.

Standard Redirectors

The standard way of inputting data to the computer is the keyboard, and the standard way for the computer to output data back to you is the monitor. These mechanisms are called stdin and stdout. In addition, error messages are also output to the monitor by default.

It's possible, however, to change these standard methods by redirecting the output of commands elsewhere. You can also change where the system gets its information. For example, the system can use a text file as a source of input instead of the keyboard. Changing these mechanisms is called redirection.

Redirection Operator	Action	Example	Result
>	Redirect the standard output to a file.	ls > file1.txt	The output of the ls command is redirected to a file named file1.txt
>>	Append the standard output to the end of the destination file.	ls >> file1.txt	The output of the ls command is appended to a file named file1.txt
2>	Redirect the standard error message to a file.	ls file3.txt 2> errorfile.txt	The output will not be displayed on the screen but is redirected to a file named errorfile.txt
2>>	Append the standard error message to the end of the destination file.	ls file3.txt 2>> errorfile.txt	The output will not be displayed on the screen but is appended to a file named errorfile.txt

Redirection Operator	Action	Example	Result
&>	Redirect both the standard output and the standard error message to a file.	ls file1.txt file3.txt &> errorfile.txt	The output will not be displayed on the screen but is redirected to a file named errorfile.txt
<	Read the input from a file rather than from the keyboard or mouse.	mail user@address < myletter.txt	The myletter.txt file is taken as the input and attached to the email message.
<<{string}	Provide input data from the current source, stopping when a line containing the provided string occurs. When placed in a script, this is called a here document.	cat <<EOF This is a here document. EOF	The cat command will use the rest of the lines in this file as input. It will stop accepting that input when it reaches the string EOF. This string can be named anything you want. The output of the cat command would therefore be: This is a here document.

This table is provided for reference and was covered previously in Lesson 4.

Use Redirection with Here Documents

One common automation technique is to use a script to connect to a remote computer and then run multiple commands. The technique is called a "here document" and is accomplished via a special redirector:

```
<< {string}
```

For example, a script connects to a remote system by using SSH. Once connected, several commands must be run. This portion of the script might look like the following:

```
COMMAND << remote-cmds
tar -cf tarball *.txt
date > datefile.txt
ip addr > IP.txt
remote-cmds
```

Observe that the string "remote-cmds" bookends the rest of the content. This string represents the start and end of the redirection. The string can be anything you wish, but it must be the same in both positions.

Review Activity:

Script Elements

Answer the following questions:

1. How might you combine the echo and read commands in a script to guide users through a process?

2. You've created a script that includes the string dev=web server. The script throws an error indicating too many arguments for the dev variable. How could you set the dev variable to see the words web and server as a single value?

3. You need to use the sed command to find a value 'server' and replace it with the value 'system' in a file named inventory.txt. What is the syntax to accomplish this?

Topic 13C

Implement Scripts with Logical Controls

EXAM OBJECTIVES COVERED
3.1 Given a scenario, create simple shell scripts to automate common tasks.

Scripts have an incredible amount of potential. Values may be declared as variables and then used throughout a script. Scripts may loop through processes multiple times until conditions are met or a specified number of executions are run. Scripts may even perform arithmetic functions and make comparisons between values. From simple to complex, scripts enable an immense amount of automation.

Understand Variables

Variables refer to entities whose values change from time to time. Most variables are set either by the operating system when you log in or by the shell when it is initially invoked. Variables are the key components that comprise the shell environment. When you want to change the details of an environment, you change its variables and their values.

Variable assignment is the act of defining a variable as having a certain value. In code, you assign values to variable names. The values in a variable may change throughout the script's execution, but this is not required. The purpose of variables is to store values for later use and to enable you to reference these values without explicitly writing them out in the code.

In Linux, variables can be categorized as shell variables or environment variables. **Shell variables**, by default, do not have their values passed on to any child processes that spawn after them. **Environment variables**, on the other hand, do get passed on.

Set Variables

To set a shell variable, simply enter `VAR=value` such as `MYVAR=123`

In order to reference a variable, you must type it in this format:

    ${VARIABLE NAME}

Bash variables are assigned as follows:

    my_str='Hello, World!'

Note the lack of white space around the equal sign (=) in these commands—this is a strict rule in Bash.

Retrieve Variables

To retrieve the value of a variable, you can enter `echo ${VARIABLE NAME}` at the CLI. For example, `echo $SHELL` will print your default shell (e.g., /bin/bash).

The act of referencing or retrieving the value of a variable is called *substitution* or *parameter expansion*. After you assign a value to a variable, you reference that variable later in the code so that you don't need to hard-code values into the script's logic.

Environment Variables

An environment variable is a variable that is inherited from parent shell processes and is subsequently passed on to any child processes. An environment variable consists of a name, usually written in uppercase letters, and a value, such as a path name.

Within the environment, variables are referenced as key–value pairs in the format `KEY=value` and `KEY=value1:value2` for variables with multiple values.

Some of the default environment variables and their functions are provided in the following table.

Environment Variable	Specifies
`HOSTNAME={hostname}`	The hostname of the system.
`SHELL={shell path}`	The shell path for the system.
`MAIL={mail path}`	The path where mail is stored.
`HOME={home directory}`	The home directory of the user.
`PATH={user path}`	The search path.
`HISTSIZE={number}`	The number of entries stored in the command history.
`USER={user name}`	The name of the user.

Environment variables can also be used to configure localization options, typically by editing the `/etc/locale.conf` file and assigning the appropriate locale to the variable. Some of these localization variables are described in the following table.

Localization Environment Variable	Specifies
`LC_*={locale}`	A collection of localization environment variables, including (but not limited to): • `LC_ADDRESS` to set the postal address format. • `LC_MONETARY` to set the format of monetary values. • `LC_MEASUREMENT` to set the measurement system (e.g., metric vs. imperial).
`LANG={locale]`	The locale to use for all `LC_*` variables that aren't explicitly defined.
`LC_ALL={locale}`	The locale to use for all options, overriding any `LANG` and `LC_*` values. Typically used for troubleshooting purposes.
`TZ={time zone}`	The system time zone. This is an alternative to using commands such as `date` or `timedatectl` to set the time zone.

Linux localization features were covered in an earlier section

Modify Variables

The export Command

You can effectively change a shell variable into an environment variable by using the export command. For example, if you have a shell variable SHL_VAR, you can enter export SHL_VAR to make it an environment variable.

You can also change the value of a variable while exporting it, including existing environment variables. You can do this by entering something similar to export SHL_VAR="New value" at the CLI. This will set the value for all child processes spawned from this shell.

No initial value

```
root@server01:~
[root@server01 ~]# echo $SHL_VAR

[root@server01 ~]# export SHL_VAR="New value"
[root@server01 ~]# echo $SHL_VAR
New value
[root@server01 ~]#
```

Create environment variable

Now has a value

Changing the value of a shell variable.

To set the value of an environment variable for all future Bash sessions, you can add an export statement to your .bash_profile file. To automate this process for new users, and to ensure those with similar job roles have the same environment variable settings, you can modify the .bash_profile file in the /etc/skel/ directory. To set the value of an environment variable system-wide, add an export statement to the appropriate file in the /etc/profile.d/ directory.

The syntax of the export command is export [options] [NAME[=value]]

Use the env Command

The env command is used to run a command with modified environment variables. By supplying the name of a variable and a value in the key–value pair format, as well as supplying a command to run, you can change the value of the specified variable for that particular command session. If the variable does not exist, it will be added to the environment. Likewise, you can use the -u option to remove the specified variable from the environment in which the specified command runs. Consider using env if you want to override values in child processes or add new ones.

Issuing the command without any arguments will display all variables in the environment as well as their corresponding values.

The syntax of the `env` command is `env [options] [NAME=value] [command]`

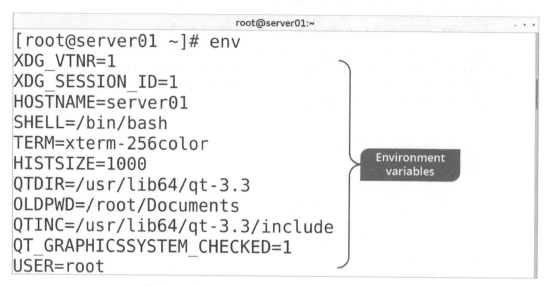

Listing environment variables and their values.

Print the Variables

You can use the `set` command without any arguments to print all shell variables, environment variables, and shell functions. This command can also enable the use of options in a shell script to change its behavior.

The following is a summary of the difference between these three commands: `export` changes the value of a variable for all child processes, `env` displays environment variables or changes the value of a variable for a specified command, and `set` displays shell variables or changes the value of shell attributes.

Use Search Paths

A **search path** is a sequence of various directory paths that is used by the shell to locate files. Paths can be assigned to the PATH environment variable. The **PATH variable** comprises a list of directory names separated by colons. You can add a new path to an existing group of path names, modify a path, or delete a path.

Usually, directories that contain executable files are assigned to the PATH variable. This enables you to enter the name of an executable at the CLI without needing to specify its full directory path. This is because the PATH variable searches its directories for the name of the executable.

Use HISTFILESIZE

HISTFILESIZE is an example of a shell variable that enables you to set the maximum number of lines contained in the command history file. It also enables you to specify the number of lines to be displayed on running the `history` command. For example, by assigning a value of 20 to this variable, the history file gets truncated to contain just 20 lines. The default value of this variable is 1,000.

The alias Command

The `alias` command is used to customize the **shell environment** by generating command-line aliases. Aliases are shorthand for longer expressions. Using aliases, you can create a short string that represents a longer command with various options and arguments. For example, you can create an alias called `myls` that executes the `ls - al` command.

The Bash shell maintains a list of aliases that you can view by using the `alias` command by itself. You can also remove aliases using the `unalias` command. By default, aliases are only maintained for the current shell and for the user who created them. To have them persist, add the appropriate alias command to .bashrc or .bash_aliases, which is called by .bashrc.

The syntax of the `alias` command is `alias [alias name[='command with options']]`

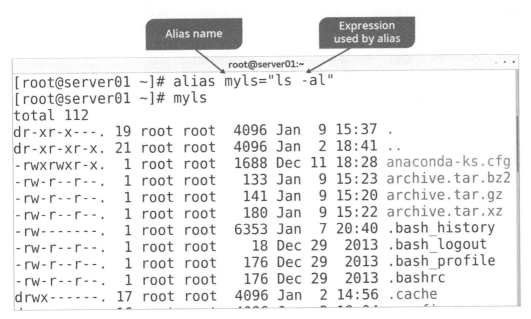

Creating an alias for a command expression.

Troubleshoot Shell and Environment Variables

You may encounter some issues when using or customizing the Bash shell environment. The following are some troubleshooting tips.

When adding an alias, check the syntax. For example: `ls='ls -la'`

If, when executing scripts or other programs, they are not stored in the normal locations for executable files, then add their locations to the PATH variable or execute them with a `. /` preceding the command.

Use the `export` command to set a variable for all shell child processes.

Configure environment variables in the ~/.bash_profile file to make the variable available to all shells. For example, if a service account requires certain environment variables, you can set them in the ~/.bash_profile for that account.

Edit the ~/.bash_profile file to change default variables.

Ensure values are set for any environment variables that a software package has a dependency on. For example, if a Java application relies on the Java runtime environment, it may only be able to find and access that runtime environment if it is referenced in the PATH variable.

Conditionals

Some scripts can remain simple, but the true power of scripting comes from being able to control the flow of logic as it executes. In this topic, you'll augment your scripting skills through the use of conditional statements and loops.

A script's logic determines how it will process written code during execution. In Bash, as in most languages, there are various ways to design the logic of the code to essentially accomplish the same results in execution. Logic is therefore important in maximizing the efficiency and readability of code.

One of the most important components for implementing programming logic is a control statement. A **control statement** begins a section of code that will define the order in which instructions are executed. By controlling the flow of these instructions, you can write scripts to follow one or more paths based on certain circumstances.

A conditional statement is a control statement that tells the program it must make a decision based on various factors. If the program evaluates these factors as true, it continues to execute the code in the conditional statement. If false, the program does not execute this code.

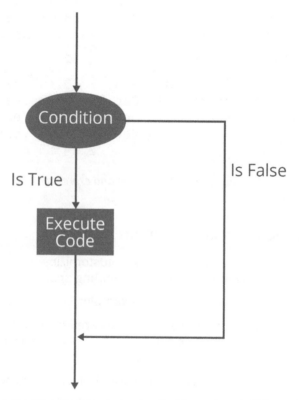

Operation of a conditional statement, executing the code only if the condition is true.

Conditional statements are fundamental to most programs and scripts because they help control the flow of executed code. For example, if a user enters some input, you might want to process that input differently based on a number of factors. The user might supply one argument and not another. Rather than executing the script as if all possible arguments were intended, you'd only execute the script with the argument the user supplied.

Use the if Conditional

In most languages, including Bash, the primary conditional statement is the if statement. An if statement contains a condition to be evaluated and one or more actions to be performed if the condition is satisfied. If the condition is not satisfied, the actions are skipped and the next statement in the script is executed. In Bash, the end of the set of instructions is indicated by the fi statement.

The following is an example of a simple if statement:

```
var=5
if [ $var -gt 1 ]
then
   echo "$var is greater than 1!"
fi
```

The if statement includes, between two square brackets, a condition to be evaluated. In this case, it's whether the $var variable is greater than 1. On the next line is the then statement, within which is the code that will be executed if the prior condition is true. Lastly, the fi statement indicates the end of the entire if statement. Because 5 is greater than 1, the message will echo to the screen. If it were not true, then nothing would happen.

The basic syntax of an if statement follows:

```
if [ <condition to be evaluated> ]
then
   <code to execute if condition is true>
fi
```

Use the if...else Conditional

The if...else statement enables a choice between two actions based on the evaluation of a condition. If the condition is satisfied, the first action is performed; otherwise, the action following the else segment is performed. If there are more than two sets of instructions, one or more elif statements may be used to specify alternative sequences of action.

The following is an example of a simple if...else statement:

```
var=1
if [ $var -gt 1 ]
then
   echo "$var is greater than 1!"
else
echo "$var is less than or equal to 1!"
fi
```

The value of $var has changed since the previous example, which means that the first `echo` command won't execute. Rather than nothing happening, the `else` statement specifies what will happen if the condition is false: in this case, it is to print a different message to the screen.

The basic syntax of an `if...else` statement follows:

```
if [ <condition to be evaluated> ]
then
  <code to execute if condition is true>
else
  <code to execute if condition is false>
fi
```

The basic syntax of an `if...elif` statement follows:

```
if [ <condition to be evaluated> ]
then
  <code to execute if condition is true>
elif [ <other condition to be evaluated> ]
then
  <code to execute if other condition is true>
fi
```

Use Exit Codes with Conditional Statements

Conditional statements like `if...else` are good at handling process exit codes. For example:

```
chmod 888 file 2> /dev/null
if [ $? -eq 0 ]
then
  echo "Permissions set successfully."
exit 0 else
  echo "Could not set permissions."
exit 1 fi
```

If the `chmod` command exits with a code of `0`, then the success message is echoed to the screen, and any other process that executes this script will receive that exit code because of the `exit` command. Likewise, if the exit code is `1`, then a custom error message is echoed to the screen. The default error message is suppressed because it is being redirected to the null device.

The case Statement

There might be times when you want to evaluate numerous conditions, such as when a variable that can hold many different values, and each value requires its own action. You could define multiple `elif` branches in an overall `if` statement, but this can make your code difficult for a human to parse. The `case` statement helps you avoid this issue.

The following is an example of a simple case statement:

```
var=blue
            case $var in
              red)
                 echo "Your color is red."
    ;; green)
                 echo "Your color is green."
    ;; blue)
                 echo "Your color is blue."
    ;; *)
                 echo "Your color is neither red,
                 green, nor blue."
    ;; esac
```

The first line in the `case` statement defines what variable it is that you're evaluating. Below that is the first condition, red, which has a closing parenthesis to indicate the end of the condition. On the next line is the action that will be performed if the color is indeed red—a message will display on the screen saying as much. The double semicolons (`;;`) indicate the end of the action.

This pattern is repeated and can go on for as many conditions as you'd like. In this case, the last condition uses a wildcard (`*`) to indicate that if the variable doesn't match any of the conditions above, then the following action will execute. The `esac` statement ends the `case` statement.

The basic syntax of a case statement is as follows:

```
case <variable> in
  <first condition>)
    <code to execute if first condition is true>
    ;;
  <second condition>)
    <code to execute if second condition is true>
;; esac
```

The Bash `case` statement varies from the C or JavaScript language `switch` conditional. While `case` stops searching for matches once a match is found, `switch` continues checking. This is a good example of slightly different functionality between languages. However, the terminology is sometimes used interchangeably.

The test Command

The `test` command is used to check conditional logic and perform comparisons. You can use the `test` command in your shell scripts to validate the status of files and perform relevant tasks. It evaluates a conditional expression or logical operation and displays an exit status. The exit status is 0 if the expression is true and 1 if the expression is false.

These codes are different from the exit codes generated upon process termination.

For example:

```
var=/etc
if test -d $var;
then
   echo "The $var directory exists!"
fi
```

This example uses the `-d` option to test whether a directory exists. There are many such conditional options you can use. Consult the man page for the `test` command to see them all.

Loops

Aside from conditional statements, another useful way to control the flow of logic in a script's code is by implementing loops. A **loop** is any control statement that executes code repeatedly based on a certain condition. In general, loops are a great way to keep a certain block of code active until it is no longer needed. There are three types of loops supported by Bash: the `while` loop, the `until` loop, and the `for` loop. All three types of loops are enclosed within the `do` and `done` statements.

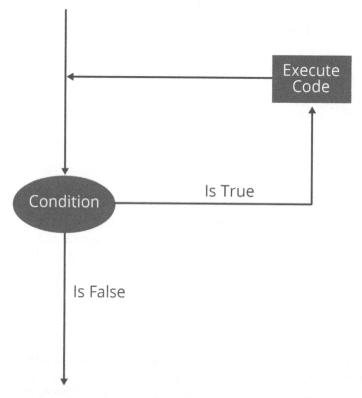

This loop will repeat a series of commands or instructions as long as the conditions on which it depends are true.

The while Loop

The `while` loop enables you to repeat a set of instructions while a specific condition is met. The expression is evaluated, and if the expression is true, the actions in the loop are performed. The execution returns to the beginning of the loop, and the expression is evaluated again. If the expression becomes false at any point, the execution breaks out of the loop and continues to the next block of code in the script.

The following is an example of a simple `while` loop:

```
var=1
while [ $var -le 5 ]
do
echo "The current number is $var."
  ((var++))
done
```

In this case, the condition being tested is whether the variable $var is less than or equal to 5. As long as the expression is true, then the code under "do" will execute. Below the `echo` command is an iterator, which simply adds 1 to the variable. This is common in any kind of loop. Without it, $var will always equal 1 and will therefore never break out of the loop.

The basic syntax of a `while` loop follows:

```
while [ <condition to be evaluated> ]
do
  <code to execute while condition is true>
done
```

The until Loop

The `until` loop is similar to the `while` loop except that the code is executed when the control expression is false. For example:

```
var=1
until [ $var -ge 5 ]
do
  echo "The current number is $var."
  ((var++))
done
```

The condition in this loop is whether $var is greater than or equal to 5. So, the code will execute until $var becomes 5, at which point it will break out of the loop.

The basic syntax of an `until` loop is as follows:

```
while [ <condition to be evaluated> ]
do
  <code to execute while condition is false>
done
```

The for Loop

The `for` loop executes a block of code as many times as specified by a numerical variable that is within the conditional part of the statement. Unlike a `while` or `until` loop, a `for` loop does not depend upon a condition being evaluated as false or true for it to stop or never begin in the first place. So, `for` loops are meant to always execute code a given number of times. This makes them ideal for processing iterable objects like arrays.

The following is an example of a simple `for` loop:

```
var=("Kai" "Ali" "Joseph")
for i in ${var[*]}
do
  echo "$i is a member of the team."
done
```

The `for` statement evaluates every value in the $var array. In this case, each value is represented by the iterator `i`, though you can call this whatever you want. It's common to name it something similar to the variable you're looping through or to simply call it `i` for iterator.

Then, the loop itself will execute three times—once for each value in the array. So, each person's name will be echoed to the screen.

The basic syntax of a `for` loop follows:

```
for i in <variable to loop through>
do
  <code to execute a specific number of times>
done
```

Looping Through Ranges with for

The `for` loop is also used to step through a range of numbers. These ranges are enclosed in curly braces, with the range itself indicated by two periods (. .). For example:

```
for i in {1..5}
do
  echo "The current number is $i."
done
```

So, this loop will iterate exactly five times.

Shell Parameter Expansion

When creating more complex scripts, it may be useful to substitute or bring in data. This data may be the output of commands within the script or variables called when the script is executed. One of the strengths of Bash scripting is its ability to bring information into the script and process it.

Shell Expansion

When a command is issued at the Bash shell, it is split into tokens or words. **Shell expansion** is the process by which the shell identifies special tokens for which it substitutes values. Variable substitution is a type of shell expansion by which the shell identifies the $ special character and then expands a variable into its actual value. In other words, in `echo $var`, the `echo` command doesn't "see" a variable; it sees whatever the value of that variable is when Bash expands it.

There are actually several more types of expansions—eight in total. Bash performs these expansions in a defined order, similar to an order of operations in a mathematical expression.

1. Brace expansion

2. Tilde expansion

3. Concurrently:

    a) Parameter expansion/variable substitution

    b) Arithmetic expansion

    c) Command substitution

    d) Process substitution

4. Word splitting

5. File/path name expansion

For the four expansions that happen at the same time, the expansion is done in left-to-right order as each appears.

Variable Substitution with Braces

As you've seen, the format `$var` is an expansion that will substitute a variable with its value. However, let's say you have the following code:

```
word=computer
echo "The plural of $word is $words."
```

This will print: "The plural of computer is." This is because Bash expects a variable that is exactly named $words even though you just intended to add a letter to the actual value. You can get around this by enclosing the variable in braces:

```
word=computer
echo "The plural of $word is ${word}s."
```

This syntax will print: "The plural of computer is computers."

Command Substitution

Command substitution is a method of shell expansion in which the output of a command replaces the command itself. This is useful when you want to include a command's output within an existing string of text. For example:

```
$ echo "The current directory is 'pwd'."
```

Notice that the command `pwd` is enclosed within backticks ('). Depending on what the current directory actually is, the output might be something like: The current directory is /root.

You can also use the format `$(command)` to perform command substitution:

```
$ echo "The current directory is $(pwd)."
```

The second format is preferred in Bash because using backticks requires escaping certain characters (including nested backticks).

Globbing

Globbing is another name for file/path name expansion. This method of shell expansion is used to replace a specific wildcard pattern with values that match the pattern. There are three special characters used in globbing: the asterisk (*), which is used to match any number of characters; the question mark (?), which is used to match a single character; and characters within square brackets ([ ]), which are used to match any of the characters listed.

The following are three examples of globbing.

```
$ cp *.txt ~/dest
```

This example with an asterisk (*) copies any and all files with a .txt extension. This is because the wildcard character appears before the period, indicating that Bash should expand any possible combination of characters.

```
$ cp ?.txt ~/dest
```

Using a question mark (?) in the syntax will only copy .txt files with a single character as a name, like a.txt and b.txt, but not ab.txt.

```
$ cp [abc].txt ~/dest
```

The brackets ([ ]) example will only copy files named a.txt, b.txt, or c.txt.

Positional Parameters

A positional parameter is a variable within a shell script that is assigned to an argument when the script is invoked. For example, you can invoke the script myscript.sh:

```
$ ./myscript.sh arg1 arg2 arg3
```

The `arg1` argument corresponds to the positional parameter $1, `arg2` corresponds to $2, `arg3` corresponds to $3, and so on. Note that the space between arguments is used to separate positional parameters.

You can reference positional parameters directly in your scripts as you would for any other variable:

```
#!/bin/bash
echo "The first argument is $1"
echo "The second argument is $2"
echo "The third argument is $3"
```

This is useful because your script can perform various operations on any arguments that are passed to it, as most scripts and commands do.

You can also set positional parameters directly in your scripts by using the `set` command. For example:

```
#!/bin/bash
set -- arg1 arg2 arg3
echo "The first argument is $1"
echo "The second argument is $2"
echo "The third argument is $3"
```

When this script is invoked without any arguments provided by the user, it will still have positional parameters $1, $2, and $3 because they were set manually.

Operators

Operations enable you to perform tasks on the variables and values that you specify in your code. In most cases, this task is the evaluation of an expression. Operators are objects that evaluate expressions in a variety of ways, while operands are the values being operated on.

There are many different kinds of operators that apply to most languages. Arithmetic operators include addition, subtraction, multiplication, division, and more advanced mathematical operations. Comparison operators include checking whether operands are equal, whether one operand is less than or greater than another operand, and more. Boolean (logical) operators connect multiple values together so they can be evaluated, and they include AND, OR, and NOT. Finally, string operators are used in operations that manipulate strings in various ways, including concatenating strings, returning a specific character in a string (slicing), verifying whether a specific character exists in a string, and more.

Some Arithmetic Operators	Description
+	Addition
−	Subtraction
*	Multiplication
/	Division

Some Boolean Operators	Description
&&	Logical AND (this and that)
| |	Logical OR (this or that)
!	Logical negation (not this)

Some Comparison and String Operators	Description
-eq	Equal to
-ne	Not equal to
-gt	Greater than
-ge	Greater than or equal to
-lt	Less than
-le	Less than or equal to

Many programming languages find common ground when it comes to representing operators in code. For example, in many languages the == comparison operator evaluates whether the operands have equal values. Therefore, the expression 1 == 2 outputs to false. Note that this particular operator is distinct from a single equal sign (=), which is used in assigning values to variables. However, some languages do not use the traditional symbols for comparison operators. Instead, they use a letter-based syntax. For example, consider that the >= operator evaluates whether the left operand is greater than or equal to the right operand. In letter-based syntax, the operator is -ge. So, 1 -ge 2 outputs to false.

Bash Operations Examples

The following is an example of an arithmetic operation in Bash. Note that expressions are evaluated when wrapped in double parentheses:

```
$((var1 + var2))
```

An example of a comparison operation in Bash follows. Note the use of square brackets and a letter-based operator:

```
[ $var1 -ge $var2 ]
```

An example of a logical operation (AND) in Bash:

```
[ $var1 -ge $var2 ] && [ $var3 -le $var4 ]
```

An example of a string operation (concatenation) in Bash:

```
$var1$var2
```

Schedule a Script

One of the biggest benefits of scripting is the ability to schedule tasks. By creating a script and then telling the system to execute the script (and everything in it), administrators can automate anything from backups to software updates to system configurations.

Both the cron utility and systemd .timer files give administrators many options for scheduling tasks.

Edit the crontab file with the following information to schedule the backup.sh script to run at 2 a.m. daily:

```
0 2 * * * /scripts/backup.sh
```

 Scheduling tasks was covered in an earlier section of the course.

Review Activity:

Logical Controls

Answer the following questions:

1. You are exploring your local (shell) variables on each system that you manage. The first variable you check is the SHELL variable. How can you check the SHELL variable, and what do you expect it to display?

2. Differentiate between for and while loops.

3. What is the purpose of file globbing in scripts?

Lesson 13

Summary

You are encouraged to use the many scripts that are available on the Internet. Apply the content of this lesson to those scripts to understand how the script functions before running it. You can also create your own scripts. Start simple, and then add complexity and features as you master each technique.

Command Reference Table

This list of commands and their associated syntax can also be found in Appendix B.

Command	Syntax	Purpose	Covered in
awk	awk [options] ['patterns {actions}'] | {file-names}	Search for specified information, and take action when that information is found.	Lesson 13, Topic B
sed	sed {'options/ address/action'} {file-names}	Modify text files, especially by searching and replacing.	Lesson 13, Topic B
find	find {where to search} {search criteria}	Search for files based on criteria other than filename.	Lesson 13, Topic B
tee	command [options] [arguments] | tee [options] {file-names}	Verify the output of a command immediately, and store that output in a file for later reference.	Lesson 13, Topic B
xargs	command [options] [arguments] | xargs [options] {command}	Commonly used with the find command to operate on each result that is found within the file or directory search.	Lesson 13, Topic B
export	export [options] [NAME[=value]]	Set the value of an environment variable for all future Bash sessions.	Lesson 13, Topic C
env	env [options] [NAME=value] [command]	Run a command with modified environment variables.	Lesson 13, Topic C
alias	alias [alias name[='command with options']]	Customize the shell environment by generating command-line aliases.	Lesson 13, Topic C

Lesson 14

Using Infrastructure as Code

LESSON INTRODUCTION

DevOps informs the use of Infrastructure as Code, a sysadmin approach to managing system deployments and configuration. By treating configuration files as code and enforcing version control and change tracking on them, organizations seek to bring greater stability, security, and automation to their environments.

The combination of orchestration tools, such as Ansible, and file management tools, such as Git, brings Infrastructure as Code to the forefront of administrator responsibilities.

Lesson Objectives

In this lesson, you will:

- Understand infrastructure as code.

- Implement orchestration.

- Manage version control with Git.

Topic 14A

Understand Infrastructure as Code

EXAM OBJECTIVES COVERED
3.4 Summarize common infrastructure as code technologies.

A new way of managing coding and system administration projects is becoming more prevalent. This new approach—DevOps—introduces a quicker software life cycle with an emphasis on automation. Sysadmins implement this to manage Linux servers via Infrastructure as Code (IaC). IaC allows version control and centralized management of server provisioning and configuration. While standard Linux text-based configuration files may still be used, other configurations formatted as JSON or YAML files may also be used.

DevOps Concepts

DevOps is an amalgamation of software development and systems operations. It is characterized by a shorter development life cycle, reducing the time between product changes and the integration of those changes in the production environment. With this shorter turnaround time, DevOps provides continuous integration and continuous deployment (CI/CD) within a faster and more reliable workflow.

Many organizations are changing their culture to shift IT staff to a DevOps structure. This impacts Linux sysadmins immensely. You can expect to work more closely with developers, deploy incremental changes quickly and often, and experience greater use of automation tools. The shared ownership between dev teams and ops teams provides robust support, along with rapid feedback to identify and correct issues.

DevSecOps integrates security practices to the entire development life cycle instead of treating security as a separate component. DevSecOps was discussed in an earlier section.

Linux administrators may immediately begin working with DevOps practices while using automation and orchestration tools, such as Ansible and Chef, or by using version control and repository software, such as Git.

Continuous Integration/Continuous Deployment and its Use Cases

Continuous Integration/Continuous Deployment (CI/CD) is a process for managing the software-development life cycle that automates feature integration and testing. It is a method used in DevOps to ensure quick and reliable changes to software.

While the CI portion of the acronym is Continuous Integration, the CD portion may be defined as Continuous Delivery or Continuous Deployment. The two steps differ slightly—Continuous Delivery pertains to uploading complete code to a repository, and Continuous Deployment pertains to deployment of that code from the repository to projection. For the most part, the two terms are synonymous.

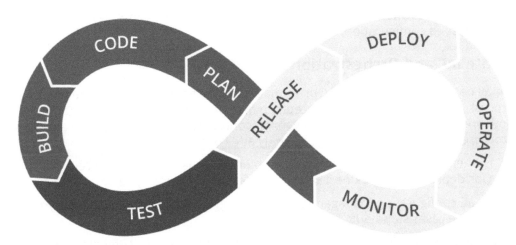

The CI/CD loop. Software development can be viewed as always in motion with no set ending, only moving on to the next phase of the process.

Once the appropriate DevOps tools are in place, how might an organization use CI/CD, and what is the role of a Linux administrator? You might be involved in the deployment of container images to a cloud service provider or the in-house development and deployment of a Python application. Your organization might use CI/CD to publish websites to internal webservers.

Linux administrators are traditionally part of the "operations" team denoted in the DevOps phrase. You're responsible for ensuring resource availability, performance, and configuration and overseeing any tasks related to the infrastructure. However, with the advent of DevOps, you'll work more closely with developers on these tasks, supporting some of the dev team's functions while handing off control of some ops roles to programmers.

To fulfill this role successfully, you'll need to familiarize yourself with automation and orchestration tools, as well as with version control.

 Automation, orchestration, and version control are covered in the remaining sections of this Lesson.

Infrastructure as Code Concepts

Infrastructure as Code (IaC) refers to the idea of centrally managing configuration files with strict version control. IaC also automates the deployment of configuration file changes. Because Linux relies on text-based configuration files, it is perfectly suited to Infrastructure as Code management.

IaC replaces manual configurations with automated practices. When configuration changes need to be implemented, such as updating the package manager repositories on a group of servers, a single configuration file is written, verified, and then automatically sent to each server, ensuring all targeted servers receive the same settings. This automation, which can work with both on-premises and cloud-based infrastructures, provides several benefits. Settings are consistent, with less configuration drift, which is especially welcome with security configurations. Automation allows changes to be rapidly implemented, addressing zero-day vulnerabilities or agile service management.

IaC management tools operate in either declarative or iterative modes.

- **Declarative**: DevOps team defines the desired configuration, and the tool accomplishes the settings.

- **Iterative**: DevOps team defines the specific commands necessary to implement the desired configuration.

Relate IaC and Orchestration to DevOps

It may be useful to think of DevOps as managing the software development process, while IaC uses similar concepts to manage system configuration tasks. Both are similar in that they rely on version control, establish testing and validation processes, and implement changes quickly and consistently.

IaC is often used by Linux administrators to provide the infrastructure required by DevOps deployments, making it part of the development life cycle.

While IaC configuration management can be used for nearly any Linux deployment, several use cases stand out:

- Quickly and consistently creating test environments for new software, patching, and learning labs.

- Deploying fresh development environments free of artifacts or leftover configurations from previous projects.

- Rapid scaling of VMs in cloud environments.

Bootstrapping

Once the installation process is complete, the system is ready for its first boot. In the past, administrators would begin to manually configure security settings, install patches and software, create local user accounts, set the root password, and complete other post-install tasks. With the DevOps emphasis on automation, these settings and others are now typically managed by `cloud-init` scripts.

As the name suggests, one common use of these scripts is the deployment of cloud-based virtual machines. These deployments are often part of a larger orchestrated process that does not leave time for administrators to perform specific tasks on each VM. The `cloud-init` scripts automate such tasks, placing each VM in a repeatable, well-known baseline state.

File Types in IaC

Many DevOps and IaC tools rely on specific files to accomplish their goals. The two most common file types are YAML and JSON. The two file types implement similar solutions, though YAML is often preferred for its simplicity and flexibility. As a Linux administrator, you will likely work with both files at some point.

JSON (JavaScript Object Notation) files are characterized by being easy for both humans and machines to process, making them ideal for passing instructions. JSON files use the .json file extension, and they use two structures. The first, name/value pairs, associates a name with one or more values, while the second, value list, outlines specific values to be used. There are many name types, including object, record, or array. Values may be a list or sequence.

YAML (YAML Ain't Markup Language) is another language commonly used for configuration files. Like JSON, it is easily read by both humans and machines. YAML files are organized by list or map. YAML is very strict on syntax, including the careful use of white space (spaces). YAML files use the .yaml file extension.

Many automation tools can consume YAML files, including Ansible and Kubernetes.

Kubernetes manages container clusters. Ansible is a robust orchestration solution. Ansible is discussed later in this lesson; Kubernetes is covered in the next lesson.

Review Activity:

Infrastructure as Code

Answer the following questions:

1. **How would an organization's change to DevOps management impact Linux administrators?**

2. **How does IaC contribute to increased system security?**

3. **Differentiate between declarative and iterative IaC management tools.**

Topic 14B

Implement Orchestration

 EXAM OBJECTIVES COVERED
3.4 Summarize common infrastructure as code technologies.

One of the tenets of DevOps is reducing human intervention. By automating tasks, DevOps hopes to reduce errors and ensure consistency. Individual tasks are automated, and combinations of automated tasks are orchestrated into pipelines that quickly respond to scalability requirements. Tied to orchestration, which is usually used for provisioning, is configuration management, which is primarily establishing the desired settings on the system. Many tools exist to do this, including Ansible, Chef, Puppet, and others.

Orchestration Concepts

DevOps emphasizes task completion without human intervention. Like scripting, orchestration and automation offer benefits that include consistent configurations, repeatable deployments, greater efficiency, fewer errors, and nonmanual scalability based on thresholds.

Orchestration enables the deployment of Infrastructure as Code configuration files. In the previous section, the example of a software-package-repository configuration was given. Once the configuration file (for example, a YAML, JSON, or plaintext file) is written, it can be integrated into an orchestration process that ensures the settings are enforced.

Compare Automation versus Orchestration

Orchestration includes two parts: automation and orchestration itself.

Automation uses a script or other engine to accomplish a single task without human intervention. One example of an automated task is the scheduled execution of a backup script. Another example is the deployment of a fully configured virtual machine (on-premises or in the cloud).

The important aspect of automation is that one task is completed.

 "Human intervention" might mean that an administrator initiates the process via a command (such as running a script) or that a particular environment threshold is met, causing the system to kick off the automated process.

Orchestration refers to a series of automated tasks that, when combined, result in a complete solution.

For example, here are five common administrative tasks. Each of these is individually automated:

1. Recognize the need for an additional database server.

2. Deploy a VM.

3. Install and replicate a MariaDB database application.

4. Enable all necessary services, and configure the firewall.

5. Make the database VM available to consumers.

However, as automated tasks, they are still initiated individually, resulting in five distinct processes. Orchestration takes the five individual tasks and consolidates them into a single event—the deployment of a fully-configured database server ready for consumers.

The important aspect of orchestration is that a series of tasks are combined into a single event that executes without human intervention.

Configuration Management

Automation and orchestration tasks are also related to configuration management, or the process of ensuring systems are configured to match security and performance requirements. IT departments have long attempted to maintain standardized settings across servers, but configuration management takes that goal to a new level through integration automation.

It's worth pointing out that configuration management via orchestration is different from provisioning via orchestration. Provisioning refers to deployment tasks, while configuration relates to defining settings after the deployment process is complete. Some organizations select one tool for provisioning and a different tool for configuration management.

Consistent configuration management is essential to avoid undocumented or unapproved changes that may result in security breaches or downtime.

Understand Agent and Agentless Solutions

There are many configuration management tools available to Linux administrators. One differentiating factor is whether those tools rely on pre- or post-installed **agent** software. There are advantages and disadvantages to both implementations. Sysadmins should investigate which type of software is best suited to an organization's needs.

Compare Orchestration Utilities

Common orchestration tools include Ansible, Puppet, Chef, SaltStack, and Terraform. Each has its own attributes and benefits. Organizations select orchestration tools based on criteria such as comfort with particular languages (for example, many teams are more familiar with Python than Ruby), agent versus agentless topologies, container support, and cross-platform support for Windows and macOS.

Ansible

Attributes of Ansible	Benefits of Ansible
Common for Red Hat Enterprise Linux deployments	Cross-platform configuration (though Ansible itself runs on Linux)
Many orchestration management tools	Configuration files are relatively easy to read and author
Agentless	Can configure containers, physical or virtual servers, and those servers may be on-premises or cloud-based
Can use declarative or imperative methods	
Stores configurations in reusable modules	
Relies on Python	
YAML configuration files	

 Ansible's management platform is hosted on Linux. However, Ansible can manage the configuration of Windows target systems.

Puppet

Attributes of Puppet	Benefits of Puppet
Enables orchestration and DevOps processes	Cross-platform configuration
Enterprise and open-source versions	Only applies a configuration if the settings would change the system (idempotency)
Uses reusable/shareable modules to contain specific automation tasks	Can configure containers and physical or virtual servers, and those servers may be on-premises or cloud-based
Agentless	
Declarative language	
Recognizes configuration files in Bash, Python, Ruby, YAML, and PowerShell	

Chef

Attributes of Chef	Benefits of Chef
Three components: • Chef Workstation for management instructions • Chef Server for distribution • Chef Nodes (target systems)	Cross-platform configuration
Uses recipes to store execution instructions and cookbooks to maintain recipe combinations for reuse	Reusable configurations
Chef uses both declarative and imperative methods	Can configure physical or virtual servers, either on-premises or cloud-based
Agent Uses the Ruby programming language	

SaltStack

Attributes of SaltStack	Benefits of SaltStack
Event-driven automation	Cross-platform configuration
Agent and agentless options	Can configure containers and physical or virtual servers, and those servers may be on-premises or cloud-based
Python and YAML	
Reusable configuration template called a state	
Imperative ordering and declarative configuration	

Terraform

Attributes of Terraform	Benefits of Terraform
Agentless	Cross-platform
Declarative language	Incremental execution to only update changed items
Uses Terraform configuration language	Focused on configuration more than provisioning
Primary/secondary topology	

 Note that Terraform's own term for their topology design has been deprecated.

Review Activity:

Orchestration

Answer the following questions:

1. How does orchestration provide scalability?

2. Differentiate between orchestration and automation.

3. Why might an organization select one orchestration tool over another?

Topic 14C

Manage Version Control with Git

EXAM OBJECTIVES COVERED
3.3 Given a scenario, perform basic version control using Git.
3.4 Summarize common infrastructure as code technologies.

If automation and configuration management relies on files that store settings and provisioning details, then it becomes important to manage those files carefully. This is another example of sysadmins borrowing a developer standard by using the Git service for version control. The files relied upon by Linux itself, or Ansible, Chef, Puppet, and other provisioning tools, may be stored in central repositories accessed, edited, and updated by many people. Git allows the tracking of changes and version control by using a simple but robust set of commands.

Git Concepts

Open-source software development, script management, and IaC are all file-based solutions. As such, proper management of files is critical. Many proprietary version-control methods exist, but in 2005, Linux Torvalds (the creator of Linux) released **Git**, a free and open-source version-control system. Since then, Git has become the de facto standard for version control.

Git excels at tracking and integrating changes, especially in the context of large, distributed software-development projects where many programmers work on different aspects of the same application. In addition to increased speed and higher levels of file integrity, Git offers support for nonlinear and collaborative development, making it useful across a number of different fields.

While Git is aimed at developers, it works for other version-control scenarios, including authoring books and articles, outlining tutorials, developing recipes, creating music sheets, and more.

There are many uses for Git, and those uses are not just for developers. Here are four use cases, three of which apply directly to Linux sysadmins.

Git Use Case: Standardized Configuration Files

You manage 15 identical Linux servers. Each server is remotely administered via SSH connections, and you must ensure the SSH daemon's configuration is identical on each server. You can maintain a copy of this (and other) configuration files in a Git repository. If you make changes to the file, the changes are stored in Git and can easily be copied to all 15 servers.

Git Use Case: Infrastructure as Code

You can use Git as a repository for standardized automation and orchestration files to manage server and network device configurations.

Ansible Server can pull configuration files from a Git repository. This enables you to ensure valid files are available to all Ansible servers, even if they exist in isolated sections of the network.

Git Use Case: Scripts

You can create a centralized script repository available to all sysadmins.

Systems administrators typically have a large library of custom scripts carefully developed over time. A single script repository provides a place to share, update, and manage these scripts, enabling significantly more collaboration.

Git Use Case: Development Projects

You can centrally manage collaborative and distributed development projects, and you can implement robust version control.

The original design of Git was targeted to groups of developers working collaboratively on projects that needed to track changes and maintain correct versions of source code. However, in-house development teams benefit from Git as much as teams distributed around the world.

 Git recently renamed a key concept in code management. The "master" branch is now called the "main" branch.

Use Git to Manage Code

To get started with Git, use an available package manager to install the `git` package. You will need a directory to serve as the local storage location for your project. Initialize a Git repository, and begin working with the Git subcommands.

Git Repositories

The core component of Git is the Git repository. This is a storage area where versions of code and related files are stored. Version control is managed within this local directory. The repository may be stored on a single developer's workstation, or this repository may be centrally stored and then cloned to the developer's workstation. Organizations may choose to have a centralized Git repository on-premises or to use an online solution like GitHub. A centralized repository is not required, however.

The git Command

The `git` command is used to manage Git repositories. Using `git`, you can create a repository, add files to the repository, commit changes to the repository, pull down files from another repository, and much more. You can perform these tasks by issuing various subcommands within the larger `git` command.

The syntax of the `git` command is `git [options] {subcommand}`

There are a number of subcommands used with `git`, and the most often-used are listed in the table below.

Subcommand for the git Command	Purpose
`config`	Set options for a repository or Git users, as well as other global options.
`init`	Create a Git repository, or reinitialize an existing one.
`clone`	Create a working copy of an existing repository.
`add`	Add files to be tracked by the Git repository.
`commit`	Update the Git repository with your changes, creating a "snapshot" of that repository.
`status`	Display the status of the repository.
`branch`	Manage branches, or pointers to specific repository snapshots after committing changes.
`merge`	Integrate changes from one branch into a "main" branch.
`rebase`	Rewrite Git history for a cleaner, more linear merge history.
`pull`	Acquire and merge changes made to other repositories and branches into the local working copy.
`push`	Upload a local working copy of a repository to a remote repository, such as a centralized repository.
`log`	Display the changes made to a local repository.
`checkout`	Switch to a specific branch to work with.
`tag`	Add a label to a repository's history, often to mark significant versions or releases.
`show`	Display information on the current branch's status.

Many of these subcommands are used in context in the following examples.

You're probably most likely to use `clone`, `add`, `commit`, `pull`, `push`, and `status` the most often.

The `merge` and `rebase` subcommands are slightly different. The `merge` subcommand integrates changes into the main branch, and these changes are tracked in the Git history. The `rebase` subcommand accomplishes the same task, but it rewrites the Git history to make it appear all changes took place in a serial fashion, when in reality they may have occurred in parallel by multiple developers. The goal is a more streamlined history that is easier to review and understand.

Git in Practice

Here are three common scenarios for using Git. The first scenario creates a local Git repository and adds files to manage. The second scenario builds on the initial design by adding branching. The final scenario covers a more collaborative situation.

Local Git Repository

In this example, you will establish a local Git repository for your code or configuration files and begin a project. Finally, you'll make an initial commit.

1. Configure global settings, including a user name and email address:

   ```
   $ git config --global user.name 'User'
   $ git config --global user.email 'user@domain.
   tld'
   ```

2. Create a directory where your project will reside. Change into that directory, and then initialize it with the `git init` command to designate it as a Git repository:

   ```
   $ mkdir /dev-project
   $ git init /dev-project
   ```

3. Add project files to the repository. These are the files that make up the actual development project you are storing and controlling with Git. Just as you have seen with Linux configuration files, in development projects you want to work with copies of the project, not the original file itself. That makes it far easier to roll back to the original project in the event of a mistake.

   In Git, you create a working copy by using the `clone` subcommand:

   ```
   $ git clone /dev-project
   ```

4. Add project files to the Git tracking system. This causes Git to begin tracking changes to the file. Use the `add` subcommand and the name of the file(s) to track:

   ```
   $ git add {file name}
   ```

5. Consider tagging commits at major release points by using the `tag` subcommand and the `-a` option:

   ```
   $ git tag -a v1.1 -m "Version 1.1"
   ```

6. Commit the changes to take a snapshot of your project. At this stage, you should also enter a message that summarizes what changes you made. Make sure these messages are clear:

   ```
   $ git commit -m 'Initial commit'
   ```

7. Retrieve the current status of changed files. If three files were being worked on for a particular step in the project but only two were ready to be committed at this time, they would show up here as "added" but not yet committed. The commit process could be executed once edits to all three files are complete:

```
$ git status
```

Continue working with your files, making commits whenever you want to differentiate the updated version against the most recent previous commit.

Branching

Optionally, you can work with Git branches. In this example, you'll work with an existing repository that another Git user has established. You'll create a new branch to work with and merge changes into the original main branch. The goal is to create a new code branch, make modifications, and then merge the code branch back into the main branch.

1. Create a branch of the main copy of the code:

```
$ git branch newbranch
```

2. Make changes, and then integrate (`merge`) those changes back into the main branch. This integrates the changes, creating a new-and-improved version of the original. At this point, the branch that was being used to create the changes can be removed. The changes are now a part of the main branch:

```
$ git merge newbranch
```

Collaboration

In this example, you'll pull another Git user's branch and push changes to the remote repository. You can also view what other changes have been made by using the git log command. This is an example process flow for collaborating with other developers using Git.

1. Pull other developers' proposed changes and merge them into the local repository (the local working copy):

```
$ git pull otherbranch
```

2. Push your own changes to a remote repository. A development or IaC environment will usually include a central repository, perhaps in the cloud, and each developer has their own local copy of the repository. Changes made locally can then be uploaded to the central repository using the `git push` command:

```
$ git push <remote repository> mybranch
```

3. See what changes were merged and what other actions were taken on the repository. Run the `git log` command inside the project directory. For example, to see all of the commits in the last 10 days, type:

```
$ git log --since=10.days
```

You can use this information to troubleshoot any issues introduced in configuration files, scripts, or any other data tracked by the repository.

4. Navigate or switch between branches of a project by using the `git checkout` command. This enables developers to focus their attention on different branches of the same project:

```
$ git checkout specificbranch
```

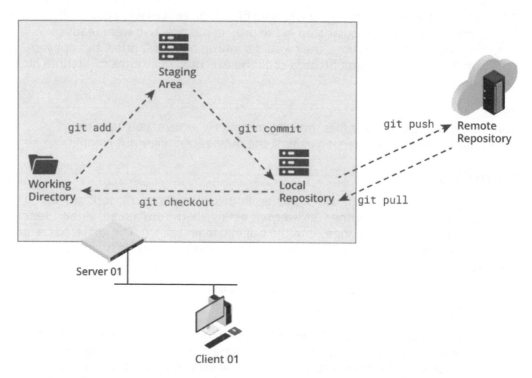

An example Git process flow. Users operate within the working directory, the staging area, the local repository, and a remote repository with various git *commands. (Images © 123RF.com.)*

Submit a git pull Request

Recall that an important part of Git is collaboration. Contributors to a project can make a git pull request that asks project maintainers to review suggested code modifications and merge them if approved. For example, a developer might be working on an open-source project that uses Git to maintain code. The developer has created a few components for the project and is ready to integrate one component with the existing code. The developer makes a git pull request to the project maintainers, who may then elect to merge the suggested changes.

The .gitignore File

You can create a .gitignore file in the Git repository. The file's purpose is to identify files that should be ignored during a commit action. For example, you may have a README.txt file or a project To-Do.txt list that does not need to be committed as part of the project but does reside in the project directory for convenience. These files are identified in the project's .gitignore file.

The *.git/ directory contains all the files Git uses to manage version control for your project. It is a single location where Git stores all of its information. The directory resides in the project directory and is created with the git init command.

Review Activity:

Git

Answer the following questions:

1. If an IT department stored all scripts written by sysadmin in a Git repository, what benefits might the department realize?

2. What is the purpose of tagging in Git?

3. Where might Git repositories be stored?

4. In what circumstances might you submit a Git pull request?

Lesson 14

Summary

Linux administrators are often deeply immersed in DevOps practices and Infrastructure as Code configuration-management projects. Linux benefits greatly from these approaches and lends itself to supporting and receiving configurations from tools such as Ansible and Git.

Command Reference Table

This list of commands and their associated syntax can also be found in Appendix B.

Command	Syntax	Purpose	Covered in
git	git [options] {subcommand}	Manage Git repositories.	Lesson 14, Topic C

Lesson 15

Managing Containers in Linux

LESSON INTRODUCTION

Containers provide fast, scalable deployments of applications on-premises and in the cloud. Administrators often orchestrate container deployments to provide consistency and agility. Containers virtualize at a higher layer than traditional virtualization solutions that support virtual machines do. Container solutions begin with a container engine that provides virtualization functionality. Next are the files that make up containers, followed by the running containers.

For all the focus on container deployments, it's important to recognize that more traditional hardware virtualization still has its place, and Linux administrators will frequently support virtualized devices.

Lesson Objectives

In this lesson, you will:

- Understand container basics.

- Deploy containers.

- Understand virtualization concepts.

Topic 15A

Understand Containers

EXAM OBJECTIVES COVERED
3.2 Given a scenario, perform basic container operations.
3.5 Summarize container, cloud, and orchestration concepts.

Containerization is a form of virtualization, but it is significantly different from VMs. Container engines virtualize at the OS layer rather than the hardware layer. A container holds a single application and everything it needs to run. This narrow focus allows containers to excel with technologies such as microservices.

Basic Container Concepts

Containers offer a different form of virtualization than the one offered by **virtual machines (VM)**. A **container** is a complete, portable solution. It contains the application code, runtime, libraries, settings, and other components—everything needed for the software to run. This complete package is portable and will run on any platform hosting a container solution. Containerized software developed on a Linux workstation runs the same way on a Windows cloud-based VM. Containers are typically quick, reliable, and lightweight. They share a single OS (usually Linux) and provide a single function.

Hardware virtualization and virtual machines are covered later in this lesson.

Containers may be deployed on physical, on-premises servers or in a cloud infrastructure. They can even be used on individual workstations. Hosting containers in the cloud provides all the usual cloud benefits: scalability, high availability, and quick deployments.

Container vs. VMs

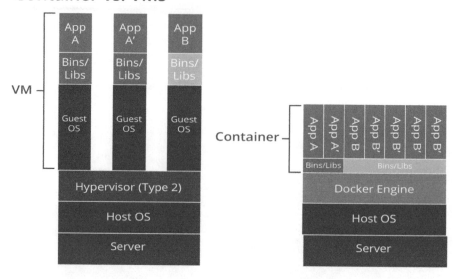

Comparing virtual machines and containers.

Identify Container Engines

Container engines are pieces of software that process user requests and run one or more containers on top of a single operating system. Selecting and installing a container engine is the first step in container deployment. Container engines use the Open Container Initiative (OCI) standard for container-image formats.

> *The Open Container Initiative (OCI) is a governance body managing open-container formats among developers of container technologies.*

Common container engines for Linux include Docker, rkt, runc, and containerd.

Images versus Containers

There are three components to a container solution. The first is a configuration file, the second is an image, and the final piece is a running container.

Using the Docker container engine as an example, the process begins with a Dockerfile, the configuration file for Docker images. The Docker container engine processes this text file. The file contains everything necessary for the container to function: source code, libraries, tools, and dependencies. Think of this file as a specifications sheet or a set of instructions.

Next, those instructions are turned into a **container image**. The image is a template for how containers should look when running. The image is built from the instructions provided in the Dockerfile. For a Docker container image, you would use the `docker build` command.

Finally, containers are run, executing instances of a container image. Many identical containers can be spawned from a single image. For a Docker container, you would use the `docker run` command. Note that this only constructs the container, it does not run it.

Containers cannot run without an image defining their configuration, and images must be built from the configuration file (a Dockerfile in the above example).

Containers are stateless, meaning that any changes to the container or applications running in it are not preserved. Persistent changes to the container occur via configuration file updates.

Review Activity:

Containers

Answer the following questions:

1. **What are three advantages of containers?**

2. **Differentiate between an image and a container.**

3. **What makes a container stateless?**

Topic 15B

Deploy Containers

EXAM OBJECTIVES COVERED

3.2 Given a scenario, perform basic container operations.
3.5 Summarize container, cloud, and orchestration concepts.

Getting started with containers only requires a container engine and one or more images. Images can be pulled from container registries or created fresh on your Linux system. Container engines have many commands to create, destroy, start, stop, and otherwise manage containers to create robust, networked, and interlinked environments.

The first portion of this section looks at container operations, such as building and starting containers. The next part covers management tasks and commands. The topic finishes by examining container registries.

Basic Container Operations

Operating a container starts with an image, and the `docker` command handles basic image-related tasks. Using `docker`, you can gather information about available images housed in a given repository, retrieve (pull) or upload (push) images to a repository, or run containers from image files.

Use the docker Command

The `docker` command is the primary management command for Docker containers. The command has many subcommands to focus its functionality.

The syntax of the `docker` command is `docker subcommand {options} {arguments}`

Here are some common subcommands used for container operations.

Subcommand for the docker Command	Purpose
`info`	Display system-wide information.
`port`	List port mappings for the specified container.
`pull`	Pull an image from a registry.
`push`	Upload an image to a registry.
`ps`	List containers.
`rm`	Remove containers.
`rmi`	Remove images.
`run`	Run a command in a container.

Configure Container Image Operations

The following steps cover the major deployment steps, using Docker as the example container engine and the `docker` command.

First, create a storage location to house the files used for containers and change into the directory:

```
$ mkdir containers
$ cd containers
```

To pull an image from a registry such as Docker Hub, the syntax is:

```
docker pull {image-name}
```

For example, to pull the Alpine Linux image, type:

```
$ sudo docker pull alpinelinux/docker-alpine
```

```
labadmin@Udesktop:~$ sudo docker pull alpine
Using default tag: latest
latest: Pulling from library/alpine
df9b9388f04a: Pull complete
Digest: sha256:4edbd2beb5f78b1014028f4fbb99f3237d9561100b68
81aabbf5acce2c4f9454
Status: Downloaded newer image for alpine:latest
docker.io/library/alpine:latest
labadmin@Udesktop:~$ ▮
```

Pulling an Alpine Linux image from a registry.

 This scenario has you using a very lightweight Linux distribution named Alpine. This is a very common container image to start with.

Display the image to confirm it was pulled:

```
$ sudo docker images
```

```
labadmin@Udesktop:~$ sudo docker images
REPOSITORY     TAG        IMAGE ID        CREATED          SIZE
ubuntu         latest     825d55fb6340    43 hours ago     72.8MB
alpine         latest     0ac33e5f5afa    2 days ago       5.57MB
```

Confirm the image is in place, and view some image details.

Recall that the image is a static template, and the container is a running instance of that image. Run a container from the image:

```
$ sudo docker run {image-name}
```

However, if you need to work within the container itself, start it interactively by adding the -it options. In this case, you will have a Bash shell:

```
$ sudo docker run -it {image-name} bash
```

You now have a running container. The Alpine image doesn't do a lot, but it serves as a starting point. It can be further customized with additional applications.

Check the status of containers on the system by typing:

```
$ sudo docker ps -a
```

```
labadmin@Udesktop:~$ sudo docker ps -a
CONTAINER ID    IMAGE       COMMAND      CREATED          STATUS
                PORTS       NAMES
4b1a1260f538    alpine      "/bin/sh"    26 seconds ago   Exited (0) 2
5 seconds ago               loving_wright
```

Review the status of containers present on the system.

Create a Customized Image

The Alpine Linux image is a good place to start, but what about customizing images? You can write a Dockerfile that specifies what additional commands should be executed when building the image. It's very common to install software into the image this way. Create a new Dockerfile, and specify a package to install.

First, open a text editor and create a Dockerfile containing the following lines:

```
FROM alpinelinux/docker-alpine
RUN apt-get install -y nano
```

```
FROM alpinelinux/docker-alpine
RUN apt-get install -y nano
```

Create a customized image.

Alpine Linux relies on the APT package manager.

The FROM line indicates which initial image will be used. The RUN line defines any commands that will be executed. In this example, RUN indicates that the nano text editor will be installed via the apt-get command.

Next, build the image. For Docker images, use the docker build command to build the image from the Dockerfile. You can add the --tag option to provide the image with a descriptive name.

```
$ sudo docker build --tag alpine
```

Verify the image was created by displaying all container images:

```
$ sudo docker images
```

```
labadmin@Udesktop:~$ sudo docker images
REPOSITORY    TAG       IMAGE ID       CREATED        SIZE
ubuntu        latest    825d55fb6340   43 hours ago   72.8MB
alpine        latest    0ac33e5f5afa   2 days ago     5.57MB
```

Output of the `images` *command, displaying two container images—one in an Ubuntu repository and one in an Alpine repository.*

Administer Containers

The `docker container` command manages attributes for specified containers. The syntax for the `docker container` command is:

```
docker container subcommand {options} {arguments}
```

Some of the more common subcommands for `docker container` are listed in the table below.

Subommand for the docker container Command	Purpose
`start`	Start a stopped container.
`stop`	Stop a started container.
`restart`	Restart a container.
`attach`	Attach local STDIN, STDOUT, STDERR to a container.
`inspect`	Display detailed information on a container.
`logs`	Display container logs.
`ls`	List existing containers.

One of the first items you must know to manage running containers is the container ID. This value is assigned to the container when it starts. To display running containers, including their container ID, type:

```
$ sudo docker container ls
```

It may be necessary to restart the container. Now that you have the container ID, type:

```
$ sudo docker restart {container-ID}
```

To stop a running container, type:

```
$ sudo docker stop {container-ID}
```

Container Registries

Container images are usually centrally stored in repositories known as registries. Registries are an easy way to share images within a community, whether that community is a single organization or the entire world. Registries are either public, meaning that they are available on the Internet to anyone, or private and available on a restricted network only to authorized users.

Many public registries exist. Docker Hub is very common, but Google, AWS, Microsoft, and many other organizations also host registries.

Container administrators upload images to a registry via a `push` command, while downloads from a registry use a `pull` command. The exact syntax depends on the container engine.

Container registries are a critical part of the DevOps infrastructure, enabling CI/CD by providing a standardized and accessible location from which automation and orchestration tools can pull images without human intervention.

Container Persistent Storage

Containers are stateless, meaning that their settings and data are not preserved when the container is destroyed. The settings and data are not available when the container is next run, either. All container configuration is stored in the configuration file (for example, the Dockerfile).

Depending on the application running in a container, it may be necessary to provide the application with access to stored data. It could also be useful to allow the containerized application to persist or store data for other services to utilize. Either way, container persistent storage refers to providing the container access to data not built into it by the build process. This may be especially important in orchestrated environments that automatically scale up the number of available containers depending on demand.

Container Networks

Containers receive network access via network drivers. These drivers are configured to match network- and container-communication requirements.

The various container network drivers provide different functions for administering containers:

- **host**: Networking between the container and host with the use of the host's network access.

- **overlay**: Connectivity between containers run by different daemons.

- **bridge**: Standard configuration for standalone containers that need network access.

- **none**: Disables networking for the container, providing isolation.

Network drivers such as **overlay** and **bridge** rely on **Network Address Translation (NAT)** to track IP addresses between the containers, hosts, and remote services.

Orchestration Concepts

Initial container deployments tend to be straightforward. A container engine is selected and installed, and a few new containers are deployed via images. Over time, however, as the containers host more complex applications and as the container topology scales, the environment needs more advanced features.

Tools such as Kubernetes provide orchestration and management features that increase the reliability and features of the simpler container environments.

Kubernetes Benefits and Use Cases

Kubernetes is a container orchestration solution. It's used to support dynamic, scalable, and intertwined container environments. The main component of a Kubernetes deployment is a pod. A pod consists of one or more containers; however, Kubernetes manages the pods rather than the individual containers within them.

The two types of pods are singlenode, housing only one container, and multicontainer, which houses more than one. Single-container pods usually house a simple application or **microservice**, with little reliance on external resources.

Multicontainer pods may have basic microservice application containers that also require specialized or complex network connectivity. Different types of containers playing specific roles may exist in the same pod. These specialized containers that facilitate communications are called sidecars (proxies), and they are part of a service mesh topology.

Some organizations will grow beyond the multicontainer environments provided by Docker. Docker builds multicontainer clusters by using a tool named Compose. Compose files can be translated into something Kubernetes can understand, allowing for an easy transition into a larger orchestrated-container environment.

Container Service Mesh

A **service mesh** is a dedicated infrastructure layer managed by code that provides service-to-service interaction in a container environment. It includes a sidecar proxy for each microservice that enables communication as the environment scales. The sidecar exists in the pod along with the application container.

Service meshes provide load balancing and traffic control benefits, as well as service monitoring and discovery.

Service mesh proxies rely on sidecar containers that work alongside container applications to enable monitoring, service discovery, and service communication. The sidecar containers support the containers that actually run the application.

The pod may house multiple containers and access various services outside the pod. To facilitate this, a special container can be configured to handle communications on behalf of the rest of the containers in the pod. This is known as an ambassador container, and it is a specific type of service mesh proxy.

Review Activity:

Container Deployment

Answer the following questions:

1. **Differentiate between running a container with the docker run {image-name} command versus with the docker run -it {image-name} bash command option.**

2. **What are some advantages of a private image registry?**

3. **How does a container registry enable CI/CD?**

Topic 15C

Understand Virtualization Concepts

EXAM OBJECTIVES COVERED
3.5 Summarize container, cloud, and orchestration concepts.

Virtual machines rely on a layer that virtualizes hardware, whereas containers rely on a virtualized operating system. A hypervisor application provides this virtualization. VMs are an essential part of today's IT deployments because they provide better resource utilization, easier scalability, and high availability. They are commonly found in both on-premises and cloud environments in production and development servers, test environments, and learning labs.

Cloud environments are built on virtualization and can host VMs in their datacenters rather than on your organization's local hardware. This can be an attractive benefit as it offloads hardware support to the cloud service provider. This section looks at a few virtualization tools and commands a Linux sysadmin may encounter.

Virtual Machines

Virtual machines are configured much like standard physical systems. An amount of memory is allocated, storage is defined, processor access is granted, and networking is configured—all of these attributes enable the VM to participate on a network just like a traditional Linux server or workstation.

Virtual machines can host applications and services.

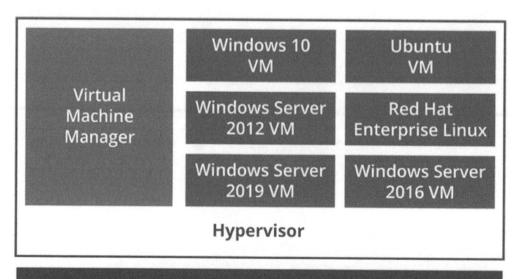

Diagram of a virtual machine configuration including a hardware layer, a hypervisor, guest VMs, and a virtual machine manager.

Virtualization Tools

Many **virtualization** host servers will run Linux without a graphical user interface. Such a configuration enables more hardware resources to be available to the virtual machines. Management of the virtual machines must then occur at the command-line. The common Linux virtualization engine is the **Kernel-based Virtual Machine (KVM)**.

The `virsh` command is an interactive shell to KVM virtual machines and includes the following subcommands.

Subcommand for the virsh Command	Purpose
`help`	Get help with the `virsh` command.
`list`	Display a list of recognized virtual machines.
`shutdown {VM}`	Gracefully shut down a virtual machine.
`start {VM}`	Start a virtual machine.
`reboot {VM}`	Reboot a virtual machine.
`create {XML file-name}`	Create a virtual machine from an XML file.
`save {VM} {file-name}`	Save the state of a virtual machine with the given file name.
`console {VM}`	Open a console to a virtual machine.

Other virtualization commands exist, including `virt-install`, which sysadmins can use to build virtual machines. The following example depicts the creation of a CentOS7 virtual machine from the command line using the `virt-install` command:

```
$ sudo virt-install --name=centos7-install
--vcpus=1 --memory=2048 --cdrom=/opt/CentOS-
7-x86_64-DVD-1804.iso --disk size=12 --os-
variant=rhel7
```

Recall that one interesting aspect of command-line commands is the ability to add them to a script. You could script the above VM deployment to automate the process, making the VM deployment fast and consistent.

```
[student@fedora ~]$ sudo virt-install --name=centos7-install --vcpus=1
--memory=2048 --cdrom=opt/CentOS-7-x86_64-DVD-1804.iso --disk size=12
--os-variant=rhel7
```

Using the virt-install command.

Linux virtualization solutions are built on top of libvirt, an application programming interface (API) that provides the software building blocks for developers to write their own virtualization solutions. Solutions can also be composed of a daemon and a management interface. Several **hypervisors**, including VMware ESXi, KVM, and QEMU, are all built using libvirt. It provides a solid foundation for Linux-based virtualization. For example, the `virsh` tool is a part of the libvirt API.

GNOME Virtual Machine Manager

The GNOME Virtual Machine Manager (VMM) utility can be used for managing connectivity to virtual machines. It enables the deployment, management, and removal of virtual machines using an intuitive graphical interface. Download and install the virt-manager package to begin using VMM.

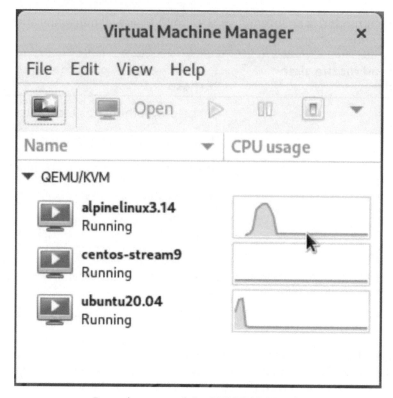

Example output of the GNOME VMM utility.

Virtual Networks

Virtualization also takes place at the network layer. Virtual machines (VMs) may have one or more **virtual network interface cards (vNICs)**. These vNICs are configured like physical NICs and are attached to virtual switches. Each virtual NIC has its own MAC address and IP address to permit the VM to participate on a physical or virtual network as an independent node. In addition, the VM can join a **Virtual Local Area Network (VLAN)**. Virtual switches are used to better manage network traffic.

Virtual machines can share a virtual bridge with the host device, which enables network access for the virtual machines. Virtual machines typically have four options for network access, each of which provides different operational functionality.

- **None**: As if the virtual machine has no NIC installed.

- **Local**: Network access only to other virtual machines on the same host.

- **Host-only**: Access only to the host computer but not to the physical network or Internet.

- **Bridged**: Access to both the physical network and the Internet.

Review Activity:

Virtualization

Answer the following questions:

1. **Differentiate between virtualization layers for VM virtualization versus container virtualization.**

2. **How might you automate a virtual machine deployment, and what command is used?**

3. **What is the purpose of the virtual bridge?**

Lesson 15
Summary

Containerization supports DevOps goals and provides an entirely new way of developing and supporting applications. Linux is the standard host for container engines, whether in the cloud or on-premises. Linux administrators need to understand the differences between containers and virtual machines and what software is necessary to support each.

Command Reference Table

This list of commands and their associated syntax can also be found in Appendix B.

Command	Syntax	Purpose	Covered in
`docker`	`docker subcommand {options} {arguments}`	The primary management command for Docker containers.	Lesson 15, Topic B
`docker pull`	`docker pull {image-name}`	Pull an image from a registry.	Lesson 15, Topic B
`docker container`	`docker container subcommand {options} {arguments}`	Manage attributes for specified containers.	Lesson 15, Topic B
`push`	*Exact syntax depends on the specific container engine.*	Upload images to a registry.	Lesson 15, Topic B
`pull`	*Exact syntax depends on the specific container engine.*	Download images from a registry.	Lesson 15, Topic B

Lesson 16

Installing Linux

LESSON INTRODUCTION

Most operating systems follow the same boot path; it's the utilities involved that vary. For Linux, the primary boot loader that manages the startup process is GRUB2. Once the system starts and the boot loader launches, it handles the process until the Linux kernel starts and takes over. GRUB2 has specific configuration requirements that involve assembling the main configuration file from a series of supporting configuration files.

When deploying Linux, you must first decide on a physical or virtual machine platform and then walk through a series of installation tasks that involve selecting source files, hardware configurations such as partitioning, and software. Once the installation is complete, you will manage post-installation tasks. These tasks consist of final security settings and updates.

Lesson Objectives

In this lesson, you will:

- Understand the Linux boot process.

- Modify boot settings.

- Deploy Linux.

Topic 16A

The Linux Boot Process

EXAM OBJECTIVES COVERED
1.1 Summarize Linux fundamentals.
2.1 Summarize the purpose and use of security best practices in a Linux environment.

The boot process consists of many steps, which begin with the hardware layer and move up through the BIOS, boot loader, Linux kernel, and authentication layers. Understanding this process is helpful for troubleshooting and performance tuning. The process requires many components, which this Topic covers.

Boot Sources

Installation files may be stored on various media and available from several sources. Most organizations will have a standard Linux distribution for deployment on internal systems.

Storage Disk

Typically the system BIOS/UEFI is configured to boot from the internal storage disk. Source files may have been copied to the disk from a remote source or from a currently installed operating system that you will replace.

USB

In this configuration, Linux would boot from a removable USB flash drive or storage disk that contains the Linux source files. The system BIOS may need to be adjusted to boot from USB storage rather than an internal storage disk or DVD drive. Typically, you must configure USB disks to be bootable.

Virtual Machine File

You can also boot from a preconfigured virtual machine configuration file specifying CPU, memory, storage, and network configurations. The hypervisor virtualization layer constructs the VM and boots it, initiating the installation from the storage media.

ISO Image

An **ISO image** is a system image, originally that of an optical disc. Today, it is a common file format for packaging and distributing images of operating systems that users can boot from to install the OS. Typically, you write the ISO image to an optical disc or USB thumb drive, insert the media into the computer, and instruct a boot environment like UEFI to boot from that media. ISOs are also commonly used to construct virtual machines.

PXE

Preboot Execution Environment (PXE) is a part of the UEFI standard that enables a client to retrieve the necessary boot loader and system files from a server over the network. The client configures UEFI to boot from PXE, and during the startup process, it will search for Dynamic Host Configuration Protocol (DHCP) servers that also act as PXE servers. Once the proper server is found, it transfers the necessary boot files to the client over the **Trivial File Transfer Protocol (TFTP)**.

HTTP and FTP

Clients can also acquire boot data over a network from content delivery protocols like **Hypertext Transfer Protocol (HTTP)** and **File Transfer Protocol (FTP)**. These are typically faster, more reliable, and more secure than the standard TFTP protocol used in PXE. Open-source implementations of PXE, like iPXE, extend PXE support to include these protocols.

Network File System

This is another network boot option. Rather than store system files on a local storage drive, a client will mount a **Network File System (NFS)** share as its root file system. The share must be prepared ahead of time and stored on an NFS server that the client can retrieve the files from. Therefore, the client does not store data locally, but rather stores it on the NFS server. DHCP, TFTP, and other network protocols communicate the necessary boot data in such an environment.

Begin the Boot Process

The boot process begins with the BIOS or UEFI configuration on the system's motherboard. Next, the bootloader starts and manages the next phase of the boot process, including the launch of the initrd. Finally, the operating system kernel loads along with drivers and modules. The kernel takes over the remaining steps of the boot process.

This section covers those steps in more detail.

BIOS/UEFI

The **Basic Input/Output System (BIOS)** is a standard for firmware interfaces stored on a computer motherboard's ROM chip. The BIOS firmware runs when the computer powers on, enabling it to test the various hardware components in a computer and run the **boot loader** to start the operating system. The BIOS has access to the ports used by basic hardware input devices like a mouse and keyboard. Users can also load up a BIOS interface instead of an operating system to make various hardware-level changes. BIOS was the dominant standard for home and enterprise computers for several decades.

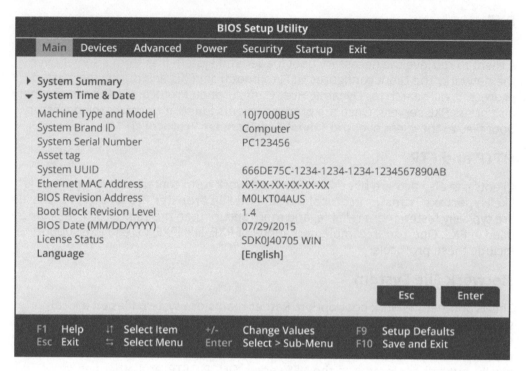

Example of a BIOS interface.

Unified Extensible Firmware Interface (UEFI) is newer firmware technology that has largely replaced BIOS by bringing with it several key advantages. UEFI runs faster than BIOS, can operate within a greater amount of memory, can access storage drives of currently unattainable sizes, can access more hardware types, and has improved security protections. Most modern motherboards, as well as the pre-assembled PCs that use them, ship with UEFI. The secure boot features of UEFI are critical.

Like BIOS, UEFI provides an environment to execute a boot loader and ultimately start up the operating system.

One secure boot feature that both BIOS and UEFI include is the ability to set a password. If this password is not provided at boot time, the system will not start. Since BIOS/UEFI firmware differs between hardware manufacturers, the process of setting this password is not consistent. However, most firmware places this password protection option in a "Security" or "Password" section.

The Boot Loader

Booting is starting or restarting a computer and loading an operating system for the user to access. A booting environment reads a small program stored in **read-only memory (ROM)**. This program then executes various operations in RAM that bootstrap the operating system and make it available for use.

A boot loader is a small program stored in ROM that loads the kernel from a storage device and then starts the operating system. A boot environment like BIOS reads the boot loader from ROM so that the boot loader can execute the necessary operations to begin the process.

Boot loaders can protect the boot process with a password to prevent unauthorized system startups. In addition, boot loaders can load more than one operating system into the computer's memory, but the user needs to select the desired operating system to use during boot.

The boot loader uses three main components that work together to load the operating system in stages.

1. The boot sector program is loaded by a boot environment on startup and has a fixed size of 512 bytes. Its main function is to load the second-stage boot loader; however, it can also load another sector or a kernel.

2. The second-stage boot loader loads the operating system and contains a kernel loader.

3. Finally, the boot loader installer controls the installation of drive sectors and can only be run when booting from a drive. It coordinates the activities of the boot sector and the boot loader.

 The most common Linux boot loader is GRUB2. Details and modifications to the GRUB2 boot loader are covered in a later section.

Load the Kernel

The initial ramdisk (initrd) refers to the root file system that is temporarily loaded into memory upon system boot. The initrd loads along with the kernel, which controls its functionality. The initrd enables the system to start in two phases. In the first phase, the system boots with the minimal set of modules required to load the main or the permanent root file system. In the second phase, when the main root file system is mounted, the previously mounted initrd file system is removed and the user-space boot process continues.

The initrd is useful because many potential variables can complicate the boot process. For example, the kernel needs to find and load the necessary device driver modules and the actual root file system itself. There's also the possibility that the root file system uses one of several advanced storage methods, like LVM or NFS, which has different mount requirements than a standard partition has. Rather than hardcode all of this behavior in the kernel and introduce bloat, the initrd's temporary root file system can handle these tasks.

The Linux **initrd image** is an archive file containing all the essential files required for booting the operating system. It can be built or customized to include additional modules, remove unnecessary modules, or update existing modules. Typically, the /boot directory stores this image.

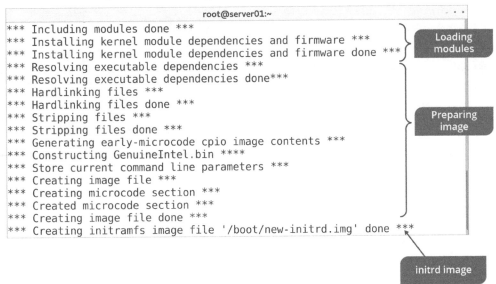

Creating a new initrd image.

The `mkinitrd` command creates the initrd image for preloading the kernel modules.

The syntax of the `mkinitrd` command is `mkinitrd [options] {initrd image name} {kernel version}`

The `mkinitrd` command uses several different options, collected in the table below.

Option for the mkinitrd Command	Purpose
`--preload+{module-name}`	Load a module in the initrd image before the loading of other modules.
`--with+{module-name}`	Load a module in the initrd image after the loading of other modules.
`-f`	Overwrite an existing initrd image file.
`--nocompress`	Disable the compression of the initrd image.

The following example creates an initrd image from the current kernel version and names the image `initrd-<kernel version>.img`

```
# mkinitrd /boot/initrd-$(uname -r).img
$(uname -r)
```

The `dracut` command can also generate an initramfs image, similar to how `mkinitrd` generates an initrd image. In fact, on some distributions, `mkinitrd` is a compatibility wrapper that calls the `dracut` command.

The following is an example of using the `dracut` command to create an initramfs image:

```
# dracut /boot/initramfs-$(uname -r).img
$(uname -r)
```

The /boot Directory

As defined by the **Filesystem Hierarchy Standard (FHS)**, the /boot/ directory contains files that facilitate the Linux boot process.

```
labadmin@Udesktop:~$ ls /boot
config-4.15.0-140-generic      memtest86+.elf
config-5.3.0-1034-azure        memtest86+_multiboot.bin
config-5.4.0-1043-azure        System.map-4.15.0-140-generic
grub                           System.map-5.3.0-1034-azure
initrd.img-4.15.0-140-generic  System.map-5.4.0-1043-azure
initrd.img-5.3.0-1034-azure    vmlinuz-4.15.0-140-generic
initrd.img-5.4.0-1043-azure    vmlinuz-5.3.0-1034-azure
memtest86+.bin                 vmlinuz-5.4.0-1043-azure
```

The /boot directory contents.

The /boot/grub directory contains configuration files for a type of boot loader called GRUB2. The /boot/grub2/ directory does likewise, but it does so for GRUB 2, which is an improved version.

The /boot/efi directory contains boot files for an EFI system partition (ESP), which is a required partition for systems that boot from UEFI. It contains boot loader, device driver, and system application files that are executed by UEFI. Boot loader files are typically named with an .efi extension.

The /boot/initramfs<kernel-version>.img file is an initramfs image, which is an alternative to initrd that uses different methods to do the same basic thing: initialize a temporary root file system on boot. Whereas initrd requires a special driver to be compiled into the kernel, initramfs does not. In addition, the initrd image is a block device formatted with a fixed-size file system, while the initramfs image is an archive file that can be sized dynamically.

/boot/vmlinuz-<kernel-version> is a compressed executable file that contains the Linux kernel itself. The boot loader loads this file into memory during the boot process to initialize the operating system. A related file is vmlinux, which is essentially the non-compressed version of the kernel used for debugging.

The Boot Process Summarized

The boot process is repeated each time your computer starts by loading the operating system from a storage device. It involves a series of sequential steps, including: BIOS/UEFI initialization, boot loader, kernel and initrd/initramfs initialization, and boot scripts.

The following is an example boot process that uses an initrd image.

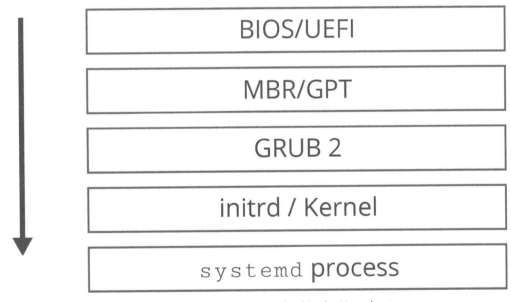

A high-level look at the components involved in the Linux boot process.

1. The processor checks for the BIOS/UEFI firmware and executes it.

2. BIOS/UEFI checks for bootable media from internal storage devices or peripherals like USB flash drives and DVD-ROMs. It locates a valid device to boot the system.

3. BIOS/UEFI loads the primary boot loader (probably GRUB2) from the MBR/GPT partition into memory. It also loads the partition table along with it.

4. GRUB2 prompts the user to select an operating system to boot. If the user does not respond, then the default operating system is booted.

5. The boot loader determines the kernel and locates the corresponding kernel binary. It then uploads the respective initrd image into memory and transfers control of the boot process to the kernel.

6. The kernel configures the available hardware drivers, including processors, I/O subsystems, and storage devices. It decompresses the initrd image and mounts it to load the necessary drivers. If the system implemented any virtual devices, such as LVM or software RAID, then they are initialized.

7. The kernel mounts the main root partition and releases unused memory. The systemd program runs to set up the user environment. It becomes process ID 1.

8. The systemd program searches for the `default.target` file, which contains details about the services to start. It mounts the file system based on the `/etc/fstab` file or .mount files and begins the process of starting services. On most systems, the selection is either `multi-user.target` or `graphical.target`.

9. If graphical mode is selected, then a display manager starts and the login window is displayed on the screen.

10. The user enters a user name and password to log in to the system.

11. The system authenticates the user. If the user is valid, then various profile files are executed.

12. The shell starts, and the system is ready for the user.

Review Activity:

Linux Boot Process

Answer the following questions:

1. **Differentiate between the older system BIOS and the modern UEFI standards.**

2. **What is the role of the initrd?**

3. **What is the /boot/vmlinuz<kernel-version> file?**

Topic 16B

Modify Boot Settings

EXAM OBJECTIVES COVERED
1.1 Summarize Linux fundamentals.
4.5 Given a scenario, use systemd to diagnose and resolve common problems with a Linux system.

The boot loader program manages the startup process. It offers OS selection choices, loads the initrd file, and loads the kernel. The GRUB2 boot loader is found on most modern Linux distributions and is highly configurable. The configuration process is different from that of other services, so this section covers that process and the tools needed.

Identify GRUB2

The **GNU GRand Unified Bootloader (GNU GRUB)** is a boot loader developed by the GNU Project that became popular on Unix-like systems. It enables users to choose which operating system or kernel version to boot in a multi-platform environment. Although the original version of GRUB was the primary boot loader for Linux distributions, it had several limitations and was eventually phased out in favor of a newer version of GRUB. This original version is sometimes referred to as GRUB legacy.

GRUB2 is more than simply a newer version of GRUB; it is a complete redesign and rewrite of the legacy GRUB system. GRUB2 offers administrators more control over the boot process, boot devices, and boot behavior. In addition, it comes with several improvements, including:

- Support for non-x86 architecture platforms.

- Support for live booting (booting an OS from storage media and running the OS entirely in memory, without installation).

- Support for partition universally unique identifiers (UUID).

- Support for dynamically loading modules that extend GRUB's functionality.

- The ability to configure the boot loader through scripts.

- Rescue mode, which attempts to fix boot issues like corrupted or missing configurations.

- Support for custom graphical boot menus and themes.

Because of these improvements, GRUB2 has become the default boot loader on almost all modern Linux distributions.

The grub2-install Command

The `grub2-install` command installs the GRUB2 boot loader on a storage device. It copies GRUB2 files into the `/boot/grub2` directory and, on some platforms, installs GRUB2 into the boot sector. However, `grub2-install` applies to BIOS systems, not UEFI. To install GRUB2 on a UEFI system, use a package manager to install the grub2-efi package. Installing this package copies GRUB2 files onto the EFI system partition (ESP) in the `/boot/efi` directory.

The syntax of the `grub2-install` command is `grub2-install [options] [device name]`

You can use these options with the `grub2-install` command.

Option for the grub2-install Command	Purpose
`--modules {module-names}`	Preload the specified kernel modules with the GRUB2 boot loader.
`--install-modules {module-names}`	Install only the specified modules and their dependencies rather than the default of installing all available modules.
`--directory {directory-name}`	Install files from the specified directory rather than from the default.
`--target {target platform}`	Specify the target platform to install GRUB2 for rather than the platform that is currently running.
`--boot-directory {directory-name}`	Specify the boot directory to install GRUB2 files to rather than the default `/boot/` directory.
`--force`	Install GRUB2 regardless of detected issues.

 You will rarely need to actually install GRUB2; it's usually part of the operating system installation process.

Configure GRUB2

The GRUB2 boot loader is highly configurable. The grub.cfg file stores the configurations, though administrators don't edit this file directly. Instead, the `grub2-mkconfig` command is executed to reference multiple configuration files and assemble a correct grub.cfg file. Any mistakes to this file can cause boot errors on the system.

The grub.cfg File

The `grub.cfg` file is the main configuration file for the GRUB2 boot loader. On BIOS systems, it is located in the `/boot/grub2/` directory. On UEFI systems, it is located in the `/boot/efi/EFI/<distro>/` directory.

```
                               root@server01:~                        _ □ ✕
#
# DO NOT EDIT THIS FILE
#
# It is automatically generated by grub2-mkconfig using templates
# from /etc/grub.d and settings from /etc/default/grub
#

### BEGIN /etc/grub.d/00_header ###
set pager=1

if [ -s $prefix/grubenv ]; then
  load_env
fi
if [ "${next_entry}" ] ; then
   set default="${next_entry}"
   set next_entry=
   save_env next_entry
```

Contents generated by command

The `grub.cfg` *file.*

This file is an executable shell script. Don't edit this file directly, as it is generated using the `grub2-mkconfig` command that leverages configuration scripts stored elsewhere on the file system. This command is covered later in this section.

The `/etc/grub.d/` directory contains scripts used to build the main `grub.cfg` file. Each script provides various functions to GRUB2 and is numbered so that the scripts can execute in a sequence. It's usually not a good idea to edit the existing scripts in this directory. If you want to add a custom script, you can place it in this directory with a ##_ file name prefix, depending on the order you want the script to be executed. You can also add your script to the existing `40_custom` file so that it executes last by default.

Observe that the /etc/grub.d directory is stored in /etc, which normally stores system configurations. However, the grub.cfg file is stored in the /boot directory. Some portions of GRUB2 are stored in each location.

Customize the GRUB2 Boot Menu

The `/etc/grub.d/40_custom` file enables the customization of the menu presented to the user during the boot process. GRUB2 offers the user a menu of installed operating systems to choose from. This choice is useful for multi-boot scenarios (more than one operating system available on the computer), booting to different Linux kernels, or booting into a rescue mode.

You can customize the menu contents by editing the `/etc/grub.d/40_custom` file, enabling an administrator to specify the order of the menu choices, provide user-friendly names, and password-protect menu entries.

The /etc/default/grub File

The `/etc/default/grub` file contains GRUB2 display menu settings that are read by the `/etc/grub.d/` scripts and built into the `grub.cfg` file. `/etc/default/grub` enables you to change options such as how many seconds GRUB2 will wait before automatically selecting the default boot option, whether GRUB2 will order kernel versions in a sub-menu, whether GRUB2 will display the menu in a graphical terminal, and more.

Display menu settings

```
root@server01:~
[root@server01 ~]# cat /etc/default/grub
GRUB_TIMEOUT=5
GRUB_DISTRIBUTOR="$(sed 's, release .*$,,g' /etc/s
ystem-release)"
GRUB_DEFAULT=saved
GRUB_DISABLE_SUBMENU=true
GRUB_TERMINAL_OUTPUT="console"
GRUB_CMDLINE_LINUX="crashkernel=auto rd.lvm.lv=cen
tos/root rd.lvm.lv=centos/swap rhgb quiet"
GRUB_DISABLE_RECOVERY="true"
[root@server01 ~]#
```

The /etc/default/grub *file.*

Use the grub2-mkconfig Command

The grub2-mkconfig command generates a new grub.cfg configuration file or updates an existing one. The grub2-mkconfig command combines the configuration file templates in the /etc/grub.d/ directory with the settings in /etc/default/grub to generate the grub.cfg configuration file. This is the proper way to update GRUB2. Do not edit the configuration file directly.

 This command is simply grub-mkconfig *on some distributions. This is a legacy command from the original GRUB program. If GRUB2 is installed, the command updates GRUB2 files.*

The syntax of the grub2-mkconfig command is grub2-mkconfig [-o {file name}]

So what does the process look like if you modify the timeout period (the amount of time the boot loader waits for an OS selection from the menu)? To update the GRUB2 configuration with a customized timeout value, the process is:

1. Edit /etc/default/grub to the desired timeout and save changes.

2. Run grub2-mkconfig -o /boot/grub2/grub.cfg

On an EFI-based system, the path to the grub.cfg file is different, depending on the distribution. The path will resemble the following one: /boot/efi/EFI/<distro>/grub.cfg

Some distributions provide a shortcut command for grub2-mkconfig. The command is update-grub (or sometimes update-grub2), and it's a substitute for grub2-mkconfig -o /boot/grub/grub.cfg

Troubleshoot Common Boot Problems

Boot problems may arise from multiple issues. Consider whether there have been recent changes to the GRUB2 configuration, BIOS, or hardware.

GRUB2 Configuration Problems

Common GRUB2 configuration problems include typographical errors in the menus, kernel paths, or other settings. Run `grub2-mkconfig` after changes to ensure the grub.cfg file reflects the most recent updates or configuration changes.

Use `update-grub` as a substitute for `grub2-mkconfig -o /boot/grub/grub.cfg`

BIOS Problems

Common BIOS problems include typographical errors in any manually defined storage devices and unanticipated boot device order.

Hardware Problems

Boot problems could also be due to a failed or missing storage device as a result of a hardware failure.

Swap potentially failed hardware with a known good device, or check for updated device drivers.

Switched System

During the boot process, it's possible that users may inadvertently switch from the GUI target to the CLI target. In those instances, it's helpful to be able to display your current environment and be able to change to a different one if needed.

To display the current boot environment, type:

```
# systemctl get-default
```

To change the default boot target from CLI to GUI, type:

```
# systemctl set-default graphical.target
```

To change the default boot target from GUI to CLI, type:

```
# systemctl set-default multi-user.target
```

 These commands were covered earlier in the course.

Review Activity:

Boot Settings

Answer the following questions:

1. **Why don't you usually need to install GRUB2 on most Linux systems?**

2. **How is working with the grub.cfg file different from working with most Linux configuration files?**

3. **What is the role of the grub2-mkconfig command?**

Topic 16C

Deploy Linux

EXAM OBJECTIVES COVERED
1.1 Summarize Linux fundamentals.

Manual Linux deployments usually guide users through the process of selecting installation media, defining partitions, selecting software, and configuring post-installation settings. While there are thousands of available Linux distributions (and you can even create your own!), the installation steps are usually the same. It's the software that guides you through the process that differs.

Break the installation process into three steps:

- Prepare the platform.

- Install Linux.

- Complete post-deployment tasks.

This section covers all three steps.

Compare Physical and Virtual Deployments

The first deployment decision is to select a platform. In many cases, virtualization is the best option. A single computer of moderate power can host and run multiple Linux virtual machines. This is usually more cost-effective than purchasing a dedicated system. New users can experiment with multiple distributions easily by using virtualization.

Common virtualization options include KVM, VirtualBox, HyperV, and VMware Workstation. Pair these with well-supported Linux distros such as Ubuntu Desktop (Debian-based), Fedora Workstation (Red Hat–based), and Linux Mint (Debian-based and very user friendly).

It's a good idea to install at least one Red Hat–derived and one Debian-derived distribution to compare package managers, included software, graphical interfaces, and other features. With so many Linux distributions there is a lot of variety, and it's worthwhile to find a distribution you're comfortable with.

Recall that since Linux is FOSS, it is easy to try out many different distributions.

Raspberry Pi

One inexpensive option for Linux is the Raspberry Pi hardware platform. These small powerful systems easily run Linux and are very affordable. While Raspberry Pi was originally created to introduce young people to development projects, many production environments use Pi today.

Linux distributions that are available for Raspberry Pi hardware include:

- Raspberry Pi OS

- Ubuntu for Raspberry Pi

- Kali Linux for Raspberry Pi

Begin the Installation Process

The details of the Linux installation process vary by distribution, but in general, you will need to select an installation source, choose software installation options, configure networking, and define system settings. Once the installation completes, it's important to update both the operating system and applications. Finally, configure any custom software or other settings required for your environment.

Distinguish Install Methods

Most Linux distributions are downloaded as ISO images and either burned to a DVD or used as startup media for a VM. A more advanced technique is to access source files from across the network. Once the installation method is selected and available, you are ready to begin the installation.

You are strongly urged to use the most current version of whatever Linux distribution you select. These versions have the most up-to-date security patches and features.

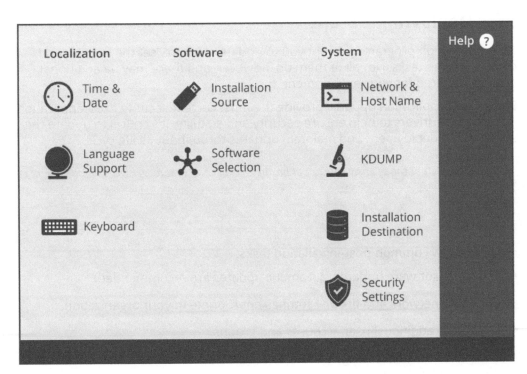

A sample Linux installation screen. Most distros start with similar-looking configuration options.

Basic Installation Steps

Each distribution has a slightly different deployment process, but all Linux installations have some features in common. The first step is to boot to the installation media. Next, you will probably need to address the following configuration areas in any Linux installation:

- Set the correct date/time for your locale.

- Select a language and keyboard for your locale.

- Select an installation source.

- Create or select a partition to install Linux to.

- Select the Linux system's role and appropriate software packages.

- Set the root password.

- Create a non-root administrative user account.

- Configure network settings.

- Complete post-installation tasks.

Non-root administrative accounts are more restricted than root user accounts. However, they are still given the authority to complete common sysadmin tasks, such as user and group maintenance, filesystem mounting, system service configuration, and system reboots and shutdowns. The root account has more privileges than are necessary for most tasks.

Post-Deployment Steps

Most installation programs prompt you to update software, set the firewall, and complete other tasks. Not all of them do, however, and there may be additional settings required for your environment, too.

System and application updates provide the most current security fixes, application features, and drivers to help ensure security and stability. It's critical to update the system upon deployment and maintain updates throughout its life cycle.

 Recall that the security concept of hardening specifies that the system should be kept up to date.

Here are a few common post-installation tasks:

- Configure software updates (automatic updates are recommended).

- Configure network and firewall settings appropriate to your organization.

- Create any additional user accounts and groups.

- Connect to network storage and other network services.

- Execute any additional configuration scripts.

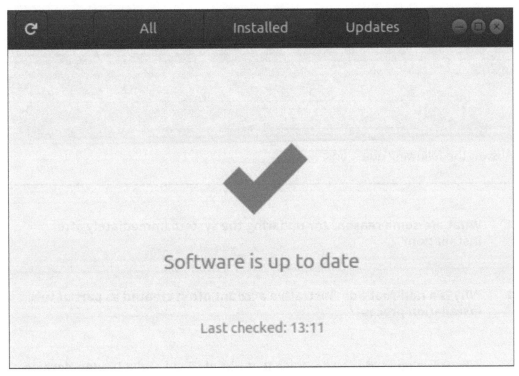

Confirmation message after bringing software up to date.

 The deployment may be automated and cloud-init scripts may execute to complete some or all of the installation steps.

Review Activity:

Linux Deployment

Answer the following questions:

1. **What are some reasons for updating the system immediately after installation?**

2. **Why is a non-root administrative account often created as part of the installation process?**

3. **Why is it a good idea to deploy a Red Hat–derived and a Debian-derived distribution at least once?**

Lesson 16

Summary

The early phase of the boot process is managed by the GRUB2 boot loader, which acquires its configuration from the `grub.cfg` file. This file is constructed by the `grub2-mkconfig` command from several supporting files. Sysadmins edit these files rather than the main `grub.cfg` file.

The Linux installation process is usually menu-driven with options that include selecting source files, defining partitions, choosing software based on the server's role in the organization, and completing post-installation configurations. It's worth noting that a password for root is set and most modern Linux distributions also create a non-root administrator account.

Guidelines

These best practices and guidelines are provided as revision tools or as quick references in your job role.

Deploying a standalone Linux system is straightforward, and the installation is typically easy. If you use a physical computer, confirm device driver compatibility before beginning.

- Select an installation platform (either a physical or a virtual computer).
- Check driver availability.
- Select a distribution that supports the role the system will play in your organization.
- Understand which package manager will be used.
- Check software compatibility.
- Select an install method.
- Plan for updates after installation.
- Create a non-root admin account.

Command Reference Table

This list of commands and their associated syntax can also be found in Appendix B.

Command	Syntax	Purpose	Covered in
mkinitrd	mkinitrd [options] {initrd image name} {kernel version}	Create the initrd image for preloading the kernel modules.	Lesson 16, Topic A
grub2-install	grub2-install [options] [device name]	Install the GRUB2 boot loader on a storage device.	Lesson 16, Topic B
grub2-mkconfig	grub2-mkconfig [-o {file name}]	Generate a new grub.cfg configuration file, or update an existing one.	Lesson 16, Topic B

Appendix A

Mapping Course Content to CompTIA Linux+ (Exam XK0-005) Objectives

Achieving CompTIA Linux+ certification requires candidates to pass Exam XK0-005. This table describes where the exam objectives for Exam XK0-005 are covered in this course.

1.0 System Management	
1.1 Summarize Linux fundamentals.	**Covered in**
Filesystem Hierarchy Standard (FHS)	Lesson 4, Topic A
/boot	
/proc	
/sys	
/var	
/usr	
/lib	
/dev	
/etc	
/opt	
/bin	
/sbin	
/home	
/media	
/mnt	
/root	
/tmp	
Basic boot process	Lesson 16, Topic B
Basic input/output system (BIOS)	Lesson 16, Topic A
Unified Extensible Firmware Interface (UEFI)	
Commands	
mkinitrd	
grub2-install	
grub2-mkconfig	
grub2-update	
dracut	
initrd.img	
vmlinuz	
Grand Unified Bootloader version 2 (GRUB2)	

1.1 Summarize Linux fundamentals.	Covered in
Boot sources	
Preboot eXecution Environment (PXE)	
Booting from Universal Serial Bus (USB)	
Booting from ISO	
Kernel panic	Lesson 8, Topic D
Device types in /dev	Lesson 8, Topic A
Block devices	
Character devices	
Special character devices	
/dev/null	
/dev/zero	
/dev/urandom	
Basic package compilation from source	Lesson 6, Topic D
./configure	
make	
make install	
Storage concepts	Lesson 7, Topic A
File storage	
Block storage	
Object storage	
Partition type	
Master boot record (MBR)	
GUID [globally unique identifier]	
Partition Table (GPT)	
Filesystem in Userspace (FUSE)	
Redundant Array of Independent (or Inexpensive) Disks (RAID) levels	
Striping	
Mirroring	
Parity	
Listing hardware information	Lesson 8, Topic A
lspci	
lsusb	
dmidecode	

1.2 Given a scenario, manage files and directories.	Covered in
File editing	Lesson 4, Topic C
sed	Lesson 4, Topic C
awk	Lesson 5, Topic A
printf	
nano	
vi(m)	

1.2 Given a scenario, manage files and directories.	Covered in
File compression, archiving, and backup	Lesson 5, Topic B
	Lesson 6, Topic E
gzip	
bzip2	
zip	
tar	
xz	
cpio	
dd	
File metadata	Lesson 4, Topic A
stat	
file	
Soft and hard links	Lesson 4, Topic A
Copying files between systems	Lesson 10, Topic C
rsync	
scp	
nc	
File and directory operations	Lesson 4, Topic B
mv	
cp	
mkdir	
rmdir	
ls	
pwd	
rm	
cd	
.	
..	
~	
tree	
cat	
touch	

1.3 Given a scenario, configure and manage storage using the appropriate tools.	Covered in
Disk partitioning	Lesson 7, Topic B
Commands	
fdisk	
parted	
partprobe	

1.3 Given a scenario, configure and manage storage using the appropriate tools.	Covered in
Mounting local and remote devices	Lesson 7, Topic B
systemd.mount	
/etc/fstab	
mount	
Linux Unified Key Setup (LUKS)	
External devices	
Filesystem management	Lesson 7, Topic B
XFS tools	
Ext4 tools	
Btrfs tools	
Monitoring storage space and disk usage	Lesson 7, Topic B
df	
du	
Creating and modifying volumes using Logical Volume Manager (LVM)	Lesson 7, Topic B
Commands	
pvs	
vgs	
lvs	
lvchange	
lvcreate	
vgcreate	
lvresize	
pvcreate	
vgextend	
Inspecting RAID implementations	Lesson 7, Topic C
mdadm	
/proc/mdstat	
Storage area network (SAN)/network-attached storage (NAS)	Lesson 7, Topic C
multipathd	
Network filesystems	
Network File System (NFS)	
Server Message Block (SMB)/Common Internet File System (CIFS)	
Storage hardware	Lesson 7, Topic B
lsscsi	
lsblk	
blkid	
fcstat	

1.4 Given a scenario, configure and use the appropriate processes and services.	Covered in
System services	Lesson 9, Topic A
systemctl	
stop	
start	
restart	
status	
enable	
disable	
mask	
Scheduling services	Lesson 9, Topic B
cron	
crontab	
at	
Process management	Lesson 8, Topic B
Kill signals	
SIGTERM	
SIGKILL	
SIGHUP	
Listing processes and open files	
top	
ps	
lsof	
htop	
Setting priorities	
nice	
renice	
Process states	
Zombie	
Sleeping	
Running	
Stopped	
Job control	
bg	
fg	
jobs	
Ctrl+Z	
Ctrl+C	
Ctrl+D	
pgrep	
pkill	
pidof	

1.5 Given a scenario, use the appropriate networking tools or configuration files.	Covered in
Interface management	Lesson 10, Topic B
iproute2 tools	
ip	
ss	
NetworkManager	
nmcli	
net-tools	
ifconfig	
ifcfg	
hostname	
arp	
route	
/etc/sysconfig/network-scripts/	
Name resolution	Lesson 10, Topic B
nsswitch	
/etc/resolv.conf	
systemd	
hostnamectl	
resolvectl	
Bind-utils	
dig	
nslookup	
host	
WHOIS	
Network monitoring	Lesson 11, Topic B
tcpdump	
wireshark/tshark	
netstat	
traceroute	
ping	
mtr	
Remote networking tools	Lesson 6, Topic E
Secure Shell (SSH)	Lesson 10, Topic C
cURL	
wget	
nc	
rsync	
Secure Copy Protocol (SCP)	
SSH File Transfer Protocol (SFTP)	

1.6 Given a scenario, build and install software.	Covered in
Package management	Lesson 6, Topic B
DNF	Lesson 6, Topic C
YUM	Lesson 6, Topic A
APT	
RPM	
dpkg	
ZYpp	
Sandboxed applications	Lesson 6, Topic F
snapd	
Flatpak	
AppImage	
System updates	Lesson 8, Topic D
Kernel updates	Lesson 6, Topic B
Package updates	Lesson 6, Topic C

1.7 Exam Objective	Covered in
Updating configuration files	Lesson 9, Topic B
Procedures	Lesson 6, Topic B
Restart service	Lesson 6, Topic C
Reload service	
.rpmnew	
.rpmsave	
Repository configuration files	
/etc/apt.conf	
/etc/yum.conf	
/etc/dnf/dnf.conf	
/etc/yum.repo.d	
/etc/apt/sources.list.d	
Configure kernel options	Lesson 8, Topic D
Parameters	
sysctl	
/etc/sysctl.conf	
Modules	
lsmod	
imsmod	
rmmod	
insmod	
modprobe	
modinfo	
Configure common system services	Lesson 9, Topic B
SSH	
Network Time Protocol (NTP)	
Syslog	
chrony	

1.7 Exam Objective	Covered in
Localization	Lesson 9, Topic C
timedatectl	
localectl	

2.0 Security	
2.1 Summarize the purpose and use of security best practices in a Linux environment.	Covered in
Managing public key infrastructure (PKI) certificates	Lesson 12, Topic B
Public key	
Private key	
Self-signed certificate	
Digital signature	
Wildcard certificate	
Hashing	
Certificate authorities	
Certificate use cases	Lesson 12, Topic B
Secure Sockets Layer (SSL)/Transport Layer Security (TLS)	
Certificate authentication	
Encryption	
Authentication	Lesson 12, Topic C
Tokens	
Multifactor authentication (MFA)	
Pluggable authentication modules (PAM)	
System Security Services Daemon (SSSD)	
Lightweight Directory Access Protocol (LDAP)	
Single sign-on (SSO)	
Linux hardening	Lesson 12, Topic A
Security scanning	Lesson 8, Topic D
Secure boot	
UEFI	
System logging configurations	
Setting default mask	
Disabling/removing insecure services	
Enforcing password strength	
Removing unused packages	
Tuning kernel parameters	
Securing service accounts	
Configuring the host firewall	

2.2 Given a scenario, implement identity management.	Covered in
Account creation and deletion	Lesson 2, Topic B
Utilities	Lesson 2, Topic A
useradd	
groupadd	
userdel	
groupdel	
usermod	
groupmod	
id	
who	
w	
Default shell	
Configuration files	
/etc/passwd	
/etc/group	
/etc/shadow	
/etc/profile	
/etc/skel	
.bash_profile	
.bashrc	
Account management	Lesson 2, Topic A
passwd	
chage	
pam_tally2	
faillock	
/etc/login.defs	

2.3 Given a scenario, implement and configure firewalls.	Covered in
Firewall use cases	Lesson 11, Topic A
Open and close ports	
Check current configuration	
Enable/Disable internet protocol (IP) forwarding	
Common firewall technologies	Lesson 11, Topic A
firewalld	
iptables	
nftables	
Uncomplicated firewall (UFW)	
Key firewall features	Lesson 11, Topic A
Zones	
Services	
Stateful	
Stateless	

2.4 Given a scenario, configure and execute remote connectivity for system management.	Covered in
SSH	Lesson 10, Topic C

Configuration files
    /etc/ssh/sshd_config
    /etc/ssh/ssh_config
    ~/.ssh/known_hosts
    ~/.ssh/authorized_keys
    ~/.ssh/ssh_config
Commands
    ssh-keygen
    ssh-copy-id
    ssh-add
Tunneling
    X11 forwarding
    Port forwarding
    Dynamic forwarding

Executing commands as another user	Lesson 2, Topic C

/etc/sudoers
PolicyKit rules
Commands
    sudo
    visudo
    su -
    pkexec

2.5 Given a scenario, apply the appropriate access controls.	Covered in
File permissions	Lesson 3, Topic B Lesson 3, Topic C

Access control list (ACL)
Set user ID (SUID)
Set group ID (SGID)
Sticky bit

Security-enhanced Linux (SELinux)	Lesson 12, Topic D

Content permissions
Labels
    Autorelabel
System booleans
States
    Enforcing
    Permissive
    Disabled
Policy types
    Targeted
    Minimum

2.5 Given a scenario, apply the appropriate access controls.	Covered in
AppArmor	Lesson 12, Topic D
Application permissions	
Command-line utilities	Lesson 3, Topic A
chown	Lesson 3, Topic C
umask	Lesson 12, Topic D
chmod	
getfacl	
setfacl	
ls	
setenforce	
getenforce	
chattr	
lsattr	
chgrp	
setsebool	
getsebool	
chcon	
restorecon	
semanage	
audit2allow	

3.0 Scripting, Containers, and Automation	
3.1 Given a scenario, create simple shell scripts to automate common tasks.	Covered in
Shell script elements	Lesson 13, Topic B
Loops	Lesson 4, Topic B
while	Lesson 4, Topic C
for	
until	
Conditionals	
if	
switch/case	
Shell parameter expansion	
Globbing	
Brace expansions	
Comparisons	
Arithmetic	
String	
Boolean	
Variables	
Search and replace	
Regular expressions	

3.1 Given a scenario, create simple shell scripts to automate common tasks.	Covered in
Standard stream redirection	
|	
||	
>	
>>	
<	
<<	
&	
&&	
Redirecting	
stderr	
stdout	
Here documents	
Exit documents	
Shell built-in commands	
read	
echo	
source	
Common script utilities	Lesson 13, Topic B
awk	Lesson 4, Topic B
sed	Lesson 4, Topic C
find	
xargs	
grep	
egrep	
tee	
wc	
cut	
tr	
head	
tail	
Environmental variables	Lesson 13, Topic B
$PATH	
$SHELL	
$?	
Relative and absolute paths	Lesson 4, Topic A

3.2 Given a scenario, perform basic container operations.	Covered in
Container management	Lesson 15, Topic B
Starting/stopping	
Inspecting	
Listing	
Deploying existing images	
Connecting to containers	
Logging	
Exposing ports	
Container image operations	Lesson 15, Topic B
build	
push	
pull	
list	
rmi	

3.3 Given a scenario, perform basic version control using Git.	Covered in
clone	Lesson 14, Topic C
push	Lesson 14, Topic C
pull	Lesson 14, Topic C
commit	Lesson 14, Topic C
add	Lesson 14, Topic C
checkout	Lesson 14, Topic C
branch	Lesson 14, Topic C
tag	Lesson 14, Topic C
gitignore	Lesson 14, Topic C

3.4 Summarize common infrastructure as code technologies.	Covered in
File formats	Lesson 14, Topic A
YAML Ain't Markup Language (YAML)	
JavaScript Object Notation (JSON)	
Utilities	Lesson 14, Topic B
Ansible	
Puppet	
Chef	
SaltStack	
Terraform	
Continuous integration/continuous deployment (CI/CD)	Lesson 14, Topic A
Use cases	

3.4 Summarize common infrastructure as code technologies.	Covered in
Advanced Git topics	Lesson 14, Topic C
merge	
rebase	
Pull requests	

3.5 Summarize container, cloud, and orchestration concepts.	Covered in
Kubernetes benefits and application use cases	Lesson 15, Topic B
Pods	
Sidecars	
Ambassador containers	
Single-node, multicontainer use cases	Lesson 15, Topic B
Compose	
Container persistent storage	Lesson 15, Topic B
Container Networks	Lesson 15, Topic B
Overlay networks	
Bridging	
Network address translation (NAT)	
Host	
Service mesh	Lesson 15, Topic B
Bootstrapping	Lesson 15, Topic B
Cloud-init	
Container registries	Lesson 15, Topic B

4.0 Troubleshooting	
4.1 Given a scenario, analyze and troubleshoot storage issues.	Covered in
High latency	Lesson 7, Topic D
Input/output (I/O) wait	
Low throughput	Lesson 7, Topic D
Input/output operations per second (IOPS) scenarios	Lesson 7, Topic D
Low IOPS	
Capacity issues	Lesson 7, Topic D
Low disk space	
Inode exhaustion	
Filesystem issues	Lesson 7, Topic D
Corruption	
Mismatch	
I/O scheduler	Lesson 7, Topic D

4.1 Given a scenario, analyze and troubleshoot storage issues.	Covered in
Device issues	Lesson 7, Topic D
Non-volatile memory express (NVMe)	
Solid-state drive (SSD)	
SSD trim	
RAID	
LVM	
I/O errors	
Mount option problems	Lesson 7, Topic D

4.2 Given a scenario, analyze and troubleshoot network resource issues.	Covered in
Network configuration issues	Lesson 10, Topic A
Subnet	Lesson 10, Topic D
Routing	
Firewall issues	Lesson 11, Topic A
Interface errors	Lesson 10, Topic D
Dropped packets	
Collisions	
Link status	
Bandwidth limitations	Lesson 10, Topic D
High latency	
Name resolution issues	Lesson 10, Topic D
Domain Name System (DNS)	
Testing remote systems	Lesson 11, Topic B
Nmap	Lesson 10, Topic D
openssl s_client	

4.3 Given a scenario, analyze and troubleshoot central processing unit (CPU) and memory issues.	Covered in
Runaway processes	Lesson 8, Topic B
Zombie processes	Lesson 8, Topic B
High CPU utilization	Lesson 8, Topic B
High load average	Lesson 8, Topic B
High run queues	Lesson 8, Topic B
CPU times	Lesson 8, Topic B
steal	
user	
system	
idle	
iowait	

4.3 Given a scenario, analyze and troubleshoot central processing unit (CPU) and memory issues.	Covered in
CPU process priorities	Lesson 8, Topic B
nice	Lesson 8, Topic C
renice	
Memory exhaustion	Lesson 8, Topic C
Free memory vs. file cache	
Out of memory (OOM)	Lesson 8, Topic C
Memory leaks	
Process killer	
Swapping	Lesson 8, Topic C
Hardware	Lesson 8, Topic A
lscpu	
lsmem	
/proc/cpuinfo	
/proc/meminfo	

4.4 Given a scenario, analyze and troubleshoot user access and file permissions.	Covered in
User login issues	Lesson 2, Topic D
User file access issues	Lesson 3, Topic A
Group	Lesson 3, Topic B
Context	Lesson 3, Topic C
Permission	
ACL	
Attribute	
Policy/non-policy	
Password issues	Lesson 2, Topic D
Privilege elevation	Lesson 1, Topic B
	Lesson 2, Topic C
Quota issues	Lesson 7, Topic A

4.5 Given a scenario, use systemd to diagnose and resolve common problems with a Linux system.	Covered in
Unit files	Lesson 9, Topic A
Service	
Networking services	
ExecStart/ExecStop	
Before/after	
Type	
User	
Requires/wants	

4.5 Given a scenario, use systemd to diagnose and resolve common problems with a Linux system.	Covered in

Timer
- OnCalendar
- OnBootSec
- Unit
- Time Expressions

Mount
- Naming conventions
- What
- Where
- Type
- Options

Target
- Default
- Multiuser
- Network-online
- Graphical

Common problems
- Name resolution failure
- Application crash
- Time-zone configuration
- Boot issues
- Journal issues
- Services not starting on time

Lesson 9, Topic C
Lesson 9, Topic A

Appendix B
Command Reference

Understanding Linux commands, the syntax and purpose is critical to being a successful Linux administrator. Appendix B is a helpful reference tool with all the Linux commands that are discussed in the course, grouped by lesson and topic order.

Basic Linux Commands

Command	Syntax	Purpose	Covered in
ls	ls [option]	List the contents of the current directory.	Lesson 1, Topic B
cat	cat [file-name]	Display the contents of a text file on the screen.	Lesson 1, Topic B
cd	cd /etc	Change from one directory to another.	Lesson 1, Topic B
pwd	pwd	Displays the present working directory.	Lesson 1, Topic B
whoami	whoami	Displays the username of the current user.	Lesson 1, Topic B
touch	touch [file-name]	Create a new empty file or update the timestamp on an existing file.	Lesson 1, Topic B
man	man [command]	Display manual, or help, pages for a specific command.	Lesson 1, Topic C
whatis	whatis [command]	Provides a brief description of the specified command.	Lesson 1, Topic C

Commands Related to Administering Users and Groups

Command	Syntax	Purpose	Covered in
passwd	passwd [user-name]	Manage user passwords.	Lesson 2, Topic A
chage	chage -options	Manage password settings.	Lesson 2, Topic A
w	w	Display current users on the system.	Lesson 2, Topic A
who	who	Display current users on the system.	Lesson 2, Topic A
useradd	useradd -options argument	Add a user.	Lesson 2, Topic A

Command	Syntax	Purpose	Covered in
usermod	usermod -options argument	Modify a user.	Lesson 2, Topic A
userdel	userdel [user-name]	Delete a user.	Lesson 2, Topic A
id	id [user-name]	Gather and display account information.	Lesson 2, Topic A
groupadd	groupadd [group-name]	Create a new group.	Lesson 2, Topic B
groupmod	groupmod -options argument	Modify an existing group.	Lesson 2, Topic B
groupdel	groupdel [group-name]	Remove an existing group.	Lesson 2, Topic B
su	su - [user-name]	Switch user to the specified user or account name.	Lesson 2, Topic C
sudo	sudo -options [command]	Exercise delegated privileges.	Lesson 2, Topic C
pkexec	pkexec program argument	Allows an authorized user to execute an action.	Lesson 2, Topic C

Permissions Configuration Commands

Command	Syntax	Purpose	Covered in
umask	umask {number}	Alter the default permissions on newly created files and directories.	Lesson 3, Topic A
chmod	chmod [options] {mode} {file/directory name}	Modify the permissions of a file or directory.	Lesson 3, Topic A
chown	Varies based on desired outcome: • Change the owner but not the group: chown {newowner} {filename} • Change both the owner and the group: chown {newowner}:{newgroup} {filename} • Change the group but not the owner: chown :{newgroup} {filename}	Change the owner, the group, or both for a file or directory.	Lesson 3, Topic A

Command	Syntax	Purpose	Covered in
chgrp	chgrp {group name} {file/directory name}	Change the group ownership of a file or directory.	Lesson 3, Topic A
lsattr	lsattr [options] {file/directory names}	List attributes of a file or a directory.	Lesson 3, Topic A
chattr	chattr [-R] [-v {version}] [+- {attributes}] {file/directory names}	Change attributes of a file or a directory.	Lesson 3, Topic A
getfacl	getfacl {filename}	Retrieve the ACLs of files and directories.	Lesson 3, Topic C
setfacl	setfacl [-bR] [-mx {acl_spec}] {file/directory names}	Change the permissions associated with the ACL of a file or directory.	Lesson 3, Topic C

File Management Commands

Command	Syntax	Purpose	Covered in
stat	stat {file-name}	Display file metadata in a relatively user-friendly structure.	Lesson 4, Topic A
file	file {file-name}	Display file information based on the file type.	Lesson 4, Topic A
ln	ln [options] {target-name} {link-name}	Create links, either hard or symbolic.	Lesson 4, Topic A
cd	cd {path}	Move your present working directory to another directory.	Lesson 4, Topic B
tree	tree {directory-name}	Display the filesystem in a hierarchical structure, perhaps making it easier to understand a directory's location relative to other directories.	Lesson 4, Topic B
mkdir	mkdir {new-directory-name}	Create directories along the specified path.	Lesson 4, Topic B
cp	cp {source-file} {new-file}	Copy a file into a new location while retaining the source file in its original location.	Lesson 4, Topic B

Command	Syntax	Purpose	Covered in
mv	mv {source-location} {destination-location}	Place the file elsewhere in the filesystem.	Lesson 4, Topic B
mv	mv {original-filename} {new-filename}	The rename command in Bash.	Lesson 4, Topic B
rmdir	rmdir {directory-name}	Remove (delete) a directory with no files in it.	Lesson 4, Topic B
rm	rm [options] {file-name}	Remove (delete) a file or a non-empty directory.	Lesson 4, Topic B
head	head {file-name}	Display the first 10 lines of a file.	Lesson 4, Topic B
tail	tail {file-name}	Display the last 10 lines of a file.	Lesson 4, Topic B
grep	grep {character-string]	Search for strings of characters within a data stream. Grep is case-sensitive unless the -i option is used.	Lesson 4, Topic B
xargs	command [options] [arguments] | xargs [options] {command}	Read from standard input and executes a command for each argument provided.	Lesson 4, Topic B
tee	command [options] [arguments] | tee [options] {file names}	Read the standard input, sends the output to the default output device (the CLI), and also copies the output to each specified file.	Lesson 4, Topic B
find	find {where to search} {search criteria}	Search the filesystem for files that match the given parameters.	Lesson 4, Topic C
locate	locate [options] {string}	Search for files and directories along a specified path.	Lesson 4, Topic C
updatedb	updatedb	Build and update a database of files based on the /etc/updatedb.conf file.	Lesson 4, Topic C
which	which {command}	Display complete path of a specified command.	Lesson 4, Topic C

Commands for Authoring Text Files

Command	Syntax	Purpose	Covered in
`tar`	`tar [options] {file1, file2 ...}`	Bundle files for easier transfer.	Lesson 5, Topic B
`gzip`	`gzip [options] [file-names]`	Reduce size of files.	Lesson 5, Topic B
`xz`	`xz [options] [file-names]`	Reduce size of files.	Lesson 5, Topic B
`bzip2`	`bzip2 [options] {file-names}`	Manage file compression.	Lesson 5, Topic B
`zip`	`zip [options] [file-names]`	Reduce size of files with archiving functionality.	Lesson 5, Topic B

Software Management Commands

Command	Syntax	Purpose	Covered in
`rpm`	`rpm [options] {package-name}`	Package management in Red Hat distros.	Lesson 6, Topic B
`yum`	`yum [options] [subcommand] {package-name}`	Software package management in Red Hat distros.	Lesson 6, Topic B
`apt`	`apt [subcommands] {package-name}`	Package management in Debian-based distros.	Lesson 6, Topic C
`dpkg`	`dpkg [options] {package-name}`	Manage software packages in older Debian-based distros.	Lesson 6, Topic C
`wget`	`wget [options] {URL}`	Download package files housed on websites from the command line.	Lesson 6, Topic E
`curl`	`curl [options] {URL}`	Download package files housed on websites from the command line.	Lesson 6, Topic E

Commands for Administering Storage

Command	Syntax	Purpose	Covered in
lsblk	lsblk {drive-path}	Display information about storage devices recognized by the system.	Lesson 7, Topic B
lsscsi	lsscsi [options]	Display information about SCSI devices.	Lesson 7, Topic B
fdisk	fdisk [options] {device-name}	Create, modify, or delete partitions on a storage drive.	Lesson 7, Topic B
parted	parted [options] {device-name}	Create, destroy, and resize partitions.	Lesson 7, Topic B
mkfs	mkfs [options] {filesystem-name} {partition-name}	Format new partitions.	Lesson 7, Topic B
mount	mount {filesystem-name} {directory-name}	Attach storage to the FHS.	Lesson 7, Topic B
umount	umount {filesystem-name} {directory-name}	Detach storage from the FHS.	Lesson 7, Topic B
df	df [options] {directory-name}	Display device storage information.	Lesson 7, Topic B
du	du [options] {directory-name}	Display device usage information.	Lesson 7, Topic B
e2label	e2label /dev/ {device name} {partition number} {label name}	Display or modify file system labels.	Lesson 7, Topic B
resize2fs	resize2fs [options] {device/file system name} [desired size]	Change the size of an ext2/3/4 file system on a device.	Lesson 7, Topic B
tune2fs	tune2fs [options] {device/ file system name}	Configure parameters associated with an ext2/3/4 file system.	Lesson 7, Topic B

Command	Syntax	Purpose	Covered in
dumpe2fs	dumpe2fs [options] {device/ file system name}	Dump ext2, ext3, and ext4 file system information.	Lesson 7, Topic B
cryptsetup	cryptsetup [options] {action} [action arguments]	Encrypt data before it is written to disk.	Lesson 7, Topic C
shred	shred [options] {file-name}	Securely wipe a storage device by overwriting contents with random data or all zeros.	Lesson 7, Topic C
iostat	iostat [options] [device names]	Display reports on CPU and device storage.	Lesson 7, Topic D
ioping	ioping [options] {file/ directory/ device name}	Generate a report of device I/O latency in real time.	Lesson 7, Topic D

Commands for Managing Devices, Processes, Memory and the Kernel

Command	Syntax	Purpose	Covered in
hwinfo	hwinfo [options] {device}	Display detailed information about hardware resources.	Lesson 8, Topic A
dmidecode	dmidecode [options] {device}	Display system information for current devices.	Lesson 8, Topic A
lspci	lspci [options]	Display information about devices attached to specific busses.	Lesson 8, Topic A
lsusb	lsusb [options]	Display information about devices attached to specific busses.	Lesson 8, Topic A
lscpu	lscpu [options]	Display CPU information.	Lesson 8, Topic A
lsmem	lsmem [options]	Display information about memory blocks.	Lesson 8, Topic A

Command	Syntax	Purpose	Covered in
ps	*The ps command supports multiple command syntax formats.*	Display process status.	Lesson 8, Topic B
sar	sar [options]	Display system usage reports.	Lesson 8, Topic B
nohup	nohup {command/ script}	Prevent a process from ending when the user logs off.	Lesson 8, Topic B
mkswap	mkswap [options]	Create swap space on a storage partition.	Lesson 8, Topic C
swapon	swapon [options]	Activate the swap partition on a specific device.	Lesson 8, Topic C
swapoff	swapoff [options]	Deactivate the swap partition on a specific device.	Lesson 8, Topic C
free	free [options]	Display the quantity of free or unused memory.	Lesson 8, Topic C
vmstat	vmstat [options]	Display the virtual memory usage.	Lesson 8, Topic C
modinfo	modinfo [options] {module-name}	Display information about a particular kernel module.	Lesson 8, Topic D
insmod	insmod {module-name}	Install a module into the currently running kernel.	Lesson 8, Topic D
rmmod	rmmod {module-name}	Remove a module from the currently running kernel.	Lesson 8, Topic D
modprobe	modprobe [options] {module-names}	Add or remove modules from a kernel.	Lesson 8, Topic D
depmod	depmod [options]	Build the modules. dep file by aggregating all instances of symbols being exported and used.	Lesson 8, Topic D
sysctl	sysctl [options]	View or set kernel parameters at runtime.	Lesson 8, Topic D
dmesg	dmesg [options]	Print any messages that have been sent to the kernel's message buffer during and after system boot.	Lesson 8, Topic D

Service Management Commands

Command	Syntax	Purpose	Covered in
systemctl	systemctl [subcommand] [argument]	Manage startup options.	Lesson 9, Topic A
service	service [options] [service] [subcommand]	Manage enabling and starting services under SysVinit.	Lesson 9, Topic A
chkconfig	chkconfig [options] [service] [subcommand]	• Control services in each runlevel. • Start or stop services during system startup.	Lesson 9, Topic A
crontab	crontab [options]	Schedule an event by editing the crontab file.	Lesson 9, Topic B
at	at [options] {time}	Run a task once at a specified time.	Lesson 9, Topic B
lpr	lpr [options] [file names]	Submit files for printing.	Lesson 9, Topic B
date	date [options] [format]	Print the date in a specified format.	Lesson 9, Topic C
timedatectl	timedatectl [options] [subcommand]	Set the system date and time information.	Lesson 9, Topic C
localectl	localectl [options] [subcommand]	View and configure the system locale and keyboard layout settings.	Lesson 9, Topic C

Network Setting Configuration Commands

Command	Syntax	Purpose	Covered in
ip	ip [options] {object} [subcommand]	Display IP address, subnet mask, and MAC address settings.	Lesson 10, Topic B
ifconfig	ifconfig [options] [interface]	Display current IP address information for each NIC recognized by the system.	Lesson 10, Topic B
iwconfig	iwconfig [options] [interface]	Provide wireless NIC configurations and settings.	Lesson 10, Topic B

Command	Syntax	Purpose	Covered in
`nmcli`	`nmcli [options] [subcommand] [arguments]`	View and manage network settings.	Lesson 10, Topic B
`ethtool`	`ethtool [options] {device name}`	Manage NIC driver and network configurations.	Lesson 10, Topic B
`hostnamectl`	`hostnamectl [options] [subcommand] [arguments]`	View system's network hostname.	Lesson 10, Topic B
`netcat`	`netcat [options]`	Test connectivity and send data across network connections.	Lesson 10, Topic C
`iftop`	`iftop [options] [-i {interface}]`	Display bandwidth usage information.	Lesson 10, Topic C
`traceroute`	`traceroute [options] {destination}`	Report the network path between the source and destination computers.	Lesson 10, Topic C
`tracepath`	`tracepath [options] {destination}`	Report the network path between the source and destination computers.	Lesson 10, Topic C
`resolvectl`	`resolvectl query {domain-name}`	Manually query name resolution services.	Lesson 10, Topic D
`dig`	`dig {domain name}`	Test name resolution.	Lesson 10, Topic D
`nslookup`	`nslookup {domain name}`	Gather information about and test name resolution.	Lesson 10, Topic D
`host`	`host {domain name}`	Gather information about and test name resolution.	Lesson 10, Topic D
`whois`	`whois [options] {domain name}`	Display hostname, FQDN, IP address, and other information about a given host.	Lesson 10, Topic D
`arp`	`arp [options]`	Discover information about known MAC addresses.	Lesson 10, Topic D

Network Security Configuration Commands

Command	Syntax	Purpose	Covered in
iptables	iptables [options] [-t table] [commands] {chain/rule specification}	Manage packet filtering and stateful firewall functions.	Lesson 11, Topic A
firewall-cmd	firewall-cmd [options]	Configure firewalld by querying and modifying zones or services as desired.	Lesson 11, Topic A
ufw	ufw [options] {action}	Configure nftables or iptables.	Lesson 11, Topic A
ping	ping [options] {destination}	Generate a response request from the sending computer, which should receive a reply from the destination computer.	Lesson 11, Topic B
traceroute	traceroute [options] {destination}	Display each hop along the network path.	Lesson 11, Topic B
tracepath	tracepath [options] {destination}	Display each hop along the network path.	Lesson 11, Topic B
mtr	mtr [options] [hostname]	Test network connection quality and packet loss.	Lesson 11, Topic B
netstat	netstat [options]	Gather information about TCP connections to the system.	Lesson 11, Topic B
ss	ss [options]	Gather information about TCP connections and display in a simple output.	Lesson 11, Topic B
tcpdump	tcpdump [options] [-i {interface}] [host {IP address}]	Determine traffic type and content.	Lesson 11, Topic B
nmap	nmap [options] [target]	Report extremely detailed information about a network.	Lesson 11, Topic B

Security Management Commands

Command	Syntax	Purpose	Covered in
md5sum	md5sum options] [file name]	Calculate the hash value of a file with the MD5 hash function.	Lesson 12, Topic B
sha#sum	sha#sum options] [file name]	Calculate the hash value of a file with the SHA hash function.	Lesson 12, Topic B
chcon	chcon {-u|-r|-t} {context value} {file or directory name}	Temporarily change the SELinux context of a resource.	Lesson 12, Topic D
apparmor_status	*No additional options or subcommands.*	Display the current status of AppArmor profiles.	Lesson 12, Topic D
aa-complain	aa- complain {path to profile}	Place an AppArmor profile in complain mode.	Lesson 12, Topic D
aa-enforce	aa- enforce {path to profile}	Place an AppArmor profile in enforce mode.	Lesson 12, Topic D
aa-disable	aa-disable {path to profile}	Disable an AppArmor profile, unloading it from the kernel.	Lesson 12, Topic D
aa-unconfined	*No additional options or subcommands.*	List processes with open network sockets that don't have an AppArmor profile loaded.	Lesson 12, Topic D

Script Implementation Commands

Command	Syntax	Purpose	Covered in
awk	awk [options] ['patterns {actions}'] | {file-names}	Search for specified information, and take action when that information is found.	Lesson 13, Topic B
sed	sed {'options/ address/action'} {file-names}	Modify text files, especially by searching and replacing.	Lesson 13, Topic B
find	find {where to search} {search criteria}	Search for files based on criteria other than filename.	Lesson 13, Topic B
tee	command [options] [arguments] | tee [options] {file-names}	Verify the output of a command immediately, and store that output in a file for later reference.	Lesson 13, Topic B

Command	Syntax	Purpose	Covered in

`xargs`	`command [options]`
	`[arguments] |`
	`xargs [options]`
	`{command}`
		Commonly used with the `find` command to operate on each result that is found within the file or directory search.	Lesson 13, Topic B

`export`	`export [options]` `[NAME[=value]]`	Set the value of an environment variable for all future Bash sessions.	Lesson 13, Topic C

`env`	`env [options]`
	`[NAME=value]`
	`[command]`
		Run a command with modified environment variables.	Lesson 13, Topic C

`alias`	`alias [alias`
	`name[='command`
	`with options']]`
		Customize the shell environment by generating command-line aliases.	Lesson 13, Topic C

IaC Commands

Command	Syntax	Purpose	Covered in
`git`	`git [options]` `{subcommand}`	Manage Git repositories.	Lesson 14, Topic C

Commands for Managing Containers

Command	Syntax	Purpose	Covered in

`docker`	`docker`
	`subcommand`
	`{options}`
	`{arguments}`
		The primary management command for Docker containers.	Lesson 15, Topic B

`docker pull`	`docker pull` `{image-name}`	Pull an image from a registry.	Lesson 15, Topic B

`docker container`	`docker`
	`container`
	`subcommand`
	`{options}`
	`{arguments}`
		Manage attributes for specified containers.	Lesson 15, Topic B

`push`	*Exact syntax depends on the specific container engine.*	Upload images to a registry.	Lesson 15, Topic B
`pull`	*Exact syntax depends on the specific container engine.*	Download images from a registry.	Lesson 15, Topic B

Linux Installation Commands

Command	Syntax	Purpose	Covered in
mkinitrd	mkinitrd [options] {initrd image name} {kernel version}	Create the initrd image for preloading the kernel modules.	Lesson 16, Topic A
grub2-install	grub2-install [options] [device name]	Install the GRUB2 boot loader on a storage device.	Lesson 16, Topic B
grub2-mkconfig	grub2-mkconfig [-o {file name}]	Generate a new grub.cfg configuration file, or update an existing one.	Lesson 16, Topic B

Solutions

Review Activity: Linux Characteristics

1. **Compare the advantages and disadvantages of GUI and CLI environments.**

CLI may be faster to work with and consume fewer resources. GUI is usually easier to work with and supports graphics-based applications.

2. **Explain how distributions differ from each other.**

Distributions tend to focus on addressing particular needs, such as an end-user workstation, multimedia editing, and high-performance service hosting.

3. **Why do servers tend to rely on CLI administration and desktops rely on GUI environments?**

Servers attempt to dedicate all possible resources to the provided services and do not usually run end-user applications that often require a GUI. Desktop systems often run user applications that benefit from or require a graphical component.

4. **How might anyone contribute improvements to a piece of free and open-source software?**

Anyone might notice a need or requirement in software, create a solution to the problem, and then release the modified software. As the cycle is repeated, the software continues to improve.

Review Activity: Interact with Linux

1. **An administrator asks you to make a change to the system's configuration. Why would you need to use Vim or Nano to accomplish this task?**

Most Linux configurations are stored in text files, so changing the configuration requires editing the text files.

2. **What types of files will be found in the /etc directory?**

Configuration files.

3. **Explain the difference between the su and sudo commands.**

The su command switches to a different user account (usually root). The user can exercise all privileges associated with that account. The sudo command allows a user to run only specific, delegated commands that normally require administrative privileges.

Review Activity: Help in Linux

1. **Name three things a man page might provide a user.**

Man pages provide a summary of the command's function, examples of using the command, explanation of options.

2. **Why might vendor websites be the best source of information about an application or service?**

The vendor site probably contains the most current information to configure the application or service, provides the version history, and supplies examples of use.

Review Activity: Troubleshoot in Linux

1. A user contacts you to find out why they cannot access a directory. Using the troubleshooting methodology, how would you narrow the scope of the problem?

Checking with another user in the same group who has the same level of access to the directory will allow you to determine whether the problem is widespread.

2. When should you escalate a problem?

Escalate a problem when you cannot solve it yourself (although it won't be good for your career if you give up too easily). You might also escalate if you do not have authorization to perform the necessary changes or if the system is under some sort of warranty.

3. True or False? Documentation should be created only at the end of the troubleshooting process.

False. The last step of the methodology is to ensure that findings, actions, and outcomes are documented, but you cannot do this effectively without existing notes. Most troubleshooting takes place within a ticket system. Ideally, a documented job ticket would be opened at the start of recording the incident.

Review Activity: User Account Management

1. Why are user passwords stored in the `/etc/shadow` file and not the `/etc/passwd` file?

The `/etc/passwd` file can be read by all processes and therefore isn't as secure. The `/etc/shadow` file can only be read by root.

2. What is the purpose of the `/etc/skel` directory?

Any files stored in this directory are automatically copied to the home directory of new user accounts. Profile files and other configurations can be easily set using `/etc/skel`.

3. Why might an administrator change a user's default shell?

The user may be more comfortable with a different shell than Bash, such as the Zsh or Ksh.

Review Activity: Group Account Management

1. Suggest at least two ways to display group membership information.

View the /etc/group file, id command, group command.

2. What command adds a user to a group?

The usermod command (usually with the -aG options).

3. What is the result if an administrator forgets to add the -a option when adding a user to a group?

The user is added to the specified group but removed from all other groups.

4. Why might a user be a member of multiple groups?

Membership in multiple groups provides access to different resources. For example, a user who is a member of both the sales group and the marketing group can be granted access to both types of resources.

Review Activity: Privilege Escalation

1. **A developer at your organization needs the ability to reboot a test server, but their account's standard privileges do not permit this. The developer requests the system's root user password in order to use su to reboot the server. Is there a more secure option that aligns with the principle of least privilege?**

A better option is sudo, which allows the administrator to delegate only the necessary task (in this case, rebooting the server). The root password combined with su would grant more than just the reboot privilege.

2. **How are the su root and su - root commands different?**

The su root command switches the user identity to that of root within the user profile settings of the original user. The su - root command switches the user identity to that of root with the root user's own profile settings.

3. **You must delegate the shutdown -h privilege to SOMEUSER. What tool is used to modify the /etc/ sudoers file, and what line must be added to that file?**

The visudo command is run to edit the file. The following line is added to the file: SOMEUSER ALL=(ALL) NOPASSWD: SHUTDOWN_CMDS

4. **Whose password must be entered with sudo? Whose password must be entered with su?**

The user's own password must be entered with sudo. The destination user's password must be entered with su.

Review Activity: User and Group Troubleshooting

1. **List at least three scenarios where you might need records of who logged in to a Linux system.**

security incident response, security audit, troubleshooting account access

2. **Another administrator asks you to explain the value of editing the /etc/sudoer's file with visudo rather than a traditional text editor. What is your response?**

The visudo editor confirms the syntax of the /etc/sudoers file. The file is very sensitive, and misconfiguration could prevent administrative access to the system.

3. **List at least three reasons a user account might be locked.**

An administrator locked the account while the user was on a leave of absence, an incorrect password was entered too many times, and password settings are misconfigured.

4. **During a security audit it is discovered that a user does not have a password set. When you check the /etc/passwd file, the password field is properly populated with the x character. What file would actually display whether a password has been set for the user?**

/etc/shadow

5. **A user places sudo before a command, but the command still fails to run. What might be the cause?**

The /etc/sudoers file is not configured for the user or for the command.

6. **An administrator asks you how to delegate Linux administrative privileges to a specific user. What group is used for such delegation?**

the wheel group

Review Activity: Standard Linux Permissions

1. How does the principle of least privilege help mitigate threats and mistakes?

It mitigates threats and mistakes by providing users with only the level of access required and no more. By not having more access than needed, mistakes such as accidental or malicious changes or deletions may be avoided.

2. What octal value is used in absolute mode to set permissions at all access for all identities?

777

3. Write the command by using symbolic mode that removes the read permission from others for fileA without impacting other permissions.

chmod o-r fileA

4. Interpret the results of the following command: chown -R USERA:sales dirA

Sets the dirA directory owner to USERA and the associated group to sales. The -R option causes the owner and group change to apply to all existing files and directories in dirA.

Review Activity: Special Linux Permissions

1. How would SGID benefit users when set on the /projects directory where multiple users are members of the associated group and need access to each other's files in the directory?

SGID assigned the group association to files created in the /projects directory, allowing group members to have access to each other's files.

2. Why might a sysadmin set the sticky bit on a configuration file?

A sysadmin might do this to keep the configuration file from being accidentally deleted by another user or by the system (for example, during an upgrade).

Review Activity: ACL Configuration

1. Explain the benefit offered by ACLs compared to standard Linux permissions.

ACLs provide additional flexibility by permitting multiple users and/or multiple groups to have different levels of access.

2. What commands are used to set ACL entries for USERA with rwx and USERB with r-- for fileA?

Run these two commands:

setfacl -m u:USERA:rwx fileA

setfacl -m u:USERB:r fileA

3. Does the ACL structure replace standard permissions?

No, ACLs enhance the existing standard permissions structure.

Review Activity: The Linux File System

1. **You are installing a new application on your Linux system. The documentation states that configuration files and log files will be added to your system. Where will these files likely be stored, and how does the FHS make such installations easier?**

Configuration files will likely be stored in the /etc directory, and log files will likely be stored in /var/log. The FHS makes it easier for developers to automate installations since directories such as /etc and /var/log are consistent across distributions. The FHS also makes it easier for administrators to understand where such files are likely to be stored.

2. **You are in the new-projects directory, which is stored in the projects directory within your home directory. What is the absolute path to the new-projects directory?**

/home/USERNAME/projects/new-projects

3. **A user submits a ticket regarding a file access issue. The first file, projectA.txt, had a second hard link named my-project.txt. The same data was available via either link. The user deleted the my-project.txt file, and the data was still available via projectA.txt. The second file, projectB.txt, had a sym link that pointed to the projectB.txt link. When the projectB.txt link was deleted, the data was no longer available via the sym link. The user wants to know why the first file is still available after a link deletion but the second is not.**

The first file still exists, and one hard link pointing to its content remains after the other hard link was deleted. Hard links point to the actual data stored on the drive. Data always has at least one hard link. When the only hard link to the second file was deleted, the sym link was broken because sym links do not point to data, they point to hard links (that then point to data).

Review Activity: File Management Commands

1. **You have been assigned a helpdesk ticket to answer a user question. The user is attempting to rename files but cannot find the rename command. What command do you teach the user?**

The mv command, and the syntax is mv {oldname} {newname}

2. **A user asks how to delete a directory named /projects containing 100 directories. The user does not want to delete the files individually and does not want to be prompted to confirm the deletion of each file. What is the appropriate command expression, and why?**

rm -fR /projects

Most Linux distributions ask for confirmation when removing files. This is tedious when many files are involved, though it's an important safety check. The -f option forces the removal without confirmation.

3. **A user complains that they redirected the output from several commands into a text file, but the only content that appears in the file is the output from the most recent command. How would you explain to the user what happened and how to correct the problem?**

The > redirector overwrites any existing content in the target file. In the future, the user should use the >> redirector to append new content to existing content in the target file.

Review Activity: File Location

1. **You are conducting a security audit and need to document user access to log files—specifically whether any files are world-readable or whether any allow rwx access to all users. How can the find command be used in such a project, and what specific command might you use?**

`find /var/log -perm 400` (for world-readable access) and `find /var/log -perm 777` (for rwx to all users)

2. **A coworker on the helpdesk team is troubleshooting an issue where a user is attempting to run a command, but the command is not executing. Your coworker needs to discover where the command executes from as part of the troubleshooting process. What command(s) can you suggest?**

The `where` command would be useful.

3. **A senior sysadmin suggests that commands such as sed, awk, and sort are just as useful in automation as at the command-line. How might commands such as these be used in automation?**

File management commands such as `sed`, `awk`, `sort`, `cut`, `paste`, `tr`, `wc`, `printf`, `echo`, and `diff` can be integrated into automation scripts to find, organize, and display information or provide configurations.

Review Activity: Text Files

1. **A user contacts you and wants an easier text editor to use than Vim. There is no GUI installed on the system in question. What text editor do you suggest and why?**

Suggest the Nano editor. It is less confusing because it does not use modes and the common commands are displayed in the interface.

2. **Explain how the keyboard responds depending on which mode Vim is currently in. How do modes add to Vim's functionality?**

The keyboard issues commands to Vim in some modes (Command and Execute) and manages content in Insert mode. By allowing Vim to respond differently to keystrokes, many actions and features are possible within the editor.

3. **Why are text editors more important on Linux systems than on other systems?**

System settings and service configurations are stored in text files. For a sysadmin to change the server's configuration, these files must be edited. Many Linux servers do not have a GUI and therefore do not have mouse-driven, menu-based interfaces. CLI text editors are the tools sysadmins use to reconfigure systems.

Review Activity: Text File Management

1. **Why is it a good practice to back up a configuration file before making changes?**

The original file can be put back in place if the updated file causes issues.

2. **Why should the integrity of a file downloaded from the Internet be checked by tools such as SHA or MD5?**

Files may be corrupted or changed during the download process. Checking file integrity with hashing tools identifies whether any changes have occurred.

Review Activity: Software Management

1. What are the software-management phases?

The phases are install, update/maintain, remove, inventory, or query information.

2. Why should administrators control software repository locations?

They should do this to ensure the availability of proper software versions, authorized software, and legitimate software.

3. Why is compiling software more common with Linux systems than with other operating systems?

The open-source nature of Linux software means there is access to the source code for customization and understanding of the software.

Review Activity: RPM Software Packages and Repositories

1. What information might sysadmins query the RPM database to retrieve?

Package version, install date, description, vendor, file locations

2. Why might sysadmins restrict certain software repositories?

Version and software control, access to approved software, maintain network efficiency by only downloading software once to the network and then distributing it

3. Why are .rpmnew files important during an upgrade?

These files maintain existing configuration file settings rather than overwriting them with vendor defaults.

Review Activity: Debian Software Packages and Repositories

1. What are the two steps for upgrading software with apt?

Use the apt update command, and then use the apt upgrade command.

2. Explain the difference between the two steps in upgrading software with apt.

The apt update command updates the database of available packages, and the apt upgrade command upgrades the actual packages.

Review Activity: Source Code

1. What is the effect of using ./ before an executable file?

The ./ causes Bash to check the current directory for the executable instead of the normal command path.

2.   Why is it more common to compile software with Linux than with other operating systems?

The source code is readily available in open-source environments and can be modified before compiling. In proprietary environments, the source code is not available and software is almost always precompiled.

Review Activity: Software Acquisition

1.   How can wget or curl be used to download files from the Internet in a way that a web browser can not be used?

They can be used in an automated file download script and a browser cannot.

2.   How might tar be used to distribute an application?

The application source code and supporting files may be bundled into a tar archive and compressed for a more efficient download.

Review Activity: Software in Sandbox

1.   What is the advantage of sandboxing?

Isolating a piece of software from any other software, the operating system, and system resources decreases its ability to damage the system.

2.   True or False? The original practice, known as chroot, that predates the current method of sandboxing, is deprecated and no longer used.

False. The practice of chroot is still appropriate in many settings.

Review Activity: Storage Concepts

1.   Explain the key differences between MBR and GPT partition tables.

MBR is limited to four partitions and a maximum drive size of 2 TB, while GPT does not have such limitations.

2.   How might quotas help sysadmins manage storage capacity on a server?

Quotas help by better controlling how much data users are allowed to store on the system.

3.   Do all RAID array designs provide fault tolerance?

No, RAID 0 Disk striping does not provide fault tolerance.

Review Activity: Storage Deployment

1.   What does /dev/sdc3 specify?

It specifies the third partition (3) on the third storage disk (c).

2.   What role does the partprobe command play in the process of adding storage?

The partprobe command checks for changes to the partition table, updating the system with any new or removed partitions.

3. **What command adds the XFS filesystem to /dev/sdb2?**

mkfs.xfs /dev/sdb2

4. **What is a mount point?**

A mount point is a directory where storage capacity is attached to the filesystem and made accessible to users.

5. **What are the three layers of an LVM deployment?**

The three layers are physical volumes, volume groups, and logical volumes.

Review Activity: Storage Options

1. **Why is RAID 5 fault tolerant and RAID 0 not?**

RAID 5 maintains parity information about stored data that can be used to recreate data missing from any one failed disk. RAID 0 does not store parity information.

2. **You purchase two 100 GB storage disks to use in a RAID 1 mirror. Assuming the entire storage capacity of both disks is at your disposal, what is the maximum amount of data your RAID 1 array can store?**

100 GB

3. **What do the Fibre Channel and iSCSI standards provide?**

They send SCSI commands to storage over network connections.

Review Activity: Storage Troubleshooting

1. **What command reports real-time disk latency information?**

ioping

2. **List the commands necessary to show configuration information for each of the three layers of LVM.**

pvdisplay, vgdisplay, lvdisplay

3. **When trying to save a file to a storage disk, you receive a message stating the drive is out of space. The df command indicates there is plenty of free space. What might be the issue?**

inode exhaustion

4. **You have added a partition to an existing disk by using fdisk. The partition is not displayed by the cat /proc/partitions command. What other command do you need to run?**

partprobe

Review Activity: Processes

1. **Differentiate between stopped processes and zombie processes.**

Stopped processes are terminating and releasing their resources. Zombie processes are child processes awaiting parent-process acceptance of their termination.

2.   Differentiate between -15 and -9 kill signals.

The kill signal -15 asks a process to gracefully exit. The kill signal -9 terminates the process ungracefully.

3.   What keys are used to cause `top` to display resources by memory consumption or by CPU consumption?

Use M to display memory and P to display processor consumption.

4.   Differentiate between the nice and renice commands.

The nice command is used to launch new processes at a specified priority, and the renice command is used to re-prioritize running processes.

Review Activity: Memory

1.   Explain the concept of virtual memory.

Because both RAM and storage drives are storage locations, if the RAM fills additional storage, space can be borrowed from storage devices and information can be swapped between the two.

2.   What is a swap partition?

A swap partition is a dedicated partition on a storage device that is used as virtual memory space.

3.   Differentiate between the free and vmstat commands.

The free command displays physical memory use. The vmstat command displays virtual memory use.

Review Activity: The Linux Kernel

1.   What is a kernel module?

A kernel module is a prewritten piece of code that adds functionality beyond what's built into the kernel.

2.   What does the output of the dmesg command display?

The output contains kernel messages covering drivers, modules, parameters, and other functions, including status and error information.

3.   Where else is dmesg output found?

/var/log/dmesg

Review Activity: System Services

1.   When using the systemctl command, how does enabling a service differ from starting a service?

Answers will vary. Enabling a service causes it to start when the system starts. Starting the service launches the service for the current runtime.

2.   What command restarts the sshd service after a configuration change?

systemctl restart sshd

3.   What are the target names for the GUI and CLI startup options?

GUI = graphical.target and CLI = multi-user.target

Review Activity: System Service Configuration

1. **A sysadmin has several virtual machines that are frequently on and off the development network. The administrator complains of time synchronization problems with applications on the VMs. What time service can you suggest to help?**

chrony

2. **Define some reasons to forward Linux log files to a central server.**

Forwarding log files makes it easier to archive logs and easier to search or parse logs.

3. **Differentiate between the at command scheduler and the cron scheduler.**

The at command is most useful for one-time commands, and cron is most useful for commands that are repeated.

4. **When would a script run if it were configured in cron with the following settings? 30 1 * * ***

It would run every day at 1:30 a.m.

Review Activity: Localization Settings

1. **Where are regional time-zone files stored on Red Hat–derived systems? And Debian-derived systems?**

On Red Hat–derived systems, see /user/share/zoneinfo. On Debian-derived systems, see /etc/timezone.

2. **True or false? The localectl command configures the system locale and keyboard settings as one collective setting that is aligned with the locale's specific cultural elements.**

False. The keyboard layout can be configured separately and independently of the locale, allowing the wide variety of keyboard layouts to be used with different locale settings.

Review Activity: Network Fundamentals

1. **Differentiate between MAC addresses, IP addresses, and hostnames.**

MAC addresses are physical addresses encoded on NICs, IP addresses are logical addresses configured by administrators or DHCP, and hostnames are logical human-friendly names assigned by administrators.

2. **Explain the difference between the Network ID and the Host ID portions of an IP address.**

The Network ID is assigned to a network segment, and all nodes on the segment have the same Network ID, making them local to each other. The Host ID is unique to each node within the Network ID to differentiate hosts from each other.

3. **List three advantages of IPv6 over IPv4.**

IPv6 has more addresses, native encryption, and more efficient routing.

Review Activity: Network Settings

1.   Why would an administrator need to use the ip link set eth0 up command?

The link was configured as disabled but is now needed.

2.   Describe the dynamic and static IP address assignment processes, and list the types of devices that likely rely on each process.

The dynamic process relies on a DHCP server with a range of available addresses. Clients lease addresses automatically, requiring no user intervention. Common devices are workstations, laptops, phones, and tablets. The static process relies on an administrator manually configuring the IP address settings, and common devices are servers, routers, switches, and other network devices.

3.   What commands are needed to refresh dynamically assigned IP settings?

dhclient -r and dhclient

4.   What is the purpose of the /etc/resolv.conf and /etc/nsswitch.conf files?

The /etc/resolv.conf file lists available nameservers, and the /etc/nsswitch.conf file defines the order for name resolution between the local /etc/hosts file and the nameservers listed in /etc/resolv.conf.

Review Activity: Remote Administrative Access

1.   A developer wants to integrate an SSH connection to a remote server into a script. The developer needs to avoid a password challenge for the SSH connection. What solution can you recommend?

Key-based authentication can be fully automated, avoiding the password challenge.

2.   Why might a sysadmin use the curl or wget commands?

These commands allow for a command-line-based download from a web server and can therefore be scripted.

**3.   What advantage does the rsync utility have over SCP and SFTP?
What disadvantage does it have?**

Advantage - It only copies changes across the network.
Disadvantage - It does not provide encryption.

Review Activity: Network Troubleshooting

1.   A helpdesk technician approaches you for help with a network troubleshooting challenge. The tech states that the workstation shows two IP addresses, neither of which matches the expected configuration. The first IP address is 127.0.0.1 and the second is 169.2540.99.42. What can you explain about each address?

The 127.0.0.1 address is the loopback address, assigned to each host to reference itself. The 169.254.99.42 address is from Automatic Private IP Addressing (APIPA) and indicates the client attempted to lease an IP configuration from a DHCP server but failed to do so.

2.   A helpdesk technician approaches you for help with a network troubleshooting challenge. The tech states that a workstation can ping a remote server by IP address but cannot ping it by name. What type of problem is this?

This is a name resolution problem.

Review Activity: Firewall Configuration

1. **How does a firewall help mitigate threats between two network segments?**

The firewall only permits allowed traffic to move between the segments, blocking unallowed traffic. For example, FTP file transfers might be blocked between the segments, or any connections at all might be blocked.

2. **What commands are necessary to persistently permit custom TCP port 9876 through the local firewalld configuration on the public zone?**

firewall-cmd --permanent --zone=public --add-port=9876/tcp

and

firewall-cmd --reload

3. **Explain the purpose of a firewall's default deny rule.**

Any traffic not matching an explicit permit rule will be blocked.

Review Activity: Network Traffic

1. **An administrator wants to better understand the structure of TCP/IP packets, including addressing, transport layer protocols, and the data payload. How would the Wireshark utility help with this understanding?**

Wireshark shows the packet headers, including source and destination MAC addresses, source and destination IP addresses, transport layer protocols and any synchronization information used, and the payload (actual data being sent). If the payload is not encrypted, it is readable by humans.

2. **A developer is working on a custom application that sends data to three different remote servers. The developer wants to see, at the network level, what data is sent to each server. What tools can you suggest to help with this, and what selection criteria might you suggest for those tools?**

Select either the tcpdump or Wireshark protocol analyzers. Wireshark has an easy-to-use GUI that can filter results, while tcpdump is easily scriptable.

3. **A junior administrator needs to generate a report displaying the operating systems running on all nodes on the 192.168.1.0/24 network segment. What command might you suggest?**

sudo nmap -O 192.168.1.0/24

Review Activity: System Hardening

1. **Explain the principle of least privilege, and provide at least two examples of its use.**

The principle of least privilege states that users and services should be given as little access to resources as possible. Examples include limiting the resources that services can access and setting file permissions for users.

2. **Explain the three components of the CIA Triad.**

Confidentiality: only authorized users can access data.

Integrity: data has not changed unexpectedly.

Availability: resources are available when needed.

3. **Explain the three goals of encryption.**

Confidentiality: only authorized users can access data.

Integrity: data has not changed unexpectedly.

Non-repudiation: the sending party cannot deny where data originated.

4. **Differentiate between symmetric and asymmetric encryption, and explain the rule associated with asymmetric encryption.**

Symmetric encryption uses one key to both encrypt and decrypt. Asymmetric encryption uses two keys (public and private). The rule is if data is encrypted with one key, only the other key can decrypt it.

Review Activity: Certificates

1. **What are some of the contents of a digital certificate?**

issuer, holder, purpose, expiration, public key

2. **Differentiate between self-signed certificates and third-party certificates.**

Self-signed certificates are created by your organization to show trust within the organization and are not trusted by outside entities. Third-party certificates are created by Certificate Authorities that are trusted by your organization and outside entities.

3. **When might checking file integrity with hashing tools be useful?**

This might be useful when performing file downloads from the Internet, file transfers on the local network, and backups.

Review Activity: Authentication

1. **What is the purpose of sssd?**

The purpose of sssd is to direct login attempts to central authenticate services.

2. **What is the relationship between PAM modules and PAM control flags?**

Modules specify an action such as an authentication attempt, and control flags manage how that action is enforced (such as whether it is required or optional).

Review Activity: SELinux and AppArmor

1. **What command displays the SELinux context for files?**

ls -Z

2. **You're troubleshooting a file-access issue and wish to see whether SELinux is to blame. What is one way you could test this by using the Permissive and Enforcing modes?**

Assuming the system is properly configured with Enforcing mode, set the system to Permissive mode with the setenforce 0 command and attempt the access again. If access is successful in Permissive mode but unsuccessful in Enforcing mode, SELinux is likely the culprit. Be sure to use setenforce 1 to return the system to Enforcing mode.

3.   Differentiate between targeted and strict policy types in SELinux.

Targeted enforces SELinux settings only on specific resources, leaving all other resources unconfined. Strict enforces SELinux settings on all resources unless the administrator deliberately excludes specific resources.

Review Activity: Script Basics

1.   What is the purpose of sh-bang, and how would you configure the value for Bash?

sh-bang lets Linux know what shell the script is written for and should execute in. Many shells have their own syntax. The sh-bang value for Bash is #!/bin/bash

2.   How does Bash handle lines that begin with the # character?

Bash ignores them, allowing script authors to insert comments, instructions, and examples.

Review Activity: Script Elements

1.   How might you combine the echo and read commands in a script to guide users through a process?

Combining the two allows the script and the user to communicate. The echo command displays instructions and questions from the script while the read command accepts user input in response to the questions.

2.   You've created a script that includes the string dev=web server. The script throws an error indicating too many arguments for the dev variable. How could you set the dev variable to see the words web and server as a single value?

You could enclose "web server" in double quotes.

3.   You need to use the sed command to find a value 'server' and replace it with the value 'system' in a file named inventory.txt. What is the syntax to accomplish this?

sed 'a/server/system/g' inventory.txt

Review Activity: Logical Controls

1.   You are exploring your local (shell) variables on each system that you manage. The first variable you check is the SHELL variable. How can you check the SHELL variable, and what do you expect it to display?

The SHELL variable can be checked with echo $SHELL and /bin/bash can be expected as the output.

2.   Differentiate between for and while loops.

for loops execute a given number of times, no more and no less. while loops execute as long as a given condition is met, whether that's zero, one, or more times.

3.   What is the purpose of file globbing in scripts?

File globbing, such as defining a list of files as *.sh, is a shorthand method of defining a list of files with a common name attribute.

Review Activity: Infrastructure as Code

1.   How would an organization's change to DevOps management impact Linux administrators?

Linux administrators would work more closely with developers, use a CI/CD pipeline to manage servers, and integrate more automation and orchestration.

2.   How does IaC contribute to increased system security?

IaC provides standardized security configurations that are easy to change to adapt to new threats.

3.   Differentiate between declarative and iterative IaC management tools.

Declarative defines both the configuration and the tools needed to set the configuration. Iterative defines the specific commands to achieve the desired configuration.

Review Activity: Orchestration

1.   How does orchestration provide scalability?

Orchestration allows administrators or automated systems to quickly provision new resources in response to spikes in demand.

2.   Differentiate between orchestration and automation.

Automation refers to an individual task accomplished without human intervention. Orchestration refers to a series of automation tasks that completes an entire deployment.

3.   Why might an organization select one orchestration tool over another?

Requirements such as cross-platform support, familiarity with particular languages, support for containers, and agent or agentless options might influence and organization's selection.

Review Activity: Git

1.   If an IT department stored all scripts written by sysadmin in a Git repository, what benefits might the department realize?

easier collaboration, better version control, centralization of resources

2.   What is the purpose of tagging in Git?

Tags identify important versions or code changes.

3.   Where might Git repositories be stored?

They might be located on the user's local workstation, on a local/internal network, in the cloud, or in a public repository such as GitHub.

4.   In what circumstances might you submit a Git pull request?

Such a request might be submitted when contributing code to a project managed by project maintainers who must approve your changes.

Review Activity: Containers

1. **What are three advantages of containers?**

Containers are scalable, offer high availability, and can be quickly deployed.

2. **Differentiate between an image and a container.**

An image is a static specification for a container. When the image is run, the executing code is a container.

3. **What makes a container stateless?**

The data processed inside a container and the changes to the container's configuration are not stored. (Note that data may be persistently stored outside the container.)

Review Activity: Container Deployment

1. **Differentiate between running a container with the docker run {image-name} command versus with the docker run -it {image-name} bash command option.**

Running the docker run {image-name} command causes the container to start up and run without establishing an administrative interface. Running a container with the docker run -it {image-name} bash command causes the container to start up and run but then launches the Bash shell within the container and establishes an administrative connection to the shell.

2. **What are some advantages of a private image registry?**

Authorized users have full control of the images stored there, including versions, image access, and change management.

3. **How does a container registry enable CI/CD?**

By acting as a central storage area for container images, the registry provides a place from which CI/CD processes can pull images as needed for rapid and automated deployments for scaling.

Review Activity: Virtualization

1. **Differentiate between virtualization layers for VM virtualization versus container virtualization.**

VM virtualization virtualizes at the hardware layer, while container virtualization virtualizes at the OS layer.

2. **How might you automate a virtual machine deployment, and what command is used?**

You might automate a VM deployment by including the virt-install command in a script that provides specifications such as processor, memory, storage, and network settings.

3. **What is the purpose of the virtual bridge?**

The virtual bridge manages network connectivity between the VM and the host server and/or the network. The bridge may allow no network access to any other system, allow network access that is limited to other VMs on the host and the host itself, or allow full network access.

Review Activity: Linux Boot Process

1. Differentiate between the older system BIOS and the modern UEFI standards.

BIOS tests hardware, manages hardware settings, and runs the boot loader. UEFI does the same but handles larger memory spaces, larger storage disks, and includes security enhancements.

2. What is the role of the initrd?

The initrd loads with the kernel and contains everything needed to boot the system. It is loaded during the initial startup phase to allow for flexible configurations.

3. What is the /boot/vmlinuz<kernel-version> file?

The file is a compressed version of the Linux kernel.

Review Activity: Boot Settings

1. Why don't you usually need to install GRUB2 on most Linux systems?

It's already installed as part of the OS installation process.

2. How is working with the grub.cfg file different from working with most Linux configuration files?

Most Linux configuration files are edited directly, but grub.cfg is assembled from a group of configuration files. Those files are edited directly.

3. What is the role of the grub2-mkconfig command?

The grub2-mkconfig command constructs the grub.cfg file from various configuration files.

Review Activity: Linux Deployment

1. What are some reasons for updating the system immediately after installation?

Updates provide security enhancements, stability components (such as device drivers), and application features. Updating is part of security hardening.

2. Why is a non-root administrative account often created as part of the installation process?

Logging in as root is usually a poor security choice, but administrative tasks still need to be completed. Therefore, a non-root administrative account is less privileged than root, but it can complete most necessary administrative tasks.

3. Why is it a good idea to deploy a Red Hat–derived and a Debian-derived distribution at least once?

It's useful to compare features such as package managers and GUI tools between the two Linux families.

Glossary

absolute mode A syntax for setting Linux permissions that uses numeric octal values to represent permissions values.

absolute path A reference to a specific location on a file system irrespective of the current working directory or combined paths.

access control list (ACL) Collection of access control entries (ACEs) that determines which subjects (user accounts, host IP addresses, and so on) are allowed or denied access to the object and the privileges given (read-only, read/write, and so on).

Address Resolution Protocol (ARP) Broadcast mechanism by which the hardware MAC address of an interface is matched to an IP address on a local network segment.

Advanced Package Tool (APT) An advanced package management utility that is used with dpkg packages on Debian-based distributions.

agent A software program that acts on behalf of some other program or service.

AppArmor A context-based permissions scheme provided with Debian-based and SUSE Linux distributions.

authentication A method of validating a particular entity's or individual's unique credentials.

automation Use of scripts to perform configuration steps without requiring manual intervention.

availability The fundamental security goal of ensuring that computer systems operate continuously and that authorized persons can access data that they need.

backup Security copy of production data made to removable media, typically according to a regular schedule. Different backup types (full, incremental, or differential) balance media capacity, time required to backup, and time required to restore.

basic input/output system (BIOS) Legacy 32-bit firmware type that initializes hardware and provides a system setup interface for configuring boot devices and other hardware settings.

block storage The storage method that breaks data into chunks and distributes the chunks across available storage space, independent of the server's file system.

boot loader A small program stored in read-only memory that loads the kernel from a storage device, and then starts the operating system.

booting The process of starting or restarting a computer and loading an operating system for the user to access.

certificate authority (CA) A server that guarantees subject identities by issuing signed digital certificate wrappers for their public keys.

Cinnamon One of the default desktop environments for Linux Mint and a fork of GNOME 3.

command mode A text editing mode that enables users to perform different editing actions using single keystrokes.

command substitution A method of shell expansion in which the output of a command replaces the command itself.

command-line interface A text-based interface between the user and the operating system that accepts input in the form of commands.

Common Internet File System (CIFS) CIFS was proposed as a means of implementing SMB version 1 as an Internet standard. SMB1 has very serious security vulnerabilities and is now disabled by default on current Windows versions. Also known as Server Message Blocks (SMB).

Compression Reducing the amount of space that a file takes up on disk using various algorithms to describe it more efficiently. File storage compression uses lossless techniques. NTFS-formatted drives can compress files automatically while ZIP compression adds files to a compressed archive. Lossy compression, such as that used by JPEG and MPEG image and video formats, discards some information in the file more or less aggressively, allowing for a trade-off between picture quality and file size.

conditional statement A control statement used in programming to evaluate whether a particular condition is true or false.

confidentiality The fundamental security goal of keeping information and communications private and protecting them from unauthorized access.

confidentiality, integrity, and availability (CIA triad) Three principles of security control and management. Also known as the information security triad. Also referred to in reverse order as the AIC triad.

container An operating system virtualization deployment containing everything required to run a service, application, or microservice.

container engine A piece of software that processes user requests and runs one or more containers on top of a single operating system.

container image A static file with executable code that can create a container on a computing system. As a static file, it cannot be changed, and it can be deployed consistently in any environment. It is a core component of a containerized architecture.

context-based permissions A permissions scheme that describes multiple types of information about processes and files that are used in combination to make decisions related to access control.

Continuous Integration/Continuous Deployment (CI/CD) Software development method combining app and platform updates, which are rapidly committed to production, with code updates, which are rapidly committed to a code repository or build server.

control statement A programming element that enables a program to execute instructions in a specified order.

cron job Scheduled task that is managed by the Linux cron daemon.

CUPS A print management system for Linux that enables a computer to function as a print server.

current working directory (CWD) The directory that the user is currently accessing.

cybersecurity Protection of computer systems and digital information resources from unauthorized access, attack, theft, or data damage.

daemon A program that runs in the background without the need for human intervention.

Dandified YUM (DNF) An improved version of the YUM package manager.

desktop environment A client to a display server that tells the server how to draw graphical elements on the screen.

DevOps A combination of software development and systems operations, this term refers to the practice of integrating one discipline with the other.

DevSecOps A combination of software development, security operations, and systems operations, this term refers to the practice of integrating each discipline with the others.

digital certificate Identification and authentication information presented in the X.509 format and issued by a certificate authority (CA) as a guarantee that a key pair (as identified by the public key embedded in the certificate) is valid for a particular subject (user or host). Also known as a certificate.

digital signature Message digest encrypted using the sender's private key that is appended to a message to authenticate the sender and prove message integrity.

distro One of several fully functional operating systems and members of the Linux family that run the Linux kernel, GNU software, and additional components. Also known as a Linux distribution.

domain name system (DNS) Service that maps fully qualified domain name labels to IP addresses on most TCP/IP networks, including the Internet.

dpkg A package management system used by Linux distributions derived from Debian Linux.

Dynamic Host Configuration Protocol (DHCP) Protocol used to automatically assign IP addressing information to hosts that have not been configured manually.

encryption Scrambling the characters used in a message so that the message can be seen but not understood or modified unless it can be deciphered. Encryption provides for a secure means of transmitting data and authenticating users. It is also used to store data securely. Encryption uses different types of cipher and one or more keys. The size of the key is one factor in determining the strength of the encryption product. Also known as cipher and algorithm.

environment variable A type of variable whose values are inherited from parent processes and passed on to child processes.

escape character A character that is used to remove the special meaning from another character so it can be interpreted literally.

execute mode A text editing mode that enables users to execute commands within the editor.

exit code A value that a child process passes back to its parent process when the child process terminates. Also known as exit status.

ext2 A non-journaled Linux file system introduced in 1993 and now the file system on some flash storage media.

ext3 Standard Linux file system that includes journaling and has since been replaced with ext4.

ext4 One of the default file systems in modern Linux versions that supports journaling and large volumes.

Fibre Channel (FC) High-speed network communications protocol used to implement SANs.

file storage A storage method where data is managed as a discrete file within an operating system's file system. Common on workstations, servers, and NAS devices.

file system Structure for file data indexing and storage created by a process of formatting a partition that allows an OS to make use of a mass storage device, such as an HDD, SSD, or thumb drive.

File Transfer Protocol (FTP) Application protocol used to transfer files between network hosts. Variants include S(ecure) FTP, FTP with SSL (FTPS and FTPES) and T(rivial)FTP. FTP utilizes ports 20 and 21.

Filesystem Hierarchy Standard (FHS) A set of guidelines for the names of files and directories and their locations on Linux systems.

Filesystem in Userspace (FUSE) Permits the creation of non-privileged virtual file systems without privileged access to the kernel by providing an interface between the two.

firewall Software or hardware device that protects a network segment or individual host by filtering packets to an access control list.

free and open-source software (FOSS) Computer code that embodies the principles of both the free software movement and the open-source software (OSS) movement.

full disk encryption (FDE) Encryption of all data on a disk (including system files, temporary files, and the pagefile) can be accomplished via a supported OS, via third-party software, or at the controller level by the disk device itself.

fully qualified domain name (FQDN) Unique label specified in a DNS hierarchy to identify a particular host within a subdomain within a top-level domain.

gedit The default GUI text editor used in GNOME desktop environments.

Git Type of version tracking software used primarily with collaborative development projects to ensure integrity and version control.

globbing A method of shell expansion used to replace a specific wildcard pattern with values that match the pattern.

GNOME The default desktop environment for most Linux distributions that run the X Window System or Wayland.

GNU GRand Unified Bootloader (GNU GRUB) A boot loader developed by the GNU Project that became popular on UNIX-like systems.

GNU nano A small, user-friendly text editor that evolved from the Pico text editor created for UNIX-like systems. Also known as nano.

GNU Parted A utility that is used to manage partitions on a storage device.

graphical user interface (GUI) An environment for passing commands to a computer by using a graphical, mouse-driven interface rather than by using text-based commands.

group An access control object that contains multiple users with similar security requirements.

GUID partition table (GPT) Modern disk partitioning system allowing large numbers of partitions and very large partition sizes.

hard link A reference to a file that enables a file's data to have multiple names on the same file system.

hardening Process of making a host or app configuration secure by reducing its attack surface, running only necessary services, installing monitoring software to protect against malware and intrusions, and establishing a maintenance schedule to ensure the system is patched to be secure against software exploits.

hash The theoretically indecipherable fixed-length output of the hashing process. Also known as hashed value.

hashing Function that converts an arbitrary-length string input to a fixed-length string output. A cryptographic hash function does this in a way that reduces the chance of collisions, where two different inputs produce the same output. Also known as message digest and cryptographic hash.

home directory A container for a user's personal files and other files specific to that user.

hop One link in the path from a host to a router or from router to router. Each time a packet passes through a router, its hop count (or TTL) is decreased by one.

hostname A human-readable name that identifies a network host.

HyperText Transfer Protocol/ HTTP Secure (HTTP) Application protocol used to provide web content to browsers. HTTP uses port 80. HTTPS(ecure) provides for encrypted transfers, using TLS and port 443. Also known as HTTP Secure.

hypervisor Software or firmware that creates and manages virtual machines on the host hardware.

I/O scheduling The process by which the operating system determines the order of input and output operations as they pertain to block storage devices.

identity and access management (IAM) Security process that provides identification, authentication, and authorization mechanisms for users, computers, and other entities to work with organizational assets like networks, operating systems, and applications. Also known as identity management (IdM) and access management.

immutable flag An attribute of a file or directory that prevents it from being modified, even by the root user.

index node (inode) An object that stores metadata about a file or directory on a file system.

infrastructure as code (IaC) Provisioning architecture in which deployment of resources is performed by scripted automation and orchestration.

init A daemon that initializes a system and acts as the parent to all processes. Also known as init daemon.

initrd image An archive file containing all the essential files that are required for booting the operating system.

input/output operations per second (IOPS) Performance indicator that measures the time taken to complete read/write operations.

insert mode A text editing mode that enables users to insert text by typing.

integrity The fundamental security goal of keeping organizational information accurate, free of errors, and without unauthorized modifications.

integrity checking The process of verifying that data has not been modified, whether intentionally or unintentionally, in any way.

Internet Protocol address (IP) Format for logical host and network addressing. In IPv4, a 32-bit binary address is expressed in dotted decimal notation, such as 192.168.1.1. In IPv6, addresses are 128-bit expressed as hexadecimal (for example, 2001:db8::0bcd:abcd:ef12:1234).

Internet Small Computer Systems Interface (iSCSI) IP tunneling protocol that enables the transfer of SCSI data over an IP-based network to create a SAN.

ISO image A disk image for OS booting and installation named after the ISO 9660 file system standard used by compact disks (CDs).

JavaScript Object Notation (JSON) A file format that uses attribute-value pairs to define configurations in a structure that is easy for both humans and machines to read and consume.

KDE Plasma The second-most common desktop environment for Linux distributions that run the X Window System or Wayland.

Kerberos Single sign-on authentication and authorization service that is based on a time-sensitive, ticket-granting system.

kernel All operating systems have a kernel, which is a low-level piece of code responsible for controlling the rest of the operating system.

kernel module A system-level object that extends the functionality of the kernel.

kernel panic A mechanism by which the system detects there has been a fatal error and responds to it.

kernel space The area of system memory in which the kernel executes the services it provides.

Kernel-based Virtual Machine (KVM) Hypervisor used to implement virtualization in Linux.

latency Time taken for a signal to reach the recipient, measured in milliseconds. Latency is a particular problem for two-way applications, such as VoIP (telephone) and online conferencing.

least privilege Basic principle of security stating that something should be allocated the minimum necessary rights, privileges, or information to perform its role. Also known as principle of least privilege.

Lightweight Directory Access Protocol (LDAP) Protocol used to access network directory databases, which store information about authorized users and their privileges, as well as other organizational information.

Lightweight Directory Access Protocol Secure (LDAPS) A method of implementing LDAP using SSL/TLS encryption. Also known as Secure LDAP.

Linux Open-source OS packaged in distributions supported by a wide range of hardware and software vendors.

Linux kernel A free and open-source monolithic kernel that manages all other resources on the Linux operating system.

Linux Unified Key Setup (LUKS) A platform-independent full drive/disk encryption (FDE) solution that is commonly used to encrypt storage devices in a Linux environment.

load balancing The technique of distributing network traffic or computing workload among multiple devices in a network.

local area network (LAN) Network scope restricted to a single geographic location and owned/managed by a single organization.

localization The process of adapting system components for use within a distinct culture, other than the culture that the system was originally designed for.

logical volume (LV) Storage capacity created from the volume group of logical volume management.

Logical Volume Manager (LVM) Software that maps physical devices and partitions to logical volumes.

loop In scripting and programming, control statement that executes code repeatedly based on a condition.

mandatory access control (MAC) Access control model where resources are protected by inflexible, system-defined rules. Resources (objects) and users (subjects) are allocated a clearance level (or label).

manual pages Built-in documentation for specific Linux commands that provides information on what a command does and how to use it. Also called man pages.

master boot record (MBR) Sector on a mass storage device that holds information about partitions and the OS boot loader.

MATE One of the default desktop environments for Linux Mint and a fork of GNOME 2.

media access control (MAC) Hardware address that uniquely identifies each network interface at layer 2 (Data Link). A MAC address is 48 bits long with the first half representing the manufacturer's organizationally unique identifier (OUI). Also known as client identifier, hardware address, and local address.

Message Digest Algorithm v5 (MD5) A cryptographic hash function producing a 128-bit output.

microservice An independent, single-function module with well-defined and lightweight interfaces and operations. Typically this style of architecture allows for rapid, frequent, and reliable delivery of complex applications.

minimum policy A policy wherein subjects and objects run in an unconfined environment with minimal configuration loaded into memory. This policy is well suited to small devices.

mount point A partition or volume mapped to a folder in another file system rather than allocated a drive letter.

multifactor authentication (MFA) Authentication scheme that requires the user to present at least two different factors as credentials; for example, something you know, something you have, something you are, something you do, and somewhere you are. Specifying two factors is known as 2FA. Also known as multifactor.

name resolution Relating easy-to-remember hostnames with difficult-to-remember IP addresses for network communications.

network address translation (NAT) Routing mechanism that conceals internal addressing schemes from the public Internet by translating between a single public address on the external side of a router and private, non-routable addresses internally.

Network File System (NFS) Remote file access protocol used principally on UNIX and Linux networks.

network interface card (NIC) Adapter card that provides one or more Ethernet ports for connecting hosts to a network so that they can exchange data over a link. Also known as network adapter.

network port An endpoint in network communication that identifies the type of Application-layer protocol used in a communication.

Network Time Protocol (NTP) Application protocol allowing machines to synchronize to the same time clock that runs over UDP port 123.

New Technology Filing System (NTFS) 64-bit default file system for Windows, with file-by-file compression and RAID support as well as advanced file attribute management tools, encryption, and disk quotas.

object storage A storage method where data is broken into chunks and managed with detailed metadata. It is very scalable and is best for data that is written once and read often.

octal number A number that is expressed using one of eight unique digits, i.e., a base-8 number system.

one-time password (OTP) A password that is generated for use in one specific session and becomes invalid after the session ends.

open-source Licensing model that grants permissive rights to end-users, such as to install, use, modify, and distribute a software product and its source code, as long as redistribution permits the same rights.

operator Programming object that can resolve the truth value of a condition, such as whether one variable is equal to another.

orchestration Automation of multiple coordinated steps in a deployment process.

out-of-memory killer (OOM killer) A feature of the Linux kernel that determines what process(es) to kill when the system is extremely low on memory.

ownership The property by which a user is allowed to apply and modify the permissions of a file or directory.

package manager A program that installs, updates, inventories, and uninstalls packaged software.

parent directory The directory that is one level above the current working directory.

partition A discrete area of storage defined on a hard disk using either the master boot record (MBR) scheme or the GUID partition table (GPT) scheme. Each partition can be formatted with a different file system and a partition can be marked as active (made bootable).

path A reference to a specific location on a file system.

PATH variable An environment variable that specifies where an application's binaries are stored on the file system.

permissions Security settings that control access to objects including file system items and network resources.

physical volume (PV) A storage device or partition allocated to logical volume management (LVM).

piping Using the output of one command as the input for a second command.

pluggable authentication module (PAM) Framework for implementing authentication providers in Linux.

preboot execution environment (PXE) Feature of a network adapter that allows the computer to boot by contacting a suitably configured server over the network.

privilege escalation The practice of exploiting flaws in an operating system or other application to gain a greater level of access than was intended for the user or application.

process Software program that has been executed and is running in system memory.

process identifier (PID) A unique integer assigned to each new process when it starts so that it can be identified by the system and users. Also known as process ID.

process management The layer of the Linux kernel that allocates execution space on the processor for different processes.

public key infrastructure (PKI) Framework of certificate authorities, digital certificates, software, services, and other cryptographic components deployed for the purpose of validating subject identities.

RAID0 Striping drive configuration that provides no redundancy against device failure.

RAID1 Mirrored two-disk redundant drive configuration with 50% capacity utilization.

RAID5 Striping with parity-redundant drive configuration supporting a flexible number of devices and better than 50% capacity utilization.

Read-only Memory (ROM) A ROM chip is a special form of memory that has data written to it during the manufacturing process and thus is not amenable to alteration.

Red Hat Package Manager (RPM) A package management system used by Linux distributions derived from Red Hat Linux.

redirection The process of accepting input data from and sending output data to a component that is not a default I/O device.

redundant array of independent/ inexpensive disks (RAID) Specifications that support redundancy and fault tolerance for different configurations of multiple-device storage systems.

relative path A reference to a specific location on a file system that is relative to the current working directory.

remote desktop A Windows remote control feature allowing specified users to log onto the Windows computer over the network and work remotely. Remote Desktop uses the RDP protocol over TCP port 3389.

router Intermediate system working at the Network layer capable of forwarding packets around logical networks of different layer 1 and layer 2 types.

script Series of simple or complex commands, parameters, variables, and other components stored in a text file and processed by a shell interpreter.

search path A sequence of various directory paths that is used by the shell to locate files.

Secure Hash Algorithm (SHA) A cryptographic hashing algorithm created to address possible weaknesses in MD5. The current version is SHA-2.

Secure Shell (SSH) Application protocol supporting secure tunneling and remote terminal emulation and file copy. SSH runs over TCP port 22.

Secure Sockets Layer (SSL) Original, obsolete version of the security protocol now developed as TLS.

Security-Enhanced Linux (SELinux) The default context-based permissions scheme provided with CentOS and Red Hat Enterprise Linux.

serial ATA (SATA) The most widely used interface for hard disks on desktop and laptop computers. It uses a 7-pin data connector with one device per port. There are three SATA standards specifying bandwidths of 1.5 Gb/s, 3 Gb/s, and 6 Gb/s respectively. SATA drives also use a new 15-pin power connector, though adapters for the old-style 4-pin Molex connectors are available. External drives are also supported via the eSATA interface.

Server Message Block (SMB) Application protocol used for requesting files from Windows servers and delivering them to clients. SMB allows machines to share files and printers, thus making them available for other machines to use. SMB client software is available for UNIX-based systems. Samba software allows UNIX and Linux servers or NAS appliances to run SMB services for Windows clients. Also known as Common Internet File System (CIFS).

service A non-interactive process that runs in the background to support an OS or application function, such as Plug-and-Play, the print spooler, and DHCP. In Windows, services can be viewed, configured, and started/stopped via the Services console, MSConfig, and the Processes tab in Task Manager. Also known as daemon.

service mesh A dedicated infrastructure layer managed by code that provides service-to-service interaction in a container environment.

set group ID (SGID) A special permission that enables a user to execute a file with the privileges of the file's group.

set user ID (SUID) A special permission that enables a user to execute a file with the privileges of the file's owner.

shell System component providing a command interpreter by which the user can use a kernel interface and operate the OS.

shell environment The mechanism by which a shell maintains settings and other behavioral details about the shell.

shell expansion The process by which a shell identifies special tokens that it substitutes values for.

shell variable A type of variable that is contained within specific shell processes and whose values do not get passed on to child processes.

single sign-on (SSO) Authentication technology that enables a user to authenticate once and receive authorizations for multiple services.

Small Computer Systems Interface (SCSI) Legacy expansion bus standard allowing for the connection of internal and external devices. Each device on a SCSI bus must be allocated a unique ID. The bus must also be terminated at both ends.

software compilation The process of translating human-readable source code into computer-readable instructions that the processor can execute.

SSH port forwarding The process of tunneling an application through the SSH protocol to encrypt data in transit.

standard error A text stream that is used as the destination for error messages.

standard input A text stream that acts as the source for command input.

standard output A text stream that acts as the destination for command output.

sticky bit A special permission bit that provides protection for files in a directory.

storage area network (SAN) Network dedicated to provisioning storage resources, typically consisting of storage devices and servers connected to switches via host bus adapters.

storage as a service (STaaS) A common cloud subscription for managing file storage.

storage quota The storage space that is allotted to a user for file storage on a computer.

strict policy In SELinux, a policy in which mandatory access control (MAC) is enforced on all subjects and objects.

superuser The local administrative account on a Linux system, typically named root.

swap space A partition on the storage device that is used when the system runs out of physical memory.

switch Intermediate system used to establish contention-free network segments at OSI layer 2 (Data Link). An unmanaged switch does not support any sort of configuration. Also known as an unmanaged switch.

symbolic link A reference to a file or directory that can span multiple file systems.

syslog Application protocol and event-logging format enabling different appliances and software applications to transmit logs or event records to a central server. Syslog works over UDP port 514 by default.

system initialization The process that begins when the kernel first loads.

systemd A software suite that replaces older init methods like SysVinit and that includes various service management tools.

SysVinit An older system initialization method that has been largely superseded by systemd.

tab completion A feature in which a command-line shell fills in the name of a command you've partially typed.

targeted policy In SELinux, a policy in which mandatory access control (MAC) is enforced on all subjects and objects marked as targeted, while discretionary access control (DAC) is enforced on all untargeted subjects and objects.

text editor An application that enables you to view, create, or modify the contents of text files.

throughput Amount of data transfer supported by a link in typical conditions. This can be measured in various ways with different software applications. Goodput is typically used to refer to the actual "useful" data rate at the application layer (less overhead from headers and lost packets). Also known as goodput and throughput tester.

token A physical or virtual item that contains authentication and/or authorization data, commonly used in multifactor authentication.

Transmission Control Protocol/ Internet Protocol (TCP/IP) Network protocol suite used to implement the Internet and most WANs and LANs. It uses a four-layer network model that corresponds roughly to the OSI model as follows: Network Interface (Physical/ Data Link), Internet (Network), Transport (Transport), Application (Session, Presentation, Application).

Transport Layer Security (TLS) Security protocol that uses certificates for authentication and encryption to protect web communications and other application protocols.

Trivial File Transfer Protocol (TFTP) Simplified form of FTP supporting only file copying. TFTP works over UDP port 69.

troubleshooting methodology Structured approach to problem-solving using identification, theory of cause, testing, planning, implementation, verification, and documentation steps.

udev A Linux device manager that automatically detects and configures hardware devices.

uncomplicated firewall (UFW) A simplified interface for configuring the iptables firewall service.

Unified Extensible Firmware Interface (UEFI) Type of system firmware providing support for 64-bit CPU operation at boot, full GUI and mouse operation at boot, and better boot security.

unit file A configuration file that systemd uses to determine how it will handle system resources that systemd can manage.

unshielded twisted pair (UTP) Media type that uses copper conductors arranged in pairs that are twisted to reduce interference. Typically, cables are 4-pair or 2-pair.

user account The credentials and profile settings that represent a subject on a computing host or network system.

user space The area of system memory outside of kernel space that includes software that accesses kernel services.

variable Identifier for a value that can change during program execution. Variables are usually declared with a particular data type.

vim Command-line text editor that extends the original vi software. Vim uses a command mode for file operations and an insert mode for editing. Also known as vi.

virtual file system (VFS) An abstraction layer that translates file system information between a real file system and the Linux kernel.

virtual local area network (VLAN) Logical network segment comprising a broadcast domain established using a feature of managed switches to assign each port a VLAN ID. Even though hosts on two VLANs may be physically connected to the same switch, local traffic is isolated to each VLAN, so they must use a router to communicate.

virtual machine (VM) Guest operating system installed on a host computer using virtualization software (a hypervisor).

Virtual NICs (vNICs) Connections between a virtual machine instance and a physical network interface card (NIC) in the host server.

virtualization Computing environment where multiple independent operating systems can be installed to a single hardware platform and run simultaneously.

volume group (VG) Aggregated space of one or more physical volumes in logical volume management (LVM).

Wireshark Widely used protocol analyzer.

XFS One of the default file systems in modern Linux versions that supports journaling and efficiency in handling large files.

YAML Ain't Markup Language (YAML) Language for configuration files and applications such as Netplan and Ansible.

Yellow Dog Update Manager (YUM) Package manager for installing, maintaining, inventorying, and removing software from the Red Hat family of Linux distributions.

Zypper An openSUSE package manager that supports .rpm packages.

Index

Note: Page numbers with *Italics* represent charts, graphs, and diagrams.

O

P